PARLIAMENT AND FOREIGN POLICY DECISION MAKING

PARLIAMENT AND FOREIGN POLICY DECISION MAKING

Parties, Politics and the Making of India's China Policy

Sibaram Badatya

P. Lazarus Samraj

KALPAZ

ISBN: 978-93-5324-238-1

First Published, 2020

Published by

Kalpaz Publications
C-30, Satyawati Nagar,
Delhi – 110052
Ph.: 011-47034999, 9811692060
www.kalpazpublications.com
E-mail: kalpaz@hotmail.com

Printed at: G. Print Process, Delhi

Contents

Preface

The Asian strategic landscape is undergoing a tremendous transformation. The strategic rise of China, India's fast-paced economic growth, Japan's giant economy, the resurgence of Southeast Asian countries and the burgeoning politico-strategic competition in Western Asia have shifted the gravity of world affairs from Europe to Asia, what is often called as the new world order of the 'Asian Century'. However, more than any other country, China and India remain juxtaposed for a new and intense politico-strategic and economic competition precariously holding the key to the future of global order. Therefore, the emergence of the Asian century and its impact on world order would be largely determined by these two prominent players whose colossal emergence presents an opportunity as well threat to the world order.

The fear of rising China is preeminent among all the important states in the world affairs. America's National Security Strategy continues to identify China as a potential threat and a challenge to US dominance. Apart from taking crucial military-strategic and diplomatic overtures, America's foreign policy has carefully treaded to engage China. Similarly, European Union and other individual countries in Europe have realigned their foreign and security policies to actively meet China's economic success. However, if geo-politics would re-emerge in China-EU interactions the possibilities of intense and overt rivalries cannot be ruled out. In this context, several other countries, like Korea, Russia, Australia and Pakistan have substantially embarked on gradually overcoming the deficiencies of their foreign policies to meet China's strategic potential.

India which has an important stake in the rise of China has not taken pro-active foreign policy measures. The changing realities of Asian and global world order requires a pragmatic and pro-active foreign policy that transcends the traditional 'ethical fences' which India has created for herself. China has cooperated in peacefully resolving border disputes with all its neighbours except India. China has accepted the de facto separation of Taiwan for the moment and abstained from forceful actions towards reunification. However, with India, China continues to claim Arunachal Pradesh which is as big as Taiwan and continues to hold on Aksai Chin. Besides, Beijing builds strategic inroads in Pakistan Occupied Kashmir (PoK) and aggressively builds ports and other infrastructure with India's neighbours in a way to strategically encircle India. Apart from the continuous Sino-India rivalry on trade, economy, and institutional participations, the above mentioned contentions between both the nations remain to be resolved. This resolution of Sino-Indian rivalry depends up on a change in India's strategic psyche. The strategies of survival whether it is war, alliance building, constructive engagement or peaceful resolution of disputes depends on the attitude of Indian policy makers. In India, Parliament a plays very important role in policy making and opinion making. In any democracy the attitude of the Parliament towards other country is considered as very important.

Parliament in a representational democracy like India is a cardinal pillar of the sovereign will. Its institutional mandate is to formulate public policies within the framework of our constitutional system. In a legalistic sense, the democratic Parliament thus reins supreme, theoretically ensuring the Executive's answerability to the Legislature. This work is an attempt to understand how the Members of the Parliament, from both the houses, understood, reacted, debated and pronounced foreign policies related to China. The executive who is assured of the legislative majority for its policy proposal considers the Parliament as a constitutional procedural device for approving the decisions of the government. This research would attempt to understand the extent to which the Indian Parliament responded to the changing realities of the emergence of China. Public policies which are triggered by the Executive are also consciously reflected in the political party's election manifesto and the Indian Parliament through its various mechanisms of accountability which holds the government responsible. A study on the changing attitude of Indian Parliament towards China is necessary when Parliament as an institution is seeking larger stakes in foreign and security policies of the nation. Therefore the origin of the research problem emanates from a conscious objective of evaluating the foreign policy of a nation and its changes from a broader and systemic level rather than a unit level perspective.

Apparently, the Indian Parliament as an institution had little formal power to affect far reaching changes in the foreign policy of the country and, beyond its role in questioning the government and overseeing financial accounts it did not wield any power. However, the debate on Indo-U.S nuclear deal in the Indian Parliament and the withdrawal of support by the

Left Party members signalled the beginning of Parliament as a proactive institution. Parliament reigns substantial authority in democracy like India and any closed loop policy making by executive committees would be tantamount to the basic philosophy of 'popular will'. By shedding light on the role of Indian Parliament this research seeks to illuminate how Indian legislature moves towards establishing a procedural control over the executives. A procedural and operational control over the government on defense and strategic affairs by the Members of the legislature would have important consequences. The present work intends to study the role of Parliament and its level of influence on India's foreign policy decision making process in general and on India's China policy in particular and to analyse the attitude of different political parties towards China. It also aims to map the attitude of Indian Parliament towards China in foreign policy engagement and draw implications for the future of India's engagement with China.

An analysis of the parliamentary debate on India-China relations requires enormous time, effort and more importantly, the support of unpublished data of parliament archives. We were fortunate to have enormous support of the officials of the Parliament Library, Ministry of External Affairs and National Archives for providing the required materials and other critical documents to complete the book. We are also grateful to our friends and family members for their love, affection and continuous support that always been our greatest source of inspiration throughout the research work and our life in general. We are also thankful to Shri Amit Garg of Gyan Books/ Kalpaz Publication for publishing the manuscript and bringing our research to the larger audience.

Abbreviations

ABHM	: Bharatiya Hindu Mahasabha
AICC	: All India Congress Committee
AIFB	: All India Forward Block
AIMIM	: All India Majlis-E-Ittehadul Muslimeen
ARC	: Administrative Reform Commission
ASEAN	: Association of Southeast Asian Nations
ASSOCHAM	: Associated Chambers of Commerce and Industry of India
BJP	: Bharatiya Janata Party
BJS	: Bharatiya Jan Sangh
BOS	: Bureau of Security
BPM	: Bureaucratic Politics Model
BSM	: Bangladesh, Sri Lanka, Maldives (Division of MEA)
CBDT	: Central Board of Direct Taxes
CBM	: Confidence Building Measures
CE	: Central Europe
CII	: Confederation of Indian Industry
CNN	: Cable News Network
CNV	: Cypher, NGO & Vigilance (Division of MEA)
CoM	: Council of Ministers
COS	: Chief of the Staff
COSC	: Chief of the Staff Committee
CPCED	: Co-operative Economic Development
CPI	: Communist Party of India
CPC	: Communist Party of China
CPV	: Consular, Passport and Visa (Division of MEA)
CT	: Counter Terrorism
CTBT	: The Comprehensive Nuclear-Test-Ban Treaty

D & ISA	: Disarmament & International Security Affairs
DAI	: Directorates of Air Intelligence
DDP	: Department of Defense Production
DDR&D	: Department of Defense Research & Development
DMI	: Directorates of Military Intelligence
DMK	: Dravida Munnettra Kazhagam
DNI	: Directorates of Naval Intelligence
DOD	: Department of Defense
DPA	: Development Partnership Administration
DRSCs	: Departmentally Related Standing Committees
DSP	: Deputy Superintendent of Police
E & SA	: East & Southern Africa (Division of MEA)
EA	: East Asia (Division of MEA)
EEZ	: Exclusive Economic Zones
EG & IT	: E-Governance & Information Technology
FICCI	: Federation of Indian Chambers of Commerce and Industry
FPDM	: Foreign Policy Decision Making
FSI	: Foreign Service Institute
FSO	: Foreign Service Officer
GBP	: Governmental Barging Model
GPM	: Governmental Politics Model
HNA	: Hsinhna News Agency
HRD	: Human Resource Development
MHRD	: Ministry of Human Resource Development
IAF	: Indian Air Force
IB	: Intelligence Bureau
ICJWGBQ	: China-India Joint Working Group on the Boundary Question
ICWA	: Indian Council of World Affairs
IDS	: Integrated Defence Staff
IDSA	: Institute of Defence Studies and Analysis
IFS	: Indian Foreign Service
IGOs	: International Governmental Organizations
INC	: Indian National Congress
INGOs	: International Non-Government Organizations

ITP	: Investment, Technology, Promotion
JD	: Janata Dal
JIC	: Joint Intelligence Committee
JWG	: Joint Working Group
KMT	: The Kuomintang (of China)
L & T	: Legal & Treaties
LAC	: Latin America & Caribbean
LAC	: Line of Actual Control
LoC	: Line of Control
LTTE	: Liberation Tigers of Tamil Eelam
MDMK	: Marumalarchi Dravida Munnetra Kazhagam
MEA	: Ministry of External Affairs
MER	: Multilateral Economic Relations
MHA	: Ministry of Home Affairs
MI	: Military Intelligence
MIB	: Ministry of Information and Broadcasting
MKP	: Mazdoor Kisan Party
MNCs	: Multi-National Companies
MNF	: Most Favoured Nation
MoD	: Ministry of Defence
MOIA	: Ministry of Oversees Indian Affairs
MoS	: Minister of State
MPs	: Member of Parliament
NAM	: Non Alignment Movement
NAM	: Non Alignment Movement
NDA	: National Democratic Alliance
NEFA	: North-East Frontier Agency
NGOs	: Non-Government Organization
NIA	: National Investigation Agency
NPT	: Non-Proliferation Treaty
NRIs	: Non-Resident Indians
NSA	: National Security Advisor
NSAB	: National Security Advisory Board
NSC	: National Security Council
NSPC	: National Security Planning Council

OBCs	: Other Backward Communities
OPM	: Organizational Process Model
OSD	: Officer on Special Duty
PACs	: Political Action Committees
PAI	: Pakistan, Afghanistan & Iran
PAK	: Pakistani Administrative Kashmir
PD	: Public Diplomacy
PIO	: People of Indian Origin
PM	: Prime Minister
PMO	: Prime Minister's Office
POTA	: Pervasion of Terrorism Act
PP & R	: Policy Planning & Research
PPC	: Policy Planning Council
PPRC	: Planning and Review Committee
PPRD	: Policy Planning and Research Division
PPS	: Policy Planning Section
PRC	: People's Republic of China
PSO	: Principal Staff Officer
PSP	: Praja Socialist Party
R&D	: Research and Development
RAM	: Rational Actor Model
RAW	: Research and Analysis Wing
RBI	: Reserve Bank of India
RTI	: Right to Information
SAARC	: South Asian Association for Regional Cooperation
SCD	: Standing Committee on Defence
SCEA	: Standing Committee of External Affairs
SCF	: Scheduled Caste Federation
SCG	: Strategic Core Group
SCs,	: Scheduled Caste
SKC	: Special Kuwait Cell
SP	: Samajwadi Party
SPG	: Strategic Planning Group
STs	: Scheduled Tribe
UDHR	: Universal Declaration of Human Rights

UGC	: University Grants Commission
UIA	: Union of International Associations
UN	: United Nations
UNES	: United Nations Economic & Social
UNP	: United Nations Political Division
UNSC	: United Nations Security Council
UPA	: United Progressive Alliance
US	: United State
USSR	: Union of Soviet Socialist Republics
VIP	: Very Important Person
WA	: Western Africa
WANA	: West Asia & North Africa
WMD	: Weapon of Mass Destruction
WTO	: World Trade Organization
XP	: External Publicity (Division of MEA)

Chapter - 1

Foreign Policy Decision Making: A Theoretical Analysis

In the modern world, no state can remain isolated from the global community. With the rise of globalization, the concept of statecraft has been reshaped and the interdependency between and among the nations has grown to a new height. The network is so visible that, an action and decision of one state is bound to affect the fate of another state. Even the domestic matters or instability of a particular state poses far reaching consequences for the entire region or even the whole world. Indeed, globalization and other forces of modernization, notably trans-boundary and global environmental changes, mean that more of what was once purely national is now the subject of Foreign Policy. Hence, each and every state should have an effective and vibrant Foreign Policy to manage the highly complex issues of modern statecraft.

Foreign Policy refers to the comprehensive and effective design of a state to deal with matter that is outstretched beyond its territorial borders. It is a complete plan to materialize the national objectives and multiply the national gain. Making this comprehensive plan or the policy is a complex process and usually, prepared by the top political leadership with the help of senior bureaucrats. The procedure of decision making as well as the policy out comes generally depends upon the working style of leadership, the structure of decision making unit as well as the nature of other internal and external factors. In an autocratic system, the decision making is generally a one act play where the supreme leader plays the decisive role, whereas in the democratic setup, the decision making is the sum of overall consensus. Hence, the decision outcome is apparently different from autocratic to democratic Foreign Policy. Hence it is essential to know how the Foreign Policy is formulated and what are the factors responsible for the successful and effective Foreign Policy?

In this regard, the present chapter attempts to answer the above questions by giving a comprehensive picture of the nature and structure of the Foreign Policy decision making process. The chapter is divided into two broad sections. The first part of the first section attempts to define the terms 'Foreign Policy' and 'Foreign Policy decision making. The second part of the first section analyses the composition and function of the decision making units in detail. The second section discusses various models and stages of Foreign Policy decision making along with its merits and demerits in detail. It also explains various factors that eventually determine the Foreign Policy decision making and its limitations. Hence, this chapter gives a theoretical foundation which is essential for the better understanding of the successive chapters on India's Foreign Policy decision making.

Conceptualizing Foreign Policy Decision Making

Cosmopolitanization of international relations has put a huge challenge in defining Foreign Policy as well as Foreign Policy decision making. Analyzing in general, Foreign Policy includes a range of activities and strategies under which a sovereign state interacts with other international players. But, the recent trend shows that Foreign Policy does not limit itself with state to state interaction but also deals with the non-state actors and international organizations. Therefore, it is essential to know what Foreign Policy is and what Foreign Policy Decision Making means. A careful study reveals that the meaning of the concepts varies from scholar to scholar. Here is an account of a brief discussion of the two debatable terms.

Defining Foreign Policy

Going by literal meaning, the word Foreign Policy can be divided into two different words- Foreign and Policy. The term 'Foreign' refers to things that exist beyond the territorial boundaries and 'policy' can be referred to as the guidelines and approaches to achieve the objectives. Therefore, Foreign Policy can be defined as the principles and guidelines to achieve the objectives existing outside the territorial border. But, the meaning of Foreign Policy in the modern time is not restricted to this simple definition and the concept is changing rapidly along with the world political environment. Thus, the modern concept of 'Foreign' is associated with deep and multidisciplinary approaches relatively different from scholar to scholar. Hence, the simple meaning of Foreign Policy can be summarized as the sum of a state's strategy to strengthen its national capacity, the approach to attain the national goal and the tools to deal with the other elements of the world. It is the desired state craft to avoid any conflict without compromising the national goal. In a narrow sense, 'Foreign Policy' is the official relationship between two states. Traditionally, Foreign Policy referred to the course of action taken by the government, more precisely by the Foreign Ministry to deal with foreign countries. But the rise of globalization has down played this argument where dealing with the outer world became more complex. The internalization of life took this issue beyond the matter of diplomat to diplomat interaction. As the fair answer to the question "What is Foreign Policy?" seems beyond the reasonable conclusion, a brief account of scholarly definitions might march ahead towards conceptualizing the term.

The first step in any investigation on 'Indian Foreign Policy' is to define the term Foreign Policy. But interestingly, being the centre of International Studies and the flash point of scholarly discussion for centuries, the term 'Foreign Policy' hardly has any unanimous definition. While one school of scholars blame for its wider scope and multidimensional characteristic, others are not ready to take the narrow approach to define it. According to Roy Jones "an attempt at an acceptable, and an accepted brief, definition of foreign policy would be to invite ridicule. The nature of foreign policy is not agreed, and one is tempted to believe that in political societies it never will be agreed".[1] Surprisingly, most of the literature on Foreign Policy didn't even attempt to define it, before debating on the issues of Foreign Policy. Perhaps due to this systematic ignorance, Charles Hermann called Foreign Policy as the "neglected concept". Going further, he asserts that, "This neglect has been the most serious obstacle to provide more adequate and comprehensive explanations of Foreign Policy." According to Hermann, the reason for this neglect is that "most people dealing with the subject have felt confident that they know what Foreign Policy was"[2], hence, feel unnecessary to define it. He believes that most of the people argued that, "we know it when we see it".[3] However, unlike other concepts of International Relations, Foreign Policy does not confine to one meaning but comprises of range of terms and activities. Based on individual perceptions, it sounds different to different people. Perhaps this is why many, if not most, Foreign Policy studies don't even attempt to define the term. However, a careful search will reveal that there are dozens of different definitions available, out of which some of the definitions have been critically discussed below.

Foreign Policy is a multidimensional concept that lies into the various corners of the state craft and bears different meaning for different people. For some it is the official and state to state relation, both between and among the nations, while others focus on therole of non-state actors and non-human factors too in definingForeign Policy. Similarly, one school defines Foreign Policy as the product of internal discourse, other takes as the result of international environment.

Literally, the word Foreign Policy is comprised of two individual words, foreign and policy. The word 'Foreign' came from the Latin word "*foris*" and "*foras*" meaning "outside"[4] and the word 'Policy' originated from the Old French word "*policie*" meaning 'civil administration'[5]. Therefore, the literal meaning of the phrase 'Foreign Policy'is the administration of the outside activities or strategy to manage of the issues that exist beyond territorial boundaries of a state. According to the Oxford Dictionary, Foreign Policy is "a government's strategy in dealing with other nations."[6] Putting it more comprehensive, Encyclopaedia of Britannica defines Foreign Policy, as the "General objectives that guide the activities and relationships of one state in its interactions with other states." It further explains that "The development of Foreign Policy is influenced by domestic considerations, the policies or behaviour of other states, or plans to advance specific geopolitical designs".[7]

In their path breaking classical work, "*American Policy: Pattern and Process*" Kegley and Wittkopf defined Foreign Policy as "the goals that the nation's officials seek to attain abroad, the values that give rise to those objectives, and the means or instruments through which they are pursued."[8] The definition while giving the comprehensive definition of defining Foreign Policy in terms of three concepts – the goals, values, and instruments, it limits Foreign Policy behaviour only to the activities of the state. Stretching the definition longer Robert Jackson and Georg Sorensen observesthat "Foreign Policy involves goals, strategies, measures, methods, guidelines, directives, understandings, agreements and so on, by which national governments conduct international relations with each other and with international organizations and non-governmental actors."[9] In the "*Changing Politics of Foreign Policy*", Christopher Hillhas given a comprehensive account of Foreign Policy.By putting it short,he wrote "a brief definition of Foreign Policy can be given as follows: the sum of official external relations conducted by an independent actor (usually a state) in international relations."[10] Similarly, for Thompson and Macridis "Foreign Policy refers to the way in which policy –making institutions and official actors "define their positions and that of their states vis-à-vis outside .... world over a period of time." [11] According to Joyce P. Kaufman "Foreign Policy refers to those decisions made within a country that are affected by and that in turn affect entities outside the country."[12]

Summarizing the above definitions it is clear that most of the scholars limited the definition of Foreign Policy to the official relation between the states and recognize the state as the only actor in the Foreign Policy decision making. But in the 21st century, non-state actors such as MNCs, INGOs as well as other international and ultra-national organizations are also playing active role in shaping foreign policies of the states and influence their international politics in many ways. For example, the 9/11 terrorist attack or the rise of LTTE has definitely been the major factor in reshaping the behaviour of the statecraft of America and Sri Lanka respectively. Similarly, the secessionist movements of Kashmir, North-eastern states as well as the Punjab have been the prime factors in determining the Foreign Policy of India for years. Even disproving the standing definitions, the United States has started negotiating with the non-state actors, the Taliban leaders for the settlement of Afghanistan issue. Besides non-state actors, and non-human factors such as earthquake, Tsunami or prolonged famine also are considered as the major determinants of Foreign Policy of a nation. *Amnesty International* for example, has been constantly perusing, directing and criticizing the nation states over any human rights violation by the respective states. Similarly, during the outbreak of Tsunami in the South and Southeast Asian nations in 2004, the whole world came forward in reconstruction process. Addressing these conceptual gaps, George Modelski defines "Foreign Policy is the system of activities evolved by communities for changing the behaviour of other states and for adjusting their own activities to the international environment."[13] Here the activities are not limited to the state, but address the whole community including various organizations or groups. James N. Rosenau views Foreign Policy as an adaptive behaviour and is contended that it "consists of all the attitudes and activities through which organized national societies seek to cope with and benefit from their international environment.[14] According to Walter Carlsnaes "Foreign policies consist of those actions which, expressed in the form of explicitly stated goals, commitments and/or directives, and pursued by governmental representatives acting on behalf of their sovereign communities, are directed towards objects, conditions and actors-both governmental and non-governmental – which they want to affect which lie beyond their territorial legitimacy."[15] Similarly, Hill limits the Foreign Policy to the official relation between the states. As the modern life has become more internationalized where relations cannot be limited to the state, Foreign Policy definitely goes beyond from diplomat to diplomat iteration. Non-official relations also play a vital role in shaping the state behaviour with others.

While national goal largely has been the focal point in defining Foreign Policy, scholars like Gibson, Padelford and Lincoln mostly stress upon the approaches to attain these goal. Highlighting the means Hugh Gibsondefines Foreign Policy as "a well-rounded, comprehensive plan, based on knowledge and experience, for conducting the business of government with the rest of the world. It is aimed at promoting and protecting the interests of the nations. This calls for a clear understanding of what those interests are and howfarwe can hopeto grow the means at our disposal. Anything lessthanthis falls short of being a national Foreign Policy."[16] Similarly, according to Padelford and Lincoln" "Foreign Policy is the key element in the process by which a state translates its broadly conceived goals and interests into concrete courses of action and to attain these objects and preserve its interests." In other words, Foreign Policy involves both a formulation as well as the approach to achieve the objectives. Cecil V. Crabb offers a simple yet very effective definition of Foreign Policy. For him, "reduced to its most fundamental ingredients, Foreign Policy consists of two elements: national objectives to be achieved, and means for achieving them."[17] Though the scholars differ in the goal andthe means, both are integral parts of Foreign Policy and carry equal importance.

The main objective of the Foreign Policy is to maximize the national interest, to maintain the state sovereignty and defend its border by enhancing its capacity.Highlighting the importance of national capacity, Hazel Smith defines Foreign Policy "as the capacity to make and implement policies abroad which promote the domestic values, interests and policies of the actor in question".[18] For F.S. Northedge Foreign Policy is the "use of political influences in order to induce other states to exercise their law making power in a manner desired by the state concerned; it is an interaction between forces originating outside the country's borders and those working within them."[19] In a different language, Norman Hill defines Foreign Policy, "as the substance of nation's efforts to promote its interests *vis-à-vis* other nations." To put it in a sentence the ultimate aim of Foreign Policyis to promote national interest and influence other's decision outcomes according to the desire of the state. However, Harmann's definition stresses upon the state's action when he defines Foreign Policy as "the discreet purposeful action that results from the political level decision of an individual or group of individuals..... (it is) the observable artefact of a political level decision. It is not the decision, but a product of the decision."[20]

Although, managing external relations is the salient feature in defining Foreign Policy, some of the present studies highlight that domestic environment also plays a significant role in determining the Foreign Policyof a state. Hence, the significance of the internal and external factors has been the centre of debate for years. While one section stresses upon internal structure such as internal leadership, domestic political setups and nature of decision making environment, others highlight the importance of international environment and world political order. For James D. Fear on the Foreign Policy is "just the domestic politics of foreign countries, or the product of their domestic politics". Similarly, Fearon describes Foreign Policy as an outcome of domestic politics and states that "some non-unitary states are choosing suboptimal foreign policies due to domestic-political interactions."[21] Carlsnaes in his earlier definition also highlights the importance of inputs of Foreign Policy and not outcomes and believes that, Foreign Policy is the product of internal political discourse.However, some balanced views havebeen emerged in recent times putting equal emphasis on bothdomestic factors and external environment. Howard Lenther for instance, believes that "Foreign Policy lies at the intersection of the domestic and international aspects of a country's life" [22] Similarly, according to Joseph Frankel "decisions taken on Foreign Policy differ from those in other fields in that they are subject to a unique interplay between domestic and foreign environments. The persons involved usually occupycertain official positions of trust and importance empowering them to act on behalf of their society in its external relations."[23] Therefore it can be stated that, for an effective Foreign Policy both internal setups and external environment play equal role in the decision making process. The decision maker has to consider the internal limitations and external compulsions while making policies.

As observed by Christopher Hill, "defining political activities are notoriously difficult and Foreign Policyhas no exception". [24] The rise of globalization and the internationalization of society push the globe into a boundary less phenomena where an attempt for segregation of aconcept such as Foreign Policy is considered as a matter of joke. Putting it orderly, Roy Jones's writes "An attempt at an acceptable, and an acceptably brief, definition of Foreign Policy would be to invite ridicule. The nature of Foreign Policy is not agreed, and one is tempted to believe that in political societies it never will be agreed."[25] Again, diverting the traditional single window concept of Foreign Policy where Ministry of External Affairs was the only active branch of government, the subject of external relation is now taken care by the various ministries. In other words the monopoly of the MEA is no more visible. This present development pushes that problem of defining Foreign Policy onto another level.

Defining Foreign Policy Decision Making

In the highly hostile international environment, it is the behaviour of a certain country which determines its fate. A single wrong move may cost heavily even to the survival of a country. Hence, an appropriate decision during the time of crisis is highly needed to guide the course of action of a state for the attainment of national interests and to deal with important international entities. Though the Foreign Policy outcomes channelize the relation of a country with other powers, it is the decision making structure which identifies the problems, explores the alternatives and takes the final call to defuse the outstanding issues. Therefore Foreign Policy Decision Making is the key to avoid the consequences and realize national interests. But interestingly, it is only in the 1970s a systematic study on the structure and function of decision making process has emerged as a new discipline, though the issues related to Foreign Policy have been the focal point of discussion for years. As a result very limited works have been attempted to define Foreign Policy decision making systematically and the concept remains far from the overall understanding of the mass. Therefore, a brief discussion to define Foreign Policy Decision Making will be appropriate, before going to discuss the issues on Foreign Policy decision making.

Foreign Policy decision making is the process by which government analyzes the existing problems, evaluate the policy alternatives and take appropriate actions to overcome the outstanding issuesas well as for the maximization of the national gain. Putting it simple, FPDM explains why the government takes such an action, how the decision is going to work out and what could be the possible alternatives and its consequences. Hence, it largely attempts to investigate the structure, approach and process of decision making rather than the policy outcomes. In decision making the ultimate aim of the actorsis to minimize the loss, multiply the benefits and resolve the problems. FPDM is an investigation to find out the alternative way to cope with international system, to avoid the conflict, to promote the national influence and to live peacefully. It is a complex process to find out the best alternatives, by various means and approaches.

Before we go on to examine the problems in detail, it isessential to define Foreign Policy decision making for the better understanding of the discipline. The word "decision "comes from the Latin root *"de"*, meaning "from", and "*caedere*" meaning "to cut". Hence, Decision in its root "*caedere*", meaning "to cut from" and making decision means to come to a conclusion or cutting yourself off from any other possibilities.[26] In simple term, decision making refers to the process to identify the problems, explore possible alternatives and to select the appropriate strategy to resolve those issues. Often 'decision making'is described as the synonym of 'making choices'. But for MacKenzie "the word does not quite coincide in modern use". He argues that the decision is a 'real choice' to meet the end as well as the approaches to attain the end. To put it simple, decision consists of the cumulative sequence of stages of choices rather than one choice to arrive into a conclusion. [27] Koontz and O'Donnel, the well-known scholars of management, the principal branch of decision making define decision making as "the actual selection from among alternatives of a course of action" [28] Whereas for George R. Terry, "decision-making is the selection based on some criteria from two or more possible alternatives." Similarly, Louis A. Allen, states that "decision making is the work which a manager performs to arrive at a conclusion and judgment."[29] According to Baumann and Deber "decision making can be defined as the situation in which a choice is made among a number of possible alternatives often involving a tradeoff among the values given to different outcomes." [30] The father of Political Science Aristotle in his classic work 'Nicomachean Ethics' defines the decision making process as a *Deliberate Appetition*, "which is a logical and psychological sequence that starts with desire, continues with violation and concludes with the act of choice."[31] Defining decision making, Mauro Maldonato writes that "Making a decision ...... means deciding which course of action to follow, among those that are possible...to maximize the expected value that is to choose the alternatives associated with the highest expected values". Further he added "The decision making process carries out a complex calculation which would include the collection of a large amount of information and of an enormous quantity of formulations for its processing."[32] In the words of Roth and Mullen "decision makingis a technique thatis designed to help arrive at the best possible choice that satisfies that higher order values and goals that have been selected".[33] Seckler-Hudson, believes that "Decision making in a government is a plural activity. One individual may pronounce the decision, but may contribute to the process of reaching the decision. It is part of the political system."[34] Summarizing the above definitions one can agree that, decision making is a process to choose the best out of the rest by analyzing the cost and consequences.In the decision making process decision makers enter into a complex process to find out some constructive conclusion. Decision making is not a one time business. It is a continuous affair to defend the previous decisions and to take supplement decisions based on the feedbacks.

From the earlier discussions on defining Foreign Policy and the subsequent analysis on decision making one can synthesize what Foreign

Policy decision making is? To put it simple, Foreign Policy decision making is the a malgamation of two different concepts 'Foreign Policy' meaning the external behaviour of a country; and'decision making'meaning choosing the right options. Therefore,Foreign Policy decision making can be referred to as the sum total of a governmental decision to guide its national interests. In other wordsForeign Policy decision making is the process to reach a conclusive approach to address the outstanding Foreign Policy complexity. In the words of Mintz and DeRouen "Foreign Policy Decision Making (FPDM) refers to the choices individuals, groups and coalitions make that affect a nation's actions on the international stage". Further he added that it is the study to understand what goes into decision that presages the activities and events. [35] Similarly, Goldstein and John Pevehouse define "(Foreign Policy) Decision making is a steering process in which adjustments are made as per the feedback from the outside world. Decisions are carried out by actions taken to change the world, and then information from the world is mentioned to evaluate the effects of these actions."[36] According to Janice Gross Stein"the Foreign Policy process is a process of decision making. States take actions because people in governments—decision makers—choose those actions".[37] Policy-making has been defined as the process by which governments translate their political vision into programmes and actions to deliver 'outcomes' – desired change in the real world.[38]

According to B. Raman "Decision-making in Foreign Policy involves the analysis and assessment of past and current data, in the light of our past experience and that of others, who had dealt with similar situations, in order to identify the need and available options for action in the future and the likely implications of each of those options for the protection and promotion of our national interests."[39] From the above definitions, it can be analyzed that Foreign Policy decision making is the process of searching the best alternative costs and consequences and choosing the best course of action to take.

Though there are multiple agencies involved in the decision making process, it is the leadership who takes the ultimate decision by examining the cost of available alternatives. As the leadership is the backbone of the policy decision, their course of action and behaviour should be close to reality. The crises management experience, capacity to study the phenomena, indefatigable attitude during difficult times, and more importantly the cognitive potentiality of the principal players of the decision making body largely shape the Foreign Policy outcomes of a country and rearrange the global political settings at large. The decision makers must have the ability to deal with and manage any uncertain development. The decision maker is constantly facing uncertainty of deciding on a course of action, knowing that the consequences associated with the selection of any given act depend up on future conditions and events, the outcomes of which are unknown at the time the decision is taken.

Models of Foreign Policy Decision Making

Decision making is a complex and ever changing process. The nature of decision outcome mostly depends upon varieties of internal and external factors, such as the leadership, the structure of decision making unit, the decision making environment etc. Interestingly, one cannot predict the similar decision out of the same decision making bodies as the surrounding environment changes time to time. In order to understand the complexity, Allision has divided the decision making style into three different models, based on the structure and functionof decision making unit. These are The Rational Actor Model (RAM), Organizational Process Model (OPM) and Bureaucratic Politics Model (BPM).

The Rational Actor Model (RAM)

Rational Actor refers to the leader who takes decision the way it should have been taken without any bias or influence. Rationality has been considered as the best way to solve the outstanding issues. It is the behavioural attitude having its very purpose. In defining rationality, Allison Grahamwrites "Rationality refers to consistent value-maximizing choice within special fiend constraints".[40] Hence, rational actor model of decision making is the process to choose the right options to achieve 'national goal' by analyzing all possible alternatives and its consequences. Rational decision making is the ability to relate means to ends.[41] The leadership under this model is open to receive new inputs. After a thorough analysis of the input information, the decision maker chooses the option that gives the highest payoff. In the words of Janice Gross Stein "Rational decision-making refers to the process that people should use to choose. In a rational decision-making process, people should be logical and orderly".[42]

Rationality is a complex phenomenon to define. There is no such standard procedure called as the rational decision making, rather it is different from person to person, situation to situation and organization to organization. The process of calculating the cost and choosing the appropriate decision is a complex task. Based on the cognitive capacity and access to information, the decision outcome might differ person to person. Therefore rational decision for one leader will not be considered rational for the other. The decision making should be logical and unbiased, without any fear or favour.

Element of Decision Making in RAM

As the maximization of national goal is the ultimate aim of the decision makers, the process of decision making involves various stages and elements. Graham Allison in his classical work *"Essence of Decision"* has discussed various stages of decision making of the rational actor model.

The Rational Actor Model is a kind of ideal approach of decision making whereas in many cases decision making has been seen as a highly politicized affair. Highly influenced by the discipline of Micro Economics, the actor under this model behaves in a mechanized way for the value maximization. The Rational Actor Model, like a chess board game always aims to acquire the optimum benefit with minimum cost. Once the assignment is stimulated into the model, the leader carefully studies the problem besides evaluating the options and related consequences. After the complex calculation of gain and involved cost, the decision maker selects the most reliable options having maximum benefit.

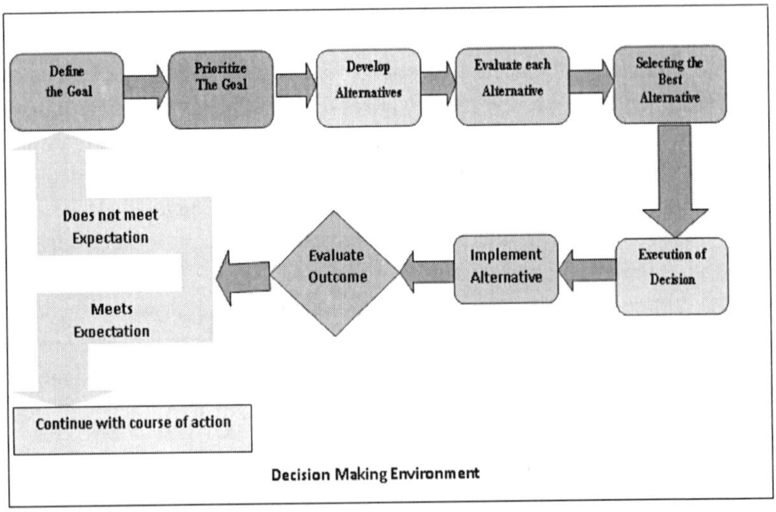

Figure - Rational Actor Model of Decision Making.

Features of Rational Actor Decision Making Model

The Rational Actor Model is the most logical form of decision making which aims to achieve the optimum benefits by choosing the alternative policies. Apart from the logical preferences, the Rational Actor Model of decision making has various other features, which are discussed below.

Open for New Information and Evidence

Under the Rational Actor Model state is the only player, hence there is hardly any room for the non-state actors or interest groups. Therefore, under this single window mechanism, the Decision Maker is heavily provided with flow of information, be it from advisors or any other reliable sources. But the leader under the model is not bound to go along with advises or input of information. The Decision maker under the RAM enjoys full freedom to go with his own cognitive interpretation sensuring maximum benefit for the nation. For good effective decision the information that has been collected should be taken from reliable sources and if possible tested before relayed to ensure bias free.[43]

Open for Discussion and Believe in Transparency

Rational actor model allows the participants to discuss the causes and consequences of the each available option in the decision making process. The decision maker also tries to acquire more and detail information by initiating discussion. Except the dictatorial regimes, most of the policy making mechanisms are practicing greater debate before coming to a conclusion, though the decision of the leader is considered supreme and absolute.

Logical and Based on Circumventive Evidence

As the RAM believes in rationality and selection of options purely based on merit and probability, it is believed to be the fairest mechanism. Hence, the decision making under this model mostly depends on circumventive evidence and reliable information.

State is the only Actor and Ignores Non-state Actors

In the rational actor model of decision making, state is the supreme and perhaps the only actor in the decision making process. The decision making also follows the standard structural model of resolving the policy obstacle. There is no place for emotions and self-assumptions in this process. Similarly, there is no place for non-state actors like NGOs, IGOs, Pressure or Interest Groups, terror organizations or other such organizations, as it goes against the very spirit of the rationality by creating space for influencing the policy decision.

No Place for Values and Notions

The first and foremost feature of Rational Actor Model is that it is purely based on the rational choice of available alternatives without any presumptions or emotion. In this model the decision maker takes decision opting for maximum benefit and the decision is purely based on merit. The decision making according to this model should be free from values, notions, emotions for the proper decision.

Believes in Maximization of Goal

The Rational Actor Model is based on the decision structure, where the appropriate decisions are taken over other alternatives according to its merit. Under this model, the decision maker chooses the best alternative option to maximize the national gain at the cost of minimum loss. As the decision maker under the RAM is free from all kinds of values and emotions, he often seems aggressive while making a decision. Similarly, to promote its only motto "the maximization of state interest" it does not believe in the give and take approach, rather aims for optimum benefit.

Believes in Interstate Business

As we have discussed, the rational decision making model does not take into account the concerns of the pressure groups or other likely organizations but recognizes state as the only player in the decision making process and, its engagement always limits to the state level institutions only. But in the modern world it seems to be far from reality. The American Administration for example, is now talking to the *Al-Qaeda* to resolve the Afghanistan blunder.

Free From Serious Blinkers

Always the decision making process under the RAM follows some standard and structural procedure and seems quite similar in its decision making process. This model heavily depends upon the prescribed seven step process, to come to the conclusion. Therefore there is no scope of unexpected turn as seen in the other models of decision making to satisfy the pressure groups or sympathize over the public opinion.

The Limitations of Rational Actor Decision Making Model

1. This model ignores the importance of the individuals involved in decision making as individuals are grownup with their own

beliefs, values, emotions, perceptions, ideologies and host of other traits which might affect their decisions. [44]

2. As the information is the key to decision outcomes, there is a possibility that the leader may not evaluate the situation correctly and may be misinformed and may choose the inappropriate policy which may hinder the national goal. Further, the leader or the advisor may tend to block out information that does not agree with what they have already believed to be accurate. President Bush, for example gave misinformation about the possible development of WMD by Iraq, which proved false after the war. Here the US government gained nothing rather than losing thousands of forces in war and made Muslim World as its enemy.[45]
3. Sometimes emotion plays an important role in making the country great. After the First World War Germany grew to a height with the help of the national emotion or in other words patronizing "nationalism". The RAM sprightly ignores the emotion and takes decision which is highly logical, which may lose the plot to radicalize the national gain.[46]
4. Often the state faces multiple problems and in the globalized world the decision making bodies are often pushed to deal with multiple and highly complicated issues at the same time. As a result the decision maker may not found enough time to study the problem and after all to calculate the available options to select for. Therefore the pressure of the overloaded issues often limits him to choose the right option because of inadequate analysis of alternatives.
5. In Rational decision making model the leader often takes decision based on the well laid principles and the decision usually seems rigid, stable and satisfactory rather than optimized one. In this model, the decision maker does not take risk to multiply the gain and does not stimulate his enthuse for the greater benefit of the nation. Therefore the pace of development remains comparatively slow.
6. Foreign Policy decision making is a two level game. Along with the international environment, the domestic politics is also considered as an important factor while making policies on external relation. But, in Rational Actor Model this domestic aspect is widely neglected.

The rational Actor Model is one of the most effective decision making models of Allison crisis management theory. Due to its logical policy preference, it opts for the appropriate policy to deal with any issue. There are some other theories, such as the Game theory, the Prospect theory and the Poliheuristic theory, which also advocate the rationality in decision making, the basic ethos of the Rational Actor Model. However, some rational actor literatures state that, decision makers including the central decision makers do not have complete freedom of action and they are not in full control of their rationality.[47] While making decision, the decision makers need to consider the other hindering factors and modify their choices accordingly. In due process, they are often forced to abandon the preferred and most effective alternative and end up with their least preferred outcome even though they choose rationally at every step along the way.

The Organization Process Model (OPM)

Decision making in the modern globalized world is not as simple as it was in the past. The emerging issues are so complex that the political leadership on its own can hardly do justice while making polices to address these issues. In this regard, there is a need of an efficient and multidimensional organization to take appropriate decisions. To overcome this problem, Graham Allison offered two more different models of decision making, such as the Organizational Process Model and the Bureaucratic Politics Model, where multiple actors and agencies work together in making policies.

According to Allison's Organizational Process Model, the policy decisions are not the result of rationality but the outcome of a large organizational discourse, which is continuously involved in formulating policies within a 'standard operating procedure'. The government, according to Greg Cashman, is a "conglomerate of large autonomous semi-feudal, loosely allied organizations".[48] Hence, the decision making in government involves large number of inter-branch organizations that are linked with each other and function under a well laid procedure of operandi. The Organizational Process Model, according to Holis and Smithis a top-down approach where the agencies usually function as per the demand of the government or the top leadership and vice versa.[49]

Decision Making Under the OPM

Allison's second model of the organizational process model has been drawn from the organizational theories. Under this model, the whole structure of decision making has been divided into several sub-agencies that are eventually arranged as the top down approach and the leader dismantles the whole problem and assignsthesub part among the small specialized agencies. The concerned authority of that particular section has to resolve the given task within the stipulated time frame. Considering the limitations of time and resource during the time of crisis, leaders often settle on the first alternative to address the issue, rather than exploring the best. Due to the sequential goal preference, the problem of control and coordination of various stake holders and the fixed ground rules (standard operating procedure) of the decision making units, the outcome often seems "satisfying"[50] rather than rational. The Organizational Process approach is highly beneficial during the time of war or war like crisis where the leader has to take decisions quickly with limited information. The organizational process model is based on the shared responsibility and shared organizational goals and procedure. The Leaders usually gravitate towards the solutions that limit short-term uncertainty.

Table 2. Organizational Process Model of Decision Making

Basic Features	Value	Shared Responsibility for organizational goal
	Alternatives	Generated based on professional efficiency and interest of percipients
	Premises	Group Consensus Mutual Respect Ample Time
Component	Key Players	Professionals
	Organizational Structure	Shared Governance
	Goals	Organizational, support through shared responsibility
	Information	Diverse, Specialized
	Timing	Lengthy
Process	Decision	Support General Welfare
	Implementation	By Effected Individuals with Wide Spread Commitment
	Result	Smooth Organizational Change
	Feedback	Through Participant Observation and Priorities

Adapted from EE Chaffe, *Rational Decision Making in Higher Education* (Boulder, CO: National Centre for Higher Education Management Systems, 1983) 17

Features of OPM

Greg Cashman has given in brief the features of Organizational Process Model, as follows:

- Under this model, the decision outcome mostly remains Satisfying, rather than optimal.
- The Organizational Process Model always believes in incrementalism. Hence, it is a positive and gradual process.
- This model of decision making is very rigid and lacks flexibility in decision making.
- Decision making under this model is carried out by qualified and experienced professionals and specialized organizations, rather than a small group of top level leadership.
- Organizational process model undertakes sequential search of alternatives and often settles on the first options, rather than choosing the best.[51]

Limits of OPM

Allison's Organizational Process Model has revolutionized the theory of decision making in many ways. Influenced by the management theory, Alison advocated the Organizational Process Model which consists of multiple agencies and institutions, rather than a single unit. Despite the ground breaking contribution to the decision making approach the organizational process model also is not far from criticism like any other model and has some of its own limitations. Some of the limitations of organizational process model have beendiscussed below:

1. The decision outcome in the OPM is shaped by perception and interest of the participants and therefore the policy is far from reasonable and effective.
2. As the ability of the individual of the decision making process is regulated, controlled and managed by the standard operating procedure, there is hardly any scope for flexibility, hence the outcomes are often satisfying rather than maximizing the benefits.
3. Each subunit or the department of the organization bears different rank of objectives and provides different value of means to achieve those objectives compared to other subunits. Therefore their setup of the objectives as per the organizational objective to solve the problem may not be same.[52]
4. The Foreign Policy problem is distributed among the various departments of the organization and subsequently the departments

divide the task among further micro units working under the department. As the different units deal with different tasksand different objectivities the coordination is the key for worthy outcome. If the coordination and communication fail, the outcome will definitely suffer. Similarly, the leaders and employers do not take time to examine all the linkages between their functional units and others in the organization.

5. Throughout the process the behaviour of the organization is monitored, controlled and managed by ground laws, i.e. standard operating procedure, and the activities of the individual are accountable to the higher authority as well as to the organization. Therefore the individuals play a safe game rather than taking risk for greater benefit. Hence the decision remains satisfied.

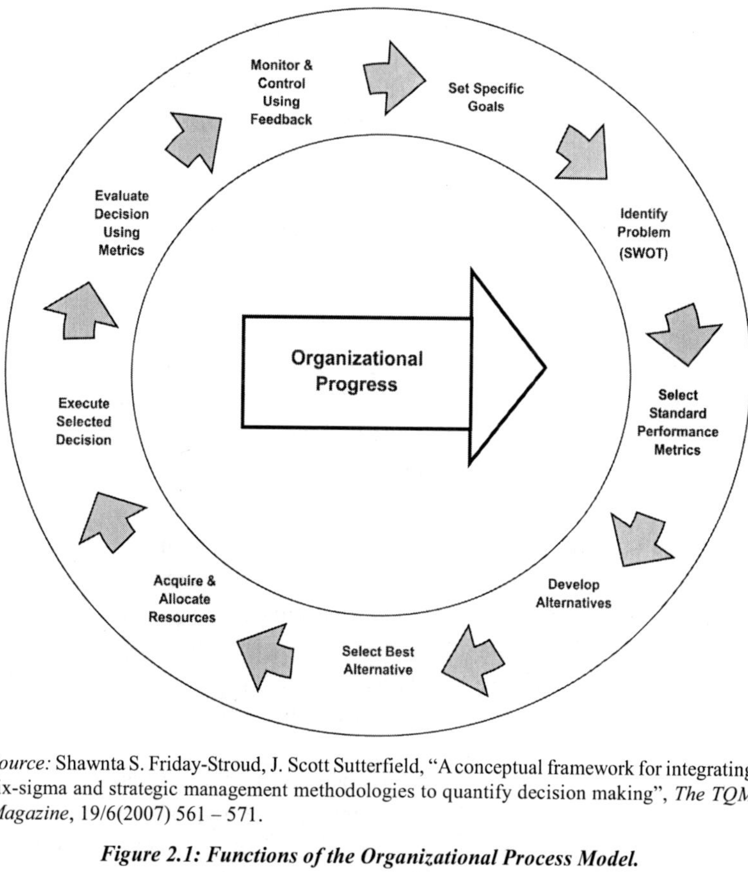

Source: Shawnta S. Friday-Stroud, J. Scott Sutterfield, "A conceptual framework for integrating six-sigma and strategic management methodologies to quantify decision making", *The TQM Magazine*, 19/6(2007) 561 – 571.

Figure 2.1: Functions of the Organizational Process Model.

6. The organization has its own style of operation and bears its organizational ideology. Hence, the leadership by default is often hijacked by the organizational ideology and constrained by the limitation of the organization.[53]

Bureaucratic Politics Model

The Bureaucratic Politics Model, which is also known as the Governmental Politics Model (GPM) or the Governmental Barging Model (GBP) is the third decision making model of Allison. According to this model, the decision outcome is a product of bureaucratic interactions and elite politics, rather than the result of rational thinking or organizational discourse. As highlighted in the "*The Essence of Decision*", the BPM believes that policy decision in general is the product of political bargaining of bureaucrats and government officials. The actors in this model are the bureaucrats and other elite leadership of the government, who selfishly engage in bargaining with the government to maximize their organizational interest using various bureaucratic channels. Under the BPM, the decisions are taken by "pulling and hauling" rather than rational choice.

Bureaucracy in Decision Making

The term bureaucracy is derived from the French word "Bureau" meaning "desk". Therefore, the literal meaning of bureaucracy may be put as "rule by desks or offices" or "desk government" as termed by Finer.[54] Looking at the size and complexity, the administration in a modern state has to be assisted by large paraphernalia of officers and subordinates. One cannot think of a modern state without adequate bureaucrats, who lead various departments of the Government and assist the Government to achieve the national goals. They also support the political leadership in making polices for the optimization of departmental objectives.

According to Alison's third model the government is not a single calculating unit, it is a blend of various organizations and individuals such as the administrators, bureaucrats and subordinates. Bureaucrats, being the important part of government are not only assisting the government, but also advising the government in policy formulation. But in popular political discourse bureaucracy and bureaucratic polices have been perceived as negative acts.[55] This argument seems more convincing when it comes to Foreign Policy decision making. Bureaucrats, who hold various significant positions, are competing with each other to present their own interest and to optimize their organizational or departmental goal. They are the key advisors to the political boss in the formulation of external policies, hence got strong source to influence the policy that suit their departmental objectives. In India for example, there are 43 Ministries and dozens of departments and divisions, which are headed by thousands of bureaucrats. Out of which, Ministry of External Affairs, Ministry of Defence, Ministry of Industry and Commerce, Ministry of Finance as well as National Security Council plays a significant role in India's Foreign Policy decision making mechanism. Each of the ministries has its own defined interests, goals, approaches and objectivities. All the departments of the government want to achieve "more missions, greater autonomy from outside interference, greater influence within the government, greater capabilities, resources, and personnel and after all a larger budget allocation".[56]

The ultimate aim of all such departments and ministries is to dominate and maintain supremacy in the administrative setups. The individuals representing various ministries and departments are having different responsibilities, resources, and sources of information and grown up with different perceptions, follow different code of operation, see one particular issue from different angles and have different stakes in policy outcome; hence their attitudes and objectives are different from each other. Similarly, being involved in the respective departments the bureaucrats inherit the organizational ideology into to their own and assume most of the matters through organizational perspective. Therefore bureaucratic agencies seem parochial in terms of objectives, attitudes and approaches. Every administrative unit tries to secure its own interest (some time their own personal interest and not necessarily organizational interest) and calculate the organizational affects (lose or gain) vis-à-vis central decision outcomes.[57]

In BPM, association of bureaucrats in decision making process is much larger than assisting and advising the supreme political boss. The bureaucrats often try to influence the decision for the sake of their departmental benefit or even for their own personal gain. As the resources are limited, each organization wants to win over the other. As a result they compete, quarrel and fight with each other to multiply their stake and to maintain supremacy over others at the time of decision making. According to Greg Cashman, the reasons for the parochialism are mostly related to their organizational sociological behaviour. Cashman believes that, all the leaders of a particular organization pose similar set of mindset, values, ideologies, objectives and approaches because they choose the organization which suits their personality or the organization selects the suitable person who can complement the departmental ideologies. If at all one's personality does not match the organizational ideologies, he or she is automatically moulded in due course of time in accordance with the organizational desire by the process of "Institutional Socialization". Therefore proliferation of organizational interest automatically becomes the ultimate aim of the individual.[58]

Core Propositions of BPM

The Bureaucratic Politics Model as projected in Graham Allison's "Essence of Decision", Morton Helper in's "*Bureaucratic Politics and Foreign Policy*"[59] and their collaborative work the *"Bureaucratic Politics"*[60] is a complex set of organizational decision process making where all the stake holders (Mainly office bearers and bureaucrats) fight among themselves to prevail their organizational interests. While Allison proposed eight different models for the Bureaucratic Politics Model [61], Professor Rosati highlighted only four Propositions.[62] However, some of the scholars of this area [63] have only outlined three core models, namely 'stand-sit proposition' which focuses on Policy preferences for decision, 'Bargaining Proposition' which discusses actors' behaviour during the decision-making processes and the 'Resultant Proposition' which refers to Decisions that are eventually adopted. Each of the propositions has been discussed in greater length below:

Stand-sit Proposition and the Miles' Law

Mostly influenced by the old adage "where you stand depends on where you sit" the first proposition of Bureaucratic Politics Model assumes that the behaviour of the decision maker also can be influenced by the organization he works.As discussed elsewhere, the institutional socialization has moulded the personal choices of bureaucrats and his policy preference. As a result, the primary objective of the bureaucrats is to pursue and realize the interests of their organization. On their own words Allison and Zelikow summarize "Where one stands is influenced, most often influenced strongly, by where one sits. Knowledge of the organizational seat at the table yields significant clues about a likely stand".[64] The bureaucrats are not the only actors who influence decision making, there are other such actors also seen involved in the competition. They come, as Allison and Zelikow writes "with baggage in tow. The bags include sensitivities to certain issues, commitments to various projects, and personal standing with and debts to groups in society… Peculiarities of human beings remain an irreducible part of the mix".[65] The stand-sit proposition highlights the ideological rigidity of the decision making actors where he cannot see beyond the selfish organizational interest. Therefore the old aphorism can be modified and put as "where you stand depends on what you see from where you sit".[66]

Bargaining Proposition

The second and most important proposition of the BPM is the Bargaining Proposition. It is the centre of the bureaucratic influences on decision making mechanism. By the name itself one can assume that it represents the politics of bargaining in the governmental decision making bodies to protest and promote its organizational interest. The bureaucrats and other stake holders compete and fight among themselves to defend the organizational goal, objective and position. They seek to maintain and even escalate their influences to 'realize the organization's mission, and to safeguard the organization's capabilities to pursue its mission'.[67] Due to the limited resources, the politics of bargaining has often intensified to grab the maximum share of the benefit. More than the resources hunting, the stake holders often engage in 'pulling and hauling'[68] for the power and position for their personal and organization gain.[69]

According to the Bargaining Proposition, the bureaucrats not just try to influence the policy making process, they also keep a close watch at the implementation level and make sure that, it complements their departmental objectives. However, the extensive use of bargaining politics often endangers the national interest. As everyone engages in bargaining, no concrete decision is possible due to their selfish bargain. Hence, they often go for mutual compromise and the policy decision often ends with mutual consensus, rather than rational.

Resultant Proposition

The third and last proposition of bureaucratic politics model is the resultant proposition. This proposition mostly attempts to study 'how the decision is adopted and under what circumstances'. According to the proposition, the policy decisions are the product of unintended compromise, though all the stake holders of the decision making engage in apprehensive competition to influence the policy outcome into their favour. Based on their official position and power structure the bureaucrats eventually settle into mutually acceptable policies. Hence, for Allison and Zelikow, the policy outcome is not the product of rational choices, rather the result of 'compromise, conflict, and confusion of officials with diverse interests and unequal influence'.[70] However it is a matter of notice that, the result of the long bureaucratic fight seventually end with nothing more than mutual consensus and compromise.

Limits of BPM

Allison's third model, the Bureaucratic Politics Model has been a new and interesting approach to investigate the Decision Making Analysis. Being a part of organizational theory, this model emphasizes the political 'Pull and haul' and its effects on decision making. Though organizational and bureaucratic support is badly needed for the effective policy and its implementation, the bureaucratic politics behind the screen ultimately achieves nothing. There is no doubt that bureaucratic politics helps the organization to find out its drawbacks and the areas for improvement, and as Max Weber assumed, it enhances the 'efficiency and rationality'.[71] Along the side of significance, the critics have put some limitations of the BPM.

The bureaucratic actors are often seen busy in the great game of maximization of self or organizational interest rather than national interest. Therefore, there is hardly any room for national goal. Secondly, there have been seen a greater fraction among the bureaucrats because of the selfish mentality and unusual efforts to win the decision making battle. As a result it is hard to unite them when there is any national crisis. Thirdly, a large amount of resources of the nation is going wasted because various organizations demand unrequited budget and staff just to poses their superiority. Fourthly, it has been seen that there is a constant inclination of professionalism among the bureaucrats while they have been socialized with the organizational approaches and ideologies. As a result they often choose stick to the practices of 'business as usual'. Following the traditional organizational values and goals, bureaucratic actors hardly think about the innovative approach to optimize the organizational mission. Therefore, the policy outcomes are often centred on conventionalism rather than creative.

The Bureaucratic Politics Model defiantly has multiplied the policy alternatives because of its multiple advocacies, but it is hardly practicable during the time of crisis. As Allison argues the political bargaining will minimize the chance of rational action and at the end the compromise on the policy outcome will hamper the national interest. However, during the time of normalcy this model will be highly effective and if properly implemented will give maximum benefit.

Process of Foreign Policy Decision Making

Decision making is a complex process involving greater risk where every single step counts. It may escalate the institution into new heights or can be the cause of its decay. Decision making has been the very part of human behaviour since history, though it involves risk. Starting from the very personal level to the organizational, national and international level the development is attached to the ability of taking right decision. In our personal life we take decision almost every day. Similarly at the national level the policy makers take decisions to carry out the growth of both domestic and Foreign Policy.

The Foreign Policy, being the most important agenda for a nation to deal with the external entities and related crisis, has been formulated with immense care. It has been prepared with such design that it will realize the national aspirations. The nation looks it as a weapon to achieve the national goal. As a result, the decision making in Foreign Policy is usually prone to complexity. Decision making in Foreign Policy passes through various steps and involves all sorts of resources including cognitive and financial. The process is so complex that, almost all the governmental agencies involve in the panning and formulation of foreign policy in some way or other. Starting from the problem identification to policy outcome, the process passes through various stages, which have been discussed below:

Stages of Decision Making Process

The decision making is not the product of instantaneous work but developed through various stages assisted by various stake holders. Be it the rational choice or organizational or governmental process the leaders make decisions phase by phase with the available resources. Each layer filters the odds and errors and contributes new developments into the process. Decision making is not a onetime task. It is a continuous process to address the outstanding problems. It is like a chess board game where every move needs a brilliant counter move and the responded move is countered with a further counter move. Therefore the process of decision in Foreign Policy is considered as a continuous practice. It is like a policy cycle as it extracts the options for the existing problem and takes decision to resolve it and again examines it and rectifies the errors and takes another decision to improve it. International environment is an ever changing phenomenon. Nations need to be engaged themselves constantly to formulate and improve their Foreign Policy to cope with the world system and optimize their national interest. Foreign Policy decision making involves several stages. These are:

Stage 1: Analyzing the Internal and External Environment

A close analysis of the domestic and international environment is essential for Foreign Policy making. It provides vital information to the decision maker and helps to construct policy options which are close to reality. A good decision maker is he who has adequate knowledge about the present situation of the internal as well as external world. As the Foreign Policy of a nation guides its behaviour in the international forum, the study of international environment provides an opportunity to read just its position in the ever changing global order with effective policy measures. Similarly, a close look on the domestic settings helps the decision makers to realize the internal constrains as well as domestic needs.[72]

Stage 2: Recognition, Classification and Defining the Problem or Opportunity

With due study of environment, the first step towards practical decision making for the standing issue is the recognition of the problem. The leaders have to identify the problem in case of crisis or opportunity with the help of the assistants. The earlier the problem is identified, the earlier it can be solved and minimize the enduring consequences. Similarly, the early breakthrough of existing opportunity will help to contribute maximum gain for the nation.

Once the problem has been identified it should be classified including related costs or benefits. The classification of problems or opportunities will make the task easier to understand it thoroughly along with its roots and affects. Based on the classification the decision makers have to define the issues. Defining of the problem includes investigating the nature of problem, depth of issues and related causalities, its causes and its effects on national interests etc. It is the most important part of decision making. If the problem is recognized appropriately the suitable measures can be taken to prevent it. If the system fails to do so it may endanger the national security and future aspiration.

Stage 3: Setting of the Goal and Criteria

The modern state has multiple Foreign Policy goals. The leaders have to set the goal and its criteria to solve the issues based on its requirement and adaptability. Along with political environment, available resources and constraints of a nation have to be taken into account while setting the goals. The goals and its approaches need to complement with each other for good decision. The short term goals to resolve the standing issues should not be contrary to the ultimate national goal. The leader can set the goal and criteria on his own or with due consultants or advisors according to the structure of decision making. The decision making should be limited to the boundary or reliable resources and should not be depended on unrealistic asserts.

Stage 4: Development of Alternative Course of Actions

After setting the goal and criteria, the state has to find out the alternative policy options to resolve the situation. The leader may take the help of advisors and subordinates to generate as much alternatives as it can. The task may be distributed among the experts and specialists who belong to different departments so that it can produce effective alternatives in minimum time. Time and resource are the main constraints of generating alternatives. If a nation is in crisis the leaders get less time to generate more policy options, hence they trial the first option until the effective one.

Stage 5: Evaluation of the Alternatives

The next step after the identification of policy alternatives is to evaluate the alternatives. Each of the policy options has to be evaluated thoroughly in terms of its merits and demerits, costs and benefits along with its contribution to achieve national goals. Sometimes some options may be beneficial for short term but may be harmful for future and vice-versa. The related future consequences have to be taken into account while considering any selection. A balanced track has to be maintained for optimum benefit. However, the state should be in a position to implement the alternative actions and the impractical options should be avoided.

Stage 6: Selection of the Best Option

The leaders have to select the best available policy option after they complete scrutiny of the alternatives. This is the crucial stage of decision making process. If the policy selection is biased or wrong the very purpose of goal optimization will suffer. The leader should remain out of the corrupt means, including presumption and emotional and try to follow maximum degree of rationality during decision making. However choosing the best is not easy, as different individuals have different approaches to look at. But the best policy alternatives should have some basic characteristics. Being complement to the very objectives of purpose and support to optimization of national goals should be the prime nature of the best alternatives. The total decision making system often engages itself to find out the best Foreign Policy options, especially during crisis. They often classify the available alternatives and prepare their rank according to their values and choose the best (often the top ranked) option for implementation.[73]

Stage 7: Implementation of Chosen Policy Option

The policy decision is only a cognitive phenomenon and worthless unless it is put into action. The policy options need to be implemented in order to solve the outstanding issues once they have been chosen. A good decision may be tarnished by bad implementation and a weak decision may be supported by good implementation. Therefore the implementation part should be equally important alike the decision making.[74] The leader usually distributes the decisions among the associated departments and agencies for its practical implementation. The policy decision should reach all these stake holders thoroughly and they should be well informed. The communication gap should be minimized and the implementers should be equipped enough for its *operationalisation. Therefore if required some structural modifications of the associated organizations should be considered to reform it so that it can meet the expectations.*

Stage 8: Conduct Follow-up Evaluations

Finding of policy alternative is not the end of homework. Periodical evaluation is immensely needed to get the feedback so that it can be readjusted with the requirement. The practical reach and limitations may vary from place to place and situation to situation. Therefore the timely follow-ups will help to achieve the Foreign Policy goals of a nation. The mechanism should be arranged to readjust its policy in the time of need. The feedbacks may be sent to the central decision making unit to correct themselves for future policies. If the policy decision fails to achieve the expectations it can be taken away and replaced with more effective policies if required.

Decision making process, as we have discussed, is a lengthy and complicated process. There are several stages in the decision making units. These stages are arranged in a vertical order where each stage complements to the next. Starting from the environmental realization to the policy follow-up, in each stage the concept is purified and the policy is delivered at last. But the Foreign Policy making process is different in different governmental settings and different environment. While in dictatorial system it seems like a one man show that tightly controls the units and often lionizes his wish, it is more participatory in democratic settings. However, the availability of resources and its rightful use mostly make the difference in Foreign Policy. Again, the decision making process is determined by the degree of reach and the desire of the nation. Major Player like United States for example, defiantly requires different level policies to dominate the world compared to marginal actors. Therefore, we can conclude that the Foreign Policy decision making process varies according to the need though the structure is the same.

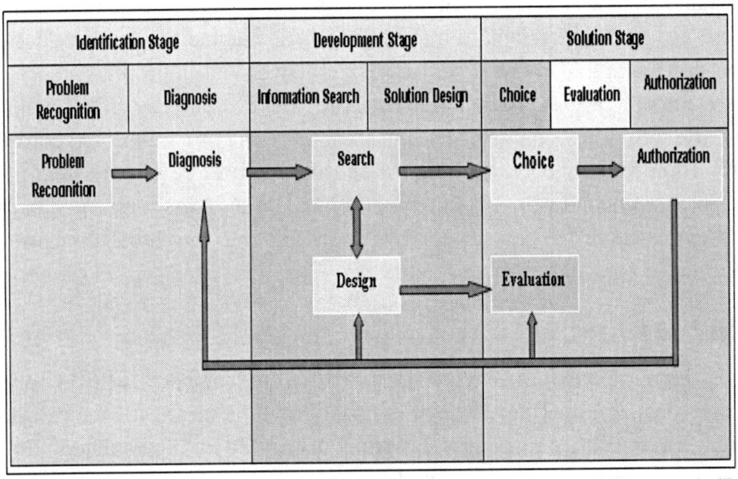

Source: Mintzberg, H., D. Raisinghani, and A. Theoret, The Structure of 'Unstructured" Decision Process. Administrative Science Quarterly 2l: 2 (June, 1976): 246-75.

Figure 1: Stages and Routines of Decision Making.

Factors Influencing FPDM

The prime intension of a country's Foreign Policy is to protect its sovereignty and optimize the national interests. The reach of one's Foreign Policy depends up on its requirement and engagement with the world communities, so as the Foreign Policy decision making. It depends upon the desire of a country and varies from country to country. But it is not the divine made instrument, nor a creation of natural process. It is formulated by the state with the help of various political settings. Therefore Foreign Policy of a nation is the product of various forces that are engaged in guiding the behaviour of the state with other world community.

Just like the human behaviour, the behaviour of a country's Foreign Policy is ever changing so as the decision making process. In fact Foreign Policy decision making of a country is highly guided, influenced, determined and channelized by various invisible factors, though we believe that it is the product of the ultimate wish of the nation or its political Leadership. There are a number of factors both internal and external at different levels: individual, state and international level that influence the behaviour of the state. The decision making process counts these factors and its significance before taking any decision.

As Foreign Policy decision making is a complex and multidimensional process, there are many actors, agents and institutions involved in this process. Besides the actors' role, there are a few other factors that affect the decision making process and the outcomes. James Rosenau beliefs that, there are five major factors that ultimately influence the Foreign Policy decision making of a state. These are external or global environment, societal environment, the governmental setting, the roles occupied by policy-makers and the individual characteristics of the policy-making elites.[75] According to Vernon McKay these factors can be dived into three broad categories, i.e. geographical, historical, and biographical issues (personality).[76] For the present research we have divided these factors into two broad categories, internal factors and external factors.

Internal Factors

Internal and external factors are two different factors that affect Foreign Policy decision making. Though Foreign Policy is meant for the external engagement of a country, it is designed, processed and formulated within the political settings well inside the country. As a result it is bound to be influenced by the domestic factors. In fact, in most of the cases the Foreign Policy is adopted just to satisfy the domestic stake holders and restricted to domestic interests. The political affiliation of the official positions of the various decision making actors also put the domestic factors at the forefront while making foreign policies. Therefore domestic politics and foreign politics are inseparable entities and equally significant as external factors. The domestic environment consists of various equally potential factors that shape the Foreign Policy decision making. For this analysis internal factors are divided into six broad categories.

Political Factors

Among all domestic factors that influence Foreign Policy decision making, political factors are the most significant ones. It is not only the decision maker who is chosen out of extensive political calculation but also the decision making settings that are grown out of political will. The head of the government, who takes decision on the external behaviour of a country, is elected politically. Hence, he is bound to be influenced by the domestic political environment of the country. In other words, the political system of a state will decide the scope and limit of the Foreign Policy choices.

Electoral Cycle

The prime motto of any political leader including the head of the government is to remain in power as long as he can. Except dictatorship regimes all remaining political settings participate in election to get authority to rule the state. Each and every initiative of them remains accountable on the eyes of the public. The public and the civil societies analyse, discuss and scrutinize the policies and decisions that are taken by the government during its tenure of rule. Addition to this, the opposite political parties try to expose the loopholes to demoralize the government. Consequently, the ruling government and the allied organizations always take the policy which favours the domestic forces. The same argument can be extended to Foreign Policy decision making process. As the leaders have to stand before the public for vote, their view will go according to the need of the domestic environment.

Secondly, during the internal crisis and challenges the government takes some significant steps to divert the internal attention. They go for war or attacking the rivalries to satisfy the home public to save the image of the government. Israeli government for example, decided to launch 'Operation Pillar of Defence' in a massive way[77] and directed the Israeli Air Force (IAF) for massive bombing on the Palestinian establishment on Gaza strip before the general election of 2013. This single incident helped the government to win the election, despite the visible differences among the coalitions on several domestic issues, including the much hyped 'Tal Law' controversy. [78] As a result, the government gained the support from most of the parties, including various opposition parties and won the election ultimately. However, there is a belief that that the operation was actually an "Election War" intended to put domestic lacunas aside and divert the public attention towards the national security.[79]

Political Settings

Political system of a country represents the formal legal institutions that govern the state. It includes its political pattern, administrative system, political leadership, people's participation, separation of power, nature of bureaucracy, freedom of press and the legal systems. Foreign Policy decisions have to come across these elements before finalized. The political pattern, the basic system of a state influences the Foreign Policy outcomes in many ways. As we have witnessed, the Foreign Policy decision of a democratic state is different from that of an authoritative or an aristocratic state. While in democracy the rule of law, public percipient, the opposition and the role of lobby group make the process so complex, that the decision makers hardly choose the 'unexpected best'. But in the undemocratic states, leaders enjoy unlimited power and hardly care for the public opinion, hence can go to any level to optimize the national goal, even to wage a war. Similarly in a democratic state the separation of power and provision of check and balances restrict the leader to misuse the power and make them accountable before the public.

Social and Cultural Factors

Social and cultural factors include the national identity, its social pattern, its religious and ideological distinctions and most importantly the non-governmental activities and actors. The leaders and the public mass grow up in a certain social environment where they inherit certain ideologies, values and beliefs that influence the policy decisions. The influence of these factors remains in the very gene of the people and leader in special. Thus, social and cultural factor is one of the significant factors in Foreign Policy decision making.[80] Further, the pressure group, media and civil Society at large carefully analyze Foreign Policy behaviour of the government and raise their concerns if things are not going along the line of their assumption.

However, social and cultural dynamics are over ruled by political factors and remain out of focal point of discussion in the Foreign Policy decision matrix. Indeed, it is the social base that motivates the decision making elites the most to make certain decisions. Major value orientations, degree of national unity, the extent to which it was industrialized are some of the variables to name among the large societal sources. Some of these are briefly discussed here:

Social and Cultural Pattern

Social customs and practices have been the drive force of the human's behaviour and eventually mechanize the behaviour of the state. The people live with a particular system and think and behave according to the system, sothat they protect and promote that pattern of society and culture. This argument does not limit into the domestic settings. If a state is socialized with these social forces it will act on the prescribed lines. Similarly, the degree of national identity also influences the external policy of the state. The state believes in one identity and stands together and eventually behaves differently as the state has multiple identities. These identities may be shaped on the basis of religion, geographic region, sects or clans, or social belief. Leaders cannot ignore one section of mass by taking hard decision. They will try to maintain balanced policy to satisfy all sections.

Religious Factor

Religion is one of the most significant variables in external policy of a country. It is so influential that the religious system governs the state in many parts of the world. Some states are created on the basis of religion and treat religion as the supreme force of the state craft. Each and every policy including, policies on external affairs goes along the line of religion in these states. Social, economic and even political settings take shapes in accordance with the religious believes. The religion is so strong that all the other factors that seem important are considered secondary. One cannot think of going against the religious belief not even the state itself. Therefore, ultimately the religion guides the Foreign Policy decision making in these kinds of states. Though the picture is apparently different in secular states, one cannot deny its influence. As religion is connected with the belief system, it is not possible to separate religion and the society. According to Pascal Boyer, this built-in religious argue is universal, possessed by all human beings, and not restricted only to the believers.[81] The government in non-secular states often mix-up the religion and policies together. In addition, the vote bank politics is also restricting the political parties from going against certain feelings of the people while formulating policies.

Role of Civil Societies and Social Actors

Social actors are those individuals and organizations who mobilize the society against or in favour of certain actions, provisions or policies of government. It can be pressure and lobby groups or media houses or individual social actors. These actors practice different strategies to pressurize the government to accept or drop the concerned provision. They organize the peoples support to peruse their goals. It can be business lobby groups or anti-nuclear activists that pressurize and try to influence the Foreign Policy option of the country. The Kudankulam anti-nuclear movement, for example tries to prevent the government to plant a Russian sponsored nuclear plant in Tamil Nadu. Similarly, media houses are also largely involved in creating social pressure against the government by highlighting the pros and corns of different policy decisions of the government.

Economic Factors

Economy is the prime force in state craft. In other words it is the economy that runs the state. Otherwise the government alone will not be able to deliver the best to the mass. Every governmental initiative needs the backing of finance to sustain. Therefore undoubtedly a sound economic environment is the ultimate aim of the policy maker. This argument is also applicable to Foreign Policy decision making. The Foreign Policy has been formulated in such a way that it secures its economic interest and attracts more funds to the state.

States search various options both soft and hard, to acquire, exploit and obtain the recourses of other country for their own purpose. They are even ready to take hard alternatives of war by citing some invalid reasons of either human rights abuses or undemocratic authoritative harassments. The golf war of 1991was initiated by the US to protect its economic security vis-à-vis uninterrupted oil supply. The Bush administration openly admitted it before the public announcing this war as 'about job, about oil, and about economic security'.[82] Even scholars believe that the motive behind the Iraq war of 2003was to restore America's energy security.[83]

Trade and Commerce

In the 21st century, trade and commerce plays a vital role in shaping the Foreign Policy of a state. Indeed, it has been prioritized compared to any other preferred variables of Foreign Policy agenda. With the liberalization of economy and market in India and elsewhere, it has been given great importance. More trades have taken place between the countries and so as the foreign relation. Various Multi-National Companies (MNCs) have taken their business across the border. Consequently, they try to influence the governmental institutions in making favourable policies, including foreign economic policies. Again, the government often consults the business houses and trade unions before signing up any foreign agreement. As a result, gradually trade and commerce become the most influential variables in Foreign Economic Policy Decision Making (FEPDM). The Federation of Indian Chambers of Commerce and Industry (FICCI), the Confederation of Indian Industry (CII) and the Associated Chambers of Commerce and Industry of India (ASSOCHAM) the apex trade unions in India in various ways try to influence the decision outcomes and pressurize the government to make policies that suit their interests. In fact some of the business icons have been selected and elected into the legislative bodies and play an active role in decision making.

Military Factor

Military remains one of the variables that influence the Foreign Policy behaviour of a country. After the world wars and subsequent security threats posed by state and non-state actors, national security has been considered as the topmost priority in every corner of the state policy. It is considered as one of the main pillars of state craft to enhance the national security environment by escalating the defence budget and importing armaments and technologies from the world communities.

Military Procurement

The huge demand of weaponry to deal with the anticipated and ongoing threats is the order of the day. Therefore countries, especially developing countries opt for the weapon procurement and technology imports from friendly states. India for instance, purchased 10 percent of the world's total arms imports during 2007-2011.[84] It affects two things. One is the change of Foreign Policy towards the donor countries and the economic impact of this deals on the domestic an international environments. While it affects the economic growth and development it cut shorts the social expenditure at domestic level, on the other hand the state has to mould its Foreign Policy as the donor centric even in the future for the weaponry maintenances. One cannot ignore this factor in Foreign Policy decision making.

Military Nationalism and Dictatorship Supremacy

In many countries the military dictators have taken the government into their hand and are administrating the state for quite a long time. They are considered as the supreme authorities in policy making, including foreign policies. They declare themselves as true patriotic forces and often choose war as the best option to resolve disputes. As a result, through history these types of countries are engaged in various conflicts. Hence, military is one of the factors which direct the Foreign Policy behaviour of a country.

Psychological Factor

Decision making is a cognitive process, whether at personal level decisions, organizational level decisions, national level decisions or even international level decisions. The leaders make policy decisions based on their psychological understanding and narratives. It is impossible to ignore their overwhelming values, beliefs, and ideologies in making any policy decision, be it at domestic or international level. The attitude of the leaders regarding foreign events matters and eventually shapes Foreign Policy of a country. Thus one can hardly ignore the psychological factor and its influence on Foreign Policy decisions.

Psychological factor that influences the Foreign Policy decision is multidimensional in nature and is not limited to any definite belief or activity. In fact the psychology of a person is inspired by various sources. The political leader, who makes foreign policies, could be influenced by the party ideology, religious ideology, own beliefs and perceptions, nationalism and national identity and political environment.[85] Along with the political ideology, social and economic ideologies also shape the cognitive perception of a person. [86] Foreign Policy in India has influenced immensely the national ideologies like Ahimsa, Swaraj, non-interventionalism, anti-colonial, and universal brotherhood. The directive principles of state policies prescribed under part IV in the Constitution of India equally guides the policies including foreign affairs. Classified into different categories of Gandhian, economic and socialistic, political and administrative, justice and legal, environmental, protection of monuments and peace and security, it directs the policy behaviour of the country. Similarly, the ideology of Jawaharlal Nehru, the chief architect of India's Foreign Policy is still visible in the conduct of India's Foreign Policy.[87]

National Ideology

Defining ideology, especially national ideology is a difficult task.[88] Gone are those days when national ideology was widely concentrated around some broad concepts: Nazism and anti-Nazism during world wars and communism and capitalism during cold war.[89] It became more complex with the rise of globalization. Attempting to explain, Quinn writes "Ideology is the intellectual simplification leaders use to explain and justify the national courses they advocate, both to others and to themselves" [90]

National ideology is the blend of social, economic and political ideology of a nation. It is a silent force which controls the policy behaviour, internal and external. For example, the Soviet Union's external relations during the cold war were leaning towards the communist forces and it offered almost everything to these states. But its attitude towards the non-communist forces had been marked as troublesome. The national ideology controls the attitude of leaders, agencies, and institutions involved in Foreign Policy decision making. In some countries, national ideologies have been clearly defied and the administration runs according to these lines. Religion has been the very psyche of the policy makers and is often considered as state ideology. It has been the ward steak of Foreign Policy for many states, especially non-secular states. Therefore it guides the national ideologies during policy formulations.

Perception and Emotion

Decision making in Foreign Policy being supposed to be logical, rational and calculative, is often driven by emotion and perception. The decision makers and the institutions take unexpected steps because of ego, emotion and presumption. Whether it is Falkland crisis or other terror and liberation movements, one thing is clear that the denial of reorganization, yearlong suppression and attempt to revenge excel the emotional level that is often transformed into war and conflict.[91] Renshon and Lerner divided Emotion into two broad categories - *Integral Emotion*, which is posed by the decision maker at the time of decision making and the *Accidental Emotions* that take place accidentally as reaction to certain issues.[92] Both types of elements influence Foreign Policy behaviour of a state. It affects all systems in its way if it is evoked and destroys the other working functions and barriers.[93] Action taken by emotion is never considered as logical and remains biased and ultimately faces severe consequences.

Nationalism and National Identity

Both National identity and Nationalism are complement to each other. It addresses the core point of unconditional love for your nation that everything is justifiable to protect and uphold its sovereignty. Though it sounds good in theory, but in practice it is the drive force for the major confrontations between the nations. Nationalism up to an accepted amount is good for the development of a nation. But excesses nationalism or ultra-nationalism teaches to hate other nations and encourages war. Since the recorded history nationalism has been the driving force of the external behaviours of a nation. Similarly, the world wars have witnessed how the ultranationalist ideas have destroyed the world.[94] Like the nationalism, national identity also determines the Foreign Policy of country. Terror organizations are apparently created in the name of nationalism and often fight to uphold their national identity.

Individual Factors

Decision making is a human centric process and needs the human involvement at every step of decision making. The decision making unit consists of political leadership, bureaucrats, intellectuals and multiple individuals, who eventually take the decisions. Hence, their personnel and other individual factors are bound to influence the very process of decision making and the policy outcomes. In this regard, a brief discussion on these factors has been given below:

Leadership

In every aspect of decision making, the leader plays an important role. Decision making has to be taken by the leaders, although other mechanisms assist and influence them during the process. For *Lloyd Jensen, it is the 'human agencies' and ultimately an individual that takes decision and not the state.*[95] It is the central and pivotal part of decision making and the nature and quality of decision is dependent on the characteristics, cognitive skill, social background, motives, beliefs and assumptions. Therefore the decision outcome is bound to be influenced by personal factor of leadership.

Decision making and the technique of decision making differ from person to person and the leaders make certain decisions out of their human cognitive, socialization, values, ideologies and perversions. The administrative pattern and types of leadership are further more contributing significantly to the decision outcomes. Decision making under an autocratic leadership is different from that of a democratic leader where he has to face more pressure to satisfy every section. Similarly, the type and nature of decision making units equally affect the decision outcomes. The nature of policy outcome is essentially different in the authoritative style of decision making, where the leader is a supreme authority of decision making unit and placed at top of decision making hierarchy, to the democratic decision making setups, where leader remains at the centre of decision making system and poses equal status among the group.[96] Therefore, leadership plays a significant role in decision making process and its activities impact the decision outcome in Foreign Policy mechanism.

Advisors and Assistants to Leadership

No doubt the leader takes the decision on behalf of the state, but in it are the advisors who help the leader to take certain decisions. In fact, most of the decisions are taken in accordance with the advice of the leadership. If the advisers are far from reality the leader automatically makes blunder. Describing about the importance of advisors to leadership David Mitchell stresses upon the various models of advisory systems and its pros and corns. He has given three different models and emphasizes how each model impacts the decision making process.[97] Whether it is rational or bureaucratic or organizational, the leader has to depend on the assistants to collect, filter and analyze the information that proceeds for decision making. The pre decision making essentials and the post decision making outcomes have to be carried out by adjunct assistants, hence naturally prone to influence the decision making process.

Geographical Factor

Geographical factor influencing Foreign Policy behaviour of a state includes the weather, atmosphere, location of a country, natural resources, population, and physical terrain of a state etc. and it is the most permanent factor that determines the Foreign Policy decisions. The United States for example, has never come under the colonial rule fully because of its geographical location being surrounded by sea and absence of strong rivalries at the borders. But in the case of India the location being surrounded by sea in the south and Himalayas in the north, it has failed to secure its borders because of the presence of strong neighbours like Pakistan in the west and China in the north and east. Similarly presence of resources enables the country to play a larger role in international politics while resource-less countries are lagging behind by depending over others and spending huge money to meet its requirements. Therefore, one can ignore or change all the other factors, but geographical factor cannot be replaced and poses wider influence in one's foreign policies.

Physical Terrain and Geostrategic Location

Physical terrain and location remains the most important and permanent factor that influences the Foreign Policy decision making of a country. As scholars rightly observed that "political geography plays a huge role in who gets what, when, and how in the game of world politics"[98]. Geography is always linked with strategic interest and economic developments and the very sustain of the country at large. The location of a state, its borders and terrain determine its development, and the national power that ultimately influences the policy decisions. If a state is engaged with border disputes and locked in a hostile strategic landscape, then it continues to spend more on security and hence, always depends on the arm supplier powers and lacks the developmental activities. The isolation of US from the rest of the world encouraged it to follow the isolated Foreign Policy Monroe doctrine. The location of Germany at the heart of Europe and surrounded by great powers during the world wars for example, pushed German politics to be linked with external environments. Separation of Britain as an island in Europe also determined its decision to remain separate from the European Union for quite a long time.

Foreign Policy decision making is also influenced by the demography along with geographic locations. Apart from the work force that mechanizes the developmental activities, the language and ethnicity and the belief system based on geographical location influence the decision that they take during their political and non-political participation. Jared Diamond, a Pulitzer Prize winner and Psychology Professor of University of California argues that, 'since the beginning of human history geography shapes each human society's culture and competitive position'. [99] Based on this theory one can agree that, interest groups like ethnic groups, NGOs, IGOs mobilize the public opinion that influence the national decision making process on foreign affairs. Hence, Glassner rightly stated "the geographical consequences of political decisions and actions, the geographical factors that were considered during the making of any decisions, and the role of geographical factors influence the outcome of political actions."[100]

Natural Recourses

Geography of a nation not only represents the sum total of the location, size and atmosphere, it also consists of natural resources. Often it is considered as the most important factor in influencing Foreign Policy decisions, as it is the heart of most of the conflicts of modern world. Most of the wars of the Middle East were fought with the prime intention to control the oil resources. Not only oil or mineral, the disputes over water emerged as the prime factor of conflict around the globe.

Lack of resources limits the state to play a larger role in the international arena, while the mineral and oil rich countries are able to influence the global policies. One cannot disagree that, the large natural resource base is a major element of national power that drives the international relation of a country. Development of nations is badly affected because of shortage of resources and it makes the country depend on other countries. Additionally, a large share of money is spent on the import of resources that undermine the economic conditions of a state. India for example, imports over ninety percent of its petroleum fuel from various countries that make the country dependent on gulf countries heavily. It courses the drain of huge amount of foreign exchanges that put pressure on the devaluation of rupee. Again, the resources can be used for various other developmental activities. Therefore, India has to maintain friendly relation with the oil rich countries and need to approach a very balanced policy toward these nations. Therefore, one cannot ignore the geographical factor in the Foreign Policy decision making process. As scholars rightly observed, "Geography frequently influences political making, just as political power influences geographical space".[101]

External Factors

Along with domestic factors, the international settings are equally influencing Foreign Policy Decision Making of a state. In other words, internal and external factors like a two track approach go hand in hand in Foreign Policy decision making. Behaviour of various states and non-state actors in global settings affects the decision making process of not just the concerning states but also other peripheral actors. India, Egypt and all the other third world countries although not involved in cold war politics, repeatedly affected the great game politics of super powers. Any change in the international sphere will affect all states. Like a wave in the pond it spreads at all directions touching all aspects of global politics, including domestic environment of states. The attack of 9/11 affected more or less all states whether strategically, economically or socially.

States are influenced more with the changes in the regional environments, especially activities of neighbours as they are closely interlinked. The actions of the neighbour or any other player that proximate to it will essentially disturb the strategic behaviour of the other states. Additionally, states are carefully watching the activities of their states especially friends and enemies and take counter actions accordingly. It is like a chess board game that you observe each and every step of your opponent and take your own decision. Similarly, your action will be prevented by counter action and so on. There are several factors that influence the Foreign Policy decision of the concerned countries.

International Treaties and Agreements

With the rise of globalization, interdependence between and among the states have raised to the next level. As a result, number of international agreements and treaties have been signed between the states to protect and promote their national interests. According to the international law "treaty is any international agreement concluded between states or other entities with international personality (such as public international organizations), if the agreement is intended to have international legal effect".[102] Therefore while making the treaties the respective states have to go along the line of international laws.

Treaties and agreements are highly influencing the external relation of a state in recent globalized world. Treaties and agreements are regarded as the safeguard of national interests during the time of crisis. The decision makers have to respect the outstanding treaties related to the ongoing issues during the time of Foreign Policy making. In some cases they try to facilitate the other states to come to the table of negotiation for an agreement that will be beneficial for both. Moreover, international treaties always prevent the international community to opt for endangering the world security and pursue for benevolent approaches for mutual benefit. The CTBT and NPT for example, have forced the countries not to proliferate nuclear weapons in some extent. Hence the importance of treaties in guiding Foreign Policy behaviour cannot be disregarded.

Strategic Deterrence

Defining deterrence is not an easy task, as there is no limit to the term adequate security and can be extended up to any stage that eventually leads to arms race.[103] But it can be termed as the ability to protect the borders and sovereignty from possible foreign interventionists. The theory of deterrence influences the Foreign Policy behaviour of a country while the whole world is betting for power according to realism. In the world of anarchists as realists believe the countries should be prepared for any possible strikes.[104] Therefore one has to be strong enough to deal with these threats either single handed or by making coalition. The deterrence theory believes that everything is justifiable to protect the national sovereignty and all the resources and policies should be directed to prevent and promote the national interest.

There are several views on how to deter the threats. While most of the scholars agree on strong national power including military, others back on the soft power to dissolve threats. After the world wars most of the countries especially super powers believed to acquire mighty military artillery like nuclear weapon to strengthen their deference.[105] However Bruce Russett believes that the strong deterrence can be achieved when there will be close economic, political, social and cultural ties that lead to interdependence between the aggressor and the target countries.[106] Therefore Russett's approach for deterrence is a soft power rather than military mightiness. Irrespective of its approaches, strategic deterrence theory has been influencing the Foreign Policy decision making for centuries. In the name of deterrence the nation states have spent huge national income and diverted a large number of human forces towards national security. Therefore, it is bound to remain as one of the factors that influence the Foreign Policy of the country.

Alliance and Counter Alliance

"Alliances are formal associations of states for the use (or non use) of military force, in specified circumstances, against states outside their membership".[107] Though, alliance is usually formed with formal agreements, there are cases of non-formal alliance or cloud alliance to deter the aggressive powers. Waltcounting the informal linkages defines alliance as a "formal or informal relationship of security cooperation between two or more sovereign states" having"some level of commitment and an exchange of benefits for both parties."[108] Out of the two definitions it is clear that alliance is a tool to maintain the balance of power at the international arena with little adjustment in the domestic institutions. While security remains the top most priority for countries around the world, they often go for alliances making to secure its sovereignty. Therefore, the states mould its Foreign Policy accordingly to maintain goodwill with alliance partners. They usually offer various defence and economic assistance to their alliance partners and exchange technologies and ideas for mutual benefit. Additionally, alliances periodically call for certain modification of their external behaviour to cope with the international scenario.

While alliance countries group together for greater cooperation against outside threats, they are indirectly threatening others with their combined power. As a result, opposite states are forced to form a counter-alliance to face the opposite alliance. It had been seen during the Cold-War when the world was divided into two different blocks and engaged to attract as many as other countries into their respective alliance. Hence, the remaining non-aligned third world countries aligned themselves to remain neutral. The Foreign Policy was remaining hoarse towards the opposite alliance partners while favourable towards its own partner countries. Therefore, it is clear that most of the Foreign Policy decisions were taken with the line of alliance and counter-alliance politics.

Regional and Global Informants

Irrespective of various models, decision making in Foreign Policy primarily relies on information. Leaders take decision after thorough analysis of various collected information. Therefore, the role of informants is crucial for any Foreign Policy decision. They provide the much needed real-time information to the decision making units. Informants can be divided into two broad different categories- official and non-official.

Official Informants

Official informants are those individuals and agencies who are officially appointed by the concerned states for collection of information from various sources. Assigned with specific task they are sent to various places to collect information and report on the mission to the concerned government. Ambassadors, consulates, trade promoters, spies and intelligence agencies to name some of them, have sent periodical reports to the government to peruse the policies according to the prescribed situations. Sometime special operations are carried out to investigate the reality so that it can be addressed affectively.

Non-official Informants

Apart from the official agencies, the government also relies on other sources of information. Agencies like News Media, Think-tanks and Research Institutes, Independent intelligence and Research Agents also help the government to collect required information. These sources, especially the independent think-tanks provide more impartial and neutral information that construct more non-biased policies. Therefore, most of the governments consider both official and non-official reports before taking critical decisions.

As information is critical in policy formation, the part of informants automatically plays a significant role in Foreign Policy decision making mechanism. They are the centre of policy formulation and their views cannot be ignored by the policy makers. The success and failure of a policy mostly depend on the ground report collected by informants. Not only that, they also follow the feedbacks and suggest for further initiatives.

Relation with Major and Regional Powers

At global stages major powers drive the course of the world order. There are no clear cut criteria to be qualified as Major Powers. While economy is the principal ward stick to call someone super power, others depend on strategic mightiness. But for a long run the great powers should possess the economic adage and strategic superiority. However there is no permanency of great power status, infact, the tag has been attached to different countries at different times. For Professor Robert B. Louden the permanent five of the Security Council are called as global powers in the 21st century.[109] These great powers bear the power to persuade and dictate the international activities directly or indecently. The potential regional players termed as 'regional powers'[110] also influence the policy decision of the surrounding countries. International politics is mostly influenced and guided by the actions of these power houses. Therefore, a modern nation can hardly ignore such players to achieve its national goals.

Countries always try to have better relation and avoid any possible collision with these powers. Extra efforts have been taken to get closer to these countries by adopting various means. Engaging with conflict may endanger the national aspirations as well as national security that lead to undermine the growth of the nation. However, maintaining good relations will facilitate more opportunity to the nation. With the rise of the new eastern giants, the centre of power has been shifted into Asia, while the countries were trying to cope with the western power houses during nineteenth and twentieth century. It poses new challenges to the decision makers to modify their Foreign Policy accordingly to have better coordination with these emerging powers. Therefore one cannot ignore the major power factor in Foreign Policy decision making.

Conclusion

A modern state needs a comprehensive and proactive Foreign Policy to attain its national objectives, to manage its external affairs for the peaceful coexistence with other states, and for the all-round development of the nation. Similarly, a successful and effective Foreign Policy requires vibrant and well laid Foreign Policy decision making machinery. Thus, success of external management depends on the effectiveness of the Foreign Policy making decision units. The Foreign Policy making units is a complex structure which consists of different actors, agencies and institutions. It takes various information and necessary inputs from multiple resources and analyses the received data to make appropriate decision. The effectiveness of the decision is often vested upon the structure and function of the decision making units. Generally, the fate of the policy outcome is influenced by the quality of leadership, which is the centre of the policy making units.

To simplify this, Prof. Graham Allison categorized the style of decision making into three broad categories – the Rational Actor Model, the Organizational Process Model and the Bureaucratic Politics Model. According to the Rational Actor model, the decision outcomes are always the product of rational choice and logical conclusion. This model is free from bias and personal influences. The decision is comparatively affective and quick and useful for the crisis like situations. Allison's second model of decision making is the Organizational Process Model. According to this model of decision making, the structure of the machinery functions like that of a large organization, where the whole assignment is divided into several sub-assignments and distributed among several specialist sub-organizations. These small units give inputs and formulate the way out formula for their share of assignment. At last all such individual assessments are merged together to take the final decision. The BPM is a lengthy and complicated process and beneficial to deal with the long term issues. The third and the last model of Allison is the Bureaucratic Politics model. Unlike, these two models, the BPM tends to consensus making rather than logical assessment. Under this model of decision making, the decision making units consist of several actors, agencies and institutions which often compete among themselves to show their supremacy and grab the maximum benefit while dealing with an issue. As a result, no concrete decision is taken during discussion and often settle data middle path or policy concessions. In this type of model, there is very little scope to achieve optimum benefit and the policy is well below the optimum level.

In all these three models, the process of Foreign Policy decision making is multi-level and multi-dimensional in character. The complex procedure of decision making in Foreign Policy passes through several stages – from identifying the issues to the reaching to a find the alternative options and finally reaching to constructive decision. In each stage the inputs are analysed and the inferior alternatives are filtered out before reaching the final decision. However, this process is not purely out of internal and external influences but eventually influenced by a number of factors such as leadership, political system, social and cultural affection, economic and military strength, geographical and international environment etc. Decision making is bound to be influenced by these factors and often forced to take unpreferred decision in Foreign Policy matters. A successful decision should have the quality to reduce these influences.

Notes

1. Roy E Jones, analysing foreign policy: an introduction to some conceptual problems (London: Routledge and Keganpaul, 1970) 1.
2. Charles F. Hermann, "Foreign Policy Behaviour: That Which Is to Be Explained," in Why Nations Act, ed. Maurice A. East, Stephen A. Salmore, and Charles F. Hermann (Beverly Hills: Sage, 1978) 25.
3. *Ibid.*
4. See Online Oxford English Dictionary, http://www.oxforddictionaries.com/definition/english/foreign?q= foreign; also see Joseph Twadell Shipley, The Origins of English Words: A Discursive Dictionary of Indo-European Roots (London: JHU Press, 2001) 72.
5. V. Kubá lková, Foreign Policy in a Constructed World (New York: M.E. Sharpe, 2001) 35. See also Oxford English Dictionary, http://www.oxforddictionaries.com/definition/english/policy; also see Julia Cresswell, Oxford Dictionary of Word Origins (New York: Oxford University Press, 2010)335.
6. See Online Oxford English Dictionary at http://oxforddictionaries.com/definition/english/foreign %2Bpolicy? q= foreign+ policy7*Encyclopaedia of Britannica*, at http://www. britannica.com/EBchecked/topic/213380/foreign-policy.
8. Eugene R. Wittkopf, Christopher Martin Jones and Charles W. Kegley, Jr., American Foreign Policy: Pattern and Process, 7th ed. (Belmont: Thomson Wadsworth, 2008) 17.
9. Robert H. Jackson and Georg Sørensen, Introduction to International Relations: Theories And Approaches, (New York: Oxford University Press, 2007) 223.
10. Christopher Hill, Changing Politics of Foreign Policy (Hampshire: Palgrave Macmillan, 2003) p. 3.
11. Kenneth W. Thompson and Roy C. Macridis, "Comparative Study of Foreign Policy" in Roy C. Macridis, Foreign Policy and World Politics, 5th Edition, (Englewood Cliffs, NJ: Prentice-Hall, 1976) 21.
12. Joyce P. Kaufman, A Concise History of U.S. Foreign Policy (Lanham, Maryland: Rowman & Littlefield, 2010) 8.
13. George Modelski, A Theory of Foreign Policy (London: Pallmall Press, 1962) 6-7.

14. James N. Rosenau, "Comparing Foreign Policies: Why, What, How," in James F. Hanrieder, Comparative Foreign Policies: Theories, Findings and Methods, ed. (New York: John Wiley and Sons, 1974) 4.
15. Walter Carlsnaes, "Foreign Policy", in Handbook of International Relations, ed. Walter Carlsnaes, Thomas Risse and Beth A. Simmons (London: Sage, 2002) 334-35.
16. Hugh Gibson, The Road To Foreign Policy (New York: Doubleday,1944) 9.
17. Cecil V. Crab jr., American Foreign Policy in the Nuclear Age, 3rd ed. (New York: Harper and Row, 1972) 1.
18. Smith, op.cit. (Note 5) 7.
19. FS Northedgeed, The Foreign Policy of The Powers (London: Faberand Faber, 1968) 9, 150.
20. Hermann (1978) 34.
21. James D. Fearon, "Domestic Politics, Foreign Policy, and Theories of International Relations", Annual Review of Political Science 1 (1998): 289-313.
22. Howard H. Lanther, Foreign Policy Analysis (Columbus: Merrill Publishing, 1974) 3.
23. Joseph Frankel, International Relations in a Changing World, Revised Edition (New York: Oxford University Press, 1988) vi-vii
24. Christopher Hill, Changing Politics of Foreign Policy (Hampshire: Palgrave Macmillan, 2003) 3.
25. Roy E. Jones, Analyzing Foreign Policy: An Introduction to some Conceptual Problem (London: Routledge and Kegan Paul, 1970)1.
26. See Online Latin Dictionary site Latdict, at http://www.latin-dictionary.net
27. W.J.M. MacKenzie, Power, *Violence*, *Decision* (New York: Peregrine Books, 1975) 176-79.
28. Harold Koontz, Cyril O'Donnell, Principles of Management: An Analysis of Managerial Functions (Tokyo: McGraw-Hill Kogakusha, 1972) 47.
29. Louis A. Allen, The Management Profession (New York: McGraw-Hill, 1964) 70.
30. Baumann A, Deber R, "Limits of Decision Analysis for Rapid Decision Making in ICU Nursing", Image: Journal of Nursing Scholarship, 21/2 (1989): 69-71.
31. As stated in Mauro Maldonato, Decision Making: Towards an Evolutionary Theory of Human Action, (Sussex: Academic Press, 2010) 8.
32. Mauro Maldonato, Decision Making: Towards an Evolutionary Theory of Human Action (Sussex: Academic Press, 2010) 18-19.
33. Byron M. Roth, John D. Mullen, Decision Making: Its Logic and Practice, (Savage, Maryland: Rowman& Little field, 2002) 22.
34. As quoted in M. Laxmikanth, Public Administration, (New Delhi: Tata McGraw Hill Publication, 2011) 159.
35. Alex Mintz and Karl DeRouen Jr., Understanding Foreign Policy Decision Making, (New York: Cambridge, 2010) 3.

36. Joshua S. Goldstein and John C. Pevehouse, International Relations, 9th ed. (New York: Pearson, 2010) 105.
37. Janice Gross Stein, "Psychological Explanations of International Conflict", in Carlsnaes, Walter, Thomas Risse, and Beth A. Simmons, eds. Handbook of International Relations, (London: Sage, 2002) 292–308.
38. Modernising Government White Paper, March 1999, as quoted in Practical Guide to Policy-Making in Northern Ireland, Office of The First Minister and Deputy First Minister, Ireland, available at http://www.ofmdfmni.gov.uk/practical-guide-policy-making.pdf
39. B. Raman, Decision-making in Foreign Policy, Research Note No. 86, South Asia Analysis Group, at http://www.southasiaanalysis.org/note86 (accessed on 20 Dec. 2012).
40. Allison & Zelikow (1999) 18.
41. W. Raymond Duncan, Barbara Jancar-Webster, Bob Switky, World Politics in the 21st Century (Boston: Cengage Learning, 2009) 130-158.
42. Janice Gross Stein, "Foreign Policy Decision-Making: Rational, Psychological, and Neurological Models", in Foreign Policy: Theories, Actors, Cases, ed. Steve Smith, Amelia Hadfield and Tim Dunne (Oxford: Oxford University Press, 2008) 102
43. Nehemia Geva, Alex Mintz, Decision Making on War and Peace: The Cognitive-Rational Debate, (Colorado, US: Lynne Rienner Publishers, 1997) 143.
44. W. Raymond Duncan, Barbara Jancar-Webster and Bob Switky, World Politics in the 21st Century (Boston: Houghton Mifflin, Cengage Learning, 2008) 145-146.
45. David A. Schultz, Encyclopaedia of Public Administration and Public Policy (New York: Fact on File. Inc, 2004) 174-175.
46. James D. Morrow, "A rational Choice Approach to International Conflict" in Decision Making on War and Peace: The Cognitive-Rational Debate, ed. Nehemia Geva and Alex Mintz (Colorado: Lynne Rienner Publishers, 1997) 12-33.
47. For detail argument see, Research article on "Foreign Policy Analysis and Rational Choice Models" by Bruce Bueno de Mesquita, available at the International Studies Association Compendium Project, at http://www.isacompss.com/info/samples/foreignpolicyanalysisandrationalchoicemodels_sample.pdf
48. Greg Cashman, What Causes War? An Introduction to the International Conflict (Lanham, Maryland: Laxington Books, 2000) 86.
49. Hollis and Smith (1990) 8-9, 196-202.
50. The word "satisficing" is a combination of two different word "satisfy" and "sufficing" popularly used by Herbert A Simonin his work Herbert A Simon,. "Rational Choice and the Structure of the Environment", (Psychological Review, Vol. 63 No. 2, 1956, 129-138), though it first coined in his work Administrative Behaviour; A Study of Decision-Making Processes in Administrative Organization (New York: Macmillan, 1947). For details see, Brown, Reva, "Consideration of the Origin of Herbert Simon's Theory of 'Satisficing' (1933-1947)". Management Decision 42:10 (2004): 1240–1256.

51. Cashman (2000) 80-82.
52. Anthony G. McGrew, Michael John Wilson (ed), Decision Making: Approaches and Analysis, (Manchester: Manchester University Press, 1982) 8-10.
53. David A. Schultz, Encyclopaedia of Public Administration and Public Policy (New York: Infobase Publishing, 2009) 175.
54. S. P. Naidu, Public Administration: Concepts and Theories (New Delhi: New Age International, 2005) 80.
55. Paul D'Anieri, International Politics: Power and Purpose in Global Affairs (Boston: Wadswarth, Cengage Learning, 2012) 156.
56. Greg Cashman (2000) 90.
57. Ibid, 89-95.
58. Greg Cashman, What Causes War?: An Introduction to Theories of International Conflict (Lanham, Maryland: 2013) 132-33.
59. Morton H. Halperin, Bureaucratic Politics and Foreign Policy, (Washington, D.C.: Brookings, 1974) 84-85.
60. Graham T Allison., and Morton H. Halperin, Bureaucratic Politics: A Paradigm and Some Policy Implications, World Politics, Vol. 24/Supplement (1972) 40-79.
61. See Allison & Zelikow (1999)182-83.
62. For detail see Jerel A. Rosati, Developing a Systematic Decision-Making Framework: Bureaucratic Politics in Perspective, World Politics, Vol. 33/3 (1981): 234-52.
63. For instance see Klaus Brummer (2009), Richard Stillman (1990), Thomas Preston (1999), Paul 't Hart (2012), David R. Berman (1985) et.al
64. Allison &Zelikow (1999) 307.
65. *Ibid,* 298.
66. Geoffrey Dudley and Jeremy Richardson, Why Does Policy Change?: Lessons from British Transport Policy 1945-99, (London: Routledge, 2001) 20.
67. Halperin (1974) 24-62.
68. Allison &Zelikow (1999) 255.
69. Allison &Zelikow (1999) 300.
70. Allison &Zelikow (1999) 295.
71. Charles W Kegley, Jr., and Shannon Lindsey Blanton, World Politics: Trend and Transformation (Boston: Wodsworth, Cengage Learning, 2011) 203.
72. Jeffrey S. Harrison, Caron H. St. John, Foundations in Strategic Management, 5th Ed., (Mason, Ohio: South- Western, Cengage Learning, 2009) 4-6; also see, Abbass F. Alkhafaji, Strategic Management: Formulation, Implementation, and Control in a Dynamic Environment, (Haworth Press, Presently Routledge, 2003) 59-80.
73. Lee R. Beach and Terry Connolly, The Psychology of Decision Making, (Thousand Oaks: People in Organizations, Sage, 2005) 1-4.
74. Pieter Johannes et al. Management Principles: A Contemporary Edition for Africa (Cape Town: Juta and Company, 2007) 152.

75 . James Rosenau, 'Pre-theories and Theories of Foreign Policy', excerpt in J. Vasquez, Classics of International Relations, 3rd Edition, (New Jersey: Prentice Hall,1996) 183.

76. Vernon McKay, African Diplomacy, 2nd Edn. (Praeger, New York, 1996) xv.

77. "Operation Pillar of Defense - Selected statements". Ministry of External Affairs, Israel, November, 20 2012, available at: http://www.mfa.gov.il/MFA/Government/Speeches+by+Israeli+leaders/2012/Operation_Pillar of Defense-Statements.htm (Retrieved March 10, 2013)

78. LahavHarkov, Shas, "Elections Bill Undercut Tal Law Alternatives", The Jerusalem Post, July 5, 2012 , available at http://www.jpost.com/DiplomacyAndPolitics/Article.aspx?id=269007 (Retrieved March 10, 2013)

79. War In Gaza: Why Now? Election Politics? Research article on Global Research, November 16, 2012 available at: http://www.globalresearch.ca/war-in-gaza-why-now/5312024, see also, Lahav Harkov, Barak: "Strikes just the beginning of IDF operations", The Jerusalem Post, November 14, 2012 , available at: http://www.jpost.com/DiplomacyAndPolitics/Article.aspx?id=291828 (Retrieved March 10, 2013)

80. Rosenau (1971) 18.

81. Pascal Boyer, Religion Explained: The Evolutionary Origins of Religious Thought (New York: Basic Books, 2001) 83.

82. Alex Mintz& Karl Derouen Jr. (2010) 130.

83. For instance see Mamdouh G. Salameh, The Oil "Price Rise" Factor in the Iraq War: A Macroeconomic Assessment, International Politics, (Vol. 2, No. III, Winter & Spring 2009) 43-57; Raymond Hinnebusch, The American invasion of Iraq: Causes and Consequences, Perceptions, Spring 2007; Alain Pilote, "Reflections on the War in Iraq, The Real Motives: Oil and Money ", Michael Journal, March-April, 2003; W. Clark, The Real Reasons For The Upcoming War In Iraq, A Macroeconomic and Geostrategic Analysis of the Unspoken Truth, available at: http://rense.com/general34/realre.htm

84. "The Top 20 Arms Importers", 2007–2011, SIPRI, http://www.sipri.org/googlemaps/2012_of_at_top_20 _imp_ map.html

85. George A. Quattrone and Amos Tversky, "Contrasting Rational and Psychological Analysis of Political Choice" in Political Psychology: Key Readings in Social Psychology, edited by John T. Jost, Jim Sidanius (New York: Psychology Press, 2004) 325.

86. Geoffrey Layman, Thomas Carsey, John Green and Richard Herrera, Party Polarization and "Conflict Extension" in American Politics: The Case of Party Activists, article presented at the American Politics Workshop, Department of Government and Politics, University of Maryland, October 7, 2005.

87. Krishan D. Mathur and P.M. Kamath, Conduct of India's Foreign Policy, (New Delhi: South Asian Publishers, 1996) 126.

88. Guy Rocher, Introduction to Sociology (Kolkata: Academic Publishers, 2004) 404.

89. We attempt to generalize the concept of national ideology. for comprehensive debate on this topic refer Bayless Manning, Goals, Ideology and Foreign Policy, Foreign Affairs, January 1976.

90. Adam Quinn, US Foreign Policy in Context: National Ideology from the Founders to the Bush Doctrine, (New York: Routledge, 2011) 3, 22.
91. Nora Femenia, 'Emotional Actor: Foreign Policy Decision Making In The 1982 Falklands/Malvinas' War in Coy, Patrick G. Coy and Lynne M. Woehrle ed. Social Conflicts and Collective Identities, (Lonham, Mariland: Rowman & Littlefield, 2000) 41-66.
92. Jonathan Renshon and Jennifer S. Lerner, "Decision - Making, the Role of Emotions" in Foreign Policy: The Encyclopedia of Peace Psychology, First Edition, Edited by Daniel J. Christie (Blackwell Publishing, 2012) 128.
93. D. Keltner, & J. S. Lerner, "Emotion", In D. Gilbert, S. Fiske, & G. Lindsay (Eds.), Handbook of Social Psychology, 5th Ed., (New York: McGraw-Hill, 2010) 271; see also, John A. Bargh, peter M. Gollwitzer and Gabriele Octtingen, Emotion, in Handbook of Social Psychology - Volume 2, edited by Susan T. Fiske, Daniel T. Gilbert, Gardner Lindzey (Hoboken, New Jersey: John Wiley & Sons, Inc., 2010) 268-316.
94. Benjamin William Moles, "Chinese Nationalism and Foreign Policy: A Cause for Concern or Patriot Games?" Research article of E-International Relations, August 18, 2012 available at: http://www.e-ir.info/2012/08/18/chinese-nationalism-and-foreign-policy-a-cause-for-concern-or-patriot-games/
95. Lloyd Jensen, Explaining Foreign Policy (Englewood Cliffs, NJ: Prentice-Hall, 1982) 13-14.
96. David Mitchell, Making Foreign Policy: Presidential Management of Decision–Making Process, (Hants, England: Ashgate Publishing, 2005) 5-16.
97. David Mitchell (2005) 1-31.
98. W. Raymond Duncan, Barbara Jancar-Webster, Bob Switky, World Politics in the 21st Century (Boston: Hunghton Miffin Publishing 2008) 235.
99. Jared Diamond, The Third Chimpanzee: The Evaluation and Future of Human Animal (New York: Harpet Perennial, 1992) 236.
100. Martin Ira Glassner, Political Geography, 2nd Edn. (New York: John Wiley & Sons, 1996). 11.
101. Duncan, Webster and Switky, (2008) 235.
102. Frederic L. Kirgis, "International Agreements and U.S. Law", Research article of American Society of International Law, May 1997, http://www.asil.org/insigh10.cfm
103. Scholars are also acknowledged on the uneasiness in defining 'deterrence theory'. For instance see Patrick M. Morgan, Deterrence Now, (Cambridge: Cambridge University Press, 2003) 1.
104. Alex Mintz (2010) 122.
105. Patrick M. Morgan, Deterrence Now, (Cambridge: Cambridge University Press, 2003) 1-8.
106. Bruce Russett, "The Calculus of Deterrence", Journal of Conflict Resolution 7/21 (1963) 97-109.
107. Glenn H. Snyder, Alliance Politics, (New York: Cornell University Press, 2007) 4.

108. Stephan M. Walt, The Origins of Alliances, (New York: Cornell University Press, 1987) 1.
109. Robert B. Louden, The World We Want : How and Why the Ideals of the Enlightenment Still Elude US, (New York: Oxford University Press, 2007) 187.
110. Miriam Prys, Redefining Regional Power in International Relations: Indian and South African Perspectives, (Oxon: Routledge, 2012) 3-5.

Chapter - 2

Foreign Policy Decision Making in India: Actors, Institutions and Procedures

The emergence of globalization and the cosmopolitanization of state craft have redefined the concept and scope of Foreign Policy. In the borderless global village when the gap between internal and external affairs is gradually narrowing down, the matter of external relation no longer remains the isolated business of foreign office only. Though the Ministry of External Affairs is the pivotal player in India's external relation, other important agencies such as the Cabinet, Ministry of Defence, Ministry of Commerce and Industry, National Security Council, Prime Minister's Office and Parliament also are contributing significantly for the planning and formulation of India's Foreign Policy. Apart from these core agencies various other peripheral agencies also are involved in Foreign Policy decision making process, which is a highly complex and multi-stage process.

In this context, this chapter analyses the process of Foreign Policy making and the role of various actors, agencies and institutions that involve in this process. The first part of the section has been further divided into ten sub-sections. In each respective sub-section the role and function of important governmental agencies like the Ministry of External Affairs, Cabinet and Cabinet Committees, Prime Minister's Office, the National Security Council, the Strategic Policy Group, the Joint Intelligence Council, Ministry of Defence, and the Parliament in the formulation of India's Foreign Policy have been discussed in detail. The second section of the chapter discusses the procedure of India's Foreign Policy decision making and analyses its structure and function.

Actors and Institutions of Foreign Policy Decision Making in India

Decision making in Foreign Policy, being the most complex process, needs multiple specialized agencies, individuals and institutions to deal with range of issues of different subjects. Though the Ministry of External Affairs is primarily responsible to deal with the matters related to foreign affairs, agencies like, the Cabinet, the Prime Minister's Office, Ministry of Defence, the National Security Council, the Strategic Policy Group and the Parliament play important role in the formulation of India's external policy. They analyse the foreign policy issues and take decisions to address these issues. In this regard, this section gives a comprehensive account on the structure and functions and the role of these agencies on India's Foreign Policy decision making process.

Ministry of External Affairs

Ministry of External Affairs (MEA) is the primary institution of Foreign Policy Decision Making in India. It is one of the oldest and important departments of Government and primarily responsible to look after the matters related to external affairs of the country. Since its formation, it has been successfully dealing with spectrum of activities related to foreign affairs of India. Though a variety of agencies and actors have been involved in Foreign Policy decision making process, it is the MEA which takes the final call on any of the issues and determine the course of Foreign Policy officially. Besides decision making, the Ministry of External affairs also plays a significant role in information gathering, processing and analyzing through its foreign missions for effective policy making. The ministry issues passports, gives consular services to Indian citizens visiting abroad and ensures their safety and security. It is also responsible for the issuance of visas to foreign tourists visiting India. Above all, the ministry plays a larger role in the planning and formulation of Indian's foreign policy. The ministry manages and coordinates the efforts of other stake holder of foreign policy decision making and channelizes their efforts to materialise India's foreign policy objects.

Evolution of MEA

The present Ministry of External Affairs, at its earlier form was established by the British East India Company on the year 1783[1] to handle the company's emerging foreign relations with South Asia, Southeast Asia and Frontier Nations (Persia, Afghanistan and Tibet).[2] Until 1833, the agency was handling both Internal and external administration of these nations for the East India Company. However, the Charter Act of 1833 has segregated the internal and external matters for the first time by setting up four different departments under the Secretariat of the Government of India. Following the act, a separate 'Foreign Department' has been established and three different branches namely, Political, Foreign and Secret Branch have been attached to it. In the year 1859, when the portfolio system was introduced, the members of Executive Council of the Governor General of India were authorized to lead these departments. Since the Foreign Department is considered very important, it remains under the supervision of the Governor General himself.[3]

Following the administrative reforms in 1914, the 'Secret Branch' was taken away from the 'Foreign Department' and the department was renamed as 'Foreign and Political Department'. The new department had two branches, the 'Political Branch' and the 'Foreign Branch' headed by two separate secretaries. While the Political Branch was assigned to look after the matter related to Princely States and other such administrative areas outside British India, the 'Foreign Branch' was put in charge to deal with the issues arising from the frontiers States. The expansion of the British Frontiers and the increasing administrative burden forced the British India Government to separate the two branches. As a result, the parental department was dismantled in the year 1937and two different departments namely, 'Political Department' and the External Affairs Department' were created.[4]

Though the new department was created to over see all matters of foreign affairs, some of the related subjects remained outside its preview. The matter of 'Overseas Indians Affair' for instance, was first attached to the 'Education Department' and later placed under the 'Composite Department of Education, Health and Lands'. Subsequently, the 'Division of Overseas Indians' was transformed into a new department called 'Commonwealth Relations Department' and assigned with additional task to manage British India' sexternal relations with Burma (the present Myanmar), Ceylon (Sri Lanka) and Malaysia, as well as to handle British High Commission at South Africa and Australia.[5] Similarly, the Indian High Commission at London was brought under the control of Department of Commerce and authorized to deal with the matters related to India's international trade.

Until 1947, India's foreign relations were taken care by the two corresponding departments 'Department of External Affairs' and 'Departments of Commonwealth Relations'. While the former was authorized to take care of India's overall external relations, the latter was set up to manage India's relations with Commonwealth Countries. This parallel system of external relations was creating unnecessary confusion and quarrels among the policy makers and caused unnecessary bureaucratic delay in the planning and execution of foreign policy. Hence, the two departments were merged together in the year 1947 and renamed as 'Department of External Affairs and Commonwealth Relations'. In 1948, the 'External Publicity Division' was taken away from the Ministry of Information and Broadcasting (MIB) and attached with the Ministry of External Affairs for optimum result. The ministry was again renamed as 'Ministry of External Affairs' by dropping the appendage 'Commonwealth Relations'. Since then the ministry has never undergone under any major structural change, though some new divisions have been created with the expansion of its functions.[6]

Structure and Organisation of MEA

Being one of the important portfolios, the Ministry of External Affairs is led by one of the senior and experienced Cabinet Ministers along with one or two Ministers of State (MoS) or Deputy Ministers to assist him. Presently, the Ministry is headed by a Cabinet Minister besides two Ministers of State. As the supreme head of the ministry, Minister for External Affairs is authorized to conduct and coordinate all the works of the ministry, whereas, the junior ministers are put in charge to look after some administrative and divisional works. From independence to 1964, except a brief break in 1952, the Secretary General used to be the administrative head of the ministry. He happened to be the prime advisor to the Prime Minister Nehru, who was also leading the Ministry of External Affairs, in the decision making on foreign affairs. To assist him the foreign secretary and two other secretaries were appointed and assigned with different works. During Nehru period the Secretary General was the supreme authority of the administrative activities and all major administrative and policy making activities functioned under his command.

In the year 1964 when Shastri became the Prime Minister, Sardar Swaran Singh was appointed as the full time Foreign Minister. With the appointment of full time Foreign Minister, the task of the policy making was transferred to the Foreign Minister and the burden of the Secretary General was drastically reduced. Therefore, the post was abolished and the Foreign Secretary was assigned to lead the administrative work of the ministry. Since then, the MEA continued to be led by Foreign Minister and Foreign secretary and the system is still in practice today.

At Present[7], including Foreign Secretary, the ministry consists of eight secretaries namely, Secretary (East), Secretary (Special Assignment), Secretary (DPA & ER), Secretary (West), Special Secretary (Americas & CPV). Below the Secretaries, there are five Additional Secretaries namely,

Additional Secretaries (IO), Additional Secretaries (AD), Additional Secretaries (FA), Additional Secretaries, (Pr Chief Controller of Accounts), and Additional Secretaries (L&T), Under the Additional Secretary, numerous Joint Secretaries Directors and Deputy Secretaries, and other administrative staffs have been appointed to assist them in various administrative works:[8]

The ministry is also divided into several administrative divisions, which is broadly Classified into two categories, (i) the Specialized and Support Divisions and (ii) the Territorial Divisions. Each of the Division has been assigned to look after the issues related to their respective Jurisdiction and the Foreign Secretary coordinates these divisions and oversees the functions of the ministry. The list of the Divisions has been given below:

Specialized and Support Divisions of MEA

1.	Administration	17.	External Publicity Division
2.	A & RM Division	18.	Finance Division
3.	Bureau of Security	19.	Foreign Service Institute
4.	Boundary Cell	20.	Haj Cell
5.	Office of the Principal Chief Controller of Accounts	21.	Investment, Technology, Promotion Division
6.	Central Registry	22.	Legal & Treaties Division
7.	Cypher, NGO, Vigilance & Inspection Division	23.	MEA Library
8.	Coordination Division	24.	Multilateral Economic Relations Division
9.	Complaints Committee of MEA against Sexual Harassment	25.	Nalanda Division
10.	Counter Terrorism Cell	26.	Parliament& VIP Division
11.	Consular Passport, Visa Division	27.	Public Diplomacy Division
12.	Development Partnership Administration	28.	Policy Planning & Research Division
13.	Disarmament & International Security Affairs Division	29.	Projects Division
14.	E-Governance & IT Division	30.	Protocol Division
15.	Energy Security Division	31.	Right to Information Division RTI
16.	Establishment Division	32.	SAARC Division
		33.	Special Kuwait Cell
		34.	UN Economic & Social Division
		35.	United Nations Political Division
		36.	Welfare Division[9]

Besides the administrative divisions, the Ministry of external affairs also consists of several territorial divisions led by specialized officers and these divisions are responsible to analyse and report the significant political developments of these regions to the government. Moreover, these divisions also coordinate and oversee India's external relation with its respective regions. These territorial divisions are as follows:

Territorial Division of MEA

1. Americas Division	9. Gulf Division
2. ASEAN Multilateral Division	10. Latin America & Caribbean Division
3. Bangladesh, Sri Lanka, Maldives Division	11. Northern (Nepal, Bhutan) Division
4. Central Europe Division	12. Pakistan, Afghanistan & Iran Division
5. East Asia Division	13. Southern Division
6. East & Southern Africa Division	14. Western Africa Division
7. Eurasia Division	15. West Asia & North Africa Division
8. Europe West Division	

Apart from the above divisions, the MEA is also supported by a large number of Foreign Missions and Posts extended across the globe. The missions are led by Ambassadors and High Commissioners, who work under the control of Ministry of External Affairs. These missions are generally situated at the capital of the respective country and in most of the cases maintain several consulates at different parts of the country. The Consulate General normally heads the consulate supported by a large number of supporting staff.

Structure of the Ministry of External Affairs

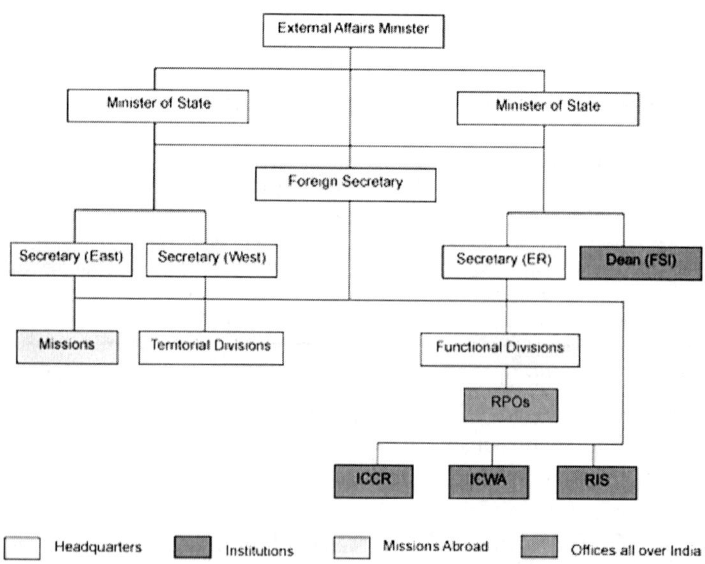

Functions of MEA

With the emergence of India as one of the aspiring global power and transformation of Indian economy, the role and function of MEA has been multiplied gradually. To deal with these emerging challenges, the role and function of the ministry has undergone constant changes to facilitate India's emerging role in the international sphere. Like any other foreign office, the prime function of MEA is to plan, formulate and manage India's external relations with other nations as well as protect and promote India's national interest at the global stage. Besides, the ministry is also responsible to setup and manage India's foreign missions and diplomatic institutions and extend consular activities to Indian and foreign nationals. Similarly, matters related to India's representatives at UN and other specialized agencies, Issues and cancellation passports and visas and protection of Indian nationals and institutions abode also come under the jurisdiction of MEA. The ministry receives reports from its foreign missions and gives the necessary inputs to the government during the Foreign Policy making. Since the attachment of External Publicity Division (XP) to the MEA, in 1948, the ministry also is responsible to publicise India's positive image among world communities. The detail functions of the MEA have been stated below:

Planning and Formulation of Foreign Policy

To deal with the increasing complexity of contemporary international relations, there is a need for careful planning and continuous pursuance of foreign policy developments over a period of time. Hence, most of the modern states set up the policy planning units within their Foreign Office long ago and formulated their external policy based on the inputs from these units. For instance, the US Policy Planning Staff and the British Policy Planning Section were created to give strategic inputs in the planning and formulation of the foreign policy of United Sates and United Kingdom respectively.[10] However, until 1663 there was no such dedicated foreign policy planning section in India under the Ministry of External Affairs. After the military disaster of 1962 war, the East Asia Research and Coordination Division was created in 1963 to conduct research and planning on China, which was later institutionalised as the Current Research Division in 1965. Since then, the Policy Planning and Research Division (as it is called now) is engaged in planning and formulation of India's foreign and strategic policy. Through the division, the MEA awards research projects to the academia, think-tanks, research organisations, and foreign policy institutes of India and assists them financially to organise seminars, conferences and studies to deliberate on various facets of India's external relations.[11] The MEA prepares a Monthly Summary of important developments and global events for the Cabinet and senior officials of Government of India, on which the government prepares its future policy.[12]

Managing India's External Relations

The prime and foremost duty of MEA is to manage India's External Relations with foreign States and international entity, such as United Nations, regional and international institutions and transnational actors. It selects and sends Indian representatives to these international entities to conduct India's external policy with the respective institutions and to report the political developments of the region. Besides, it also takes necessary steps to maintain good relations with States which have signed Special Treaty with India like Bhutan, and Nepal and handles the issues related to France and Portugal over their former colonies Pondicherry, Goa, Daman and Diu.

Diplomatic and Consular Activities

The ministry is responsible to setup and manage India's foreign missions, posts and consulates abroad and appoints India's representatives to run these missions. Using these diplomatic channels it reaches out to foreign states and conveys India's positions and concerns on significant international events. Through these missions, it provides necessary information and guidance to Indian and foreign nationals. Likewise, all matters related to the power, privileges and functioning of Indian and foreign representatives, diplomats and U.N. Officials also come under the supervision of MEA. In case of necessity, the ministry can give or deny clearance to any non-scheduled chartered flights of foreign diplomats.

Matters related to VISA, Immigration and Pilgrims

Besides managing India's external relations, MEA is also responsible for the issuance and cancelation of Passports to the Indian nationals and granting visas and travel documents to the foreign visitors. Similarly, under Reciprocity Act, 1943 (9 of 1943), the ministry also handles the issues related to Immigration to India from the Republic of South Africa or any other countries. The Ministry has the authority to grant or reject the travel permission to foreigners for Himalayan expeditions and travel to Protected Areas other than those with which the Ministry of Home Affairs is concerned.

Apart from immigration, the MEA facilitates travel arrangements for traders and pilgrims from India to holly places outside India such as, Tibet and Pakistan and vice versa. The Ministry manages the administration of Port Haj Committee Act, 1959 and the Indian Pilgrim Ship Rules, 1933, and Pilgrim parties from India to Shrines in Pakistan and vice versa. Further more, the Protection and restoration of non-Muslim shrines in Pakistan and Muslim shrines in India under Pant-Mirza Agreement of 1955, evacuation of non-Muslim from Pakistan and protection of rights of the minority communities in India and Pakistan also come under the preview of Ministry of External Affairs.[13]

Management of India's Foreign Assistance Programme

Economic aid and foreign developmental assistance has been the important tool of foreign policy. Despite being a developing country, India has been running a foreign aid programme since 1960s and its aid budge thas been continuously increasing since the economic reforms period that started in 1991. More precisely, India's aid budget rose from 13.4 Crores Indian rupees (about US$ 40.3 million) in 1966, to 6967crores Indian rupees (over US$ 1.06 billion) in 2014.[14] The MEA is responsible to manage India's Economic and technical assistance to foreign nations. It also deals with all matters related to grant of loans and credits to Nepal, Bhutan and Bangladesh and recovery of advances granted to the evacuees from Burma, Malaya, etc., during the years 1942-47 and residual work related to refugees given asylum in India during World War II.

Besides financial assistance, the MEA also handles the 'Indian Technical and Economic Cooperation (ITEC)' Programme, which was instituted to extend India's technical and economic assistance to foreign countries on September 15, 1964.[15] Though the programme was launched as a bilateral programme to finance technical cooperation programmes for African countries under the Special Commonwealth African Assistance Plan Programme, it has been extended to other Asian and Latin American countries. In addition, grants of Scholarship to foreign students, excluding scholarship to Non-Resident Indians (NRIs) and Political pensions paid to foreign refugees and descendants of those who rendered services abroad also come under the functions of MEA.

Matters of Detention and Extradition

The trend of international crime has been constantly upward since the rise of globalization. Often, criminals migrate to other countries to escape from the legal action and prosecution. Being situated in the present epicentre of terrorism, India is one of the uncommon victims of international crimes such as terrorism. To curb the menace of trans-national crime, the Ministry of External Affairs has been authorized to initiate the diplomatic negotiations with other states for the Detention and Extradition of criminals and accused persons from India to foreign and Commonwealth countries and vice versa. The ministry also deals with the general administration of the Extradition Act, 1962 and handles matters related to preventive detention in India for reasons of States connected with External and Commonwealth affairs.[16]

Materialisation of International Treaties and Agreements

Since independence, several Political treaties, agreements and conventions with foreign and Commonwealth countries have been signed by government of India to facilitate India's national interest. The Ministry of External Affairs has been assigned to conduct all ground work to form the draft and finalize the treaty. Moreover, it also ensures the rectification and implementation of the treaties, agreements and conventions conducted with foreign nations and United Nations and deals with all issues raised out of the existing treaties. The MEA also works for the Protection and preservation of Non-Muslim shrines in Pakistan and Muslim shrines in India in terms of Pant-Mirza Agreement of 1955.

Matter Related to Persons of Indian Origin and NRIs

The MEA is responsible for the protection of Persons of Indian Origin (PIO)and Non-resident Indians (NRI) residing abroad and deals with their concerns and grievances. Before the formation of Ministry of Overseas Indians in 2004, the MEA was also put in charge to oversee all matters relating to Overseas Indians, all emigration under the Emigration Act, 1983 (31 of 1983) from India to overseas countries and the return of emigrants and works relating to totalization agreements, protection and welfare of Overseas Indians and exemption from payment of Social Security. The ministry is in charge for collection and dissemination of information concerning admission of NRI/PIO students to various educational, technical and cultural institutions in India wherever discretionary quota for NRI/PIO students exists, in consultation with the Ministry of Human Resource Development and the Ministry of Culture and awarding of Scholarship to NRI/PIO students for study in India under different schemes in consultation with the Ministry of External Affairs.

Matter Related to United Nations

The coordination and implementation of all matter related to United Nations, Specialized Agencies and other International Organisations is also one of the primary responsibilities of Ministry of External Affairs. It sends the Indian representatives to the UN and to the specialized agencies and presents India's voice at the international forum. It also takes steps to Implement the reporting obligations, in coordination with the concerned Ministries, required under the United Nations and international conventions, to which India is a State party, including the protection of Human Rights.

Matter Related to Indian Foreign Services

Being the primary institution for conducting Foreign Policy, the Ministry of External Affairs is also responsible to manage all matter related to Indian Foreign Service (IFS) including Indian Foreign Service Board. It also deals with issues associated with the appointment and regulation of diplomats and other foreign officers working under the ministry and the management of Foreign Service Training Institute (FPI).

External Publicity and Cultural Activities

External publicity has been one of the important elements contemporary to international politics. It has been widely used by sates to project their positive image to the world since world wars and cold war.[17] Looking at the importance of the External Publicity, the External Publicity (XP) Division was set up in ———— and subsequently attached to the MEA in the year 1948. Since then, The Ministry continues to articulate the position of the Government of India on various foreign policy issues in the international and domestic media, through press conferences, regular press briefings, backgrounders, dissemination of statements, effective use of the MEA website and through electronic communications. The ministry also setup the Public Diplomacy Division in 2006 to update the policy decision of the Indian foreign policy on daily basis and to reach out to the scholars, thinks tanks, and media through its outreach activities.[18]

Similarly, the Indian Council for Cultural Relations (ICCR) was also set up in 1950 to promote India's cultural heritage abroad by organising a large number of exhibitions, conferences, seminars, cultural events and lecture-demonstrations abroad. Through the 37 Cultural Centres and 95 Chairs in universities abroad, the ICCR administers a large number of scholarship schemes for overseas students on behalf of the Government of India and other agencies and works as the nodal agency for the welfare of international students in India. With the help of these two divisions the MEA works to develop India's positive image abroad.[19]

Matter Related to Sea and Land Borders

It is the responsibility of the ministry to administer the matters related to Law of the Sea, including the Indian Territorial Waters, Contiguous Zone, Continental Shelf and Exclusive Economic Zones (EEZ), questions of international law arising on the high seas including fishery rights; piracies and crimes committed on the High Seas or in the air, offences against the Law of Sovereign States committed on land or the High seas or in the air, legal matters concerning the International Seabed Area and Authority etc. Besides sea border, demarcation of the land frontiers of India and matter related to border raids and incidents also come under the jurisdiction of the MEA.

Protocol and Ceremonial Functions

Along with all other administrative activities, the MEA is also responsible to facilitate the foreign visit of the Indian ministers, diplomats and official delegations and arranges to offer necessary protocols during the visit. The ministry also extends necessary protocols and conducts the ceremonial activities for foreign and Commonwealth Visitors and Diplomatic and Consular Representatives to India. It also deals with matters associated with the Hospitality Grant of the Government of India. [20]

The Cabinet and Cabinet Committees

In most of the Parliamentary systems of the government like India, the important decisions on issues of national and international affairs are decided by the cabinet. Cabinet is the inner most circle of Council of Ministers (CoM) which often consists of the senior most ministers of the government. Being the closest allies of the Prime Minister, the cabinet including Prime Minister itself, takes decisions on subjects of national importance and approves the policy proposals. The Prime Minister, being the executive head of the government generally calls the meeting of the cabinet to discuss major issues and follow the policy accordingly. But, during the time of Nehru, the cabinet was apparently the rubber stamp for policy approval, while most of the decisions were taken by Nehru himself. The cabinet meets once in a week during normal time and can hold multiple meetings at the time of emergency.

Composition of the Cabinet

The cabinet is a premier section of the Council of Ministers, selected from both the houses of the Parliament. Like other ministers, the President appoints the cabinet and distributes the portfolio as per the advice of the Prime Minister. Most of the members of cabinet are selected form Lok Sabha, though it has been seen that some significant members are also selected from Rajya Sabha. Former Prime Minister H. D. Deve Gowda, I. K. Gujral and Manmohan Singh for instance, were the members of Rajya Sabha and led the cabinet during their Prime Ministership. The members remain in cabinet as long as the President wishes. However, the President has the power to expel any member of the cabinet or change the portfolio among the ministers on the advice of the Prime Minister. In recent years, composition of the cabinet seems abalanced group of regional leadership and the representation of important communities—Muslims, Sikhs, SCs, STs and OBCs.[21]

The Cabinet Secretariat, headed by the Cabinet Secretary has been set up to look after the business of the cabinet. The Cabinet Secretary is not the member of the Cabinet, rather a senior Civil Servant of the government of India appointed to assist the cabinet in policy making and implementation. As per the Government of India (Allocation of Business) Rules 1961, the Cabinet Secretary deals with all matters related to the Cabinet Committees and promote the inter-ministerial coordination within the Cabinet.[22]

Function of the Cabinet

Being the powerful institution of the government, the cabinet performs various important functions. It leads the government and is responsible for the smooth functioning of the government and developmental activities. As a top decision making body of the government, the primary task of the cabinet is to approve new policy proposals and supervise over its implementation. But in practice, the whole function of the government comes under the preview of cabinet except some formal practices. Hence, the role of the cabinet is multidimensional in nature. The function of the cabinet is divided into four different categories, which have been discussed below:[23]

Approve all New Policy Proposals

Before making any policy or placing the bill for parliamentary approval, all new policy proposals and draft legislations require the cabinet's approval. Usually the Prime Minister calls the meeting of the cabinet and seeks their view on the proposed policy of important issues. After thorough discussion, the cabinet gives necessary suggestions and carry out necessary changes to the draft proposal. After the approval of the cabinet, the draft proposal is usually sent to the Parliament for approval. During the drafting state of the policy proposal, the cabinet has the right to reject or approve or modify the draft. But, normally it approves the proposal with some changes, as the cabinet has been consulted over the proposal during its conceptualization. Therefore, the decision of the cabinet is crucial for any policy and ultimately the future of the nation.[24]

Recommend all Major Appointments

Under the Indian Parliamentary system, the President is the formal head of the state and the entire government machinery runs on his name. He appoints the heads of the major administrative and judicial institutions, including Governors, Ambassadors and other diplomatic representatives, the Chief Justice and other Judges of the Supreme Court, the Chief Justices and other Judges of the High Courts, Attorney-General and Auditor-General of India and various commissions such as the Finance Commission of India, the Election Commission of India, Union Public Service Commission, Scheduled Class and & Scheduled Tribe Commission, Minority Commission and Joint Commission for a group of States etc. But in practice, it is the cabinet, the inner most circle of the council of Ministers that recommends these appointments and the President is duty bound to obey the advice of the Council of Ministers under Article 74 of the India Constitution. Apart from advising on key appointment, the Cabinet also advises the President for their transform and even removal.[25]

Settle Interdepartmental Disputes

The third major task of the cabinet is to resolve interdepartmental disputes and facilitate interdepartmental coordination. As different departments of the government work under different organisational structures and ideologies, it is normal to have attitudinal differences on certain policies and this leads to unnecessary administrative delays for the policy decision. Being the senior club of council of ministers, it is the duty of the cabinet to identify the dispute and address the issue by taking necessary measures. The cabinet calls the meeting and invites the two parties to present their concerns and takes appropriate action to resolve the issue, after thorough discussion. Generally, the cabinet adopts the middle path or the synthesized approaches to please both the parties during the time of dispute settlement.

Coordination of Developmental Activities

In the Parliamentary form of government, the Council of Ministers is answer able to the Parliament for its policy for the formulation and implementation of public policy. As the core of the Council of Ministers and the senior most executive body, the cabinet is directly responsible for the success and failure of government policies. The 'sails together and sinks together' provision leaves no option for the cabinet than to lead the government and guide the developmental activities. Hence, the cabinet coordinates between the departments and ministries and provides all necessary helps to complete the pending tasks. It supervises recent ongoing works and guides them for its implementation. The cabinet also follows the policy implementation, analyses the feedbacks and takes further action to resolve the issues for optimum result. [26]

Role of Cabinet in Foreign Policy Decision Making

Cabinet, being the top most decision making body of the government, determines the course of external relation of the country by giving necessary directions. The member of the cabinet is the most trusted colleague of the Prime Minister and assists and advises him/her during the time of Foreign Policy crisis. In the case of any such crisis, the Prime Minister calls the urgent meeting of the cabinet where the issues are put for discussion and the members put their views and opinions. As the representative of the department, the members present the concern and opinion of the ministry of department on that matter before the cabinet. After the discussion the cabinet takes the appropriate decision to resolve the issues.

But during recent times, the formation and policy making of the cabinet has become the product of political bargaining and negotiation.[27] In the post Narshima Rao era, coalition became the only source to form the government, hence compelled the Prime Minister to form the coalition cabinet in order to satisfy the coalition partners. In case of any issue, the Prime Minister has to negotiate with the partner members and sometimes has to go along with their views to save the government.[28] India's decision to vote in favour of UN Resolution against the Human Rights violations by the Sri Lankan Army towards native Tamilians is one of the finest examples of such cases. The United Progressive Alliance (UPA) led coalition government of India voted in favour of the resolution, to please its coalition partner DMK, who threatened to pull back its support from the government, if the government did not supported the UN resolution.[29] In order to save the government, the UPA government voted in favour of the resolution, despite the constant warning of the Foreign Policy experts against the decision[30].

The role of the cabinet is very vital in Foreign Policy making and in resolving the Foreign Policy crisis. It also takes other decisions to strengthen India's internal and external security in collaboration with Ministry of Home Affairs and Ministry of Defence respectively. For a comprehensive Foreign Policy, the cabinet also takes combined efforts by taking several ministries into confidence. For example, in collaboration with MEA, Ministry of Commerce may work to enhance the trade and business, and HRD ministry for education development.

Cabinet Committee

In the Parliamentary system of government, all power is vested with the Council of Ministers, especially with cabinet, the top most group within the Council of Ministers. However, with the growing volume of complex tasks in the recent years, the cabinet hardly has time for extensive scrutinisation of the referred policies and fruitful recommendation. Therefore, the cabinet committees have been setup to assist the cabinet in policy formulation, coordination and supervision of the government. The committees are responsible to resolve the intradepartmental conflict and ensure greater cooperation among the ministries and departments. Various specialized cabinet committees have been set up to deal with specific issues of their area of domain and pass its suggestions and recommendations to the cabinet for decision making and it is upto the cabinet to incorporate or reject the suggestions.

Types of Cabinet Committees

The cabinet committees are largely divided into two different categories, the Standing Committees and the *ad hoc* Committees. The standing committees are those permanent committees that are formed regularly and deal with certain subjects on regular basis. Though the structure of the committees changes from time to time, the function of the committees remain almost permanent. However, if the government wants, it can modify its role or even close down the committee. But so far, some of the committees have remained unchanged since formation. Now eleven standing committees have been formed to look after different subjects. The list of the cabinet committees is given below:

(1) Appointments Committee of the Cabinet.
(2) Cabinet Committee on Accommodation.
(3) Cabinet Committee on Economic Affairs.
(4) Cabinet Committee on Parliamentary Affairs.

(5) Cabinet Committee on Political Affairs.

(6) Cabinet Committee on Prices.

(7) Cabinet Committee on Security.

(8) Cabinet Committee on World Trade Organisation Matters.

(9) Cabinet Committee on Infrastructure.

(10) Cabinet Committee on Unique Identification Authority of India related issues.

(11) Cabinet Committee on Investment[31]

Apart from the above standing committees, some *ad hoc* cabinet committees have also been set up to deal with the non-permanent issues. These committees are formed from time to time and are assigned a particular task to perform. When the task gets over, the term of the committee automatically comes to an end.

The number of the cabinet committees varies from time to time, and government to government. At time of need, the Prime Minister may form additional specialized committee to deal with the emerging crisis and decide on the nature and size of the committees. In the year 1948 there were only two committees, namely the Defence Committee and the Economic Committee.[32] However, the numbers increased subsequently and in 1957 the entire structure of the cabinet committee was changed and ten new committees were set up. In 1977, when the Janata Government decided to dismantle unnecessary administrative setups, the number of the cabinet committees were minimized and reduced to six.[33] Hence the size of the cabinet committees never remains constant and is subject to the requirement of the government. At present, eleven Cabinet Committees are working in assisting the cabinet in policy formulation and coordination.[34]

Composition and Function

Being the specialist advisory body, cabinet committees are setup to assist the respective ministry for the planning and formulation of public policy on various important subjects. Normally, the Prime Minister becomes the chairman of the cabinet committees and selected members of the Cabinet and Council of Ministers become the members. As per the requirement, the membership of each cabinet committee can vary from eight to fifteen. Besides the respective minister, some special invitees are also attached to the committees, who also become the part of the committees. However, the committee system is so big that almost all the ministers of the government eventually become the member of some committee or other. Looking at its massy character it has been observed that, the cabinet committee has been used to designate the unhappy Parliamentarians who have not been given a cabinet position.

The main function of the cabinet committee is to look after the various activities of the ministry and give policy direction to their respective department. Being the body of expertises, the cabinet committee plans and formulates the public policies of the government. It also oversees the emerging issues of the department and takes appropriate steps to resolve that. The committee holds regular meetings where these issues are brought for discussion. It also works like a coordinating committee and clarifies the huddles that emerge out of interdepartmental conflicts. But now, the committee system has been criticized because of its irresponsible attitude and irregular activities.

Role of the Cabinet Committees on Foreign Policy

Though none of the cabinet committee deals with the subject of foreign affairs directly, it does not mean that foreign affairs remain out of its preview. Moreover, Administrative Reform Commission used recommendation to setup a cabinet Committee of Foreign Affairs, which was eventually played down by the government.[35] Never the less, while formulating policies, most of the cabinet committees indirectly deal with the issues related to Foreign Policy and take important steps on the subject which affect India's external relations.The Cabinet Committee Security or Economic Affairs, for instance, is meant to look into the matter related to security and economic affairs, which is not far from the subject of foreign affairs. The policy decision on national security and economic affairs is bound to affect the conduct of India's foreign relation. Again, the weapon procurement or technology transfer which is the subject of security committee is directly linked to the foreign affairs, where the diplomatic negotiations are highly essential.

Beyond its subject, the cabinet committees also work together to resolve the disputes and promote India's national interest by making several policies. Having said that, it does not mean that none of the committees have been formed to look after the issues of foreign affairs. During the Chinese invention in 1962, an important committee namely, the 'Emergency Committee' was setup to deal with the matter on national emergency. Chaired by the Prime Minister himself, the committee performed remarkable tasks and was given high priority by the Nehru government. Because of its vibrant character the committee acted likethe 'inner cabinet' where all important, both internal and external matters were discussed. The committee was so active that the meeting of the cabinet was held almost every day and some times more than once in a day, hence "virtually replaced the cabinet as the supreme decision making body in the Government of India"[36] and the committee was playing the prominent role during the time of Rann of Katch dispute with Pakistan in 1965, but later lost its predominant position gradually.

Similarly, the committee on World Trade Organisation Matters also works to resolve issues related to India's concerns at WTO. The committee constantly keeps eye on the recent development on the field of global trade and takes action accordingly to promote India's foreign trade. Cabinet Committee on Economic Affairs and committee on investment are responsible to improve India's economic conditions and to attract the foreign investment into the nation, hence indirectly related to the matter of foreign economic affairs.

But the cabinet committee is gradually losing its faith and often becomes the spot to settle the unpleased party members who have been denied a place in the cabinet. The committees now have become show pieces and hardly offer any meaningful inputs. Most of the cabinet committees were not carried forward by the successive governments and were abolished intentionally, hence lost the credibility and potentiality when they were reconstituted later. Similarly, the meetings of the committees were not been organized regularly, hence several important matters were not discussed. In addition, instead of handling the significant issues,the committee only covered the issues that were referred to them. Therefore, the cabinet committees gradually became less institutionalised and more polarised and have lost its importance today.

The Prime Minister's Office

Prime Minister, in the West minster model of constitutional democracy, is the head of the government, head of the Council of Ministers, the Chief Executive of the Government and the overall epicentre of governance in India. Being the "first among equals", the Prime Minister plays a crucial role in the politico-administrative system of the country and oversees the day-to-day functioning of the Union Government. In the conduct of his enormous responsibility the Prime Minister is assisted by the Prime Minister's Office (PMO). Consisting of senior level bureaucrats and important personalities, the PMO provides the secretarial assistance and crucial advise to the Prime Minister and works as the centre of the policy making in the Indian democratic setup. It coordinates various central agencies, like, Cabinet, Cabinet Committees, Council of Ministries and other such state holders to sort out all the interdepartmental hurdles in the public and Foreign Policy execution. Besides, observing the progress of developmental activities, the PMO passes necessary information to the Prime Minister so that he can take his own decision at the time of need.

During the time of Nehru, the Prime Minister's Secretariat (as PMO was called earlier) became the centre of Foreign Policy Decision Making, as Nehru was handling both the MEA and PMO simultaneously. In addition, the leadership of Nehru was so influential, that the role of the cabinet was minimal and mostly accepted Nehru's views on administration.[37] Even, the PMO used to send orders directly to the executives, by passing the cabinet and the cabinet committees. There is a belief that, Nehru had taken many decisions on Kashmir issue without consulting the cabinet, not even discussing with his deputy Sardar Patel.[38] Following the legacy, his successors equally enhanced the influence of the PMO in decision making. Hence, by 1970s it became the"de facto coordinator and supra-ministry of the Indian government".[39] Since then, the PMO has undergone several changes with the changes in the government. In spite of changes, it continues to remain the centre of governance and plays an important role in the planning and formulation of national policies of India.

Composition and Function

The Prime Minister's office consists of a group of senior bureaucrats and expertise to assist the Prime Minister in various administrative and coordination activities. Presently, the PMO consists of officers like Principal Secretary to PM, National Security Advisor, Additional Principal Secretary to PM, Public Relation Officer, Information Officer, four Joint Secretaries to PM, Private Secretary to PM, two Private Secretaries, four Officers on Special Duty (OSD), eleven Directors, Five Under Secretaries to deal with subjects like Funds, Public Affairs, and Administration, and a Reference Officer. Apart from these bureaucrats, supporting staff shave also been attached to the PMO to assist in the day-to-day business of the office.[40]

The main responsibility of the Prime Minister's Office is to give secretarial assistance to the Prime Minister and assist him to take appropriate policy decision. It works as the coordination centre between various stake holders of governance and update the recent developments to the Prime Minister for decision making. It also assists the prime Minister in maintaining links with President, Council of Ministers, Governors, Chief Ministers, representatives of the foreign governments to India and other such important institutions of the country. [41] Being the office of the head of the government, the PMO also works as the head of various ministries and departments. Though most of the administrative matters are attained by the respective minister, important files are often referred to the PMO for Prime Minister's consent. Besides, the PMO over looks the overall administrative activities and addresses the outstanding hurdles in policy implementation in coordination with the respective departments. The jurisdiction of the PMO may extend over all subjects which have not been allotted to any Ministry or Department and is also responsible to answer the question of general issues and non-allotted subjects. As the highest institution of the nation, the PMO also looks into large number of public requests and grievances. To deal with such types of cases the Prime Minister's Office has setup two important divisions such as, the anti-Corruption Unit and Public Wing, through which it addresses these grievances. Similarly, the office has been divided into several geographical and provincial sections and each one of them has been assigned to look after the issues arising out of the region. Along with the departmental activities, it also coordinates various cabinet committees and brings their concerns before the Prime Minister. Since the Prime Minister is the Chair Person of the Planning Commission, all related files are referred to the PMO for clearance. After all, as the highest office of the country the ultimate task of the PMO is to ensure the perfect functioning of the central administration and timely execution of the governmental activities.[42]

Role of PMO in Foreign Policy Decision Making

The Prime Minister's Office is one of the most powerful institutions in Indian Foreign Policy decision making mechanism. The PMO, in the Parliamentary system like India, is one of the most significant institutions of Foreign Policy decision making. Being the top most administrative organisation, the PMO is responsible for the planning, formulation and execution of all internal and external policies. The Prime Minister has been the central figure in foreign policy decision making. Since independence, the role of the Foreign Minister has never been crucial, as India never had one who was independent, and who was politically powerful enough to leave his personal imprints in foreign policy.[43] Though the management of the external affairs remains under the exclusive jurisdiction of Ministry of External Affairs, the decision of the Prime Minister remains the deciding factor on any policy formulation. Any successful Foreign Policy making depends on the degree of the administrative coordination between the PMO and the Ministry of External Affairs. Hence the main task of the PMO is to coordinate the different ministries and put extra efforts to clear administrative obstacles on matters of foreign affairs and ensures the optimisation of the national gain. All important matters on Foreign Policy and national security need the Prime Minister's approval before implementation.

The Prime Minister in India, often signs the international treaties and agreements with other nations. In this stage the PMO becomes the centre of the diplomatic relations. Even though the Prime Minister deals with the diplomatic relations of India when he/she visits the foreign nations, he grants the authorization to the Head of the foreign Missions to sign any agreement on behalf of the Indian Government with other countries. PMO is put in charge to approve the proposals for the appointment of Indian Heads of Missions abroad which was primarily the subject of the MEA.

After the formation of the National Security Council (NSC) and with the appointment of the National Security Advisor, who used to be the Principal Secretary to the Prime Minister, the role of the PMO has increased into many folds. The National Security Advisor, as the Member of the PMO, provides necessary advice to the Prime Minister in matters of foreign and security affairs. Hence the PMO plays an important role in India's Foreign Policy decision making. However, the role of the PMO and the degree of influence is very much contingent on his personality, leadership quality and the stability of his position within the political system. In foreign policy, the Prime Minister becomes the central figure when he shows personal interest in the international affairs and the decision making constraint within the PMO. In this regard, the country can witness the PMO centric foreign policy and the customized version of Prime Minister's perception towards the international politics. However, when the prime minister remain detached from the foreign affairs, the decision making process became more diffused and collective.

The National Security Council (NSC)

National Security Council (NSC) is the apex advisory body to the Government of India which gives advice to the Prime Minister and the government on the matters related to India's National security, Foreign Policy and Defence. Although the Prime Minister and the cabinet take the final decision on any importance matter of foreign and defence policy, in recent years, the NSC has emerged as a major stake holder in the shaping of India's foreign and security policies. Headed by the National Security Advisor (NSA), the NSC also assists the government to formulate other significant policies that directly or indirectly affects India's national Interest, such as policies on economic and energy security. The NSA plays an important role in any policy making and the government takes its advises seriously. Apart from the NSA, the council consists of eminent professionals and possesses immense potential to influence the national policy decisions.

Evaluation of NSC

The National Security Council, at its present form was constituted in 1999 by the NDA government under the Prime Ministership of Atal Bihari Vajpayee to reorganise the much criticized national security settings and to fulfil its election manifesto.[44] Many seem this development as one of the bold and essential step for the BJP led coalition government whereas many attempts have been made to form such councils before. Following India's catastrophic defeat in the 1962 Sino-Indian border war, there was a huge voice to reorganize India's military complex by establishing the NSC. But Nehru and the subsequent governments never put any effort in this direction and the demand was thrown into cold storage.[45] Later in 1970 the Administrative Reform Commission (ARC) 1966-1970 although recommended to establish 'National Security Planning Council (NSPC)' and all party 'National Defence Council' to strengthen Indian national security, it was never been accepted by the government.[46]

Beating all expectations, the coalition government of National Front led by V.P. Singh took the great step to restructure India's national security settings by setting up the National Security Council on 24th August 1990. The main intention of the council was to "take a holistic view of national security issues in the light of the external, economic, political and military situations and their linkages with our domestic concerns and objectives."[47] Besides fulfilling its election manifesto, the national front government was keen on improving the national security management by establishing NSC which was being neglected by the dominated Congress led governments. [48]

Following the US and the British model V.P. Singh's NSC consisted of Prime Minister as the Chairman, Minister of Defence, Minister of Finance, Minister of Affairs, and Minister of External Affairs. It also had a provision to include other central and Chief Ministers, and experts at the time of need. The NSC was a three tire structure, where the NSC was the top most institution. Below the NSC there was Strategic Core Group consisting of bureaucrats followed by the National Security Adversary Board.[49]

Although, the council was constituted with a lot of expectations and promises, it met only once in 1990 before its collapse. The opposition was very much critical on the council and its function. And ultimately with the defeat of the V.P. Singh government, the NSC was put into the back seat. The successive governments were not in favour of maintaining the council, which they believed unnecessary.

In 1999 the pragmatist BJP came to power which promised a lot in its election manifesto to revamp India's security and nuclear policy if brought to power. After forming government, the Vajpayee led National Democratic Alliance (NDA) government took two major steps. First it showed the green signal to conduct the nuclear test and secondly, it appointed K.C. Pant Committee to suggest comprehensive steps to re-establishing advanced National Security Council.[50] Based on the recommendation, the government reconstituted the NSC with some structural change within eight months after coming to power on 19 November 1999.[51] The New body unlike the old one created a new post of National Security advisor (NSA) whose prime duty was to give necessary advice to the prime Minister on the matters related to India's national security. The eminent Foreign Service Officer Brajesh Mishra was appointed as the first National Security Advisor.[52]

Members of NSC

The New National Security Council of India consists of eminent personals from different ministries and agencies. At the top, the Prime Minister of India is appointed as the Chairman of the council whereas the executive head is the National Security Advisor. Other members of the council are Minister of Defence, Minister of External Affairs, Minister of Finance, Minister of Home Affairs, and Deputy Chairman of the Planning Commission. Apart from these permanent members, other Central Ministers and Experts can be invited to attend the meeting of NSC and present their view as and when needed.[53] Except the appointment of NSA, the council is almost the replica of the old one. However, unlike the old one, the newly formed National Security Council does not include the Chief Minister as the non-permanent member at the time of need.

Structural Organisation of NSC

National Security Council, India's apex decision making body on national security and Foreign Policy is a three tier organisation consisting of three different agencies. At the top Strategic Planning Group (SPG), a bureaucratic decision making body has been constituted to make long term strategic policy of India. Below the SPG there is a multi-disciplinary National Security Advisory Board (NSAB) to advise the Prime Minister on national security. At the bottom the Joint Intelligence Committee (JIC) has been created to be the secretariat of the NSC and to assist the government in formulation and implementation of the national security policies. The detail structure and function of these decision making bodies have been discussed below:[54]

The Strategic Policy Group

In the three-tier National Security Council, Strategic Policy Group is the top most decision making body responsible for formulating and implementing India's strategic policies. It is a bureaucratic body that consists of the top most bureaucrats of the country who take the major decisions at the time of crisis. Headed by the Cabinet Secretary, the SPG also works as the coordinating agency to handle the matters related to national security policies. The group is also assigned to make long term strategies for India's military doctrine. Similar kind of bureaucratic forum called Strategic Core Group (SCG) for the first time had been set up in 1990 by the V.P. Singh government. But it was comparatively small and inactive which later collapsed with the end of National Front government. SPG at its present form was established by the NDA government in 1999 with much larger professional body and much responsibility.

Composition of SPG

The SPG is mostly a bureaucratic body consisting of several top most bureaucrats of different organisations that are directly or indirectly associated with the national security establishments of the nation. The Group is headed by the Cabinet Secretary besides other seventeen bureaucrats such as Secretaries of the important ministries like Home, Defence, Finance, Foreign, Defence Production, Revenue, Atomic Energy & Space, head of the RAW and IB, Chiefs of Staff of the Indian Army, Navy and Air Force, CBDT Chairman, Governor of the Reserve Bank of India (RBI), Scientific Advisor to the Defence Minister and Chairman of the Joint Intelligence Committee (JIC).[55]

Functions of SPG

Being the highest strategic decision making body within National Security Council, the Strategic Policy Group is responsible to formulate India's long and short term strategic blue prints. It also coordinates different ministries, departments and agencies with respect to national security matters. The group constantly observes the national and international security environment and takes necessary steps to dissolve the possible threats. While

Joint Intelligence Committee (JIC) is responsible to handle the short time threats, the SPG is normally focused to meet the long-term strategic concerns. The SPG prepares India's strategic planning and its execution.

Though the functions of SPG are good in theory, its performance in practical aspects is below expectation. Its members are mostly the top most bureaucrats and Defence chiefs and hardly do justice to their additional jobs at this group. Analyzing the same concern in terms of India's Nuclear doctrine, strategic analyst P.R. Cherry pointed out that, "The strategic policy group comprised serving officials; they were included on the bases of their appointments, not any special expertise in strategic issues. These busy persons had neither time nor the inclination to delve into intricate security issues, and were hardly likely to be concerned with the intricacies of a nuclear doctrine." [56] Similarly, eminent strategic thinker K. Subrahmanyam writes, "The Indian system is not a satisfactory one. The chiefs are not able to do justice to both their roles as operational commanders of forces and chief planners of future requirements of the services and its long-term preparedness."[57] Trying to give some solution to the problem he further states, "There isa good case to separate the two functions, devolve the operational responsibilities to theater the commanders and merge the service headquarters with the Ministry of Defence. In that set-up, the civilian Defence secretary will deal with budget and accounts, coordination with other ministries and states and foreign procurement. The service chiefs will look after housekeeping of the services, professional advice to the minister and long-term defence planning." [58]

The National Security Advisory Board

The National Security Advisory Board (NSAB) is the second layer of the three tired National Security Council. It has been constituted to give advice to the government for matters related to national security and development. The board includes the expertise from different disciplines and agencies. Most of the members of the NSAB are eminent professionals, academicians, scientists, administrative experts, and retired bureaucrats. It is the only advisory body outside the government and responsible to give much professional advices to the Prime Minister and the government regarding military and non-military matters. The concept of a Non-governmental professional advisory body was first developed in 1990 by the V.P. Singh Government. But it was reformed and re-established by the A.B. Vajpayee led NDA government in 1999. Since then, it has been the prime advisory body for the government in policy formulation and implementation.

Composition of NSAB

The NSAB consists of professional expertise from various subjects. Most of the members are not associated with politics and chosen from outside the government machinery. Hence advisory body seems more specialized and professional. It is headed by the Prime Minister and consists of persons with exceptional knowledge on foreign and strategic policy, Defence and national security, economic development, science and technology. The size and composition of the board remains unchanged and mostly depends on the will of the government. However, the total number should not be more than thirty.[59] Presently the board comprises of twenty three experts.

Functions of the NSAB

Headed by an eminent personal as the Chairman, NSAB is an advisory body that provides long-term forecast and analysis to the government. The board meets once in a month or more if needed and discusses the recent developments and its impacts on Indian security scenario. Along with military issues, non-military issues like problems of science and technology, foreign collaboration, diplomatic engagement and national development are the part of discussion. After thorough analysis the board recommends the policy option to the government. Apart from that the NSC also approaches the Board to study some issues and give its suggestions to the government. While the Joint Intelligence Committee is responsible to look after the short term security challenges, the NSAB is meant to analyze and advise on the long term threats.

Although the NSAB has prepared the draft paper on Indian nuclear doctrine, the much expected advisory body is not far from criticism. The major criticism has been its huge size. The board consists of twenty three members presently from different backgrounds, hence it is very difficult to reach any conclusion when it comes to decision making. Looking at this issue, the South Asian strategic experts Stephen Cohen and Sunil Dasgupta write, "Since the NSAB had only advisory standing, and some members were working journalists, creating a serious conflict of interest, its work was regarded skeptical by many observers. The NSAB was not representative of all views; its members bickered publicly, and a number of the original members were removed when the group was reconstituted in early 2000".[60] Another point of criticism is how the advisory body will be allowed to see the secret classified documents. Similarly, the domination of the ex-bureaucrats in the board is also a major drawback for the board, as they will always defend most of the decisions taken during their time.[61]

Joint Intelligence Committee

Information plays a crucial role in the successful formulation of an effective Foreign Policy. Finalizing anything without insufficient data may put the whole project under risk. Not only the quantity, the quality as well as the source of information are also important for the successful Foreign Policy making. The government also consults agencies and takes their advices into account while making any decision on foreign policies. The head of the agencies is a part of the decision making body and assists the government to make the Foreign Policy more practical with the firsthand information. Therefore, almost every country of the modern world has setup multiple intelligence agencies to collect much needed firsthand information on various matters related to Foreign Policy. These agencies have created a large intelligence network throughout the world and works as per the direction of the authority for the collection of vital information. Besides collecting information, the agencies also carry out specific task based on its strategic requirements. Big powers like US, UK, Russia and France are maintaining very large and powerful intelligence agencies and spending huge money for their capacity enhancement.

Following the constant security threat from its neighbours as well as terrorist organisations, India has setup multiple intelligence agencies to combat internal and external threats. The combined Joint Intelligence Committee (JIC) which is the premiere intelligence system which combines Intelligence Bureau, Research and Analysis Wing and the Directorates of Military, Naval and Air Intelligence is set up to give necessary intelligence inputs to the government during the time of Foreign Policy formation and implementation. Each of the agencies acts individually and collects relevant information for India. While Intelligence Bureau (IB) was set up in 1947 to conduct intelligence surveillance for both the domestic and external set ups, the Military intelligence (MI) was responsible to provide intelligence inputs for military organisations. Later the government established a dedicated external intelligence branch known as Research and Analysis Wing (RAW) under the direct control of PMO and in charge of IB for domestic surveillance. To prevent terror activities, the National Investigation Agency (NIA) was set up in the year 2008. But the critics say that the performance of the Indian intelligence agencies is not up to the mark and far behind than to the others.

Structure and Composition

India is having multiple intelligence agencies to perform multiple tasks. Each of the agencies is assigned certain subjects to handle with. In 1965 all these agencies were brought under a single umbrella called the Joint Intelligence Committee. The Joint Intelligence Committee, as the highest intelligence assessment organisation of India was set up for better inter-agency coordination and collection and analysis of the intelligence data for the country. But the formation of the JIC is not a new idea. In fact it was first set up in 1948 as a subcommittee of the Chief of the Staff Committee (CSC) and headed by a joint secretary of the MEA. But its performance was not up to the mark especially its failure during the Sino-Indian Border war.[62] Hence it has been restructured and upgraded later to meet the modern challenges.[63] At present, JIC is headed by a full time secretary level officer having its own secretariat which works under the Cabinet Secretary. The committee works like a super structural agency which collects data from the agencies like Intelligence Bureau (IB), Research and Analysis Wing (RAW), Directorate of Military Intelligence (DMI) Directorate of Naval Intelligence (DNI) and Directorate of Air Intelligence (DAI), and makes its own independent assessment based on the data and report of the Cabinet.[64]

The Joint Intelligence Committee consists of several experts from different intelligence agencies. The members are as follows:

1. One Additional Secretary of the Cabinet Secretariat as the full time Chairman
2. One Additional Secretary as representative of the MEA
3. One Joint Secretary as representative of the Defence Ministry
4. One Joint Secretary as representative of the Ministry of Home Affairs (MHA)
5. Joint director of IB
6. Joint director of RAW
7. Director of Military Intelligence (DMI)
8. Director of Naval Intelligence (DNI) and
9. Director of Air Intelligence (DAI)
10. Air Commodore from Defence Ministry as Member Secretary[65]

Apart from these core members, the committee also consists of a large number of intelligence and assessment officers from different branches of the government as well as numerous supporting staffs and assistances.

Functions of JIC

Being the top most intelligence agency of the country, the Joint Intelligence Committee has been assigned with multiple assignments to deal with. Some of the functions have been discussed below:

Collection and Assessment of Intelligence Data: The main responsibility of the Joint Intelligence Committee is to compile and analyze the intelligence data from different sources. It is neither engaged with anti real-time spying activities nor conduct intelligence mission to collect the information. It largely depends upon the other intelligence agencies like IB, RAW, DMI, DNI and DAI for the collection of raw data. It does not rely upon any one agency on certain information, rather crosschecks the same with other such agencies to assess the validity of the data. After proper confirmation it prepares reports about the developments and sends to the cabinet for further action.[66]

Coordination and Direction to all Intelligence Agencies: The Joint intelligence committee works like a coordinating agency between various intelligence agencies. Often the agencies do not pass certain information to other agencies because of the professional competition. Hence there is more chance of intelligence failure. It had been experienced during the India Pakistan war of 1965 and Chinese aggression of 1964. To avoid this, the JIC coordinates among the agencies for maximum information on any particular subject. It collects certain information from one agency and directs the other specialized agencies to dig further for more information.

Apart from the coordination work, the JIC is also responsible to ensure maximum professionalism among all intelligence agencies. It takes several steps to enhance the level of efficiency among the intelligence officers. Sometimes it directs the agencies to conduct certain task based on the demand of the government. In case of any difficulty, it asks other agencies to assist the concerned agency in any particular intelligence operation so that more information can be obtained.[67]

Advises the Government in Decision Making: Besides the operational functions, the Joint intelligence committee advises and assists the Prime Minister and the Cabinet in decision making on matters related to foreign affairs, national security and Defence. The JIC reports all the recent developments on the national and international scenario and analyzes how it is going to affect India's interest. In some cases the government seeks advices of the Committee before making any policy and order the JIC to evaluate the possible upcoming challenges. The committee not only gives pre advices, it also keeps track on the implemented policies and provides related feedbacks to the government so that it can be rectified later.[68]

The Joint Intelligence Committee has been one of the important organisations that actively participates in the decision making process on India's foreign affairs. It gives necessary intelligence inputs and advises the government on various matters related foreign to relations. In any Foreign Policy crisis it has been asked for essential consultation and guidance.

Ministry of Defence

Defending national territory and sovereignty is the main priority of the country's Foreign Policy. Hence, Ministry of Defence (MoD) has been one of the important components of the decision making body on India's foreign affairs. It works like the coordinating agency between the government and armed forces and gives additional military support to the government in implementing the foreign policies if necessary. The Ministry actively participates in decision making process and the government seeks the view of the MoD before taking any decision on matters related to Defence and national security.

Organisational Structure of the MoD

Ministry of Defence is headed by the Defence Minister, who is one of the prominent members of the Union Cabinet. Besides the Defence Minister, one or two Junior Ministers or Minister of Sates rank are appointed to assist the Defence Minister. They lead some of the departments and branches of the ministry and look after the day to day work of the divisions or the departments. The Defence Secretary is the executive head of the ministry and supervises the official and administrative task of the ministry. There used to be subsequent Secretaries, Joint and Additional Secretaries along with necessary officers to assist the Defence Secretary in various ministerial activities.

For the effective organisational performance and optimal outcome, the Ministry of Defencehas been divided into four different departments, namely, Department of Defence (DOD), Department of Defence Production (DDP), Department of Defence Research & Development (DDR&D) and Department of Ex-Servicemen Welfare and also Finance Division for each department. Headed by Secretaries, each department is assigned with a certain task to perform and to resolve the issues related to their subject.[69]

Department of Defence (DOD)

Out of all four departments, Department of Defence (DOD) is the most important branch of the Ministry of Defence. It is headed by a secretary who has been selected through all India civil service examination. The DOD consists of the Integrated Defence Staff (IDS), offices of the three service staffs and other major administrative centres responsible to look in to the matter regarding the budgetary and administrative activities of the whole ministry. It also takes part in the decision making process on India's foreign and security policy and deals with the matters related to cabinet and the Parliament. It also works like the connecting way between the government and the armed forces and coordinates all Defence related activities. Most importantly, the department looks into the matter of foreign Defence cooperation including armed procurement, joint development and joint practices with other countries.[70]

Department of Defence Production (DDP)

Headed by a secretary, the Department of Defence Production (DDP) is responsible for the production and supply of necessary defence equipment to the Indian armed forces. The department was first set up in 1965 to make India self-reliant in defence requirements. The department was assigned with two different tasks, the production weaponry and supply of other logistic items. Besides the administrative works, the department identifies the present and future Defence requirements and encourages the R&D activities to produce the same. It coordinates various public and private sector Defence production units and supervises the projects. Indinization of imported Defence equipments and spare parts is one of the core responsibilities of the DDP.[71]

Department of Defence Research & Development (DDR&D)

The Department of Defence Research and Development (DDR&D) was created to meet India's technological needs in Defence sector. It is led by a Secretary who is also the Scientific Advisor to the Defence Minister. The DDR&D works to give the Research and Development (R&D) support to the Defence production unit and makes them self reliable in making advanced weapons. The department has a network of 48 research laboratories across India, through which it plans and develops the technical blue print for the future needs of the Indian armed forces.[72]

Department of Ex-Servicemen Welfare and also Finance Division

The Department of Ex-Servicemen Welfare is responsible to look into the matters related to its large ex-serviceman community. The department has been working to ensure the post retirement benefits to the Indian armed forces and settlement of injured unfit solders. It also runs several welfare schemes for the ex-service personals and kind of the killed solders, including establishment of several vocational training centers.

Along with these departments the Ministry consists of three parallel organisations of the Service Headquarters, the headquarters of the Indian Army, Indian Navy and Indian Air Force (IAF). Each one of the Headquarters works under their respective Chief of the Staff (COS). The headquarters is further divided into several branches, and sub-branches and each of the branch is headed by a Principal Staff Officer (PSO). The Headquarter of Indian Army for example, has been divided into four major branches and under the leadership of a PSO, each of them has been assigned with different responsibilities to perform.[73]

Several coordinating and inter-service agencies have been set up under the Ministry of Defence for the efficient handling of complex issues and optimal outcome. Each of the committee is tasked with certain subjects to handle. The Defence Minister's Committee and the Chief of the Staff Committee are the two major committees under whom various other committees work. The Defence Minister's Committee is responsible to deal with most important problems related to inter-service management and is further divided into two subcommittees, Principal Personnel Officers Committee and Principal Supply Officers Committee. Similarly, the Chief of the Staff Committee (COSC) is comprised of three service chiefs, chaired by the longest serving chief. The COSC looks into the matters regarding joint Defence planning and execution.[74]

Role of MoDin Foreign Policy Decision Making

Maintaining national security is one of the fore front/and dominating agenda for the Foreign Policy decision makers. The aim of majority of the Foreign Policy initiatives is to protect the national sovereignty and territory. In the modern age the role of the Defence ministry has been significantly increased due to rise of international conflict and terrorism. Besides protecting the national borders, it also protects and promotes the national interest abroad. Hence, Ministry of Defence has been one of the important players in India's external policy making body. Before making any decision, the government consults the Defence ministry for their inputs, as the Defence backup is highly necessary behind any decision.

The Defence Minister has been the part of decision making body and gives his observation on behalf of the Ministry on matters directly or indirectly related to national security and Foreign Policy. He is also an important member of the union cabinet who takes the decision for the government. Apart from the political affiliation, his official position as the Defence Minister has enough to say in national policy making process. Similarly, as the member of the Cabinet Committee on Security and the National Security Council he also guides decision making on India's foreign and security policies.

Apart from the Minister of Defence, the Defence Secretary, the three Chiefs of the Staff and Secretary of the Defence production division also participate in decision making process as the members of Strategic Policy Group, the important decision making body on foreign on Indian external policy. They are invited for all the meetings of the SPG and actively participate in the decision making process. In case of any strategic or Foreign Policy crisis, the three servicing chiefs of the staff are asked to present their view on the issues, that significantly impact the decision outcomes. With regard to issues of Chinese incursion for example, the army chiefs brief the cabinet committee about the issues and its possible reactions.[75]

The Defence ministry collects the intelligence data on the matters related to security and international strategic development through its various intelligence agencies like Directorate of Military, Naval and Air Intelligence and shares its concerns with the government. Based on these and other intelligence reports, the government determines its Foreign Policy and external engagements. Being a part of the Joint Intelligence Committee, Defence intelligence agencies also analyze the intelligence data and advise the government in policy making.

In international relations, Defence cooperation and Foreign Policy go hand in hand. This theory got strong support after the introduction of the concept of Military Industrial Complex. There is warm relation between producing and buyer nations. The buyer adopts a friendly Foreign Policy towards the suppliers or vice versa. Hence, the Ministry of Defence plays a decisive role in extending India's Defence cooperation to foreign countries. It also advises the government on matters related to foreign Defence cooperation, Joint training and exercise, and Joint Defence production. Beside the foreign Defence cooperation activities, the ministry has a larger say in purchasing foreign Defence equipments and sale of Indian products to foreign countries. In fact it completely rests with the MoD to decide on the purchase of the foreign weapons.

Despite earning a lot of scope in decision making, Ministry of Defence comparatively plays minimal role in India's Foreign Policy making. The government has not shown greater interest to take Defence Ministry, especially the chief of the armed forces into account before formulating

India's Foreign Policy. Its role is very limited in shaping the country's external relations compared to its counterparts of US, Russia, China and other advanced countries. Even Pakistan's Defence Ministry has greater scope to play in foreign affairs than that of India. The Defence agency actively participates in matters regarding foreign affairs in these countries. But witnessing the consequences due to excessive role of military in non-military activities that eventually lead to Military coup (*d'etat*), the role should be confined with consultative rather than decisive in non- military activities.

THE PARLIAMENT

In the Westminster system of government, Parliament is the center of governance and plays an important role in policy making. According to the Constitution of Indian, the Parliament, the supreme legislative body has the absolute power to make policies on any item under the union list, including foreign affairs. Being the highest democratic institution of the country, the Parliament can also influence the course of Foreign Policy decision making by using various instruments. Though the process of policy making has been dominated by the bureaucratic agencies, the Parliament still plays a major role in shaping India's external relations.

Structure and Composition

The Parliament of India is comprised with three democratic institutions- the President of India, the Lok Sabha (House of People) and the Rajya Sabha (Council of States). The President is the head of the state and all the administrations run on his name. The bill can be made into law only after the President's approval. He authorizes the government to run the administration and takes necessary decisions on behalf of the country.

The Lok Sabha, the lower house of the Parliament is the most powerful institution and responsible to make laws and policies for the nation. The members of the house are elected directly by the citizens of the country through universal franchise of voting. The party that gets majority in general election forms the government for five years subject to maintaining majority in the house. The leader of the majority party is appointed as the Prime Minister by the president. The president also appoints the members or council of ministers and authorizes them to run the government. The members, known as ministers are put in charge to lead various ministries and enjoy absolute power to take necessary actions on behalf of the ministry.[76]

The upper house of the Indian Parliament is Rajya Sabha. It consists of members from all 35 provinces elected through indirect election. The share of membership to the house has been divided among the provinces on the basis of its population. Elected by the members of the state legislative bodies, the members represent the state at the house for five years. Unlike the Lok Sabha, the Rajya Sabha is a Permanent house and two-third of its members retire every two years. The house is headed by the Vice-President, who is the ex-officio Chairman of the house.[77]

Besides the Houses, the Parliament also consists of several Parliament committees to deal with several important functions of the Parliament. There are two types of standing committees-the Standing Committees and the ad hoc committees. The standing committees are permanent and constituted to help the Parliament in resolving the existing issues during the process of legislation, whereas the ad hoc committees are set up to resolve certain temporary issues and automatically expiries with the completion of the task. Besides the Parliamentary standing committees, there are some Departmentally Related Standing Committees that deal with the matters related to the respective departments.[78]

Functions of the Parliament

In a democratic country like India, Parliament plays an important role in the country's governmental administration. As the representative of the people's will, the function of the Parliament touches every aspect of the state craft and reshapes the perceptive of the governance according to the will of the people. Though some believe that the task of the Parliament is limited to making policies for the country, the Parliament is empowered to supervise each and every governmental agency and guides them to attain the national goal.

The primary responsibility of the Parliament is to make laws and policies for the nation. Article 246 of the Indian Constitution empowers the Parliament to legislate any matter listed under the union list.[79] Besides the Union list that contains 98 items, the Parliament is also authorized to make any legislation on subsequent items of Concurrent List along with state authorities under article 246 (2).[80] Foreign affairs, the gist of present discussion also falls under the Union list (item 1 to 21) on which the Parliament has exclusive rights to legislate any policy.[81] Similarly article 253 empowers the Parliament to legislate or amendany law for the successful implementation of international treaties, agreements and conventions.[82]

Parliament's responsibility is not limited to legislating policies. Guiding executive agencies for the successful implementation of those policies is also equally an important task of the Parliament. In case of administrative failure to achieve the target, it is answerable to the Parliament. The oppositions criticize the government using the Parliamentary procedural devices like Questions Hour, Calling Attention Notices, Half-an-Hour Discussions, Private Members' Resolution, Discussions on Matters of Urgent Public Importance, etc.

The Constitution of India also empowers the Parliament to amend the constitution for the sensible reforms according to the need of the time and to avoid unnecessary administrative obstacles. Some parts of the constitution are flexible for amendment and need simple majority, whereas other parts need at least two third majority to amend.

Role of the Parliament on Foreign Policy Making

In a Parliamentary democracy like India, Parliament is the centre of the governmental administration and enjoys unique and supreme position in the administrative and institutional hierarchy. Its supremacy over all institutions and exclusive power to legislate any policy for centre and state[83] has empowered the Parliament of India as the significant player in making governmental policy, including Foreign Policy. The constitution of India has given power to the Parliament to legislate policies on subjects associated with foreign affairs and Defence. Items 1 to 21of the union list that directly or indirectly deal with matters related to Foreign Policy and diplomacy come under the preview of Parliament on which it can make policies. Similarly, the Parliament can pass any law to facilitate the implementation of International treaties irrespective of the distribution of power between centre and states.

The government is also accountable to the Parliament. Therefore the Parliament can seek information and ask the government to clarify its stand on certain policies. If the Parliament is not on favour of the governmental performance, it can drive out the government. Using various Parliamentary provisions, it can also influence the external policy of the government and also force the government to alter the existing policy with a new one.

The Parliament through adopting various means controls and influences the executives that are the fore front players in shaping India's Foreign Policy. Controlling budgetary allotment and passing necessary resolution, it can force the executive to act according to the will of the Parliament. Hence the matter of foreign affairs is not far from the control of the Parliament.

Similarly, the Parliament has several standing committees that play a major role in shaping the country's administration. To oversee the performance of the Ministry of External Affairs and Ministry of Defence, the Parliament has set up two important standing committees – the Standing Committee of External Affairs (SCEA) and the Standing Committee on Defence (SCD). These two committees keep tracking the performance of the ministry and in many ways also influence the external policies of India.

Being the representative of the will of the people it should play the central role in the Foreign Policy making of the country. But looking its present contribution in India's Foreign Policy making process, it seems that the role of Parliament has been neglected and pushed to play the role of a secondary agency in decision making. The large size and delayed decision making forces the government to put the executive and other agencies to lead the decision making on matters related to India's Foreign Policy.

PRESSURE GROUPS AND MEDIA

Joining politics and participating political process is not the only way to take part in policy formulation, but the voice of the non-political groups, associations and organisations is also an important source of influence in shaping the governmental policies. These associations known as pressure or interest groups are in some way able to influence the governmental policies to suit their interests using various informal channels. The groups are visible in all forms of government, though they are highly active in democratic setups. They articulate and carryout the interest of a particular section of people and pressurize the government to address their concerns through non-political approaches. While most of the pressure groups participate in domestic issues, some of the organisations do pose interest in Foreign Policy related matters. However, it is hard to categorize these organisations because of the close link between the domestic and external activities. Due to its organisational and influential activities, the groups are able to enlarge its role in governmental activities and decision making. Being the largest democracy in the world, Indian administrative setups are not far from these influences. Groups like business houses, arms lobby groups, International Non-Governmental Organisations, overseas Indian religious and cultural associations are some of the organisations that actively work to influence India's Foreign Policy.

Business Houses

Business groups are the largest, perhaps the most active and the most dominating instituitions among the interest groups. As Professor Anthony J. Nownes rightly observed "any way you silence, business dominates the world of interest groups representation".[84] To support his argument he states that, in Washington DC approximately one fifth of the 20,000 active interest groups are business houses, where nearly one seventh belongs to trade unions and a combined share of the business, trade organisation and business pressure groups comprises nearly half of the interest groups.[85] Because of shadow proximity to the government machinery and economic influences, these groups are some what able to manipulate the policy decision on their favour.In America alone more than 50 percent of the federal Political Action Committees (PACs) are affiliated with the business houses.[86]

The politics of interest groups in India is not far away from the American scenario. Affiliation between business groups and political setups is a well known fact in India. But until 1990s the influence was limited to domestic systems and the business associations hardly showed any interest in India's external policies. Business associations like Confederation of Indian Industries (CII), The Associated Chambers of Commerce and Industry of India (ASSOCHAM), the Federation of Indian Chamber of Commerce and Industry (FICCI) have been constantly watching the international trade, fascicle and monetary policies of the government. Using their "invisible channels" these groups try to influence the MPs, ministers and bureaucrats through money and other means to cleanup administrative interruptions and to create favourable business environment to suit their trade. But it was not the case before economic liberation, where the Indian business farms were not active in international trade and commerce. Krishna Menon, one of the key technocrats of India's external policy during Nehru era also confirms that no business farms tried to influence India's foreign policies during his tenure in the Parliament.[87] Similarly, other foreign ministers and figure heads also deny any involvement of business houses in the Foreign Policy decision making process.[88]

However, the trend has drastically changed after the liberation of India's economic and the gradual emergence of powerful business groups in India. Following the economic liberation, the government showed special interest to promote Indian exports besides attracting foreign investment into India. Several special cells have been set up under the MEA to resolve the disputes and to promote India's trade exports. The Government seeks the opinion and concerns of the business houses before declaring any new policies.

The MEA also has been in close contact with business association and makes necessary arrangements to facilitate their involvement in internal market. The whole diplomatic setup is put in service to facilitate the Indian farms working abroad. Now-a-days a group of business delegations is accompanying important state officials during their high-level official visits to foreign countries. The active involvement of business groups to influence the trade and economic policies is a well known fact. But the point is, the levels of influences are not limited to mere business interest. It directly and indirectly also affects the policy decision of Indian's external engagements.

Arms Agents and Lobby Group

Analyzing the statistics, arms trade remains one of the ever growing phenomena. In spite of economic slowdown, the total global military expenditure has been recorded as US $1756 billion,[89] whereas the total conventional arm trade has touched US$ 28172 million[90] mark. The SIPRI data base reveals that the US remains the highest arms supplier, whereas India has emerged as the largest arms importer with nearly US $ 4764[91] million worth of arms purchase. While the trend of arms trade is increasing in the third world countries, the mighty military industrial complex has reportedly hired some local agents to propagate and promote their arms sale in the respective countries. Mostly a retired Defence personnel is chosen to be appointed as the arms agent, and the influences the decision of the government officials to purchase their weapons by bribing their former colleagues at the Defence establishments. This phenomena is not limited to Indian context, rather has become a global issue. In US the lobby of these agents is so strong that the government many times has reviewed its decision on not to sale arms to any particular country. The New York Times has openly acknowledged in its report how the Regan administration changed its decision to sale its weapons to Iran during 1980s.[92] Similarly, well known scholars have repeatedly exposed these inside stories recently.[93]

The nexus were not limited to the Defence setups, but politicians, ministers and key decision makers are reportedly connected with these mediators directly or indirectly. This case can be easily understood by analyzing the Bofors scandals of India, where the media source exposed the nexus between the politicians and arms agents and their influence in the political decision making of the country.[94] Since then, number of such type of scams have been witnessed, including the recent Augusta Westland VVIP chopper deal, and the political nexus with armed deals has become the known fact.[95]

With the growing controversy of scams in weapon procurement, Indian government banned the Defence personnel to act as an arms dealer besides restricting any involvement of third party in arms deal. But it seems ineffective with the recent break of other scandals. Even in these cases, the officials shared some classified documents with the armed dealers.[96] The cash rich agents were also able to reach the political parties, Politicians, Ministers and key decision makers that decide India's foreign policies. As the Defence procurement and Foreign Policy remains complement to each other, influencing the Defence setup is bound to affect the decision on foreign affairs of the country. Therefore, their indirect involvement in the country's Foreign Policy cannot be denied.

International Nongovernmental Organisations

The role and influence of the Non-Governmental Organisations (NGOs), the so called voice of people[97] in the Foreign Policy making have drastically increased in the recent past. According to the Union of International Associations (UIA), at present estimated 57721 active organisations are functioning worldwide, while their number was merely 9,521 during 1978. In India itself there are more than 6239 such organisations working at various sectors. The report says[98] that most of such organisations are linked and funded by the foreign sources, though some of them are only limited to the domestic sources. Besides this, the International Nongovernment Organisations (IGO) have their branches in India that are constantly criticizing the policies of Indian government towards its citizens.

These organisations are using various means of pressuring the government to change their policies not only related to developmental activities but also policies on national security and foreign policies. The famous IGO Amnesty International for example has been very critical towards the human rights violation by the Indian security forces in insurgency-prone areas of India and has been pressuring the world community to put sanctions on India against the violation. These anti-India campaigns constantly pose severe challenges to the Indian Foreign Policy to meet its goal, while the image of the country is damaged due to the adverse propaganda. However, the organisation remains silent about the human rights violation by the insurgents. Later it was found that the information was provided by the Indian NGOs to the Amnesty International.[99]

In some cases, the foreign intelligence agencies have been found to use the NGOs to collect classified information on the country's security and Foreign Policies. The investigation revealed that this sensitive information was collected by the Indian NGOs on the direction of its foreign headquarters knowingly or unknowingly. These nexus exposed when the NGOs like Asia Foundation and the Congress for Cultural Freedom, were found to have foreign hand behind their intention before they were closed down.[100] Similarly, the NGOs were found to act as clandestine agencies of the foreign country and involved and funded the secessionist movements of the country. The 2001 case of the Douche NGO and its connection with North Eastern insurgency movement is one of the examples of the foreign involvement.

Analyzing these concerns, it is clear that the NGOs and the IGOs have been very active in influencing the governmental policies including Foreign Policy. By mobilizing the people supports inside the country and by pressuring the international community some way or other they were able to influence the external policy of the country. Be it the anti-nuclear movement or the matter of the human rights violation or the so called indigenous people's movement, these organisations always criticize the governmental policies and propagate anti-Indian campaign that poses serious concern for the external relation of the country.

Academia and Think Tanks

In the modern time, decision making is not entirely left to the traditional governmental agencies, but inputs from non-governmental intellectual resources like academia and think-tanks also have been the part of the process. The vibrant research institutes and professional experts on national security, strategic policy and foreign affairs play a vital role in shaping Foreign Policy of the country. Being independent from all sorts of political and bureaucratic authoritative influences, these civil society organisations give most neutral and dependable inputs to the policy makers to make their choices for the policy formation. James G. McGann, Director of the Thinks and Foreign Policy programme of Foreign Policy Research Institute has categorically analyzed the role of Think Tanks on Foreign Policy. According to him, these organisations perform the following functions:

- Playing a mediating function between the government and the public that helps build trust and confidence on public officials;
- Serving as an informed and independent voice in policy debates;
- Identifying, articulating, and evaluating current policy issues, proposals and programs;
- Transforming ideas and emerging problems into policy issues;

- Interpreting issues, events and policies for the electronic and print media thus facilitating public understanding of domestic and international policy issues;
- Providing a constructive forum for the exchange of ideas and information between key stakeholders in the policy formulation process;
- Facilitating the construction of "issue networks";
- Providing a supply of personnel for the legislative and executive branches of government;
- Challenging the conventional wisdom and standard operating procedures of bureaucrats and elected officials.[101]

In India, the impact of research institutes is comparatively low. The reason may be the absence of structured research institutes for a quite long time and the lack of resources to do research for initial phases of the post functional period. Until 1950s scholars, diplomats, professionals and journalists were brought under a formal organisation to form India's first ever think tank- the Indian Council of World Affairs (ICWA).[102] Later in 1955 the Indian School of International Studies was established under the hood of ICWA to facilitate the research activities on India's foreign affairs. This institution was later merged with Jawaharlal Nehru University in 1970 to produce future researches.[103] Similarly, the Institute of Defence Studies and Analysis (IDSA) was established under the guidance of Ministry of Defence to promote independent research on India's Defence and strategic policy and to help the government to formulate the policies.[104] Now a number of research organisations are working on various contemporary issues in India that have been constantly the source of influence for India's external policy.

Similarly, a large segment of the internationally reputed scholars and professionals are also slowly emerging to lead the academic exercise on the domestic and international affairs. Over the last four decades the public forums and academic communities have been drastically multiplied. As a result, debates on various international affairs have taken place that eventually helped the policy makers to understand the situation better.

Government of India, especially the Ministry of External Affairs and Ministry of Defence have been actively patronizing and encouraging the research institutes to carry out meaningful research projects by various means. They mostly award research projects through University Grants Commission (UGC) to professionals and various research institutions and area study centres attached to universities. Grants are also granted to independent research institutes to conduct research activities to facilitate the government with new ideas for policy making. To inculcate new theories and alternatives, the government also funds to hold conferences and seminars on burning national and international issues.[105] The IDSA and ICWA and other such institutes get huge share of fund to conduct research on various issues of foreign and defiance policy.[106] Apart from these research projects and think-tanks, the MEA also gives huge sum of funds to organize seminars and conferences on various issues as well as supports the Centre for Advanced Study of India, University of Pennsylvania for its scholarly contribution.

Some Scholars believe that, think tanks are part of the political elite or one among other such institutions that try to influence.[107] Whatever be the role, it is proved that these intellectual bodies play a greater role in influencing, shaping and altering the Foreign Policy behaviour of a country. They have been successful in articulating new ideas and alternatives to deal outstanding issues. They publish the policy briefs and research papers to publicize the failures of the government and suggest policy measures for short term and long term issues. Though thinks tanks and academia were most influential during early phases of their existences, their role has been gradually declining due to mushrooming of such institutes and lack of producing standard research. Nevertheless the eminent research institutes have been the most influential in determining Indian Foreign Policy.

People of Overseas and Non-Residential Indians

According to the data released by Ministry of Overseas Indian Affairs (MOIA) about 2,19,09,875 (nearly 22 million) overseas Indians are living in different corners of the world out of which more than 10 million people are working abroad and known as Non-Residential Indians (NRIs) and over 11 million are People of Indian Origin (PIO) settled abroad.[108] Extended to almost all the countries of the world, these overseas Indians are major components that shape India's external engagements. Apart from sending huge money back home, these Overseas Indians also work as the back channel agents to promote greater economic and foreign engagements in India.

Most of the overseas Indians migrated as agricultural labourers and business men during nineteenth century, whereas in some cases the British officials transported large number of Indian labourers abroad to assist in plantation works. But during those early days, the attitude of the Indian government was negative and they paid least attention to protect the interest of the Overseas Indians residing abroad. The government also failed to use its diplomatic assets to put pressure on other countries when those Indians were suffering. In Fiji for example, when the ethnic Indians were attacked and their elected Prime Minister of Indian origin was overthrown out of power, the government did nearly nothing to resolve the problem.[109] Similarly, the government was inactive to react when large numbers of people of Indian origin were evacuated from various African and Southern Asian countries. More surprisingly, the Indian government sent its armed forces to fight against Sri Lankan Timilians who are ethnically Indians.[110]

But soon the Indian government realized the importance of overseas Indians in promoting its international relation abroad. The MOIA was established in May 2004 to address the interest of the overseas Indians. The MOIA was encouraging NRI and POIA association to promote Indian internal relation. The huge percentage of overseas Indians in US, UK and other advanced countries is always influencing the Foreign Policy of the respective states toward India and vice-versa. Scholars believe that the surprise turn of the US policy towards India's favour is due to the constant lobby of the Indian-Americans. The story is replicated in other countries also. As result, the Indian government is able to break the ice and establish deeper relationship with other such countries.

Public Opinion and Media

In India and other democratic republics the authority is vested over the citizens and the Constitution empowers them to decide the fate of the country through their representatives. The people elect their representatives to govern the country according to their will. They are accountable to the public, and making of any policy should have the backing of the public mandate. But others believe that the people have little or no knowledge about the state craft and mostly concerned about the short term issues. Hence, they should not necessarily be the part of decision making process and it should be left to the experts, representatives and bureaucrats to manage.[111] However, the relation between the public opinion and policy making is a complex issue and one of the flash points of debates for years.[112]

Despite this, public opinion has been one of the most influential factors of policy making and Foreign Policy is not an exception to this. There are several reasons to support this argument. First and foremost, in democracy the government runs with the support of the public. If the public opinion turns against the government, then there is every chance for the fall of the government. Therefore any elected government cannot ignore the public opinion and is bound to act according to the trend of the public opinion. Moreover, the public opinion has its influences on all sections of state crafts, including the psyche of the policy makers, bureaucrats, and experts.[113] As a result, these groups sometimes by ignorance take decisions in accordance with the public opinion. Sometimes the public opinion is seemed to have linked to nationalism or regionalism, hence gradually developed into the national or regional ideology and in many ways influences the national policy making process.

There are various sources and medium of public opinion and in modern hi-tech age these sources have been multiplied. Interest groups, political parties, social activists, Media, NGOs and other civil society actors are some of the sources and mediums. Although, all these sources and means have been mobilizing public opinion up to a level, media is the most effective and omnipresent mean. It playsa major role not only in highlighting the concern and bringing the issue into the public domain, but also sometimes successfully creates a new debate on any particular national and international issue. When the news papers highlight some issues at the frontline, the topic automatically becomes the important issue in national front, though it might be a low profile issue.

By highlighting some issues the media is able to mobilize a huge public opinion in favour of oragainst any issue. Besides the general mass, many organisations, experts, and professionals are also often seen carried away by the debates of the news media and convinced to the media arguments, they also directly or indirectly work to mould the government policy in the desired way. As a result, the government is forced to readjust its policy to that particular issue. This effect in US is termed as the CNN effect.[114] But the public opinion often intends to highlight the important issues rather than controlling the Foreign Policy[115] and the media often plays the role of an effective "pressure group", a "critical observer" and "participant" in policy formulation.[116].

In democratic countries the media has been very active and somewhat successful to influence the policy making. However, in the non-democratic setups the media has been highly controlled by the government which is very particular about not to allow them to mobile public anti-government opinions. In Saudi Arabia and in China for example, the media has been highly censored and used as a tool to highlight the positive sides of the government, not the loopholes. Media is often used as an instrument to launch a false propaganda campaign to show one country as the enemy of the nation and to win the sentiment of the people.

Public opinion in India has been mostly cantered on the matter related to domestic policies. However with the emergence of electronic media, gradually public opinion has turned towards issues related to India's Foreign Policy. The live broadcast of terrorist attack of 26/11 for example, was able to mobilize greater public opinion to break all peace talk with Pakistan and even to lunch armed operation against Pakistan. Similarly, on the Kandahar Plane hijacking or India's miscalculation over the Pakistan incursion into Kargil or on any such matter the media has been constantly critical to the government policies and successfully highlights these issues before the public. The recent Chinese incursion into the Ladakh region also mobilized greater public anger when the story was publicized by the electronic media.

But often, media creates unnecessary public hypes and broadcasts impartial and sometimes false news to attract greater public attention. As a result, the opinion of the people turns against government and creates obstacle for the government. Similarly, some issues related to foreign and security policies are thrown to public knowledge, when the authority wants to maintain secrecy. It further creates problem for the policy makers to deal with the situation. Despite the drawbacks, media has been the eye opener to the public and the important source of educating the mass about the government policies. It also plays the role of an affective pressure group, the important source of policy influence, the critical observer of government policies and one of the actors of the policy formulation.

STRUCTURE AND PROCESS OF FOREIGN POLICY DECISION MAKING

Process of decision making in Foreign Policy is a complex phenomena, which involves several active agencies and organisations. In a modern democratic third world country like India, the process is so politicized that, it is almost impossible to reach a conclusion on any matter. As a result, the decision is always taken out of consensus of the view of all agencies rather than a logical outcome. But in some cases the decision making is rational and effective. The decision making process mostly depends upon the domestic and international environments and personality of the leadership.

India's Foreign Policy behaviour has been reactive rather than proactive.[117] Hence, the Decision making largely appears to be defensive. Decision making during Pakistan's aggression into Kashmir, the first external crisis of India since its independence, was reactive to the Pakistan's

Kashmir policy. Similarly, during the successive India-Pakistan wars of 1965, 1971, 1999 and the India-china war of 1962 the decision making seemed reactive to the opponent's aggressive policy rather than proactive to defend its border. Secondly, the Foreign Policy making tradition in India had been driven by idealism and idealist perspective of world order. It was widely visible during the 1950s and 60s when Nehruvian ideology was the drive force of India's Foreign Policy. The decision to refer the Kashmir issue to UN, the refusal of permanent membership at UN Security Council were some of the cases of India's idealistic decision making tradition.

In the earlier period the decision making process in Foreign Policy was mostly based on single window model, where decision making was purely vested on Nehru, the Foreign cum Prime Minister. He was assisted by a small group of trusted colleagues and bureaucrats and avoided consulting persons beyond the inner circle. In most of the cases he used to decide the course of action on many important issues without even consulting the advisors. He threw his decision to the cabinet and asked the members to agree on his decision rather than listening to their opinions. Hence the decision making on Foreign Policy during Nehru era was mostly like closed box model.

But gradually the tradition changed and decision making now-a-days seems more democratic and pluralistic. Today, the process of decision making largely depends upon large number of agencies and organisations. Though the MEA and the PMO remain the most important institutions of India's Foreign Policy decision making process, organisations like cabinet, Defence establishment, Intelligence agencies, and independent research institutions and public opinion are equally responsible in shaping India's Foreign Policy.

Policy making process mostly follows the input-output theory. When the data and information are put inside the decision making unit the policy decision comes out in the form of outputs.[118] Though the design of structure and institutions of decision making differ from state to state they are mostly performed on the basis of the above model while making Foreign Policy decision. Based on the input-output model, India's Foreign Policy making process passes through three important stages while making policy decisions. The first stage is the collection and input of information, the second stage is the assessment and analysis of the collected and processed data and the third stage is the decision making and implementation.

Collection and Input of Information

Information is crucial for any decision making process. The decision makers take any call of any policy based on the information input and not by assumption. In Foreign Policy decision making, the role of information is very important as it determines the course of the country's relation to the rest of the world. The Ministry of External Affairs, the prime agency of Foreign Policy decision making is largely responsible to collect the information and other research data to make the Foreign Policy. Generally the data is collected through the Indian missions established abroad. These Indian missions normally send their monthly reports on the recent political developments of the respective country and its implication on India. Besides the monthly report, the missions also inform the MEA about the important major incidents that highly impact India's national interests. Similarly, India's permanent UN Mission also updates the MEA regarding the recent international scenario and crisis. Additionally, the periodical notices and memorandums of the missions of the foreign countries in India help the ministry to collect the latest information and concerns of the country that eventually help while taking decision. These sources are known as the traditional diplomatic sources of MEA in collection of policy information.

Besides the diplomatic sources, the government also uses its intelligence and other agencies to collect important data for Foreign Policy decision making. India has multiple intelligence agencies like Intelligence Bureau, Research and Analysis Wing and the Directorates of Military, Naval and Air Intelligence to collect important intelligence data within and outside the country directly and indirectly related to India's national interest. These agencies pass their information to the Joint Intelligence Committee (JIC) that analyze the data, gives its periodical and special report to the government for consideration.

Information is also collected from the open sources like media reports, books, journals and research reports of research institutions, interviews of the eminent experts and Foreign Policy debates. The government spends huge money on Foreign Policy research through various research institutions and universities. The reports are the important source of information for policy making.

Data collection, the first step towards Foreign Policy decision making is a continuous process. The embassies, consulates and intelligence agencies send periodical reports and information to the government. Sometimes the government engages its agencies and institutions to collect special information on certain important issues on which the government is going to take decision. After having proper information the government makes policies.

Analysis and Processing of the Information Data

After the collection of the information, the government through, the designated agencies and organisations, analyzes the data based on the Foreign Policy objective. Territorial Divisions of Ministry of External Agencies, Joint Intelligence Committee other such agencies are setup to do the analysis work and find out its implications on India's national interests. Along with intelligence agencies, bureaucratic institutions also engage themselves in researching the pros and cons of the information data at various angles. Generally each of the issues is handled by an individual or small group of officers. However, sometimes a huge team of specialists are engaged to analyze and interpret the intelligence data based on the significance of the issue. After preparing the analysis report, the agencies and organisations pass the report along with its valuable inputs, observations and recommendations to the government or to the decision making body to take final decision.

Policy Planning

When the information data are analyzed at various angles, they are often referred to the decision making body for final decision on any particular Foreign Policy related issue. The decision making body in India generally comprises of political and bureaucratic leaderships, advisors, and policy planning groups.

Role of Bureaucratic Leadership

Bureaucratic leadership is not the ultimate boss of Foreign Policy decision making. They work under the political leadership and assist them in decision making process. But certain powers are given to the bureaucratic leadership to address and the bureaucratic leadership takes decisions on lower level issues while the important matters are left to the political leaderships. But all the activities and any major development on the matters related to the foreign affairs are normally brought to the notice of the political leadership.

Role of Political Leadership

The political leaders, being the chief of the decision making body, mostly take final decision on behalf of the country. As the political leaders lack actual knowledge and experience on foreign affairs management they mostly depend on the bureaucrats to handle Foreign Policy issues and crisis. Similarly the political leaders also depend on large number of experts and bureaucrats for advice in decision making.

Role of Advisors

In the Foreign Policy decision making process, the policy advisors play an important role. They not only give timely advice to the decision makers, but also act as mediators in between various stake holders of the decision making process. Before taking any important decision, the leaders consult the issue with experts and official advisors; and their views, observations and advices are the determinants of the policy outcomes.[119] Advisory agencies like the Strategic Planning Group (SPG) and National Security Advisory Board (NSAB) and other such agencies give their advices and inputs during the policy making process.

The National Security Advisor (NSA), being the most important one advises the Prime Minister and the government in many significant matters of national security. In order to give its comprehensive inputs, the NSA receives all necessary information on the recent development and briefs in advance before any meeting. The role of the NSA in decision making is divided into three steps. The first is guiding the policy making process on issues related to national security and foreign relations that maximize the national gains. Second, the NSA helps the government to take the best possible and timely decision on any outstanding issue or crisis. Thirdly, it oversees the process of implementation of the policy decision taken by the decision makers. Therefore the NSA works as the coordinating agency besides advising the government.[120]

Role of Core Foreign Policy Decision Making Agencies

Foreign Policy making process is highly complex in nature and needs interplay between several institutions and agencies along with a number of individual actors. While the top political authorities take most of the final decisions, they largely go with the advice of these institutional setups. Hence the role of these institutions is more than advisory. Various institutions view the issues from various angles and give necessary inputs to the policy proposals to make the decision more comprehensive.

PMO and Cabinet: The Prime Minister's office and the cabinet are the most important players in the Foreign Policy decision making process. Though the Foreign Minister is officially responsible to make a decision on issues related to India's foreign policies, the role of the Prime Minister as the head of the government is equally important in decision making process. Similarly, the cabinet and the cabinet committees also play a major role in Foreign Policy decision making. In case of any issue the cabinet, the inner circle of the government meets and decides the future course of action on any Foreign Policy issue. Important Cabinet committees like Cabinet Committee on Economic Affairs, Cabinet Committee on Political Affairs and Cabinet Committee on Security take the leading role in decision making process.

National Security Council: Being India's apex decision making body on national security and Foreign Policy, National Security Council plays avery important part in decision making process. It is a three tier organisation that consists of three different agencies. At the top Strategic Planning Group (SPG), a bureaucratic decision making body has been constituted to make long term strategic policy for India. Multidisciplinary National Security Advisory Board (NSAB) has been set up at the middle to advise the Prime Minister on India's foreign and national security matters. At the bottom the Joint Intelligence Committee (JIC) has been created to be the secretariat of the NSC and to assist the government in formulation and implementation of the national security policies. Hence, the National Security Council as a whole is playing a major role in shaping India's foreign policies.[121]

Policy Planning and Research Division: Policy Planning and Research Division (PPRD)is the nodal agency responsible to plan India's external policy based on the intelligence and bureaucratic information. Headed by Deputy Secretary, the PPRD like the Policy Planning Council (PPC) of US State Department and Policy Planning Section (PPS) of the British Foreign Ministry is setup to plan and shape India's foreign relations with the rest of the world.[122] It gives policy outlines, suggestions, guidelines, observations and other necessary directives to the Policy Planning and Review Committee (PPRC) that is primarily responsible for preparing the external policy of India. Though research no longer remains the important task of the division, still the division plays substantial role in planning India's Foreign Policy.[123]

These core policy planning and advisory agencies take part in Foreign Policy decision making process. The government and Ministry of External Affairs formulate India's foreign policies after discussing the issues with these agencies. In the process of decision making, the agencies present their observations, inputs and recommendations and help the government to reach the best possible policy conclusion.

Reaching at the Decision and Implementing

The actors and the advisory agencies discuss the matters extensively and assess the pros and cons of the possible alternatives. After ensuring positive outcome the decision making body opts for the best possible alternative. The proposed actions or the alternative proposals are referred for implementation. The duty of the decision making body does not end here. It keeps constant observation on the implemented policies and its feedbacks. The government, if feels that the policy is not upto the mark or remain below the expected result, it sometimes replaces the policy with a new one for better result. The aim of the new policy addresses the lacunas of the previous decision and readjusts according to the demand of the environment.

Conclusion

While most of the third world countries have been suffering due to lack of proper institutional setups for Foreign Policy management, India has been in advantage with well established Foreign Policy setups. The Indian National Congress (INC) and the western educated leadership of INC have been in a way acquainted with the external affairs state craft. The INC has been successfully propagating its stand and the atrocities of the British government before the world stage. Many of its leaders attend the international conferences and successfully conduct meetings with important delegations of different states. After independence the legacy of the Foreign Policy management has been successfully carried out by the Indian government. As a result, India has been at the fore front of the third world movements including the Non Alignment Movement (NAM).

Foreign Policy decision making in India was Prime Minister centric. During his tenure, Nehru, the chief architect of India's Foreign Policy used to be the centre of the Decision making process. He used to be the fore front decision maker of India's foreign affairs. Being in charge of both External Affairs and Prime Minister during most of his tenure, he used to take most of the important decisions and the role of cabinet and advisors were limited. The Nehruvian style of decision making is still seen in practice in the Indian Foreign Policy decision making units. Though all the stake holders of the decision making body express their view, it is the Prime Minister whose decision generally prevails.

Secondly, the process of Foreign Policy decision making is the end product of bargaining and consensus, rather than rational. The bureaucrats, departments and organisations and other players of the decision making unit try to dominate over others by prevailing their views on certain issues. As a result most of the times the decision making process remains tensed. Now with the emergence of regional political parties and regional supremacy with the mix of coalition politics, the regional parties also try to play larger role in foreign affairs that make the process very complex. Therefore the decision outcomes are out of consensus and balanced. However, the government sometimes takes hard steps to take rational decisions during the crisis.

Like most of the democratic countries, the inter-departmental conflicts and power game, most of the time, have jeopardized the decision making process. In order to maintain the departmental supremacy, some organisations are seen to hide some of the information that are supposed to be passed to the other departments or agencies. The function of JIC, PPRD and other such organisations and departments hesitate to share the information and are not willing to cooperate with others in most of the cases. As a result, the country pays the price for the inaccurate decisions.

Bureaucrats are the dominant forces of the whole process of decision making. Because of the pivotal role of bureaucracy in formulating and implementing the Foreign Policy for the country, they often try to influence the decision making process for their own benefits. Both in civil and military departments, the bureaucrats enjoy some sort of monopoly in decision making process. They are the drive force of the policy making as most of the political leadership lack experience and practical knowledge of Foreign Policy management. The lobby of the bureaucrats often downplays the right policy choice and bar the political leadership to take right steps. The idea of establishing the NSC was first proposed in 1962. But the constant bureaucratic pressure barred the government to setup the same for decades, as the bureaucrats feared that they would lose their hold if the neutral experts and military bosses were brought into the decision making process through NSC.

Though many agencies and factions have tried to jeopardize the Foreign Policy decision making process in India, still the process remains effective and successful throughout the years. Many times the government has taken bold, surprising and unusual steps to maximize national interest. The ideological driven decision making process is transformed into pragmatic at the time of need. That's why India still remains one of the vibrant players of world politics.

Notes

1. Siuli Sarkar, Public Administration In India, (New Delhi: PHI Learning, 2010) 872 J. Bandyopadhaya, Making of India's Foreign Policy, 3rd Edn, (New Delhi: Allied Publishers, 2006) 164; and R.B. Jain (2001) 340.
3. R.B. Jain, Public Administration in India: 21st Century Challenges for Good Governance (New Delhi: Deep and Deep Publications, 2001) 340.
4. Shriram Maheshwari, Indian Administrative Year Book 1990 (New Delhi: Concept Publishing Company, 1992) 7.
5. J. Bandyopadhaya (2006) 164; and R.B. Jain (2001) 340.
6. Jain (2001) 341; and Sarkar (2010) 87.
7. As of Apr 17, 2015.
8. Organisation and structure of Ministry of external affairs, published under the official web sites of MEA. http://www.mea.gov.in/organisation-structure.htm (17 May 2013).
9. Organisation and Structure of Ministry of External Affairs, MEA web site 10Bandyopadhyaya, The Making of India's Foreign Policy, 201-02.
11. See answer to Rajya Sabha, Unstarred Question No.2877,http://mea.gov.in/rajya-sabha.htm?dtl/24593/Q_NO_2877POLICY_PLANNING_DIVISION_IN_MINISTRY.
12. MEA Outcome Budget 2013-2014, Ministry of External Affairs, Govt. of India. http://mea.gov.in/Uploads/PublicationDocs/21546_MEA_Outcome_Budget_2013-14_English.pdf.
13. R. B. Jain, Public Administration in India: 21st Century Challenges for Good Governance (New Delhi: Deep and Deep Publications, 2004).
14. MEA Outcome Budget 2013-2014, Ministry of External Affairs, Govt. of India. http://mea.gov.in/Uploads/PublicationDocs/21546_MEA_Outcome_Budget_2013-14_English.pdf.
15. Indian Technical and Economic Cooperation Programme, Ministry of External Affairs, Govt. of India. http://www.itec.mea.gov.in/?1320?000.
16. Rajya Sabha Questions, http://rajyasabha.nic.in/rsnew/question/ministry_sub/external.pdf.
17. J. Bandyopadhyaya, The Making of India's Foreign Policy (New Delhi: Allied Publishers, 2006)194.
18 *Ibid.* 197.
19. MEA Annual Report 2012-13, Ministry of External Affairs, Govt. of India. http://mea.gov.in/Uploads/Publication Docs/21385_Annual_Report_2012-2013_English.pdf.
20. R. B. Jain, Public Administration in India: 21st Century Challenges for Good Governance (New Delhi: Deep and Deep Publications, 2001) 341-33.
21. Robert L. Hardgrave, Stanley A. Kochanek, India: Government and Politics in a Developing Nation, (Boston: Thomson Wodsworth, 2008) 95.
22. Functions of the Cabinet Secretariat, as stated at the official web site of the Cabinet secretariat of India http://cabsec.nic.in/about_functions.php (18 May 2013).

23. M.V. Pylee have divide the task of the Cabinet into four stages. For detail see M.V. Paylee, Constitutional Government in India, 4th ed. (New Delhi: S. Chand & Co., 1984) 284.
24. For a detail study on the faction of the British Cabinet, which is the source model of Indian Cabinet see John P. MacKintosh, British Cabinet, 3rd Edn., (London: Methuen & Co., 1981) 268.
25. N. Jayapalan, Indian Administration, Vol. 1., (New Delhi: Atlantic Publishers, 2001) 118.
26. Simon James, British Cabinet Government, 2nd Edn. (London: Routledge, 2002) 50-51.
27. Juliet Kaarbo, Power and Influence in Foreign Policy Decision Making: The Role of Junior Coalition Partners in German and Israeli Foreign Policy, International Studies, Quarterly, Vol. 40, No. 4 (Dec., 1996), 501-530.
28. After the Norshima Rao government since 1996 no political party wins the clear majority, hence made coalition government.

29 "India votes against Sri Lanka at UNHRC in Tamils case, DMK hits out at UPA", The Indian Express, Mar 21, 2013,. http://www.indianexpress.com/news/india-votes-against-sri-lanka-at-unhrc-in-tamils-case-dmk-hits-out-at-upa/1091351/.

30 "Government must reject DMK demand on Sri Lanka", The New Indian Express, 14th May 2013. http://newindianexpress.com/editorials/Government-must-reject-DMK-demand-on-Sri Lanka/2013/05/14/article1588662.ece.

31 "Composition and Functions of the Cabinet Committees", published by the official web site of the Cabinet Secretariat of India, http://cabsec.nic.in/files/archive/cabinet_committees_30.08.2011.pdf.

32. N. Jayapalan, Indian Administration, Vol. - I, (New Delhi: Atlantic Publishers, 2001) 136.
33. Siuli Sarkar, Public Administration In India (New Delhi: PHI Learning, 2010) 89.
34. The last cabinet committee has created when there were slowdown on Investment has seen. To boost the investment the government has set up the Cabinet Committee on Investment with the Notice No. 1/11/3/2012-Cab. Dated Jan 2, 2013 http://cabsec.nic.in/showpdf.php?type=cci_notification.
35. S.R. Maheshwari, The Administrative Reform Commission (Agra: Laxmi Narain Agarwal, 1972) 509-10.

36 Michel Brecher, Nehru's Mantle: The Politics of Succession in India, as quoted in N. Jayapalan (2001) 139.

37. J. Bandyopadhaya, The Making of India's Foreign Policy: Determinates, Institutions, Process and Personalities, 3rd Edn. (New Delhi: Allied Publishers, 2003) 135-36.
38. Bandyopadhaya, The Making of India's Foreign Policy, 84.
39. Roxane D.V. Sismanidis, "Foreign Relations (of India)", in India: A Country Study, edited by James Heitzman and Robert L. Worden(Federal Research Division: Library of Congress, 1995) available online at http://lcweb2.loc.gov/cgi-bin/query/r?frd/cstdy:@field(DOCID+in0168).

40. This information has collected from official website of the PM's Office, Government of India, http://pmindia.gov.in/pmsoffice.php, and the RTI report of "Name, Designation and Emoluments of PMO Officials [As on 31.07.2012]" also available at http://pmindia.nic.in/ salaryjul2012.pdf.
41. Siuli Sarkar, Public Administration in India (New Delhi; PHI Learning, 2009) 67.
42. As mentioned at the official web site of PMO Office, Government of India, http://pmindia.gov.in/ pmsoffice.php.
43. Harish Kapur, Foreign Policies of India's Prime Ministers (New Delhi: Lancer Publishers, 2013) 5.
44. In its election manifesto of BJP promised to re-establish National Security Council and review India's nuclear policy if voted for power. For detail see, Chapter 8 of BJP's the BJP's Election Manifesto 1998 at http://www.bjp.org/index.php?option=com_content&view=article&id=412:chapter-8&catid=75&Itemid=501.
45. D. Shyam Babu, "National Security Council: Yet another Ad Hoc Move?" In Security Beyond Survival, edited by P.R. Kumaraswamy (New Delhi: Sage, 2004) 89.
46. Shyam Babu (2004) 90.
47. Anit Mukherjee, Failing to Deliver Post-Crises Defence Reforms in India, 1998-2010, Institute of Defence Studies and Analysis Occasional Paper No. 18, (New Delhi, IDSA, March 2011) 11.
48. Jerrold Elkin, India, in The Defence Policies of Nations: A Comparative Study, 3rd Edn., edited by Douglas Murray, Paul R. Viotti(London: John Hopkins University Press, 1994) 476.
49. The Gazette of India, Part I, Section I, 22 September 1090, 652-53.
50. Anit Mukherjee (2011) 13.
51. S. P. Agrawal, Information India: 1997-98 and 1998-99: Global View (New Delhi: Concept Publishing Company, 2002) 203.
52. Stephen F. Burgess, India's emerging security strategy, missile Defence, and arms control, INSS Occasional paper 54, (USAF Institute for National Security Studies, Colorado, June 2004) 21.
53. The Gazette of India, Part I, Section I, 19 April 1999, 4-8.
54. Agrawal, (2002) 203.
55. Sunil Dasgupta, "India: The New Militaries", in Coercion and Governance: The Declining Political Role of the Military in Asia edited by Muthiah Alagappa, (Stanford: Stanford University Press, 2001) 114.
56. P.R. Cherry, "India's Nuclear Doctrine: Confused Ambitions", The Nonprolife ration Review, (Vol. 7. No. 3, Fall winter 2000) 125.
57. As quoted in Karsten Frey, India's Nuclear Bomb and National Security, (Oxon: Routledge, 2007) 57.
58. As quoted in Frey (2007) 5.

59. Shyam Babu (2004) 93.
60. Stephen P. Cohen, Sunil Dasgupta, Arming Without Aiming: India's Military Modernization (Washington DC: Brookings Institution Press, 2010) 104.
61. Shyam Babu (2004) 96.
62. NS Sisodia and Sujit Dutta, India and the World: Selected Articles from IDSA Journals, Volume 1 (New Delhi: Institute for Defence Studies and Analysis and Bibliophile South Asia, 2005) 98.
63. Bandyopadhyaya (2003) 154.
64. Ravinder P. Singh, Arms Procurement Decision-making Processes: China, India, Israel, Japan, South Korea and Thailand (New York: Oxford University Press, 1998) 54; also see , Paul Todd and Jonathan Bloch, Global Intelligence: The World's Secret Services Today (London: Zed Books, 2004) 184-85.
65. Bandyopadhyaya (2003) 155.
66. Ravinder P. Singh (1998) 54 ; and AR Saluja," Indian Intelligence Organisation: Need for a Comprehensive Knowledge Management", Indian Defence Review (Vo. 16, No.2, Jan-Mar 2008) 82-88.
67. Behram A. Sahukar, "Intelligence and Defence Cooperation in India" in Intelligence Cooperation Practices in the 21st Century: Towards a Culture of Sharing, edited by Musa Tuzuner (BG Amsterdam, Netherlands: IOS Press, 2010) 35.
68. Ashley J Tellis, India's Emerging Nuclear Posture: Between Recessed Deterrent and Ready Arsenal (Santa Monica, US: Rand Corporation, 2001) 448.
69. "Organisational Set-Up And Functions of Ministry of Defence", as states on the official website of the Ministry of Defence, http://mod.nic.in/aboutus/welcome.html.
70. Ministry of Defence, Government of India.
71. *Ibid.*
72. *Ibid.*
73. Organisation And Functions of The Raksha Mantralaya (Ministry of Defence), available at the official site of the National Academy of Defence Financial Management (NADFM) http://nadfm.nic.in/learning/Study %20and%20 Training%20Materials/ Orientation%20CouseAAOs,%20SO(A)-83.01/ Orientation%20Course-AAOs,SO(A)/Orientation%20Course.doc.
74. Pramoda Kumar Panda, Making of India's Foreign Policy: Prime Minister and Wars (New Delhi: Raj Publications, 2003) 34.
75. "Army Chief briefs Cabinet committee on in cursion", the Hindu, New Delhi, May 1, 2013 http://www.thehindu.com/news/national/army-chief-briefs-cabinet-committee-onincursion/article 4673416.ece.
76. *Our Parliament* (New Delhi: Lok Sabha Secretariat, 2009) 1; available at the official site of the Parliament of India http://164.100.47.132/LssNew/our%20 Parliament/Folder01.pdf.
77. *Ibid.*
78. Subash Kashyap, Our Parliament (New Delhi: National Book Trust, 2007) 190-91.

79. B.K Sharma, Introduction to the Constitution of India (New Delhi: PHI Learning, 2007) 273.
80. Sharma (2007) 275; for detail discussion of the legislating power on Concurrent List refer, Background Paper on "Concurrent Powers of legislation under list III of the Constitution" published under the official website of Ministry of Law and Justice, Government of India http://lawmin.nic.in/ncrwc/finalreport/v2b3-3.htm.
81. Constitution of India, published under the website of Ministry of Law and Justice, Government of India, http://lawmin.nic.in/olwing/coi/coi-english/Const. Pock%202Pg.Rom8Fsss%2835%29.pdf, (Apr. 10, 2013).
82. "Treaty-Making Power under our Constitution", Consultation Paper prepared by National Commission to Review the Working of the Constitution, Government of India on January 8, 2001, Ministry of Law and Justice, Government of India..
83. The central government can legislate laws and policies for state on versos grounds. During president rule Parliament can make law on the items of state list for the state. Similarly the Rajya Sabha can also make laws on the state list for state by passing the necessary resolution. See, "Special Powers of Rajya Sabha" in Rajya Sabha- An Introduction, published under the official website of Rajya Sabha. http://rajyasabha.gov.in/rsnew/about_Parliament/rajya_sabha_introduction.asp.
84. Anthony J. Nownes, Interest Groups in American Politics: Pressure and Power (New York: Routledge, 2013) 54.
85. *Ibid.* 54.
86. *Ibid.*
87. Bandyopadhyaya (2003) 115.
88. *Ibid,* 115.
89. "Summary of World Military Expenditure in 2012", SIPRI Data Base 2012, http://www.sipri.org/year book/2013/03.
90. SIPRI Data Base 2012. http://armstrade.sipri.org/armstrade/html/export_values.php.
91. TIV of arms imports to the top 50 largest importers, 2012-2012, SIPRI Data Base 2012, http://armstrade.sipri.org/armstrade/html/export_toplist.php (13 June 2013), also see, Paul Holtom, Mark Bromley, Pieter D. Wezeman and Siemon T. Wezeman, "Trends in International Arms Transfers 2011", SIPRI Fact Sheet, March 2012.
92. Jeff Gerth, Arms Dealers Linked to U.S. Policy Shift, New York Times, January 16, 1987, http://www.nytimes.com/1987/01/16/world/arms-dealers-linked-to-us-policy-shift.html.
93. For detail understanding refer, Andrew Feinstein, The Shadow World: Inside the Global Arms Trade, (New York: Picador, 2011).
94. Raman Kirpal, "Back in the Line of Fire", Tehelka, Issue 2 Volume 8, January 15, 2011, http://tehelka.com/ back-in-the-line-of-fire/; "What the Bofors scandal is all about", CNN IBN, Apr 26, 2012, http://ibnlive.in.com/news/what-the-bofors scandal-is-all-about/252196-3.html; "Chronology of the Bofors Scandal", Daily News Analysis, Feb 27, 2007, http://www.dnaindia.com/india/1082262/report-chronology-of-the-bofors-scandal; "Key players in Bofors Scandal", Headlines

Today, New Delhi, April 28, 2009, http://indiatoday.intoday.in/story/Key+players+in+ Bofors+scandal/1/39264.html.

95. "Another Bofors Scam In The Making: BJP On Italian Chopper Deal", Tehelk Daily, New Delhi, Feb 13, http://tehelka.com/another-bofors-scam-in-the-making-bjp-on-italian-chopper-deal/ See also, Sandeep Unnithan,Guns and Butter in Billion-dollar Arms Deal: Indian Army at the mercy of shadowy arms dealers, lobbyists, India Today, September 21, 2012, http://indiatoday.intoday.in/story/billion-dollar-arms-deal-in-army-gun-manufacturers/1/221665.html.
96. Navy war leak case: All you need to know about Ravi Shankaran, India Military News, http://indianmilitarynews.wordpress.com/tag/war-room-leak/.
97. The term have popularly used in many places to represent the NOG, for instance see, John Dumbrell, David M. Barrett, Non-Governmental organisations: the voice of people, U.S. Foreign Policy agenda, (Vol. 5, No. 1, March 2000) 28-32.
98. The Union of International Associations (UIA) data base http://www.uia.org/ (accessed on June 14, 2013) .
99. Krishna S. Rana, Inside Diplomacy (New Delhi: Manas Publication, 2000) 367-68.
100. Bandyopadhayaya (2003) 122.
101. James G. McGann, "Think Tanks and Policy Advice in the US", Research Paper, Foreign Policy Research Institute, Philadelphia, August, 2005, 3.
102. C. Raja Mohan, The Making of Indian Foreign Policy: The Role of Scholarship and Public Opinion, Institute of South Asian Studies (ISAS) Working Paper, No. 73, 13 July 2009.
103. Introduction to School of International Studies, JNU, available at http://www.jnu.ac.in/sis/.
104. Raja Mohan (2009).
105. Annual Report 2010-12, Ministry of External Affairs, Government of India, 167-173.
106. Annual Report 2011-12, 167.
107. James G. McGann, (2005) 17.
108. Data released by Ministry of Overseas Indian Affairs, Government of India, available at http://moia.gov.in/writereaddata/pdf/NRISPIOS-Data(15-06-12)new.pdf.
109. For Detail refer, Paul Spickard, Race and Power in Fiji, Research article published by University of California, Santa Barbara, available at http://www.education.ucsb.edu/socialjustice/spickard.pdf; also see, A. C. Cato, Fijians and Fiji-Indians: A Culture-Contact Problem in the South Pacific, Oceania, Vol. 26, No. 1 (Sep., 1955), 14-34.
110. Bandyopadhyaya (2003) 123.
111. For instance see, Paul D'Anieri, International Politics: Power and Purpose in Global Affairs (Boston: Cengage Learning, 2011) 134.
112. Ole Rudolf Holsti, Public Opinion and American Foreign Policy, Revised Edition, (Michigan: University of Michigan Press, 2009) 234.
113. D'Anieri (2011) 139.

114. Many scholars have use the term while discussing the affects. For instance see, Steven Livingston, Clarifying the CNN Effect: An Examination of Media Effects According to Type of Military Intervention, Research paper, John F. Kennedy School of Government, Harvard University. 1997; Piers Robinson, The CNN effect: can the news media drive Foreign Policy?, Review of International Studies (1999), 25, 301–309; Ekaterina Balabanova, Media Wars and Politics: Comparing the Incomparable in Western and Eastern Europe, (Hampshire, England: Ashgate Publishing, 2013) 8-11.; Piers Robinson, The CNN Effect: The Myth of News, Foreign Policy and Intervention (London: Routledge, 2002); Brigitte Lebens Nacos, Robert Y. Shapiro, Pierangelo Isernia (ed.), Decision making in a Glass House: Mass Media, Public Opinion, and American and European Foreign Policy in the 21st Century (Maryland: Rowman& Littlefield, 2000) 2; also see, D'Anieri (2011) 141.
115. Bandoyopadhyaya (2003) 126.
116. Partha Pratim Basu, Press and Foreign Policy in India, (New Delhi: Lancer Books, 2003) 18-21.
117. Many scholars have termed India's Foreign Policy as reactive, for instance see, K.R. Gupta & Vatsala Shukla, Foreign Policy of India, Vol. 1, (New Delhi: Atlantic Publishers, 2009) 109; Robert L. Hardgrave, Jr., Stanley A. Kochanek, India: Government and Politics in a Developing Nation: Government and Politics in a Developing Nation (Boston: Thomson Wadsworth, 2008) 478; Ashok Kapur, India - From Regional to World Power (New York: Routledge, 2013); David M. Malone, Does the Elephant Dance?: Contemporary Indian Foreign Policy (Oxford; Oxford University Press, 2011); M. Srinivas Chary, The Eagle and the Peacock: U.S. Foreign Policy Toward India Since Independence (Westport, US: Greenwood Publishing Group, 1995) 57; Rajpal Budania, India's National Security Dilemma: The Pakistan Factor and India's Policy Response (New Delhi: Indus Publishing, 2001) 262; Anjali Ghosh, op. cit, India's Foreign Policy, (New Delhi: Pearson Education India, 2009) 358.
118. For more information see, Richard J. Norton, "Understanding the Policy-Making Process:A Guide to Case Analysis", Case Studies in Policy Making, 12th Edition, Edited by Hayat Alvi and Nikolas K. Gvosdev, (Newport, US Naval War College 2010) 5-10.
119. For a comprehensive discussion on advisors on Foreign Policy decision making see Steven B. Redd, The influence of Advisers and Decision Strategies on Foreign Policy Choices: President Clinton's Decision to Use Force in Kosovo, International Studies Perspectives, Volume 6, Issue 1, 2005; Margaret G. Hermann and Thomas Preston, Presidents, Advisers, and Foreign Policy: The Effect of Leadership Style on Executive Arrangements, Political Psychology, Vol. 15, No. 1, Special Issue: Political Psychology and the Work of Alexander L. George (Mar., 1994) 75-96.
120. Ivo H. Daalder and I.M. Destler, "How National Security Advisor See Their Role", in The Domestic Sources of American Foreign Policy: Insights and Evidence, edited by Eugene Robert Wittkopf, James M. McCormick (Lanham, U.S.: Rowman & Little field, 2008) 187.

121. D. Shyam Babu, "National Security Council: Yet Another Ad Hoc Move?" In Security Beyond Survival, ed., P.R. Kumaraswamy (New Delhi: Sage, 2004) 83-102.

122. Shashi Tharoor, Pax Indica: India and the World of the Twenty-first Century (London: Penguin UK, 2013) 87.

123. Banndyapadhyaya (2003) 200-090.

Chapter – 3

Role of Indian Parliament in Foreign Policy Decision Making

Foreign Policy Decision Making is a complex process which involves multiple actors, agencies and institutions. Though the Ministry of External Affairs plays a pivotal role in shaping India's Foreign Policy behaviour, the Cabinet, Ministry of Defence, Ministry of Trade and Commerce, Prime Minister's Office and National Security Council also are extensively involved in determining India's external policy. Apart from this, the Parliament, in any democratic setup is considered as one of the important institutions in Foreign Policy decision making. Being the centre of world's largest democracy, Indian Parliament is also playing an important role in determining India's Foreign Policy behaviour.

This chapter provides a comprehensive analysis of the role of Indian Parliament in the formation of Indian external policy. Being the main chapter, it further discusses a brief historical evolution of the Indian Parliament and its structure and function to understand the decision making procedure of Indian Parliament. The subsequent sections of this chapter describe the role of various procedural devices of Indian parliament like the parliamentary question, Motion, resolutions, debates and discussion as well as their utility in the floor of the house in influencing India's Foreign Policy.

Thus, this Chapter under the broad umbrella of Indian Parliament explains the various sub-topics such as structure of Indian Parliament, the functions carried by the Parliament and the Parliament as an instrument of accountability, to have a clear picture of the skeleton framework of Parliament.

Indian Parliament: History, Structure and Functions

Indian Parliament took the shape after undergoing several changes tracing the path from Charter Act of 1833 which sowed the seeds for the institutional specialization by clearly differentiating the law making and executive decision making. The Government of India Act 1935 authorized Indian representation in the Parliament. However, the transition from the Charter Act of 1833 to the Government of India Act of 1935 was not smooth and was constantly influenced by the successive national movements and struggles.

The structure of Indian Parliament consists of the President and the two Houses namely, Rajya Sabha, the upper house and Lok Sabha, the lower house. The mode of election of the members, tenure of members, and number of seats allocated for both the houses have been explained under the following subheadings. The functions of the Parliament are portrayed elaborately where the policy making as the major function of the Parliament takes the prior position by explaining the influence of the Parliament on public policy outcomes. In addition, T.J. Lowi's classification of public policy into four typologies namely distribution policy, redistribution policy, regulatory policy and constituent policy is mentioned to have a clear picture of the different kinds of public policies.[1] Indian Parliament performs certain important functions such as law making, political and financial control over executive, administrative accountability, amending the constitution and informational role which have been explained in detail in the following subheadings. The next subheading deals with the arena of Indian Parliament acting as an instrument of accountability. The fundamental principle of the Indian Parliament is to effectively serve as an instrument of accountability over the executive, and the instruments used by the Parliament in the exercise of accountability such as censure motion, committee system, opposition and no confidence motion have been discussed. Public policy is seen as a natural result of the legislative and executive interaction. The two important instruments of accountability in the hands of Parliament namely ministerial responsibility and administrative responsibility have been clearly illustrated.

The Fundamental Framework

The Preamble reflects the rich philosophy of Indian Constitution. It states that the sources of all are the people of India. It elucidates the objectives which the Constitution seeks to establish and encourage. The Preamble, therefore, is a fundamental fabric of the Indian Constitution which pictures its essence with magnanimity reaching its culminating point. The picture of a 'democratic republic', which the Preamble envisages, is democratic not only from the political but also from the social standpoint. The Preamble envisages a democratic form of government along with a democratic society infused with the spirit of 'justice, liberty, equality and fraternity.[2] Moreover, the Preamble also states a representative form of Government through Parliament in the Centre and State legislatures in the periphery which has become the cardinal pillars of assuring the envisioned democracy in India. In this regard, Indian Parliament as a premier institution assumes special significance because it is here the sovereign will of the people finds expression.

A Brief History of the Indian Parliament

Representational bodies in India had existed since ages, and a close examination of Indian classical literatures like Kautilya's Arthashastra, Panini's Ashtadhyayi, Aitareya Brahman including Mahabharata reveal historical evidences of functioning republics during those periods.[3] In its modern connotation, however, Parliamentary institutions own their origin to India's association with the British government. Parliamentary institution, as envisaged by the British, underwent a sea change after relentless struggles for institutionalizing a system of representation and accountability. Therefore, it would be right to claim that the Indian Parliament in the hands of Indians acquired its true meaning and character. The first faint beginning of a Central legislature for India is from the Charter Act of 1833. However, it was just the beginning and the Charter Act of 1833 did not push with huge reforms or changed the existing equations though it introduced important changes in the system of Indian administration. Institutional specialization in the Government by differentiating law making and executive decision making was made in the Governor-General's Council. The Act was created for the first time, the Government of India having authority over the entire territorial area possessed by the British in India and ended the activities of East India Company.[4]

The Indian Council Act of 1861 was considered the prime charter of the Indian legislature as it sought to make better provisions both for the Constitution of the Council of the Governor-General and for the local government. The Council of the Governor General was reconstituted with five members, and for the purposes of legislation, the Governor-General was authorized to nominate to his Council, not less than six and not more than twelve additional members, of which half were to be non-officials. There was no provision explicitly in the Act to the appointment of Indians for the post of non-officials in the Council However, the House of Commons gave assurance to that effect.[5] In so far, this Act marked a significant advancement from the previous acts and for the first time, it accepted the important principle of representation of non-officials in legislative bodies.

The British government continued this tradition and introduced a number of such Acts.[6]

One of the important Acts is the Indian Council Act of 1909. The Indian Council Act of 1909 was passed to give effect to the Morley-Minto reform proposal of 1908 and how far this act made changes in the Constitution and functions of the Indian legislatures hitherto unimagined. The maximum number of members in the Indian Legislative Council was raised from 16 to 60. Similarly members in the Legislative councils of Provinces were also doubled. The Act specifically required that the members of the Legislative Councils should include elected as well as nominated members. Functions of the Legislative Councils were also quadrupled. The members could move resolutions on the Budget and on any matter of public interest. They also had the privilege of asking supplementary questions. This Act can be termed as a colossal reshuffle in the structure of Indian legislatures.[7]

However the Act of 1909 reforms also created the communal system in the Indian electorate and provided representation and reservation of seats in Councils for special interests like Muslims thereby sowing the seeds of separatist tendencies in India. If legislative reforms were a triumph for the Congress, this system of 'divide and rule' through separate communal electorate was more victorious for the British.

One of the major turning points in the evolution of the Indian Parliament is the Government of India Act of 1919. This act introduced 'dyarchy' and the Legislature took over law making functions from the Governor-General's Council. At the Centre, the Indian Legislative Council (formerly called as the Governor-General's Legislative Council) was replaced by bicameral legislature consisting of a Council of States as Upper House and the Legislative Assembly as Lower House.[8] The Council of State was to consist of not more than 60 members, and out of these not more than 20 members were to be officials. The Legislative Assembly was fixed at 140 members from whom 100 would be elected, 26 nominated and the rest as nominated non-officials. The first Council of State had a total of 60 members, out of which 34 were elected, 20 were nominated and 6 nominated as non-officials. As a result the first Legislative Assembly came into being in 1921 and had 145 members out of whom 104 were elected (52 by General, 30 by Muslim, 9 by European, 7 by Landowners, 4 by Commercial and 2 by Sikh constituencies), 26 officials and 15 nominated as non officials.

Though the 1919 Act established diarchy, the Governor-General was directly responsible to the Secretary of State for India and through him to the British Parliament. The Act could not explicitly provide more powers in the field of legislation and was constantly subjected to the checks of the Governor-General who sought to keep the sovereignty of the British Parliament intact. However, the creation of the Central Legislature increased the legislative activity. The Budget, except for certain reserved heads, was subject to the vote of the Council; the members had broader freedom of speech and could move resolutions and motions or adjournments. Moreover, the members grew more critical of the government which increased the scope of the legislative activity of the country. In the words of Subash Kashyap "The emergence of the Central Legislature was a matter of historic importance. For the first time it gave the representatives of the people a voice in making laws and influencing Governmental policies. It also played a great role in the shaping of the political destinies of the country. While the country was fighting to overthrow foreign domination, the representatives of the people assembled in the Legislature carried the battle into the House the existence of a highly critical Legislature which encouraged the exercise of care and discretion on the part of the Executive and instilled in it a consciousness of its obligation to the people."[9]

Finally, the Government of India Act of 1935, created a scope of real Indian representation in the Parliament. According to this Act, the Governor General was to have a Council of Ministers, not exceeding ten in numbers to aid and advise him in the exercise of his functions except where he was required to exercise his functions in his discretion or in his individual judgment[10]. The Act sought to create a federal structure in India with His - Majesty, represented by the Governor-General, together with the Council of States and the House of Assembly. The Council of State was to consist of 156 representatives of British India and not more than 104 representatives of the Indian States while the House of Assembly was to consist of 250 representatives of British India and not more than 125 representatives of the Indian States. The Act provided that no bill would become law unless agreed to by both Houses and assented to by the Governor-General; both the houses were therefore given equal powers except in the field of finance. Money bills could be introduced only in the House of Assembly, but the Council of States had the powers to amend the bill and the Governor-General on the other side had the powers to resolve the differences between the two houses by summoning a joint session.[11]

Such a long and tumultuous history of the Indian Parliament has endowed it with a unique feature of self sustainability. Today it is showing promising signals of prosperity though Indian politics has fallen into a bottomless pit. As a beacon light for a representational democracy, Indian Parliament is evolving itself from a nascent stage to maturity and much of its success depends upon the functions and processes within the system. This research is a humble attempt to understand those functions and processes pertaining to one of the sensitive public policies of our times – Defence and Strategic policy with particular reference to nuclear and missile policy making.

Structure of the Indian Parliament

Article 79 of our Constitution clearly postulates that "The Parliament of India consists of the President and two Houses. The lower House is called the House of People (Lok Sabha) while the upper House is known as the Council of States (Rajya Sabha).[12] Our Constitution has adopted the Parliamentary system of Government which effects a harmonious blending of the legislative and the executive organs of the State in as much as the executive power is wielded by a group of members of the Legislature who command a majority in the popular Chamber of the Legislature and remain in power so long as they retain that majority.

The President

The President of India is a part of the Legislature, and the head of the Union Executive. The President is elected by an indirect election, in accordance with the system of proportional representation by means of single transferable vote. The Electoral College to elect the President consists of the elected members of both Houses of the Parliament, the elected members of Legislative Assemblies of the States and the elected members of the Legislative Assemblies of Union Territories of Delhi and Pondicherry.

The Rajya Sabha

The Upper House of the Parliament is also known as the Council of States. The members of Rajya Sabha are elected by the members of the State Legislative Assemblies in accordance with the system of proportional representation by means of single transferable vote[13] . The number of representatives from each state in Rajya Sabha is based on its population and as such there is no uniformity in representation. The strength of Rajya Sabha as envisaged by the Constitution must be not more than 250 members, of which 238 members are elected by State and Union Territories and the 12 members are nominated by the President.[14] The members of Rajya Sabha have a fixed term of 6 years and one-third of the members retire at the expiration of every second year in accordance with the provision made on that behalf by Parliament by law[15].

The Lok Sabha

The Lok Sabha is the lower House of the People. The members of the Lok Sabha are directly elected by the people who are above 18 years of age and who are entitled to vote in the elections of Lok Sabha unless and otherwise disqualified under law (Art 326). Article 81(1) of the Indian constitution provides that the Lok Sabha shall consist of not more than 530 members chosen by direct election from territorial constituencies in the State and not more than 20 members chosen from the Union Territories. The President may nominate not more than two members of the Anglo-Indian community. The strength of the Lok Sabha as envisaged by the Constitution is therefore 552 and the ratio in which it is allotted is based on the population of the States. The Lok Sabha has a fixed term of five years from the date appointed for its first meeting. However the House may be dissolved under certain circumstances as envisaged by the Constitution.[16]

The structure of the Indian Parliament indicates the accommodative jurisdiction in relation to the other two organs of the Government. The Parliament does not reign supreme and sovereign and much of its powers are constrained by the Constitution. As a reflector of the sovereign will of the people, the structure of the Parliament has given unto itself uniqueness quite decisive in itself.

Functions of the Parliament

Public Policy is a scheme devised by the State in pursuit of certain objectives and as David Easton notes, it is "the authoritative allocation of values for the whole society[17]". The elucidation of objectives for which a policy is required is done by the Government through articulating its rationale. T. J. Lowi classifies public policies into four typologies; distributive policies which are concerned with the distribution of new resources ; redistributive policies which are concerned with changing the distribution pattern of existing resources; regulatory policies which are concerned with regulation and control of activities and constituent policies which are concerned with the re-organization or establishment of institutions[18]. In this sense, a Government may pursue a purposive course of action or choose not to pursue the actions which are consistent with the development policy.

Based on the institutional approach to policy analysis, it is important to understand the extent of influence of the Parliament on the structures of policy making in India. On the frontiers of policy making, the Parliament performs the following important functions[19]:

Law Making and Legitimization Role: Conceived as the traditional function of the Parliament, law making has an identity in its own right under the Constitution of India. The Parliament can make laws on the Union and the Concurrent Lists of the Seventh schedule of the Constitution and this feature exclusively assigns the Parliament a uniqueness unraveled by any other institution. While the Parliament by itself does not evolve any law, its scrutiny, review, examination and discussion of the public policy designed by the Government to translate into a law, serve as an established pathway in the law making process.

Political and Financial Control over the Executive: Public policies emanating from the Government have to be rationalized to the legislature. The constitutional provision of collective responsibility of the Council of Ministers to the legislature and the Parliament's control over the Executive's budget are well established. Passing of the no confidence motion, defeating the Government in a major issue of policy, adjournment motion and defeating the Government on financial measures are some of the mechanisms of accountability held by the Parliament to check the Executive dominance on public policies.

Administrative Accountability: Administrative accountability is the Parliament's indirect evaluation of public policy carried on by the bureaucracy. This ex-post-facto check is necessary on the grounds that the public policy, which is a purposive course of action, cannot be efficacious if the administration is not able to act in conformity to the needs of the Government. In this regard, the accountability is technical and indirect through the ministers concerned. The various procedural devices like the Parliamentary committees, Questions, Calling Attention Notices, Half-an-Hour discussions, Private Members' resolution, Discussions on matters of urgent Public importance are some of the mechanisms through which the Parliament holds the administration accountable albeit indirectly through the ministers.

Informational Role: To call for information is perhaps the most significant function of the Indian Parliament. The right of the Parliament to be informed cannot be held in void unless any divulging of information is detrimental to the national interest or security. The Government feeds the Parliament with information in regular intervals through the submission of reports, laying of papers on the table of the house or placing the documents in the Parliament library. Based on the information received, the Parliament may throw light on the deficiencies and highlight the shortcomings. The role of the Fourth Estate i.e. the Press is unsurpassable in enabling the Parliament to keep abreast of information. Through the Question Hour, Calling Attention Motions, Half-an-Hour Discussions and other procedural devices available to the Parliament, the Parliament extracts information from the Government and holds it accountable.

Amending the Constitution: Parliament has a unique responsibility in amending the Constitution. In accordance with Article 368, the amendment of the Constitution can be initiated only by the introduction of a Bill in either house of the Parliament with the support of the majority of not less than two thirds of the members of each House present and voting, and ratified by the President. It may be noted that though the role of the Parliament in other functions may be diluted through other functional procedures, amendment of the Constitution is still the ultimate prerogative of the Parliament alone.

To conclude we can say that, much of the functions of the Parliament as envisaged by the Constitution and as theoretically elucidated are more of a myth than reality. The Government which commands the majority in the Parliament could circumvent the conventional functions of the Government. Mechanisms of accountability can seldom have attention when majority of the Parliament slides with the Government. Executive, administrative and informational control of the Parliament therefore remains vulnerable to the Governmental dominance.

The Role of Indian Parliament in Foreign Policy Decision Making

Indian Parliament, being the top most democratic institution and the ultimate voice of the nation and supposed to play a key role in formulating foreign relations of a country, now perhaps possesses less control compared to the other governmental Departments of governmental activities. The increasing nature of complexity in the Foreign Policy management and the cost of delayed decisions encourage the bureaucrats to lead the mission while pushing the parliamentary control into the backseat. With the rise of globalization that interlinks every aspect of the state craft including external affairs and emergence of new trends and aspects of Foreign Policy behaviour, the decision making process in Foreign Policy is ultimately accelerated into a new era of complexity. Our day to day activities are no longer personal or state level and somehow connected with international trends. Hence, new specialization departments have been created and specialized officers have been appointed to deal with these new challenges while the whole process of external relation of a nation is traditionally used to be led by one or a group leader. It tends to rise to a new system of Foreign Policy management naming organizational management model, where a group of specialized people or bureaucrats are appointed to deal with certain issues to deliver maximum benefits.

Besides the emergence of bureaucratic supremacy in Foreign Policy management mechanism, several international bodies have been set up to deal with the issues that are traditionally addressed by the domestic agencies. These organizations are often regulated by the national government and the parliament hardly has been consulted or any interference hardly ever seen from the parliament side. Hence, the national agencies like the Parliament are gradually losing their command in Foreign Policy decision making.[20] Out of all the limitations, the parliament still plays a crucial role in conducting Foreign Policy in several ways. In fact, it is the most important agency which ultimately takes responsibility for its failure or success. The role of Parliament in Foreign Policy decision making is broadly discussed below:

Parliament and Foreign Policy Decision Making in India

Parliament plays a significant role in Foreign Policy making in India. In fact, the parliament enjoys complete authority in making laws, for both domestic and foreign affairs, of this country. Thus, the part influences Foreign Policy activities in many ways. Though, some believe that the Parliament enjoys limited and minimal inputs in foreign affairs as compared to domestic affairs, it has been well established that domestic policies too can influence the foreign policies significantly.[21] Article 246 of the Indian Constitution which distributes powers to the Union Government and the states authorize the Parliament to legislate on all aspects of external affairs of this country.[22] Item 10 of the Union List under the Seventh Scheduled of the Constitution specifically empowers the Parliament to formulate appropriate laws regarding foreign affairs. [23] In addition, items listed from serial number 9 to 21 of the Union List include war and peace, diplomacy, matters regarding UN, and international treaties and agreements under the supervision of the Parliament. Apart from the policy formulation, the Parliament is influencing the Foreign Policy decision in many ways using various tools. Using its budgetary control, it can slash down various allocations on military, Defence, foreign aid and other such peripherals as well. Similarly by opening of new offices and branches and neutralizing the performance through resource control of such agencies that deal with the Foreign Policy activities, the Parliament can indirectly control the external policy of the country. Thus, one can agree that the Parliament plays a vital role in Foreign Policy making in India. Its role can be divided into three broad categories – Policy formulation, policy shaping, and policy alternation.

The Role of Parliament as a Legislating Body

Parliament in India being the super most legislative body is empowered to enact laws for the items prescribed under the union list. It introduces, discusses and passes legislations for both domestic and international affairs. Article 246 of the Indian Constitution authorizes the Parliament to make laws for the nation. Clause one (1) of the article says, "… Parliament has exclusive power to make laws with respect to any of the matters enumerated in List I in the Seventh Schedule (in this Constitution referred to as the "Union List)"[24] Out of the allotted 97 items of the Union List, items 1 to 21 are directly or indirectly related to the foreign affairs on which the parliament can make laws. Items under these sections deal with Military forces and management (items 1 to 4), diplomacy (item11), UN (item12), international treaties and agreements (item14) war and peace (item 15), foreign jurisdiction (16) citizenship and alliances (item 17) and more particularly item 10 of the list grants exclusive power to the Parliament to legislate any matter related to the foreign affairs.[25] Similarly under Article 253, the parliament also posseses exclusive power to legislate or amend laws for the successful implementation of the international treaties, agreements and conventions. The Article reads "Notwithstanding anything in the foregoing provisions of this Chapter, Parliament has power to make any law for the whole or any part of the territory of India for implementing any treaty, agreement or convention with any other country or countries or any decision made at any international conference, associated or other body."[26] In addition, the Parliament also makes laws for other non-Foreign Policy subjects and can control each and every step of administration including the mighty executives that practically controls external policy. Hence, law making power has ultimately empowered the parliament to have control over the foreign affairs decision making. Given below is a brief account of the law making procedure of the Indian Parliament:

The Legislation Process of Indian Parliament

As the Parliament is regarded as the symbol of the general will of the people, policy making in critical areas including foreign affairs often requires the parliamentary authorization through legislative process. As the supreme legislative body in India, the Parliament makes laws on the subjects listed under Article 246 of Indian constitution. Furthermore, Article 253 also empowers the Parliament to modify or make a new legislation for the items listed under the state subject to facilitate the foreign treaties and agreements.

Parliamentary legislative procedure, being the key instrument for the formulation and modification of public policy, is very complex under the Indian parliamentary system. It requires a long parliamentary procedure prescribed by the Constitution of India, under which a draft bill has to be introduced and approved by the Indian parliament to become an Act. The bill can be broadly divided into two categories, the ordinary bill and the financial bill. In terms of ordinary bill, it has to be introduced by any member of the Parliament with the prior notice of seven days stating its intention and significance. If the government or the concern ministers introduce the bill, it will be known as the governmental bill or else called private bills.[27] According to the statistics, only 14 private bills have been passed so far by the Parliament while six of these were passed in 1956 alone. It also shows that not even a single private bill has been passed since 1970.[28]

Mostly, the legislation has been sought to address the existing legal fissure and to strengthen the administrative mechanism of the country. As soon as the proposal comes to enact law for any specific issues, the concerned member or ministry prepares its blue print and finds out its political, legal, financial, and administrative implications. They also consult with other concerned ministries and agencies for their inputs. In some cases, the consultation is also sought from other stake holders including professionals, NGOs, civil societies, interest groups and trade unions. After a thorough scrutinisation of the draft proposal, it is sent to the cabinet for approval. In the cabinet meeting, the pros and cons of the proposal are thoroughly discussed and necessary corrections are incorporated with the draft. Following the approval of the cabinet, the legislative technocrats and departmental experts give the bill the final shape and make it creditable to be introduced into the parliament.[29]

Before the introduction to either house, the bill needs to be made available for the reference of the members and the copy of the bill has to be circulated among the members, at least before the proposed date of introduction. President's recommendation is a must for the introduction of the non-ordinary bills, such as, financial and Constitution amendment bills.[30] After the introduction of the bill, the minister reads out the bill and places the bill before the house for discussion. If the bill gets introduced, it is sent to the gazette section for publication in the official gazette.[31] However, in some cases, a draft bill can be published in the gazette without going through leave motion with the approval of the speaker.[32]

The second stage, being the crucial phase of legislation, consists of two stages. In the first stage, the bill seeks external inputs from the Standing Committees and public opinions and incorporates their views into the bill, whereas in the second stage, the bill receives internal inputs from the exhaustive Parliamentary debates and discussions. In the first stage of the second reading, a general discussion on the principles and provisions of the bill is used to take place without going into deep clause by clause discussion. Here it is up to the house whether it will be simply taken into consideration or referred to a select committee of the house or joint committee of the two houses or for circulation for the purpose of eliciting public opinion thereon.[33] The motion for any proposed amendment by members is allowed under this stage as per the rule 75 of the procedures of the house.

If the bill is referred to the parliamentary committee, the committee analyzes the bill clause by clause like the houses do. If the committee becomes satisfied, the bill can be passed with majority vote or can be challenged by members for amendment of certain clauses. The committee can also seek opinion and suggestions from experts and interest groups that are suppose to be affected by the bill. After rigorous analysis, the committee returns back the bills to Lok Sabha Secretariat with its feedbacks, suggestions and recommendations. Then, the Secretary General of Lok Sabha presents the report in the Parliament for discussion.[34] After obtaining the report from the committee it is up to the member or minister to move the motion to re-refer the bill to the new committee or for further public opinion or to take into consideration for further proceedings.

A general debate takes place if a motion moves to consider the bill. Then a copy of the bill is distributed among the members so that they become aware of the pros and cons of the bill. When the recommended bill for consideration is placed before the house, a thorough discussion takes place on each and every clause of the bill and the members are allowed to move amendment motion for any particular clause or a group of clauses and the amendment is also discussed, adopted or rejected by the majority vote. If the amendment is accepted, it is included into the bill for further proceedings.[35]

After a lengthy clause by clause discussion and its approval carried out during the second stage of second reading, the bill enters into the third stage of reading. In this stage, the introducer of the bill moves a motion seeking the approval of the bill. The members are allowed to have a discussion over the bill if required. But the discussion is limited to the argument in favour of or rejection of the bill without citing any further detail if it is necessarily required to know the ground.[36] Only formal, verbal or consequential amendments are allowed in this third reading stage. After the bill is formally passed the speaker has the power to correct the patent errors and ask such other changes in the bill as are consequential upon the amendments accepted by the house.[37] For the passing of an ordinary bill the house requires a simple majority of the attended members. As the government enjoys majority in Lok Sabha, it hardly faces any difficulty in passing an ordinary bill.

Once the bill is passed in one house, it is referred to another house for approval. Like the previous house, it has to pass through the same prescribed stages for its concurrence. However, if the house brings any amendment into the original bill and referred the amended bill to the house where it originated, it has to be reintroduced into the originated house once again, and need to be passed there. If it is agreed on the amended version of the bill it is referred to the President for his assent. After presidential assent, the bill becomes the law.

However, when a bill is rejected by another house or if the bill keeps on pending for more than six months following the disagreement between both the houses on the bill, the President asks for a joint sitting of both the houses to resolve the deadlock. With the due consultation of the Chairman of Rajya Sabha and the Speaker of Lok Sabha it is fixed for a joint sitting in the parliament according to the provision laid on the clause (3) of Article 118. In the joint sitting voting takes place on the bill. Based on the voting majority, the bill is passed or rejected. However, the fact is that only three bills have been passed since the enforcement of the Constitution. These are the Dowry Provision Bill of 1961, The Banking Service Commission (repeal) Bill of 1978 and The Pervasion of Terrorism Bill (POTA) of 2002. Generally, the Lok Sabha is in a decisive advantage to pass the bills, due to its numerical superiority.[38]

After the approval of both the houses or passed at the joint sittings, the bill is sent to the President for his assent. The President may give his assent or ask for certain information or clarification or simply return the bill to the house for reconsideration. However, if the bill is resent to the President after it is approved by the houses with the due procedure of rules, the President has to sign on the bill and it is transformed into an Act. The President can keep the bill with him as long as he wishes, where the bill automatically comes to end.[39] Once the President signs the bill, it becomes an Act from that particular day.

Legislation process for Money Bill is different from that of the ordinary bill. The money bill can only be introduced in Lok Sabha, and the Rajya Sabha plays a nominal role in this matter. The Rajya Sabha cannot amend the money bill passed by Lok Sabha, but can give its recommendation for the amendment. Whether the Lok Sabha accepts the recommendation for the amendment or rejects the proposal, it is considered to be passed by both the houses. In the latter case, it is deemed to be passed without the approval of Rajya Sabha. Similarly, if the Rajya Sabha keeps the money bill pending for more than fourteen days, it is considered to be passed by Rajya Sabha. Similarly, the procedure for the Constitution amendment bill is a complex one and varies from article to article. While amendment to some article (under article 368) is easy and can be done by simple majority, others are very rigid to amend and require absolute to special majority depending on the importance of the articles. Therefore, the procedure for the amendment of Indian Constitution is partially flexible and partially rigid and different from the procedure that follows during the passage of the ordinary bills.[40]

Parliamentary Legislation as an Instrument to Shape Indian Foreign Policy

As we have discussed, the Parliament enjoys adequate power to formulate or amend any law in India that ultimately guides the governance and policy initiative, including Foreign Policy. Hence, it plays a crucial role in formulating the Foreign Policy of India. Similarly, under Article 253 the Parliament is empowered to bring the required legislation to facilitate the international agreements. Therefore, there is no doubt on Parliament's role in bringing new laws to influence Foreign Policy. It can also legislate or enhance or curtail the executive power that is used to have larger role to play. Legislation regarding military forces and war and peace similarly places the Parliament at the decisive stage on Foreign Policy making mechanism. It can direct the force to go for war or legislate on maintaining peace by ending war. Further, trade and commerce and economic affairs remain on the preview area of the Centre on which the Parliament can pass any law in favor or against certain trade policies. Starting from the border settlement to the UN affairs the Parliament is awarded with immense power to make law that influence, guide or change the Foreign Policy of the country.

Parliamentary Acts Related To Foreign Affairs
• The Imports and & Import (Control) Act, 1947 • The Imports (Control) Order 1955 • The Exports (Control) Order 1988 • The Customs Act, 1962 • The Foreign Trade (Dev.& Reg.) Act, 1992 • Securities and Exchange Board of India Act, 1988, 1992 • Foreign Trade (Regulation) Rules 1993 • Foreign Trade (Exemption) Order 1993 • The Foreign Exchange Management Act, 1999 • National Investigation Agency Act 2008 • The Civil Liability for Nuclear Damage Act, 2010 • The Atomic Energy Act 1962 • Environmental (Protection) Act, 1986 • The Emigration Act, 1983 • The Citizenship Act, 1955 • The Citizenship (Amnd.) Act, 1986, 92, 2003, & 05 • Passport (Amendment) Act, • The Passport Act, • The Haj Committee Act, • The Extradition Act, • The United Nations (Security Council) Act, • Foreign Exchange Management Regulations, 2000 • Companies Act, 1956 • Constitution 100th Amendment Act 2015 (LBA Agreement)
Institutions Created to Guide Foreign Policy
• The National Security Adviser(NSA) • The National Security Council (NSC) • Securities and Exchange Board of India (SEBI) • National Investigation Agency (NIA) • The Research and Analysis Wing (RAW) • The Atomic Energy Regulatory Board (AERB) • The Atomic Energy Commission (1948)

The Role of Parliament as the Institution of Influence

"Influence" refers to the capability to modify or change someone's behaviour in the desired way. Marriam-Webster Dictionary defines it as "the power or capacity of causing an effect in indirect or intangible ways".[41] To be particular it refers to "the power to shape policy….." [42] In politics influence plays a major role in deciding policy options, be it the influence of vote, media or parliament. It occurs when such actors communicate with other actors or agencies to alter their policy behaviour.[43] Parliament being the highest agency of governance in India also plays crucial role in influencing policy behaviour of the country.

Apart from the legislative powers, the Parliament also has enough ability to influence India's Foreign Policy behaviour. The Parliament, by using its various techniques, rectifies the existing disorder in the Foreign Policy behaviour. As the representative to the voice of the people, it tries to modify and read just the external policy of the country. The prime tool of influence is the floor of the Parliament itself. The members of the house raise the concerns related to Foreign Policy during the debate session of the Parliament. Among the Parliamentarians, there used to be a group of expertise who keep tracking the global developments and raise voice against the perceived odds in the form of questions, discussion and motions. But the parliamentary involvement and its influence on Foreign Policy was limited when the Nehruvian monopoly was ruling over the Indian Foreign Policy decision making environment.[44] Till Chinese war, the view of the Parliament especially from the ruling party was unrealistic for it was not in line with the public opinion. It is the Shastry era that revolutionized the concept of the Parliamentary involvement in the Foreign Policy shaping. The Parliamentarians tried to adopt the available techniques to approve, guide and supervise the external policies of the country. The tools used in this regard were the question hours, debates and discussions, parliamentary committees, financial control and motions and resolutions on the matter of foreign affairs.

Tools and Techniques of Parliamentary Influence on FPDM

Under its various rules, the Parliament of India enjoys absolute power to debate and discuss a range of issues related to the domestic and external affairs. It controls, supervises and influences the policy of government by using several tools and techniques. Through these tools, it tries to minimize the governmental errors and modify and alternate the policy direction as per the public opinion. As the voice of the people, the Parliament keeps its concerns for the benefit of the people. The instruments of parliamentary influence on Foreign Policy are as follows:

Debate and Discussion

Debate and discussion has been the integral part of the parliamentary democracy. The Indian Parliament has the right to discuss various issues on its floor of Parliament and tries to pressurize the government for the policy improvement. Generally, the debate comes out of the question hour, during the process of passing resolution, during budgetary discussion, ministerial statement or during the period of half an hour discussion. The Parliament, being the ultimate forum to discuss the national and international issues that affect the national interests, makes its observations on the large range of issues. Additionally, by using the tools of discussion and debate the Parliament puts a check on the governmental monopoly.

Along with the domestic issues, significant amount of Foreign Policy related matters also have been the subject of the parliamentary debate and discussion. As parliamentary debate has been an important instrument of influence and control of the policy making in India, a large number of issues make into the floor of the house for discussion. The subjects of the debate on Foreign Policy issues happens to be the matter related to strategic relations, CTBT and NPT, India-Pakistan war, incursion in to Indian Territory, problems of Tibet, India's neighbourhood policies and India's relations with major powers.

Generally, the oppositions raise various questions related to the foreign affairs and matters of public importance in the Parliament. They bring various resolutions to initiate the discussion, besides using other parliamentary provisions. The main objective of such initiatives is to criticize the recent government policies and to put pressure on the government to readjust their stand, and modify according to the wish of the Parliament. Hence, one may agree that it is a discussion between the government and its alternatives.[45] Both the houses have been seen in debating such issues. However, the Lok Sabha has been playing more important role in Foreign Policy making in India than Rajya Sabha.

The intensity of the Parliamentary debates on matters of foreign affairs is normally interlinked with the international political environment. If the international situation remains tense, the debate in the Parliament escalates to noisy and animated. The house gets divided in discussed matters and each group attacks the other's stand over the issue. But when the global scenario looks peaceful, the parliamentary debate remains calm and infrequent.[46]

The tool of Parliamentary debate has been effective to influence policy making in India. It is a symbol of parliamentary supremacy over the Executive on the policy making and guidance. By debating and discussing on certain policies, the Parliament informally scrutinizes the matter and asks further clarification from the executives on the particular issue. Similarly, during the debate the member has the right to criticize the ministration showing the administrative loopholes and suggesting some policy modifications, adjustments and alternatives. The mechanism of the parliamentary debate helps to remind the administration of their duties and keep pressuring them to attain their goals. Therefore the parliamentary debates and discussions influence every aspect of the Foreign Policy of India.

Though the concept seems nice in theory, the effectiveness of parliamentary debate has never turned into constructive policies in practice. Generally debates are put for discussion, when the issue loses its significance. Often, the members apparently fight against each other, making the atric attitude in the Parliament and lacks professionalism while raising the issues. The Parliament is an important forum to bring out the administrative lacunas of the government for discussion. But, neither the government nor the opposition is serious in this regard. Quite often, the information is tempered and presented incompletely to camouflage the facts. Similarly, a very few members participate in the debate on matters of Foreign Policy, and lack expertise while raising the issues. Hence, the debate often seems generic and ritualistic and is considered as low standard.

Question Hour

Out of all the privileges that the Indian Parliament enjoys to influence and control policy direction, question hour is the most significant tool. The Question Hour is the first hour or the opening hour of every sitting of the parliament generally held in between 11.00 a.m. to 12.00 noon for five days in a week from Monday to Friday.[47] Normally the sitting of the house does not take place on Saturday. However, if the sitting is extended up to Saturday it will continue without question hour. Similarly, the question hour is not held during the extended period of the parliamentary session.[48] The provision of the question hour upholds the democratic principles of the country, because through this mechanism the people of the country can ask questions and get clarifications from the government through their representatives. In other words members of the parliament are free to ask questions regarding any matter of governance at their respective houses. It is not only exposing the government's failures, but has been the most reliable and favourite method to have control over the executive monopoly.[49]

Types of the Parliamentary Questions

Question hour has been practiced in both the houses since decades and has been the useful mechanism to expose the loopholes of the government policies. It has been divided into the three broad categories, (i) Starred Questions, (ii) Unstarred Questions (iii) Short Notice Questions.

Starred questions are those questions which are answered orally on the floor of the house, whereas the Unstarred Questions, unlike the starred are not responded with oral answers and responded with written answers. Generally, supplementary questions can be raised related to the starred questions, if the member is not happy with the preliminary answer provided by a minister. These types of questions are marked with an asterisk mark to be easily distinguished.[50] As the answers are presented in written form under the Unstarred Questions, no supplementary question can be asked. The written questions are printed in the 'official report of the sitting of the house for which it is put down' and presented by the minister in the floor of the Parliament.[51]

The short notice questions are related to the 'matter of urgent public importance' that are supposed to be brought to the preview of the minister or parliament. Any member can ask this kind of question and seek oral answer from the concerned ministry with a shorter prior notice compared to the ordinary questions that need prior notice before at least ten days. It is up to the Speaker or Chairman to decide the urgency of the matter and ask the minister to answer the question on an early possible time. The time for the answer is fixed according to the desires of the minister and chair of the house. If there is a shortage of time for the answer of the question, the Speaker or Chairman directs to place the question as the first question of the question hour the next day. Though the members are eager to put short notice questions frequently, only one such question is allowed to take place for a particular day based on its merits. The discussion for the short notice questions is held after the question hour of each sitting.[52]

Though most of the questions are directed towards ministers and government officials, private members may ask to answer the parliamentary questions referred to them by other members. In this case, the area of responsibility of the member should be the subject matter of the question.[53] No supplementary question can be raised and no short notice question can be directed to any private member as the government officials and ministers are responsible to run the government. This type of questions hardly takes place in the Parliament, especially in Lok Sabha.

Half-an-Hour Discussion

Half-an-Hour Discussion refers to the discussion taking place during the last thirty minutes of sitting on the matter of public importance arising from the recent question hours. Other than the budget session, it is normally held for three days in a week based on the question of Starred, Unstarred or Short Notice Question that is discussed on the floor of the house.[54]

According to the clauses from 2 to 5 of rule 55, if any member wishes to raise the matter for a discussion he/she has to give notice in writing three days in advance from the date of discussion. In the notice, the member has to mention the reason for raising the discussion on a particular matter. The Lok Sabha Speaker or the Rajya Sabha Chairman has to decide on the merit of the notice for discussion. He/she enjoys full power to consider the notice or return the same. If a house receives more than two notices that are admitted by the Speaker or Chairman, the secretary-general of the respective houses shall hold a ballot to prefer one over the other for the first discussion. However, the second one will be put in the waiting list for discussion. The Speaker or the Chairman asks the respective minister to respond to the raised questions on a pre-fixed day. The member who served the notice may give a short statement and the members (Not more than four) who have pre-intimated the Speaker may question on the purpose of the "further elucidating any matter of fact".[55] At the end, the minister asks to reply to the question. No formal motion shall be introduced or voting will be held during the discussion. In Lok Sabha, only one notice for half-an-Hour discussion is allowed and a member cannot ask more than two questions in a particular session.[56]

Role of Question Hour in Influencing the Foreign Policy

The Question Hour plays an important role in the parliamentary democracy in India. It has been the prime instrument to control the monopoly of the government and the executive branch, and make them accountable to the people. The members, by asking questions, expose the loop holes of the government to the public domain and simultaneously bring a lot of matters to the government's focus. Briefly, the Question Hour helps in both directions to strengthen the governance both internally and externally. As discussed elsewhere a healthy domestic environment is the prime requirement for the vibrant external policies. The country can play a bigger role in international sphere if the internal situation remains supportive. Therefore, it indirectly facilitates India's Foreign Policy while dealing with the internal issues.

The role of parliament is very much required to polish the Foreign Policy by raising various questions on the floor of the house. In most of the cases, the government hides certain issues of foreign affairs and presents a rosy picture before the country. But with the help of the provision of questions, the members, especially the oppositions, bring out these issues to the public domain and pressurize the government to take appropriate actions to rectify it. Previously, the Parliament was not interfering into the foreign affairs and mainly focused on domestic issues. But after the Chinese intrusion there were changes and it started playing played a significant role in foreign affairs.

The parliamentary questions also help the government to know the concerns, grievances and expectations of the people. However the government occasionally opts for the traditional way to deal with the issues. Through the questions and related discussions, the government is able to know the alternative ways to deal with the situation. Through the questions, the members expose the faults and scandals before the nation and educate the people against the governmental loop holes. As a result, people try by various means to pressurize the government to mould their improper policies.

Primarily, Parliamentarians are more interested to raise questions that are mostly related to their respective constituencies or issue of domestic affairs and show little interest to debate on matters of the international affairs unless it becomes the media flashpoint. The reason might be lack of interest and adequate knowledge on foreign affairs among the parliamentarians. Secondly, due to India's limited role in the world politics, the subject of foreign politics remains the secondary matter for most of the policy makers in India. But, after the economic liberation, India gradually emerged as one of the major players in the international politics, which often attracted the attention of the political leadership. With this significant development, the issues of Foreign Policy apparently dominated a sizable share of Parliamentary discussion and the influence on Indian parliament seemed gradually increasing day by day. By using the tool of questions hour, the Parliament brings the government to the knee to clarify certain issues. If the members are unsatisfied with the function of the government, they move various motions to curb the government. In this process, the mistakes of the government come to the public domain and help the government to address the issues. Due to the question hours, the government also identifies the concern of the people and the matter of priority to perform, hence it helps to redefine the national objective.

The Ministerial Statements

Following the Question Hour, the concerned minister presents his statement regarding the matter of discussion. If the matter seems important mostly the oppositions raise the additional questions to bring out further clarifications, hence often it leads to a mini debate. During the time of no confidence and censure motions, the minister is also asked to explain his stand before putting his resignation. This provision becomes the tool of parliamentary control on policy making. At the time of making a statement, the minister is criticized by the opponents due to his policy failure that helps in appropriate policy formulation in future. So far, several ministerial statements have been made regarding foreign policies and on Chinese issues during different occasions.[57]

Parliamentary Motions

"A motion is a proposal made by a member to the House that the House does something or order something to be done or express an opinion with regard to some matter."[58] Motion, in different forms is able to restrict the government from misusing its power and put a check on ministerial and executive monopoly on public will. In other words, it has been an important tool to control, manipulate and alternate governmental policies in various ways. It helps to raise urgent issues of public importance before the house within a short notice while the question hour discussion and short notice questions need more time in advance to be raised in the Parliament.

To start a motion, the person needs to obtain the floor by seeking the permission from the Chairman of the Rajya Sabha. After obtaing the floor, the mover moves the motion and needs to be supported by the second person to proceed further. The Parliament acts on the proposed direction, if it is approved by the house by a majority vote.

Types of Motions

Unlike the question hour, motion also can be moved by the government or private members. While the government motions are aimed to obtain the house to introduce any policy initiatives, private motions are meant to generate opinion of the house on certain issues. Mostly the motions moved by private members criticize the governmental loopholes and alternate the ongoing policies. Though various kinds of motions have been practiced in the Indian Parliament, it can be divided into three broad categories- the substantive motion, the substitute motion and the subsidiary motion.

1. The Substantive Motion

Substantive Motion is a new proposal to the house by the members to look into certain issues or propose certain policies to get approval from the house. This kind of motion comes first as an independent proposal rather than a follow-up. By raising this category of motion, the member(s) seek the interval of the house on the business of the government or governmental process. Adjournment Motion, Privilege Motion, Motion of Thanks, Censure Motion, Call - Attention Motion, Cut Motions, No-Confidence Motion, Motion of Election and Removal of the Presiding Officer of the houses are some of the motions of this category.

Adjournment Motion

Adjournment motion is meant for the adjournment of the house and draws the attention of the house towards a matter of urgent public importance involving serious consequences. It is a procedure that keeps the normal business of the house aside and raises the discussion on the matter that severely affects the country's security and stability. The adjournment motion can be raised on any ordinary issue, it can only propose the matters that have "a direct or indirect relation to the conduct or default on the part of the Union Government and must precisely pin-point the failure of the Government of India in the performance of its duties in accordance with the provisions of the Constitution and Law."[59] However, the matters falling under the state list cannot be admissible under the motion. But, the matter of constitutional development or atrocities against SC, ST and minorities that need the intervention of central government, may be considered into the motion. Notice for such motion should be given by 10.00 hours on the day on which the motion is proposed to be introduced.[60]

Privilege Motion

The Constitution of India extends certain rights and immunities to the members for the effective discharge of their parliamentary functions. But in certain cases, the members misuse their privileges and misguide the house, especially giving wrong information. In this case the member can raise the privilege motion to ask questions on the Breach of Privilege. This parliamentary tool is often used by the opposition to put a check on the ministerial monopoly and loop holes of provided information. An advance notice should be given to the Speaker or Chairperson before 10.00 am of the sitting. If the Speaker feels that the notice given by the member under this provision is a matter of urgent public importance he may prefer the motion to be moved over the normal business of the house and no debate will take place. However, the chair may be asked to clarify certain questions provided by the members. [61]

Calling Attention Motion

Calling Attention Motion is meant to bring the matters of public importance to the attention of the government. By raising this motion any member can ask questions to the concerned ministers on the floor of the house following supplementary questions and demand clarification and short discussion from the government. On the other side, it gives a chance to the government to present the case more precisely and clarify the doubts of public interest. But in practice, this motion is often used to bring out the loopholes and criticize the government before the Parliament.[62]

With the prior permission of the Speaker of Lok Sabha and the Chairman of Rajya Sabha any member may call the attention of the government or minister to a matter of urgent public importance and ask him to give clarifications and present the developments before the house. The concerned minister may surface the details or ask for some time to reply. The member may raise some supplementary questions to seek more information. There is no provision of Calling Attention Motion in Rajya Sabha. It is the "Motion for Papers", that is working as the call attention motion of Lok Sabha. Generally, the important issues of national and international affairs which significantly affect the security and stability of India are discussed under the Calling Attention Motion. List of issues from the Chinese incursion to the recent Italian marine shooting at the coast of Kerala has been discussed in the parliament in the form of calling attention motion.[63]

No-Confidence Motion

No-Confidence Motion is the foremost mechanism available to the Parliament to check and hold the executive. The no-confidence motion, which is introduced by the legislators and passed by a majority, would eventually lead to the fall of the government. Approval of the No-confidence Motion against the government means that the government has virtually lost the confidence of the house to run the administration and therefore deemed to be unfit to continue the business. This type of motion is raised to test the constitutional validity of the government. When majority of the members are against any particular decision of the government, they introduce No-Confidence Motion to root out the ruling government. Generally, no-confidence motion is moved by the members of opposition parties and is introduced in the house of Lok Sabha. Unlike the censure motion, that expels the concerned ministers, no-confidence motion targets the whole bench of government. It is not necessary to show any reason to introduce the motion and can be moved at any point of time. The procedure to introduce the motion is similar to the procedure of any other motions and has to be notified before 10.00 am of the sitting of Lok Sabha. According to the Constitution, the Council of Ministers is bound to resign if no-confidence motion is adopted by the Lok Sabha.

No Confidence Motions can be an effective deterrent only when the Government commands a small majority. In coalition Governments, where no single party dominates, the strength of No-Confidence Motion is the highest. A qualitative reflection on the No-Confidence Motion suggests that parties should be allowed to pass the Motion of No-Confidence only when an alternative coalition Government is agreed upon. This would ensure stability and rationality in using this instrument of accountability. "Implicit in this proposal is an important assumption that when small parties in the Parliament bring down Governments, they do so largely for their own benefit. This ability to bring down the government through No-Confidence Motion should not be confused with holding the government accountable to Parliament. Thus, while No-Confidence Motions are critical mechanism of the executive's accountability to Parliament, they can sometimes have perverse consequences".[64]

Censure Motion

Censure motion is a motion that is moved against the ruling party or any particular group of ministers for its failure to perform its duty in a desired way. Generally, the opposition parties move the motion to criticize and stop certain policies (including Foreign Policies) and actions that they feel against the benefit of this country. Before the admission of the motion into the house, the motion should clearly identify its objective and the charges against the government. Though the objectives of no-confidence motion and censure motion seem to be the same, there is a visible difference. While No-confidence motion targets the whole government and forces the ruling government to resign, censure motion is moved against a single or a group of ministers.[65]

To move a Censure Motion, no such leave is required in the house and the government has to decide its date and introduce it into the house directly. No specific provision describes the procedure to raise the motion. However, the general rules prescribed to move a motion is applicable to such motions[66] and may be admitted as a No-Day-Yet-Named Motion.[67] If the motion is adopted by majority vote, the government has to seek the confidence of the house. Like the no-confidence motion, censure motion can only be introduced into Lok Sabha.

Cut Motion

To check the monopoly of the ruling party, the members of the Parliament have been empowered by the constitution to oppose a demand in the financial bill discussed by the government. It is known as the Cut Motion. If the Parliament passes a cut motion and the government does not have the number to defend it, it is bound to resign.[68] As a motion of financial matter, cut motion can only be introduced into the Lok Sabha.

The Cut motion is divided further into three categories. The first category is the *"Disapproval of Policy Cut"* which is meant for the disapproval of the policy cut by passing the motion mentioning 'that the amount of the demand be reduced to one rupee.' The second type of cut motion is the *'Economy Cut'*. This motion is intended to reduce the amount of demand up to a certain point. And the third category of the cut motion is the *'Token Cut'*. The objective of this motion is to highlight certain grievances within the sphere of the responsibility of the government. Usually the title of the motion is "The amount of the demand be reduced by Rupees 100."[69]

The Speaker plays a crucial role in deciding whether a cut motion clears the prescribed criteria given under rule 210 of parliament procedure and should be allowed to move or not.[70] Any member who wants to raise the motion is given one day in advance or else it may be canceled with someone's objection.[71] If the motion is introduced into Lok Sabha, a discussion of a general character may take place without going in to the detail of the grant.[72] If the Lok Sabha approves any of the cut motion, the government is considered to be in minority as it failed to defend itself against the motion. Therefore they are obliged to resign.

The Substitute Motions

Substitute motions are those motions that are moved as a substitute of the original motion suggesting an alternative option to the previous proposal.[73] The Substitute motions aim to promote the opinion of the house independently and not dependent over the original motion.[74] While the original motion is on process, a substitute motion maybe moved before the discussion until the original motion takes place. The substitute motion should contain the similar subject matter that proposed earlier in original motions with intension to express the opinion of the house. As both the motions are moved at the house, discussion is allowed on both original and substitute motions together. However, the house can only vote on the body of the substitute motion, not to adopt the whole substitute motion.[75] If the house adopted the substitute motion, the body of the original motion will be replaced with substitute motion and if suggested for amendment, the original motion may be amended with a majority vote.[76]

The Subsidiary Motions

The Subsidiary motions, also known as the dependent motion, moves as a follow up of other motions of the house. It cannot stand independently and seems meaningless with the support of the original motion. It also cannot initiate the decision of the house without the reference of the original motion.[77] The subsidiary motion is further divided into the following three sub-categories:

The Ancillary Motions

Ancillary motions are those motions that are generally considered as the tools to conduct regular business of the house. It proposes whether the bill will be referred to a standing committee or that the bill be taken into consideration or that the bill be passed.[78]

The Superseding Motions

The members of the Parliament raise the superseding motion to supersede the question over the ongoing debate of the previous question. It also seeks to refer to the bill to a select or joint committee or recalculate for eliciting further opinion thereon.[79]

The Amendments

Amendment motion refers to the motion that moves to propose a new policy for the original motion by raising subsidiary motions. Sometimes, the motion even moves to replace or modify the whole or a certain section of the previous motion, bill or resolution.[80]

The Resolutions

Resolution has been one of the significant tools of the parliamentary influence over the foreign policies. Using their power privileges, parliamentarians raise discussions on 'general public interest'.[81] It may be moved to record the approval or disapproval of certain government policies or present the opinion or comment of the houses on certain governmental actions, or persuade for immediate actions and bring the attention of the houses to the matter of general public interest or the matters that the Speaker of Lok Sabha feels appropriate.[82] Resolutions may be introduced into both the houses and may be moved into any of the houses like general motions.[83]

The nature, character, and objectives of the Motions and resolutions are almost the same. They bear lots of similarities which are not easy to be distinguished. Though the content and the subject matters remain the same, it is the procedural formality that differentiates one from the other. However, some visible differences in both the cases do exist. The important difference of this kind is that, while majority of the resolutions are passed through voting, some of the motions appeared are accepted by the house through voice votes or head count method.[84]

Types of Resolutions

Based on its nature and characteristics, the resolutions are divided into three categories. They are Private Member's Resolution, Government Resolution and Statutory Resolution, which are briefly discussed below :

Private Members' Resolutions

Resolutions that are moved by the members other than the ministers are called the private members resolutions. Often, these types of resolutions are moved to bring the matter of the general public interests before the government and demand suitable actions. Any private member can move a resolution in either of the house, provided the prior notice should reach the secretary general of the respective house at least two days in advance. The names of such applicants are selected by ballot and only three proposals for Lok Sabha and five for Rajya Sabha are allowed to move in sitting.[85] If the Speaker admits, the selected resolutions will be included into the list of the business of the house. The member is allowed to move the resolution in the house on an allotted day. Generally, the last two and a half hours of a sitting of every alternative, Friday are reserved for the private members resolution.[86] The concerned minister and the other interested members are allowed to reply to the resolution and a discussion takes place before it is adopted.

Government Resolutions

The resolutions which are introduced by the ministers are known as the Government Resolutions. The procedure for adoptability of such resolutions is almost equal to the private members resolution. If the minister wants to move the resolution he/she has to give prior notice to the Secretary General of the house and get fixed the time of the proceeding. After the resolution is introduced, the debate on the resolution takes place and suggested for appropriate actions if adopted by a majority vote.[87]

Governmental resolutions are the most important techniques of the parliamentary control over foreign policies. Normally, the resolutions are moved to get the approval of the Parliament on the related international treaties, conventions and agreements or declaring war or peace with any country or recording its observations and concerns on certain policies of the national and international affairs.[88] The resolution passed by the Lok Sabha against the Pakistani resolution which criticizes the execution of Afzal Guru, the resolution against the human rights violations by the Sri Lankan Army towards native Tamilians and the resolution against Chinese aggression are some of the examples that show the significance of this tools in influencing Indian Foreign Policy decision making.

Statutory Resolutions

Statutory resolutions are tabled with the pursuance of a provision in the Constitution or an Act of Parliament. The notice to move the resolutions can be submitted to the secretary general by the ministers or private members. But at the same time certain enactments are exclusively required to table a resolution with a specified period of time. The resolution if get adopted is brought before the house for discussion and directs the government to take suitable actions if passed with a majority vote.[89]

The resolutions being the powerful tool for the Indian Parliament to influence the Foreign Policy decision making process have largely been able to guide the external policies of the country. As the legitimate authority to adopt and execute the policies, the Parliament so far has utilized the privileges, and passed several resolutions on various international issues. Similarly the international treaties, agreements and conversions are also brought into the Parliament in the form of resolutions and trialled before the Parliament or the formal will of the people for further course of action. Moving a resolution is also one of the frequently used procedural devices in the Parliament. According to Rule 172, resolution as a procedural device is available to the members and the ministers to raise a discussion in the House on a matter of general public interest[90]. Rule 171 provides that unlike motions in general, forms of resolutions can be moved in both the Houses. Therefore a resolution moved in the Lok Sabha would be to convey approval or disapproval by the House of an act or policy of the Government or convey a message; or commend, urge or request an action or call attention to a matter or situation for consideration by the Government, or in such other forms as the Speaker may consider appropriate. On the other hand, a resolution moved in Rajya Sabha would be a declaration of opinion by the House on any other matter that the Chairman considers appropriate. The efficacy of resolutions in the Parliament to provide a pathway and serve as a procedural device in the Parliament and policy making process has been so far reduced into just a formality.

Role of Parliament as an Instrument of Accountability

The fundamental tenet of the Indian Parliament is to effectively serve as an instrument of accountability over the Executive. This institutional responsibility has been rendered dysfunctional because of Parliament's own predilection towards delinquency. The instruments that the Parliament uses for exercising its accountability such as the censure motion, no confidence motions, committee system or opposition have become highly politicized and no meaningful attempts have been taken to ensure the efficacy of public policies. The technicality of public policies such as, the foreign, Defence or strategic policies – together with the inability of the Parliamentarians to comprehend the characteristics of specificities are the major institutional challenges that the Parliament faces. According to Professor Jain, the capacity of Indian Parliament to enforce accountability is hinged upon various external circumstances including the position and personality of the chief executive and the constitutional system.[91] Though the constitutional system enables members to initiate and influence the policy proposals, the impact of these processes is hampered by certain extra-constitutional factors. The chief among them are (a) the absolute party majorities of the Government in the central legislature (b) the gradual decline in the stature of men who constituted successive Parliaments in comparison to the ones which followed after independence and (c) the attitude of the majority of the leaders towards opposition. "The fact that Indian economy is globalizing has also eroded the power of Parliament in two respects. Much of the economic decision making is now increasingly governed by international treaties, and the Indian Parliament is one of the few Parliaments in the world that does not have a system of effective treaty oversight in place. These treaties are fait accompli by the time they come to Parliament. Second, India, like many other countries, is restructuring its regulatory framework with more powers being delegated to non-elected institutions. This process of delegation can increase transparency and accountability, but Parliamentary oversight of these institutions remains very weak.[92]" It must also be noted that when Parliament abdicates its fundamental responsibility and engages in horse trading, name calling and theatrics, the real accountability of democratic institutions to the public would become fictitious and a select group of elites would usurp power to the extent of being hidden dictators in their respective public spheres.

Accountability of the Executive to the Legislature

Following the Westminster model of the United Kingdom (albeit changes according to Indian customs and conventions were made) the Legislative and Executive interface constitutes the primordial feature of the Indian Constitution. Viewed in a theoretical lens, the executive and the legislature share unhindered mutuality and any public policy is a natural and normal culmination of the efforts of both the Executive and the Legislature. In the words of Subash Kashyap, "the Council of Ministers may in a sense be described as the grand executive committee of the Parliament charged with the responsibility of the Government on behalf of the parent body [Parliament]...In as much as the Council of Ministers is drawn from and remains part of the Parliament and responsible to the Lok Sabha, the relationship may be said to be that of a part to the whole or that of the delegate to the principal and one of interdependence." In this sense the roles of executive and the legislature eventually overlap but the spirit remains the same[93]. The extent to which this unity in role differentiation is understood, however, remains a well guarded secret.

The functions of the executive are distinct from that of the legislature. It initiates, defends, accelerates, formulates, and executes proposal in the Indian Parliament which eventually metamorphoses into a public policy. The executive plays a steering role in the Indian Parliament. The legislature on the other hand performs that of the directing role; it sees that the vehicle driven by the executive is in consonance to the needs and aspirations of the people. In this regard, the legislature plays an active role in criticizing, scrutinizing, evaluating, and extracting information from the executive. To deliberate, discuss, and ventilate public grievances is also a legitimate role of the legislature[94]. Two important instruments of accountability in the hands of Parliament are: ensuring ministerial responsibility and administrative accountability.

Ministerial Responsibility

As to the Ministerial responsibility, the Constitution follows in the main the English principle except as to the legal responsibility of individual Ministers for acts done by or on behalf of the President84.[95] The principle of collective responsibility is codified in Art 75(3) of Indian Constitution which states "The Council of Ministers shall be collectively responsible to the House of People".

The Ministerial responsibility to the Parliament is based on (1) the constitutional provision of the responsibility of the Council of Ministers to the popular house of the Parliament; and (2) Parliament's control over the budget.[96] Here it must be noted that the collective responsibility of the Council of ministers has two important connotations: "the first that all the members of a Government are unanimous in support of its policies and exhibit that unanimity on public occasions, although while formulating the policies, they might have differed in the cabinet meeting; the second that the Ministers, who had an opportunity to speak for or against the policies in the Cabinet are thereby personally and morally responsible for their success and failure."[97] Thus the political nature of the Parliamentary control over the executive ensures that the continuance of office depends upon the ability of the Council of Ministers in not losing the confidence of the popular house. The executive on its part works towards attaining highest confidence levels in the floor, and the legislature, on the other hand, works towards scrutinizing the confidence of the executive and eventually ventilating public grievances. Ministerial responsibility to the popular house is ensured by various parliamentary mechanisms, such as parliamentary question, motion, resolution, presence of strong opposition, etc.

The Opposition

Ministerial responsibility to the House of Parliament is also ensured through the system of opposition. The members of the opposition party are the strongest evaluators of the policies of the Government, and theoretically their critical reflections on a policy proposal of the Government would provide clarity and purposiveness in public policy. In a Parliament where the Government controls the majority, the role of opposition would be minimum and policy outcomes will reflect only the Government's position. However, when the Government does not control a substantive majority in the Parliament, the role of opposition in throwing the bargaining lever is to the extent that the policy making could be shaped by the opposition. The members of the opposition can also be the legitimate policy makers of the Government in the future. Hence, to pose credibility in their role as thoughtful policy makers, substantive suggestions, criticisms and opinions are expected from the opposition.

In reality, opposition members do not effectively hold the ministers accountable for several reasons. One, the issues raised by the members are mostly reactive than proactive which is one of the prominent organizational weaknesses of Indian political system. Therefore, much of their discussions are rhetorical. Two, unlike the United Kingdom, the system of shadow cabinet is absent in India which hampers any specialist advice to the ruling Government. Therefore there is little scrutiny over the matter discussed by the Government. Third, opposition today raises matters for the sake of criticizing or overthrowing the Government on flimsy grounds. Members of the opposition see the ruling Government as enemies and opposition is cast on virtually every policy proposal emanating from the Government. Eventually, there is a huge waste of time, money and resources in deliberations rather than actions.

Budgetary Control

The Constitution ensures the supremacy of the Lok Sabha in financial matters. At the beginning of every financial year, the President shall ask to lay down the statement of the estimated receipts and expenditure of the Government of India before both the Houses. This is known as the "annual financial statement." [98] According to Article 113 of the Indian Constitution, the estimates as related to other expenditure shall be submitted in the form of demands for grants to the House of the People, and that House shall have power to assent or to refuse to assent, to any demand, or to assent to any demand subject to a reduction of the amount specified therein. No demand for a grant shall, however, is made except on the recommendation of the President.

The financial system, therefore, starts with the presentation of Annual Financial Statement (i.e) the budget. After the presentation of the budget there is a general discussion of the Statement as a whole in either house. This discussion would largely be generalistic relating to a policy and would also involve reviewing and criticizing the Government. In this regard grievances of the people are voiced. Neither motion nor voting is made at this point. Beyond general discussions, the Rajya Sabha would not be entitled to participate in voting for grants. The special prerogative of the Lok Sabha in this regard is the voting of the grants. According to Article 113(2) of the Indian Constitution the estimates are submitted in the form of demands for grants on the particular heads after the general discussion and it is followed by a vote of the House on each of the heads.

The most important tenet of the Indian Constitution in the budget is that it is laid down according to Article 265 which reads that "no tax shall be levied or collected except by authority of law". In other words, the Constitution states that the Executive cannot impose any tax without the formal approval of the legislature.

In brief, a check on budget is one of the important tools in the hands of the Parliament to hold the Government accountable. During general discussions on the budget, the members deal with the general aspects of the fiscal and economic policy. There is a clear reflection of the mood of the house on the budget and the Government gets an idea as to how a particular proposal will be taken at the subsequent stages. It is only during the discussion on the demand for grants, the policy and the working of the ministry comes for detailed scrutiny by the Parliament. Time is allotted to each ministry for discussing demands relating to that particular ministry. It is open to members to disapprove a policy pursued by the ministry or to suggest measures for economy in the administration or to focus attention of the ministry to specific local grievances. The members can do so by moving a subsidiary motion to the main motion for demands for grants. These subsidiary motions are called Cut Motions. There are three types of Cut Motions. The most drastic is the Disapproval of Policy Cut which says that the amount of demand be reduced to Re.1. It implies that the mover disapproves of the policy underlying the demand. Then there is Economy Cut which seeks to reduce the demand by a specific sum with a view to effect economy in the expenditure. The form of this motion is that the amount of the demand be reduced to a specified sum and lastly the *Token Cut* which says that the amount of the demand be reduced by 100 rupees. The object of this motion, which is the most widely used form of Cut Motion is to voice a particular grievance for which the Government of India is responsible." [99] In recent times, after 1994-95, Standing Committees examine and discuss the demand for grants and report to the House.

The efficacy of financial accountability of the Parliament is also sceptical. "The most important fact is that while committees can examine the budgetary grants of various ministries, there is no Parliamentary scrutiny and control of public borrowing. In India, the Constitution and the laws place no limits on the extent of public borrowing."[100] The nature of caretaker Government in utilizing the contingency fund, without any authorization of the Parliament, has also been criticized.[101]

To conclude, the institutional challenges the Indian Parliament faces in holding the executive accountable is theoretically strong, but in practice it suffers from anomalies quite distinct in itself. Instruments of accountability have been seldom used to ensure good governance and in defence and strategic policy making, Parliament is relegated to the status of non-performer. Administrative accountability is used by the Indian Parliament on most foreign and defence policy making, which will be discussed below.

Indian Parliament and the various components attached to it are explained in detail to have a clear picture of the history and functions of the Parliament. The constructive face of the Parliament reveals the fact that it has been the oldest Parliamentary democracy which performs various important functions of which public policy making is taken in the main frame of the study. In this research the Parliament is seen from the lens of policy making, which comes with the reflection of the influence of the Parliament on policy making issues. It is equally important to understand the flaws and short comings of the Parliament which will bring out many suggestions for the betterment. Though the Indian Parliament exercises effective instruments to have checks on accountability of executive to legislative, it is still in the grey side on the aspect of security and Defence policy making. It has become highly politicized and no meaningful attempts have been made to ensure the efficiency of the important public policies. Indian Parliament being a non-performer in the issues of Defence and strategic policy making is due to many reasons, some of which are the technical difficulties in understanding the base of Defence and Strategic policies and the inability of the Parliamentarians to understand the characteristic features of the India's strategic intent which poses an institutional challenge to the Parliament.

Role of Parliament as the Channel of Diplomacy

Apart from legislation and policy scrutinisation, the parliament also works as the channel of bilateral and multilateral diplomacy and directly involves in transnational communication/Interaction/negotiation, which is popularly called as the 'Parliamentary Diplomacy'. The term Parliamentary diplomacy refers to a wide range of activities undertaken by the members of parliament, or parliament as an institution, to increase mutual understanding between countries and to improve scrutiny of government.[102] In terms of foreign policy, 'parliamentary diplomacy' is the "means by which two or more parliaments conduct an ongoing dialogue with regard to key bilateral and international issues".[103] The direct engagement of parliament in international relations provide greater scope for the legislators to understand the international issues better and help to resolve outstanding issues.

Role of Parliamentary Diplomacy in Foreign Policy Decision Making

For its traditional business to debate and discuss the issues of external relations, the modern parliaments have dramatically extended their sphere of involvement in foreign policy decision making in the recent years, and engage in direct interaction with foreign delegations and institutions on external affairs. This direct involvement, often called as 'parliamentary diplomacy' is multidisciplinary in nature which can be divided into two broad categories of analysis, the legal analysis and the political analysis. In the legal aspects, the parliament examines the "institutional competence of regulated Parliaments in the area of international relations of the country" and in the political aspects, the parliament interacts with other foreign parliamentary delegations through various multilateral events. However, in general, parliamentary diplomacy refers to "the activities carried out by the Parliament in international relations, both within the limits of institutional competence and as a central factor of internal political scene." [104]

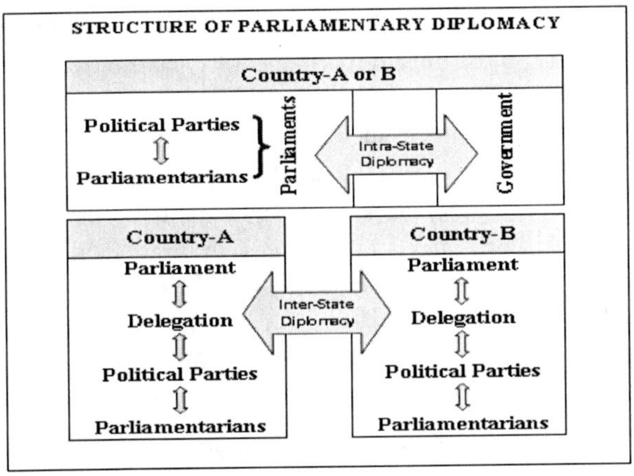

Though the term 'parliamentary diplomacy' has been widely discussed in recent years, it is not a new concept. In 205 BC, the Roman Senate for instance, had played significant role in, first suing for peace and then sanctioning war with Philip V of Macedon after the failure of the Treaty of Phoenice.[105] During the Cold War period, it has been a powerful mechanism to dialogue on bilateral security cooperation in Europe. In the subsequent years, the parliamentary diplomacy served as a testing ground and a means of harnessing the resources of East-West dialogue and, through parliamentary diplomacy, broke the impasse on many occasions when government negotiators were unable to progress.[106] More recently, the emergence of various regional and international organizations, such as SAARC, European Union and United Nations has provided a new shape to the parliamentary diplomacy, which has been further adopted by most of the modern democracies. The parliamentary diplomacy normally performs the following activities:

- Establishment of Bilateral friendship groups, mostly comprised with respective parliamentarians between the countries to understand each other and to review the bilateral issues.

- Materialisation of mutual cooperative agreements between the parliaments and the establishment of inter-parliamentary bodies to promote the bilateral relations between the countries on various subjects of mutual interest.
- Institutionalised and regular interaction between the regional and sub-regional parliamentarians to identify and understand the regional issues and promote regional consensus to address the issues.
- Regular exchanges of parliamentary delegations and study groups, political parties and parliamentary committees between the countries for the smoothening of the governmental rigidity and the strengthening of their bilateral ties.
- Periodical hosting of bilateral, regional, and international level meetings, conferences, and conventions of inter-parliamentary organisations and study groups to share and learn the new developments of parliamentary practices.
- Organization of regional and international conferences with parliamentary committees from neighbouring countries on mutual apprehensive issues to understand and resolve the issue.
- Organisation of bilateral and multi-lateral meetings of inter-parliamentary organisations, parliamentary committees and parliamentarians between the concerned and effecting countries to examine and resolve conflicts.
- Organisation of international colloquiums and other confidence-building measures in order to promote common understanding on existing mutual conflicts.
- Work carried out by individual parliamentarians such as envoys to promote peace processes. They take part in *ad hoc* working groups on particular issues.
- Periodical meetings between parliamentarians and accredited ambassadors to understand the existing bilateral issues and resolve it.
- Continuous bilateral and multilateral technical, procedural and experience sharing cooperation between parliaments and parliamentary committees.
- Establishment of political ombudsmen's offices mandated to investigate inter alia actions taken by a political party that are likely to constitute a breach of an agreement between political parties.[107]

India has been practicing the parliamentary diplomacy since independence. On various occasions, Indian parliamentary delegations, speakers, parliamentarians and various political parties visited the neighbouring and other democratic countries and interacted with the foreign delegations. Similarly, foreign parliamentary delegations come to India regularly to discuss and understand Indian democratic experiments. India has been participating in the Assembly of Inter Parliamentary Union (IPU) regularly, which provides an ideal platform to our parliamentarians to interact with world leaders and study their successful parliamentary practices. Apart from IPU, India also participates in the Annual conference of Association of SAARC Speakers and Parliamentarians, Commonwealth Parliamentary Conference, Commonwealth Speakers and Presiding Officers Conference, G-20 Speakers' Consultation Meeting and Third World Conference of Speakers of Parliaments regularly. Besides the summit level participation, Indian parliamentary delegation usually visits neighbouring countries and discusses various issues with the respective parliamentarians. Former Speaker Meira Kumar for instance, visited Pakistan with the Indian parliamentary delegation and discussed various issues with her Pakistan counterparts, which has helped to improve the bilateral relation between India and Pakistan.[108] Similarly, she also led several parliamentary delegations to Slovenia, Belarus, Myanmar, Canada, Sri Lanka, New Zealand, Uganda, Pakistan, Chile, Uruguay and Paraguay, Iran, Japan, Denmark, Sweden, Vietnam, Panama, Mexico, United Kingdom, Kenya, Mongolia, Hungary, Luxembourg, Bhutan, Mauritius and Austria during her ten years of service as the Speaker of Lok Sabha.[109]

Despite the contribution of parliamentary diplomacy in conflict resolution, it neither imitates nor replaces the traditional governmental diplomacy. It works just as a channel of diplomacy between conflicting parties and provides a platform to understand each other's stand. Being unshackled by instructions from governments, the parliament diplomacy is an effective instrument to put across views which the official government representatives are not able (or willing) to convey. It can supplement government diplomacy because members of the parliament can be more flexible when engaging in diplomatic activities. They are not, after all, bound by the positions taken by the government and can transcend their own government's interests. Parliamentary diplomacy provides a forum to smoothen and to deal with misunderstandings, complementary to and enriching and stimulating traditional forms of diplomacy. The personal contacts between members of parliament of different states are likely to enhance mutual understanding and establish alternative channels beneficial for bilateral relations between countries.

Role of Parliamentary Committees as an advisory body in Foreign Policy Decision Making

As the Parliament has been over loaded with legislative and administrative tasks, it can hardly spare time to scrutinize and discuss the matters coming before it. Additionally, with its huge size, it is difficult to make concession among the members of the Parliament to make some policies. Therefore, the role of the Parliamentary committee is highly obliged which not only scrutinizes the matter carefully, but also makes important suggestions to bring the efficiency to the Foreign Policy of the country. While playing the mediatory role between the executives and legislators, the Parliamentary Committees are taking appropriate suggestions from all the available sources and tune the policies to maximize the national interests. In some cases, it also reaches to the people and affects organizations for their valuable inputs.

Types of Committees

Looking at the nature of composition and function, the parliamentary committees are broadly divided into two types, the ad hoc committees and the standing committees. While the *ad hoc* Committees are specially created to look after some specific jobs temporary in nature, the standing committees are constituted more or less on a continuous basis. A brief discussion of the committees has been given below :

The *ad hoc* Committees

Ad hoc committees are created for a special purpose, mostly to examine as well as to review a particular task. These committees are always temporary in nature and cease to exist as soon as their task gets completed or submit their report. The *ad hoc* committees could be further divided into two categories- the *ad hoc* committees of special assignment and the Select or Joint Committees on bills. The *ad hoc* committees of special assignment are setup, either by the two Houses on a motion adopted on that behalf or by the Speaker/Chairman to analyze and report on particular matters at times of requirement. Committees like the Five Year Plan Committee, Committees for Amendment of Election Law (1970), Shah Nawaz Committee on the Death of Subhash Chandra Bose (1956), Balwant Rai Mehta Committee on the Working of the Community Development Programme (1952) and the National Extension Service (1953), Ashok Mehta Committee on Panchayati Raj (1977), Narasimham Committee on Banking Sector Reforms (1998), Sachar Committee on Condition of Muslims (2005), Srikrishna committee on Telangana (2010), etc. are some of the examples of the ad hoc committees of special assignment which were set up for a special purpose and ceased after the end of the respective assignment. The Select or Joint Committees on Bills are primarily constituted by either house of the parliament or jointly to scrutinise specific bills of the parliament. For these kinds of committees, the rules and procedures are usually laid down by the direction of the Speaker of Lok Sabha or Chairman of the Rajya Sabha respectively. They scrutinize the contents and procedures and incorporate public opinions into the bills. They due verifications and they send back the bill to the parliament for legislation.[110]

The Standing Committees

The second type of committees are the Standing Committees which function permanently and constituted in both the houses of parliament and in some cases jointly by both the house to deal with the important business of the house. The primary responsibility of these committees is policy formulation and execution. The Financial Committee, House Committee, Scrutiny Committee, and Service Committee are some of the standing committees to name a few.[111] Based on the nature and style of function of the standing committees, it can further be divided into six broad categories as follows:

Financial Committees: Being answerable to the public, the Parliament exercises its power of executive accountability over the executives. Using the parliamentary committee system, it scrutinizes and oversees the working of various departments. To carry out these tasks of parliamentary supervision over various governmental schemes, three financial committees, namely the Committee on Estimates, the Committee on Public Accounts and the Committee on Public Undertakings were formed on 10th April 1950. While the Committee on Estimates and Public Accounts constitute the members of the Rajya Sabha, the Committee on Public Undertakings constitutes members from the Lok Sabha. These committees examine the governmental expenses and give valuable recommendations to the government for better financial management.[112]

House Committees: The transcendence of participatory democracy depends upon the smooth functioning of the parliamentary system. Hence, a group of parliamentary standing committees have been constituted to deal with the day-to-day business of houses as well as to facilitate the meaningful and uninterrupted functioning of the parliamentary proceedings. They scrutinize the bills and procedure of parliamentary proceedings and organise parliamentary questions and debates. Committees such as the

Committees Absence of from Sittings of the House, Business Advisory Committee, Committee on Private Members Bills and Resolutions and Rules Committee are some of the examples of these types of committees.[113]

Enquiry Committees: Enquiry Committees are meant to look after the matters related to parliamentary petitions and privileges. They review, consider and report on petitions presented to the House and analyse questions involving breach of privilege of the House or of the members of any Committee. Committees that are coming under this category are Committee on Petition and Committees on Privileges.[114]

Security Committees: The Security Committees have been setup to scrutinize parliamentary questions, debates and papers laid on the tables of the parliament and check the constitutional validity of the matter that are referred to the parliamentary discussion. The committees also follow the promises and assurances of the ministers that have been made in the floor of the parliament. These types of committees include, the Committee on Government Assurances, Committee on Subordinate Legislation, and Committee on Papers Laid on the Table, and The Committee on the Welfare of Scheduled Castes and Scheduled Tribes.[115]

Service Committees: Service committees have been constituted to facilitate various schemes and services to the members of the parliament and look after the issues related to their salaries and accommodation. Committees like General Purposes Committee, House Committee, Library Committee and Joint Committee on Salaries and Allowances of the Members of the Parliament are some of the examples of Service Committees.

Departmental Related Standing Committees: Apart from the above parliamentary committees, several special standing committees have been setup to look after the issues related to various important ministries and departments. Known as the Departmental Related Standing Committees (DRSC), these special committees play a significant role in scrutinizing and overseeing the functions of the various activities and schemes of the respective departments. The structure and function of the DRSC have been discussed at a greater length separately.[116]

Composition and Function of the of Parliamentary Committees

The procedure for the composition and strength of the parliamentary committees varies from committee to committee. In general, the members of the committees range from 15 to 30. These members are either elected or appointed by the House by the motion, or nominated by the Chairman in the case Rajya Sabha or by the Speaker in the case of Lok Sabha. However, the members of the select or joint committee are appointed on a motion adopted by the respective house.

Other Committees

Apart from the above mentioned Standing Committees there are some committees of special importance which are often called as the 'Watch dog' of the Indian Parliament. The primary function of these committees is to scrutinize the function of various ministries, departments as well as other governmental agencies and ensure administrative accountability. These are, the Committee on Subordinate Legislation, the Committee on Government Assurances and the three financial committees, namely the Committee on Estimates, the Committee on Public Accounts and the Committee on Public Undertakings. While the Committee on Estimates and Public Accounts are constituted out of the members of the Rajya Sabha, the members of the Committee on Public Undertakings are drawn from the Lok Sabha. The Committee on Estimates, the Committee on Public Accounts, the Committee on Public Undertakings and DRSCs hold significant power to scrutinize the governmental expenditure and Policy formulation.

Departmentally Related Standing Committees

After years of careful study of its experiments in major democratic countries such as United Sates, United Kingdom and Australia, the system of Departmentally Related Standing Committees (DRSC) was set up in India to review and facilitate the policy making process of various ministries. These committees were setup following the approval of both the houses in April 1993 and replaced the old system of 'Subject Committee' of 1989 which was first constituted to assist the three important departments such as Agriculture, Science and Technology, and Forests. As a result, seventeen Departmentally Related Standing Committees, including the Standing Committee on External Affairs were set up in April 1993. After considering the satisfactory performance of the DRSC system for a decade, the Parliament of India increased the numbers of standing committees to 24 in July 2004.[117]

The jurisdiction of these committees is confined to their respective Ministries and Departments and gives important policy advice to their respective ministries on all the matters of administration. These Committees are Committee on Commerce, Committee on Home Affairs, Committee on Human Resource Development, Committee on Industry, Committee on Science & Technology, Environment & Forests, Committee on Transport,

Culture and Tourism, (all from Rajya Sabha) Committee on Agriculture, Committee on Information Technology, Committee on Defence, Committee on Energy, Committee on External Affairs, Committee on Finance, Committee on Food, Civil Supplies and Public Distribution, Committee on Labour and Welfare, Committee on Petroleum & Chemicals, Committee on Railways, and Committee on Urban and Rural Development (all from Lok Sabha). While the first six Standing Committees are constituted out of the members of the Rajya Sabha, the rest of the committees are drawn from the Lok Sabha.[118]

The members of each of the Departmental Related Standing Committees are drawn from both the houses on the ratio 2:1 and the overall membership of each committee should not be more than 45. Out of which 30 should be nominated from Lok Sabha and the remaining 15 should be from Rajya Sabha. The speaker nominates the Chairman of the committee who leads the committee after due consultation with the various party leaders.[119] The term of the committee members is one year.[120]

The primary function of the standing committees is to review the functioning of the respective ministry and to scrutinize the important policies and legislations for the ministry. It also analyses the annual report and the long term national policy documents that are referred to the parliament. The committee gives its feedbacks and suggestions on various government policies and other administrative responsibilities of the ministries.

Role of Parliamentary Committees in Foreign Policy Making

The institutionalization of the parliamentary committee system is one of the significant developments in the Indian parliamentary democracy and the most important instrument of parliamentary influence on foreign policy decision making. Along with the parliament, the committee system also works as a complementary mechanism to guide, recommend, scrutinize and felicitate the procedure of policy formulation and execution. The uniqueness of the parliamentary committee is, its members are drawn from both, ruling and opposition parties which enable them to take a balanced view on crucial policy decision. Besides promoting parliamentary influence on policy making, the committee system also works as an important check on the executive powers and governmental monopoly on policy planning.

The three financial committees, which often called as the 'watch dog' of governmental expenses, have greater influence in foreign policy formulation by exercising their financial control. The Estimate Committee examines the financial allocations and checks the bad expenses of governmental agencies. It also suggests alternative policies and recommends measures for economic improvement. Though the estimate committee does not make policies, its work is closely allied to policy formulation. As a result, it minimizes the bureaucratic monopoly and ensures parliamentary involvement in policy making. So far, the estimate committee has prepared several reports to External Affairs Ministry. The Estimate Committee during the second Lok Sabha for instance, produced the 138th report, on the financial management of the Ministry of External Affairs in 1960-61 and suggested several administrative measures for effective financial administration of Foreign Office and Indian Missions abroad.[121] Similarly, the estimate committee of the third Lok Sabha also issued the 12th report on the recommendations taken by the 138th report and produced several suggestive reports on the working of International Trade Ministry after a thorough analysis of their functioning.[122] The Estimate Committee of the sixth Lok Sabha also prepared a similar report in 1978 which pushed further administrative reforms. [123] The Public Accounts Committee, which ensures the proper spending of allocated amounts and maintain high standards of administrative accountability in financial matters also has the power to scrutinize the accounts of the various ministries, including the financial records of Ministry of External Affairs. The committee also inspects suspicious activities of the ministries and takes action against the individuals and organizations in case of any irregularity. Apart from the financial detention of foreign policy, the committee also plays a decisive role in arms purchases from foreign countries, which is one of the important aspects of India's foreign policy.[124] The committee has prepared four reports on the appropriation accounts and audit reports for a group of ministries, including the Ministry of External Affairs. Similarly, the public accounts committee also tabled the 57th report on the expenditure incurred by the External Publicity Division of the Ministry of External Affairs in the parliament for appropriate decision.[125]

In addition to the financial committees, the standing committees are also empowered to influence the foreign policy behaviours of India. Out of all the standing committees, the Committee on Subordinate Legislation and the Committee on Government Assurance pose larger impact in influencing India's foreign policy. While the Committee on Subordinate Legislation ensures the uniformity of the procedure in law making and examines the constitutional limits of the administrative authority in policy making, the Committee on Government Assurance ensures the materialization of the parliamentary promises, assurances and undertakings that are made by ministers in the floor of the parliament and responds to the parliamentary questions, and reports the unimplemented promises to the concerned ministries.[126]

These two committees check on the power of the government monopoly and minimize the misuse of the parliamentary privileges on policy making. Though their effect on the process of foreign policy decision making remain relatively minimal, these committees are still empowered to scrutinize the legislation process which eventually guides the course of India's foreign policy by ensuring prescribed legislative process in policy formulations and materialization of the ministerial promises. On the other hand, the government often respects the suggestions and recommendations made by the committees and takes proper steps to address their concerns.

Consultative Committee on External Affairs

Consultative committees are informal committees which assist the government in framing policies. The tradition emerged out of the informal practice of the then Prime Minister Jawaharlal Nehru, where he used to consult various issues of Indian foreign policy with the interested members of the parliament. During the Nehru administration informal meetings for important ministries were held on regular bases, were latter followed by his successors. This practice was later developed in other ministries and has been institutionalized. Subsequently, in 1969, the discussion to setup such kind of informal committees and their modus operandi with leaders of the opposition parties was initiated and decided to name these committees as "Consultative Committees". The enacted guidelines for the constitution and the function of the committees were also subsequently approved by the Cabinet.

Constitution and Functions of Consultative Committee

The Consultative Committee comprises of members from both the houses of parliament. Generally, the process of constituting the consultative committee for various ministries starts after the general election and as and when necessary. After the constitution of the Council of Ministers, the Minister of Parliamentary Affairs invites the members of different parties to be the members of the committee, out of which the members for the Consultative Committee are nominated from both the houses. The strength of the Consultative Committees varies from time to time and ministry to ministry, but should not be more than 40 at any given point.[127] The Consultative Committee on Ministry of External Affairs and Overseas Indian

Affairs is currently having 27 members excluding the External Affairs Minister, who is also the ex-officio Chairman of the committee. The committees meet about four times in a year. Before the meetings the ministry of parliamentary affairs discusses with the members of the committee about the issues for the agenda. During the meeting the minister offers only oral answers on the agenda items and neither the written notes nor the minutes of the meeting are put on circulation due to security reason in external affairs.[128]

Though the Consultative Committee on External Affairs is an important instrument in influencing India's foreign policy, it has no authority or responsibility in practice, mostly due to its informal character. At best, the members can make recommendations to the ministers on certain policies of the government, but is not obliged nor can be compelled to materialize their suggestions.[129] But nevertheless, the meetings of the Consultative Committee minimize the gap between the government and the opposition leaders and ensure clarity in policy making. Due to the confidentiality in committee proceedings, the working Consultative Committee is never disclosed to the public, hence its effectiveness has never been put on test. In addition, the minister often refuses to pass out information to the members of the committee and mislead the committee with wrong information. But, the committee meeting is often used as a platform for the interested parliamentarians to seek sensitive information that have not been placed in the floor of the parliament due to its confidentiality. This committee process reduces the burden of the parliament which enables the parliament to discuss the important matters of internal interest including matters related to foreign affairs.[130]

Standing Committee on External Affairs

The Standing Committee on External Affairs (SCEA) was first set up on April 8, 1993 along with other sixteen Departmental Related Standing Committees. The prime objective of the committee is to assist the policy makers in the formulation and management of India's Foreign Policy. As a consulting body in policy making, it analyzes the referred proposals and gives its report after thorough research and inputs.

Composition and Tenure of SCEA

The Standing Committee on External Affairs is one of the important committees in parliamentary committee system in India. Being a joint committee, it consists of the members from both the houses. The overall membership of the committee has been fixed as 31. While the Speaker of Lok Sabha selects 21 members, the remaining 10 members are nominated by the Chairman of Rajya Sabha. However, a minister is not eligible to become the member of the committee. If a Member is appointed as a Minister, he or she ceases to be the Member of the Committee. The Speaker also nominates the chairman of the standing committee. Considering its multidimensional tasks, several sub-committees or Study Groups have been created within the committee to deal with different specialized tasks. The standing committee also consults with various subject experts at the time of need. The tenure of the Standing Committee on External Affairs is one year from the date of its constitution, unless the Lok Sabha is dissolved earlier. [131] The present strength of the Standing Committee on External Affairs (2014-2015) is 28 out of which, 20 members are elected from the Lok Sabha and the reaming eight members are represented by Rajya Sabha. The committee is presently chaired by the opposition member Dr. Shashi Tharoor of Indian National Congress Party.

Functions of Standing Committee on External Affairs

The functions of the Standing Committee on External Affairs are multidimensional in nature. It examines the cases referred to it and gives its inputs regarding the proposal. It has some sub-committees and study groups to focus on different jobs of their area of specialization. The committee is assisting two different ministries in policy formulation, the Ministry of External Affairs (MEA) and the Ministry of Overseas Indian Affairs (MOIA). The subjects coming under the standing committee are defined time to time considering its importance. The subjects for the standing Committee on External Affairs 2012-2013 are:

1. Restructuring of Indian Foreign Service and functioning of Indian Missions and Posts abroad
2. Passport Seva Project-targets and achievements
3. India's Energy Diplomacy
4. India's Economic Diplomacy
5. Rendering and administration of scholarships by ICCR
6. Welfare of Indian workers abroad
7. Problems being faced by Indian Students abroad
8. Reforms in Emigration System[132]

Based on these issues the standing committee performs different tasks as discussed below:[133]

Assessment of Demands for Grants and Bills

Following the budgetary presentation, the Standing Committee on External Affairs examines the demands sought by the ministry and presents its report to the house. Based on the committee report, the house takes the decision and sanctions the budget for the ministry. In the case of any bills referred to the committee, it presents its report after thorough investigation on the issue.[134]

Examination and Reporting of Ministerial Annual Reports

The committee examines the various actions of the Ministry of External Affairs and Ministry of Overseas Indian Affairs and prepares its report based on its observations. It also makes some recommendations over certain policies and presents it on the house by its Chairman. So far 34 reports have been prepared and presented before the house.[135] The ministry is requested to take actions based on its observations and recommendations.

Analyzing Basic Long Term Policy Documents

Including other policies of the Ministry Of External Affairs, the standing committee also is authorized to analyze the long term government policies related to the matter of external affairs. Thus, the committee may study certain policies and ask clarification regarding the policies and make its observation before the house so that the lacunas can be rectified.

Briefing by Government Officials

If the committee asks for the briefing of important international development, the officials of the Ministry of External Affairs are bound to give details of certain issues. In this way, the committee gets updated of the governmental stands and keeps the watch over the executives on controlling the foreign policies. Several important matters have been briefed to the committee by the officials on regular basis.

Interaction with Foreign Delegations and Dignitaries

The members of the standing committee meet various Foreign Parliamentary delegations visiting India to facilitate meaningful interaction and understanding on global and bilateral issues. This meeting also helps the committee members to gain practical knowledge on the working procedure of other vibrant standing committees of foreign countries.

Undertaking Study Tours on Related Subjects

For the practical understanding of the issues, the standing committee undertakes study trip to the areas and institutions related to its interests with the prior permission of the Speaker of the Lok Sabha. These on-the-spot study enables the study groups of the committee to examine the issues thoroughly so that it can give better observation. So far the study groups have visited various passport offices and foreign missions to analyze its functions.[136] Apart from these works it also helps the ministries in several other ways including giving consultation to the parliament regarding the matters of external relations.

Parliamentary Committee in Legislating Policies on Foreign Affairs

Policy making in critical areas including foreign affairs often requires the parliamentary authorization through legislative process. As the supreme legislative body, the Parliament makes laws for the nation under the provision of Article 246 of Indian Constitution which empowers the Parliament to pass new legislations on any items of the Union List. Going further, Article 253 also empowers the Parliament to modify or make a new legislation for the items listed under the state subject to facilitate the foreign treaties and agreements. Under the Indian parliamentary system, the procedure to legislate new Law is very complex in nature and requires a long parliamentary exercise. According to the Indian constitution, a draft bill has to be introduced into either house of the parliament and need to pass through various stages before the President's approval to become an act. Under the first stage of second reading the bills are usually referred to the select or joint committee for discussion.

After introducing in either house of the parliament and having brief discussion about the significance of the bills in the floor of the house, the bills are passed to the second stage. In the first stage of second reading, a general discussion on the principles and provisions of the bills takes place without going into deep clause by clause discussion. Here it is up to the house whether it will be simply taken into consideration or referred to a select committee of the house or joint committee of the two houses or for circulation for the purpose of eliciting opinion thereon.[137] However, under the rule 74, no money bill will be referred to the Joint Committee. The motion for any proposed amendment by members is allowed under this stage as per the rule 75 of the procedures of the house.

Select Committee is a team of members drawn among the members of the respective house, whereas Joint Committee consists of the members from both the houses in the ratio of 2:1. Once the bill is referred to one of these committees, the respective committee calls the meeting of the members and analyzes the bill clause by clause as the houses do. If the committee becomes satisfied, the bill can be passed with majority vote or can be challenged by members for amendment of certain clauses. For further improvement of the draft bill, the committee can also seek opinion and suggestions from experts, interest groups and affected communities and incorporate their feedbacks into the report. After rigorous analysis, the committee returns back the bills to Lok Sabha Secretariat with its feedbacks, suggestions and recommendations. Then, the Secretary General of Lok Sabha presents the report in the Parliament for discussion.[138] Refereeing the bill to the select committee is one of the significant provisions of the parliamentary democracy which further enhances the quality of the legislation and ensures policy inputs from expertise as well as the general public. The committee system offers a platform to the general citizens to convey their opinion on the redraft legislation and facilitate public participation in the legislative process. The government usually respects the suggestions and recommendations of the committee and incorporates the feedbacks into the legislation.

The Parliamentary Committee system is one of the important institutions of India's parliamentary democracy which upholds the true spirit of democracy in policy making by offering the oppositions a platform to participate and reflect their concern in the policy making alongside the government. Due to the overburdening of responsibilities and lack of time for the thorough scrutiny of policies of important nature, the parliament often refers a bulk of its business to the parliamentary committee for review. Consisting of both ruling and opposition members, the committee scrutinizes the referred policies and gives valuable recommendation to the government in foreign policy formulation. The meeting of the parliamentary committee is often used as the platform to understand and address the concern of the opposition parties and the decision of the committee is usually respected by the government. The committee system puts the government accountable to the public spending and checks on the government's monopoly in policy planning. It also minimizes the bureaucratic influences on policy making and facilitates larger role for parliamentary influence on decision making. Being the association of foreign policy experts, the Consultative Committee and the Standing Committee of External Affairs, guides the government on various matters of foreign affairs. The government often seeks the inputs of both the committees before taking any significant decision on foreign affairs. Analyzing the greater engagement of the parliamentary committee, former Foreign Secretary J.N. Dixit appreciated the role of the committee system and credited the Standing Committee for creating space for the greater engagement of parliament on external affairs.[139]

However, like the parliament, the role of parliamentary committee in foreign policy making is limited to raising questions, asking clarifications and passing recommendations to the government. The consultative committees have no authority or responsibility in foreign policy formulation. Moreover, the government is not under any obligation to incorporate the committee's advises and recommendations. The provision of confidentiality in committee meeting further deters to review its function and minimizes its accountability. Often the meeting ends without any decision or superficial recommendations. The ministers sometimes mislead the committee with ill information and refuse to pass adequate information, mainly citing the nature of confidentiality. This is why the committee system has achieved no such major back trough in foreign policy formulation since its induction into Indian parliamentary system. The committee system, which developed from British Parliament and practiced in other parliamentary democracies works as a norm than as a constraint of foreign policy in these states. Nevertheless, the adoption of committee system has facilitated the parliamentary role in policy making and put a check on government's monopoly over foreign policy decision making. Its works as a watch dog and ensures the accountability in the government. They also highlight the important issues of the government's policy and suggest measures for maximization of national gain in external affairs.

Role of Parliament as the Institution for the Rectification of International Treaties

International treaties are the mutual agreements among the nations to enhance the level of engagement on certain areas. The Vienna Convention on the Law of Treaties which came in to force since 1980 defines treaty as "an international agreement concluded between the States in written form and governed by international law, whether embodied in a single instrument or in two or more related instruments and whatever its particular designation."[140] According to the above definition, International Treaties take place between the states. Going one step ahead, Article 38 (1) of the International Court of Justice argues that the treaties not only occur between the states but also take place between the states and international organizations.[141]

As no state can remain isolated and estranged in the globalized world, international treaties have become the effective instrument to establish and escalate the relationship between and among the nations. Generally international treaties are signed between the sovereign governments on behalf of the respective countries on matters regarding foreign relations, trade, environment, defence and strategic, war and peace, communications, ecology or finance. Hence, the treaties have immense potential to influence both internal and external policies of a country. However, the prior approval of the international treaties by parliament before implementation is not a universal procedure. The Parliament's approval of the international treaties and agreements are mandatory in Denmark, Netherlands, Norway, Switzerland, Luxemburg, Laos, Indonesia and Japan, whereas in India, Canada, U.K. and most of the British Commonwealth countries, the Parliament's nod is not compulsory to implement the signed treaties unless it involves serious consequences.[142]

Under the Constitution of India, the Parliament is empowered to make any law on the items listed under the central list without any limitations. Matters related to foreign affairs of the union list that includes entries 13, 14, 15 and 16 also come under the legislative command of the parliament which reads as follows:

13. Participation in international conferences, associations and other international bodies and implementing of decisions made there at.
14. Entering into treaties and agreements with foreign countries and implementing of the treaties, agreements and conventions with the foreign countries.
15. Matters related to war and peace, and
16. Issues related to foreign jurisdiction.[143]

To be more specific, the Indian Parliament is authorized to make law regarding the entry 14 of the union list which reads "Entering into treaties and agreements with the foreign countries and implementing of treaties, agreements and conventions with foreign countries".[144] Furthermore, article 253 also empowers the Parliament to make laws to implement the treaties. Headlined with "Legislation for giving effect to international agreements" the article further states:

> "Notwithstanding anything in the foregoing provisions of this Chapter, Parliament has power to make any law for the whole or any part of the territory of India for implementing any treaty, agreement or convention

with any other country or countries or any decision made at any international conference, association or other body".[145]

The above discussion has made it clear that, the Parliament has immense power to make laws for implementation of the international treaties.

As discussed above, treaty making in India and rectifying is different from that of the US and some European countries. Generally, the treaty making is initiated by the executives who first start negotiations with the other party using diplomatic channels. After discussion with the political boss, the executives prepare the draft keeping the prime objectives of the treaty in mind. When the provisions of the treaties get finalized, the representatives of the two sovereign states (usually the chief of the executives) sign the treaty. Then the copy of the treaty is introduced as a resolution for discussion.[146]

When the treaty is placed before the Parliament for discussion, the Parliament discusses on it like that of the other resolutions but cannot rectify the treaty according to the desire of the Parliament. Further, by enjoying the support of the majority the government gets pass the treaty and hardly faces legislative blockade. The floors of the Parliament are open for critical discussion on the treaty.[147] The Parliament cannot make judgment on the provisions of the treaty or the treaty as whole. Though several attempts have been made to change it by introducing constitutional amendment bills, none of them have succeeded so far.[148] However, India ratified the United Nations Convention Against Corruption following the 2003 U.N. General Assembly. The Lok Sabha debated on the Bill which centred on Articles 252 and 253 of the Constitution and adopted the Lokayuktas Bill on December 27, 2011 to implement the ratification.[149]

Factors Eclipsing Parliamentary Role of Foreign Policy Making

The Parliament is an important institution of a democratic system of India and an integral branch of governance. It has been empowered to legislate laws and policies for the government, identify the administrative errors and rectify it after debate. But in practice, policy making has been the business of the executive domain and 'Foreign Policy' is not an exception to this practice. The Parliament in India is not responsible to make Foreign Policy directly. However, it is able to influence the course of the Foreign Policy a bit through various Parliamentary mechanisms. Hence, the scope of the Parliament in making, guiding and supervising the Foreign Policy is very limited. Various factors are eclipsing the role of the Parliament in managing Foreign Policy of India. These factors are discussed below:

Party Affiliation and Personality Cult in Parliament

Although the Parliament plays an important role in shaping the Foreign Policy of the country, it works under certain pressures, lobbies and influences. More than that, it is the party ideology which dominates over the cognitive behaviour of a member during the Parliament debate. Similarly, leadership at some time also minimizes the influence of the Parliament's role in decision-making. The Foreign Policy making during Nehru period, for example was a one man show and the Parliament had little influence over the policy behaviour. First of all Nehru was an icon of a great personality and enjoyed the confidence of the mass. Secondly, his personal hold on decision making was so vast that others had little role to play. Thirdly, his image was so popular and acceptable for the people that it was not easy to oppose his decision at the floor of the Parliament. Therefore other members, especially party men had no way to support him. Moreover, majority of the members belongs to the ruling party of the government that makes policies. Hence they cannot go against the decision of the party. Therefore the Parliamentary debates have very little scope to influence the governmental decisions.

Executive Supremacy

Though the Parliament legislates and approves policies, the executives, in practice make policies for the government and get it approved by the Parliament. There are several reasons behind the domination of the executives in policy making. Firstly, the executives are Permanent agencies and therefore, have greater experience compared to the political heads who are elected for five years and possess less experience. Secondly, the executives are part of the larger organization which includes expertise of different areas and make all round policies while political boss lacks. Thirdly, it is the executives who implement the policies hence and possess the first hand information regarding the concerned issue. Apart from that, the political leaders are busy in politics and pay interest towards the policy formulation. Therefore, the executives enjoy supremacy in policy making, including Foreign Policy.

The superior, commendable role played by the executives has undermined the role of the Parliament in Foreign Policy making. While the executives make the decision for the government, the Parliament has limited scope to modify it. Often it has been seen that, most of the policies have been formulated by the executives and implemented with or without the approval of the cabinet and never presented before the parliament for discussion. Therefore the authoritative role of the executives has pushed the role of the Parliament into a secondary level in the Foreign Policy making.

Supremacy of the Cabinet

In India, the cabinet plays a significant role in the policy making process. It is an elite institution which is directly responsible for each and every matter of the government and enjoys more power compared to any other institutions, including the Parliament. It remains more influential in the policy making because of its proximity to the government and decides the fate of a decision in India. Most of the policies pass over to the Cabinet before they are introduced into the Parliament to decide. In case of any lacuna, it asks the executives to include new provision rather than seeking alternatives from the Parliament during the time of discussion. It also bypasses the Parliament and makes policies without introducing the proposal into the Parliament. Though it is answerable to the Parliament, in reality it always poses sufficient political backing to maintain its dominance in government.

Confidentiality in Foreign Affairs

The Parliament in its true spirit is an institution to raise questions, debate and discuss the internal and external issues of the country and make policies to address these issues. Hiding anything from the public domain is against the basic ethos of the parliamentary system. However, matters related to national security, diplomacy and Foreign Policy need to be kept secret in order to protect them from reaching the hands of the enemy country. The government may deny disclosing such details on the floor of parliament. Hence, the parliamentary tools seem ineffective to discuss matters of these secretive nature, such as Foreign Policy.

Delay in Parliamentary Decision Making

The international environment is so fickle and vast that the time allotted for the Parliament is not sufficient to analyze and understand the emerging issues. It is also very difficult for the members to raise and debate certain issues within the allotted time in the Parliament. Neither the questioner nor the minister who responds to the questions can do justice to the issue when the Parliament awards them mere two to three minutes each. Secondly, due to the time factor, limited questions are allowed to each member, and they are allowed to raise issues at certain times. As a result, most of the

Parliamentarians are interested in raising the local issues of their respective constituencies to win the votes rather than wasting time on the international issues.

Less Preference to Foreign Affairs

The Members with knowledge on the Foreign Affairs are comparatively less in the Indian parliament. Except some experts, the Foreign Policy remains a less prioritized issue for discussion in the Parliament for most of the members. It can be seen by analyzing the data of the Parliamentary debate. As more people are acquainted with the regional and national issues, they often prefer to raise the internal issues and hardly participate in discussion in matters of foreign affairs. It restricts the debate and discussion of matters related to Foreign Policy to certain level. As a result, the influence of the Parliament has been limited to issues on the foreign affairs.

Narrow Scope for Legislation

The issues related to the Foreign Policy crisis needs negotiation rather legislation. There is nothing hardbound rule book called 'Foreign Policy' of a country according to which the country must interact with others. Rather, it is a flexible idea to negotiate with the rest of the world and hardly need legislations to guide it. Moreover, the international treaties and agreements which are not mandatory are get approved by the Parliament if it does not involve or affect the financial and other serious concerns. As a result most of the treaties are signed without the approval of the Parliament. In case it is introduced into the Parliament, it cannot amend or modify any provision rather than approve it.

Parliament as a Machinery of Delay and Slow Process

The Matters and issues of Foreign Policy need to be addressed instantly for the maximum gain. The delay in handling the issue may cost amenity to the country's security and sovereignty. But in the Parliament any system of decision making is such a slow process that takes months and years together to reach any conclusion. The delay arises due to the size of the Parliament and passing of the proposal by multiple stages and the Parliamentary agencies. Consisting with the people of different interests and opinions, the Parliament is unable to take quick decision to address the issue and seems unfit to deal the matter of foreign affairs which requires quite actions.

Practice of Unprofessionalism in Parliament

Parliament is supposed to be the place of highly professionalism to debate and discuss important issues of the country and formulate the policies addressing these issues. But in recent past, the members apparently lack basic morality and they fight with each other with no point. Without going detail into the government proposal, the opposition in many occasions opposes important bills with no reason. In the recent past most of the precious time of the Parliament has been washed away due to the boycott and non-participatory approach of the oppositions in the Parliament sessions. Sometimes, important bills are turned into a law without proper discussion in the Parliament. If at all the members take part in the discussion, their arguments lack the logic. Therefore, the Parliament, on many occasions, fail to identify and criticize the weakness of the government on the matters of Foreign Policy.

Conclusion

Being the highest institution and the ultimate voice of the people, the Parliament, in a democratic state like India plays an important role in the formulation and implementation of foreign policies in a variety of ways. It can legislate on any matter that comes under union list, including matters related to foreign affairs. The Parliament also influences the course of Foreign Policy by approving or rejecting any government proposal related to Foreign Policy and can create any specialized agencies and government institutions to deal with the matter related to foreign affairs like Foreign Service Institute and National Security Council; or merge or modify the function of the existing machinery or create new posts like National Security Advisor. Using its power of sanction, the Parliament can influence the making of Foreign Policy by reducing or increasing the overall or partial budgetary allotment to Ministry of External Affairs or Ministry of Defence or other allied agencies which might affect India's Foreign Policy behaviour. In addition, Parliamentary debates and discussions are also considered one of the prime instruments to influence the process of Foreign Policy discourse. The opposition and the other members of the Parliament point out the mistakes and give suggestions for better policies, during the Parliamentary debates. The Parliament poses unparallel power to withhold, pass or reject any bill or resolution that is directly or indirectly related to India's external policy. Members of the Parliament also move adjournment, No-Confident or Cut-Motion, raise short or half-an hour discussion on any specific or an overall issue of the Foreign Policy.

Consultative committees of the Parliament, especially Standing Committee on Foreign Affairs has been playing significant role in shaping India's Foreign Policy behaviour. After all, the Parliament is considered as the face of the government and its behaviour and activities are always paid significant attention among the world communities.

But in practice, the Parliament despite all its powers and privileges has never been considered as one of the core actors of Foreign Policy decision making in India. Government always bypasses the Parliament while making decision on important issues of foreign affairs. Though, the Parliament is empowered to legislate on any matter on foreign affairs, not many issues on the foreign and the Defence policies have been referred to the Parliament for legislation. Unlike United States or Australia, it is not mandatory for international conventions, treaties and agreements to get approved by the Parliament before coming into practice. In Indian context, it is supposed to be the document of secrecy for optimum result and its open discussion in the parliament before actualization might endanger the entire goal of the treaty. Therefore, many of the treaties, such as the India–China Agreement of 1954, the Tashkent Agreement of 1965, the India-Soviet Agreement of 1971 and the Simla Agreement of 1972 have never been referred to the Parliament for debate before the conclusion of the treaty. Even the Parliament sometimes is delicately kept in dark on several national policies and serious issues on a number of occasions. The Parliament committees, which are supposed to guide the course of Foreign Policy, are often divided by the party ideologies, and the decisions that are coming up become the byproduct of negotiation rather than rational. That's why M.C. Chagla, the Ex-foreign Minister under Indira Gandhi government termed Consultative Committee on external affairs as " more of an agency for getting policies accepted and muting criticism than for influencing Foreign Policy".

Despite this, on many occasions the Parliament significantly influenced the Foreign Policy of India. For instance, Nehru's Foreign Policy towards China in the early periods used to be soft despite several border violations due to the overwhelming support of the Parliament. But, following the constant pressure in Parliament, Nehru forced to restructure his policies during late 1950s. The Parliament also successfully pressurized the Nehru government to disclose every single document on China, which was tabled in the form of white papers in the Parliament for discussion. Similarly, during the Hungarian Crisis of 1965, Nehru initially turned towards Soviet, but after the stiff pressure from the opposition in the Parliament, he changed his stand subsequently. Prime Minister Indira Gandhi also changed her stand from separation to united Czechoslovakia during the 1968 Czechoslovak crisis by the influence of strong opposition in the Parliament. To conclude, we can say that, the Parliament played a very minimal role in India's Foreign Policy decision making until 1960, but with the emergence of strong opposition and other national parties, the influence of the Parliament has increased significantly

Notes

1. Theodore J. Lowi, "Four Systems of Policy, Politics, and Choice", Public Administration Review, Vol. 32, No. 4 (Jul. - Aug., 1972), pp. 298-310.
2. D.D. Basu, "Introduction to the Constitution of India 0148", 19th Ed. (New Delhi: Wadhwa and Co. Law Publishers, 2001) 23.
3. R. K. Mookerjee, Local Government in Ancient India, (New Delhi: Oxford University Press, 1920) 34.
4. Sri Ram Sharma, Constitutional History of India (New Delhi: Atlantic Publishers, 1955) 52-54.
5. N. Jayapalan, Indian Administration, Volume 2 (New Delhi: Atlantic Publishers, 2001) 40.
6. Parmatma Saran, The Imperial Legislative Council of India from 1861 to 1920: A Study of the Inter-action of Constitutional Reform and National Movement with Special Reference to the Growth of Indian Legislature Upto 1920 (New Delhi: S. Chand & Co., 1961) 32-55.
7. Jayapalan, Indian Administration, 40-41.
8. Amiya Chatterji, Constitutional Development of India (New Delhi: Atlantic Publishers, 1958) 66-67.
9. Subash Kashyap, Our Parliament (New Delhi: National Book Trust, 2007) 12. .
10. *Ibid.* 16.
11. Verinder Grover, Constitutional Schemes and Political Development in India: Towards Transfer of Power (New Delhi: Deep and Deep Publications, 1994) 574-76.
12. P M Bakshi, Constitution of India, (New Delhi: Universal Law Publishing, 2010) 106.
13. Article 80 (4).
14. S.G Deogaonkar, Parliamentary System in India (New Delhi: Concept Publishing Company, 01-Jan-1997) 44-45.
15. Article 83 (1); Representation of the People Act, 1951 Section 154 (1).
16. Deogaonkar, Parliamentary System in India, 43-44.
17. David Easton, The Political System (New York: Knopf, 1953) 129.
18. T. J. Lowi, "Four Systems of Policy, Politics and Choice", Public Administrative Review, Vol. 32, No. 4, (1972): 298-310.
19. Referred from Subash Kashyap, Our Parliament (New Delhi: National Book Trust, 2007) 52-70.
20. Antonio Cassese, ed, Parliamentary Control Over Foreign Policy (Alphen aan den Rijn, Nederlands: Sijthoff & Noordhoff International Publishers BV, 1980) vii.

21. Many scholars have proven that there is close nexus between the domestic politics and Foreign Policy decision making. For more discussion refer James M. McCormick, (2012), Dina Spechler, (1978), Thomas Risse-Kappen, (1991), Michael Smith, (2004),Alastair Smith, (1996), Jack S. Levy, (1988), Michael McFaul, (1997), Robert D. Putnam (1988), Henry A. Kissinger (1966).
22. Parvinrai Mulwantrai Bakshi, Subhash C. Kashyap, The Constitution of India (New Delhi: Universal Law Publishing, 2002) 101.
23. Constitution of India, published under the official website of Ministry of Law and Justice, Government of India, http://lawmin.nic.in/olwing/coi/coi-english/Const.Pock%202Pg.Rom8Fsss%2835%29.pdf, (Apr. 10, 2013).
24. P. M. Bakshi, S. C. Kashyap, (2002) 101.
25. Constitution of India, Ministry of Law and Justice, Government of India.
26. "Treaty-Making Power under our Constitution", Consultation Paper prepared by National Commission to Review the Working of the Constitution, Government of India on January 8, 2001, Ministry of Law and Justice, Government of India..
27. For detail see abstract 3 of the Parliamentary Procedure "Private Members' Bills and Resolutions", published under the Parliament of India, available at official website of Parliament of India at: http://164.100.47.132/LssNew/abstract/private_members.htm (Apr.10, 2013).
28. Devika Malik, Rohit Kuma, Indian Parliament at 60 years: Facts & Statistics, CNN IBN, May 14, 2012, PRS Legislative Research, http://ibnlive.in.com/news/indian-Parliament-at-60-years-facts—statistics/2577943. html.
29. Subhash Kashyap, Our Parliament, (New Delhi: National Book Trust, 2003) 165-66.
30. *Rules of Procedures and Conduct of Business in Lok Sabha*,14th ed., (New Delhi: Lok Sabha Secretariat, 2010) 32.
31. Rule 73 of the Parliament Procedures, see *ibid*, 35.
32. Rule 64 of the Parliament Procedures, see Rules of Procedures and Conduct of Business in Lok Sabha,14th edn., (New Delhi: Lok Sabha Secretariat, 2010) 32.
33. Rule 74 of the Parliament Procedures, see *ibid*, 35.
34. Kashyap, (2003) 167-68.
35. Kashyap (2003) 168-69 and research article on "How a Bill Becomes an Act", published by Parliament of India web site. http://Parliamentofindia.nic.in/ls/intro/p5.htm.
36. Rule 94, Clause 1 of the Parliament Procedures, see Rules of Procedures and Conduct of Business in Lok Sabha,14th edn., (New Delhi: Lok Sabha Secretariat, 2010) 43 also see "Legislative Process" Published in the official website of Parliament of India, Government of India. http://164.100.47.132/LssNew/abstract/legislative_process.htm.
37. Rule 95, Rules of Procedures and Conduct of Business in Lok Sabha, 43.
38. Kashyap (2003) 171.
39. *Ibid.*
40. Kashyap (2003) 175-77.

41. See Marriam-Webster online Dictionary, at http://www.merriam-webster.com/dictionary/influence.
42. See Oxford Online Dictionary http://oxforddictionaries.com/definition/english/influence.
43. Michele Merrill Betsill, Elizabeth Corell, NGO Diplomacy: The Influence of Nongovernmental Organizations in International Environmental Negotiations (Cambridge: MIT Press, 2008) 24.
44. Naheed Murthza, Parliament and Foreign Policy: Reflection of India-China Relations (New Delhi: CADPLAN Publisher, 1998) 79.
45. Leon D. Epstein, "British Foreign Policy" as quoted in Naheed Murtaza, Parliament and Foreign Policy: Reflection on India-China Relations. (New Delhi: CADPLAN Publisher, 1998) 102.
46. Paul Martin "The Role of Canadian Parliament in the Formulation of Foreign Policy" Parliamentarian, L, (October, 1969) 262.
47. Under the Rule 32 of Parliament Procedure, see, Rules of Procedure of Indian Parliament (Lok Sabha Secretariat, New Delhi) 15.
48. S.G. Deogaonkar, Parliamentary System in India, (New Delhi: Concept Publishing Company, 1997) 79.
49. Hoshiar Singh, Public Administration: Theory and Practice (New Delhi: Pearson Education India, 2012) 231.
50. Research, Documentation and Information Services, Lok Sabha Secretariat, Parliament of India, the Ninth Lok Sabha, 1989-1991: A Study (New Delhi: Northern Book Centre, 1992) 100.
51. Ibid, 100.
52. Kashyap (2003) 120, 124; and Lok Sabha Secretariat (1992) 100 & 101.
53. Rule 40 of the Parliament Procedure.
54. Rule 55 (1) of the Parliament Procedure.
55. This provision have included into the rule book sub-clause by Lok Sabha on 9-5-1989.
56. see "Half-An-Hour Discussion" in Rules of Procedures and Conduct of Business in Lok Sabha,14th edn., (New Delhi: Lok Sabha Secretariat, 2010) 27-28.
57. For details see Naheed Murtaza (1998) 100.
58. *Rajya Sabha at Work*, published by Rajya Sabha Secretariat, Parliament of India, New Delhi, 2006, 637.
59. Abstract to the business of Parliament, Parliament of India, http://164.100.47.132/LssNew/abstract/ adjournment_motion.htm.
60. Rule 57 of the Parliamentary Procedure of India.
61. SwarajThapa, The Privileges in a Privilege Motion, The Indian Express, Mar 24, 2011 at http://www.indianexpress.com/news/the-privileges-in-a-privilege-motion/766468/.
62. Kashyap (2011) 134-137.
63. "BJP to move motion in Parliament today on Italy's refusal to send back marines", India Today, New Delhi, March 13, 2013; and Ashish Mukherjee, "BJP to move

motion in Parliament today on Italy's refusal to send back marines for trial",, NDTV News, March 13, 2013.

64. Kapur and Mehta (2006) 10.
65. Kashyap (2011) 150.
66. Rule 184-89.
67. Kashyap (2011) 151.
68. S.K. Das, Encyclopedic Dictionary of Public Administ ration, Vol. 2 (New Delhi: Sarup & Sons Publication, 2000) 462.
69. M. Laxmikanth, Public Administration, (New Delhi: Tata McGraw-Hill Publication, 2011) 358.
70. Under Rule 211 of Parliament Procedures; for further discussion see U. N. Gupta, Indian Parliamentary Democracy (New Delhi: Atlantic Publishers, 2003) 287.
71. See Rule 212 of Parliament Procedures.
72. Rule 214 (3) of Parliament Procedures.
73. Kashyap (2011) 141.
74. "Motions", Chapter VII of the hand book of the Parliamentary procedure in India, available the official web site of Parliament of India, http://Parliament ofindia.nic.in/ls/direct/dirp7.html.
75. Rule 185.
76. Kashyap (2011) 141-42.
77. *Motions and Resolutions in Parliament* (New Delhi: Lok Sabha Secretariat, 2009) 3.
78. Ibid.
79. Kashyap (2011) 142, see also Motions and Resolutions in Parliament (2009) 3.
80. Kashyap (2011) 142-43.
81. Under Rule 172 of procedure of Indian Parliament. Detail can be seen at 'Resolutions', Rules of Procedure and Conduct of Business in Lok Sabha, (New Delhi: Lok Sabha Secretariat, 2010) 62.
82. Motions and Resolutions in Parliament (New Delhi: Lok Sabha Secretariat, 2009) 10.
83. Rule 171 of the Parliamentary procedures.
84. Kashyap (2011) 145.
85. Rule 30 (4), and 170 of Parliamentary procedure.
86. Kashyap (2011) 146.
87. *Motions and Resolutions in Parliament* (New Delhi: Lok Sabha Secretariat, 2009) 13; and Kashyap (2011) 146-47.
88. Kashyap (2011) 147.
89. Kashyap (20110 and Motions and Resolutions in Parliament (2009) 16.
90. Rules of Procedure and Conduct of Business in Lok Sabha, Rule 172.
91. R.B. Jain, "Parliament and Policy in India", Asian Journal of Public Administration, Vol. 6, Issue 2 (1984) 127-152.

92. Devesh Kapur and Pratap Bhanu Mehta, "The Indian Parliament as an Institution of Accountability", Democracy, Governance and Human Rights Programme Paper, United Nations Research Institute for Social Development, No. 23, January, 2006.
93. For a comprehensive overview of the legislature and executive interface refer, Subash Kashyap, "Executive Legislature Interface in the Indian Polity", The Journal of Legislative Studies, 10/2 (2004): 278-294.
94. Subash Kashyap, "Parliamentary Procedure: Law, Privileges, Practices and Precedents Vol. 1, (New Delhi, Universal Law Publishing Company, 2000) 80-82.
95. D.D Basu (2001) 189.
96. Articles 75, 114-116 and 265. As cited in Subash Kashyap (2004) 281.
97. D.D. Basu (2001) 190. His citation shows Common Cause, A Registered Society v. Union of India, (1999) 6 S.C.C 667 (para 3): A.I.R 1999 S. C. 2979.
98. Article 112. As stated in D. D. Basu (2001) 218.
99. Kashyap (2007) 157-158.
100. Kapur and Mehta (2006) 24.
101. The caretaker Government cannot go to the house for approval because the house stands dissolved.
102. Frans W. Weisglas, Gonnie de Boer, "Parliamentary Diplomacy" The Hague Journal of Diplomacy 2 (2007) 93-99.
103. Parliamentary Diplomacy, AGORA, http://www.agora-parl.org/resources/aoe/parliamentaryinstitution/parliamentary-diplomacy.
104. George Noulas, "The Role of Parliamentary Diplomacy in Foreign Policy" Foreign Policy Journal, October 22, 2011.http://www.foreignpolicyjournal.com/2011/10/22/the-role-of-parliamentary-diplomacy-in-foreign-policy/.
105. Daniel Fiott "On the Value of Parliamentary Diplomacy" Madariaga Paper , Vol. 4, No. 7 (Apr., 2011)http://www.ies.be/files/Fiott%20Parliamentary%20Diplomacy.pdf.
106. David Beetham, Parliament and Democracy in The Twenty-First Century: A Guide to Good Practice (Geneva: Inter-Parliamentary Union, 2006) 173.
107. "Parliamentary Involvement in International Affairs", A report by the Inter-Parliamentary Union (IPU) to the Second World Conference of Speakers of Parliaments, New York, 7-9 September, 2005. www2.ohchr.org/english/issues/development/docs/ipu.doc.
108 "In a first, Meira Kumar to visit Pakistan" Hindustan Times, New Delhi, Feb 08, 2012. http://www.hindustantimes.com/newdelhi/in-a-first-meira-kumar-to-visit-pakistan/article1-808209.aspx.
109. See Profile of Meira Kumar, Office of the Speaker of Lok Sabha, http://speakerloksabha.nic.in/former/meirakumar.asp.
110. S.G Deogaonkar, Parliamentary System in India (New Delhi: Concept Publishing Company, 1997) 223-24.
111. Kashyap (2011) 190.
112. Lok Sabha, Parliament of India, the Ninth Lok Sabha, 1989-1991: A Study (New Delhi: Northern Book Centre, 1992) 37.

113. "Parliamentary Committees", Parliament of India, http://parliamentofindia.gov.in/ls/intro/p21.htm.
114. *Ibid.*
115. Virendra Kumar, Committees And Commissions In India Vol. 1 : 1947-54 (New Delhi: Concept Publishing Company, 1976) xv-xvi.
116. *Ibid.*
117. "Parliament Committees", Parliament of India, http://parliamentofindia.gov.in/ls/intro/p21.htm.
118. *Ibid.*
119. Singh Hoshiar, Indian Administration (New Delhi: Pearson Education, 2011) 78.
120. V. K. Agnihotri, Handbook on the Working of Ministry of Parliamentary Affairs (New Delhi: Concept Publishing Company, 2004) 44-45.
121. J. Bandyopadhyaya, The Making of India's Foreign Policy (New Delhi: Allied Publishers, 2003) 97.
122. Judhih M. Brown, 40.
123. Bandyopadhyaya, 97.
124. Jayantanuja Bandyopadhyaya, A General Theory of Foreign Policy (New Delhi: Allied Publication, 2004) 209.
125. Brown, 41.
126. Kaul and Shakdher 712-13.
127. V.K. Agnihotri, Handbook on the Working of Ministry of Parliamentary Affairs (New Delhi: Concept Publishing Company, 2004) 79-84.
128. Subhash Shukla, Foreign Policy of India (New Delhi: Anamika Pub & Distributors, 2007) 2015-16; Agnihotri 79-84.
129. Sita Ramachandran, Decision-making in Foreign Policy (New Delhi: Northern Book Centre, 1996) 25.
130. Brown, 42-43.
131. "Standing Committee on External Affairs Lok Sabha" published at official web site of Parliament of India, at http://164.100.24.208/ls/committee/drsc05.htm.
132. *Selection of Subjects by the Standing Committee on External Affairs*, as published under the Bulletin of the Lok Sabha, Part-II, No. 4567, dated November 1, 2012.
133. Rules Relating To The Department-Related Parliamentary Standing Committees, published under the official website of the Rajya Sabha, at http://rajyasabha.gov.in/rsnew/rs_rule/rulesdrpscs.asp (cited on April 3, 2013).
134. "Standing Committee on External Affairs Lok Sabha" published at official web site of Parliament of India, at http://164.100.24.208/ls/committee/drsc05.htm.
135. A list of such reports can be seen at the official website of Parliament of India at http://164.100.47.133/ls/committee/exaff/annexureII.htm.
136. "Standing Committee on External Affairs Lok Sabha" published at official web site of Parliament of India, at http://164.100.24.208/ls/committee/drsc05.htm.
137. Rule 74 of the Parliament Procedures, see *ibid*, 35.
138. Kashyap, (2003) 167-68.

139. J.N. Dixit My South Block years: memories of a foreign secretary (new Delhi: WBSPD, 1996) pp. 431.
140. Vienna Convention on the Law of Treaties 1969, United Nations, Treaty Series, Vol. 1155, 331, at untreaty.un.org/ilc/texts/instruments/english/conventions/1_1_1969.pdf.
141. Silvio Fazio, The Harmonization of International Commercial Law, (AH Alphen aan den Rijn, Netherlands: Kluwer Law International, 2007) 31; for a comparative and detail study on the definition of international treaties refer Duncan B. Hollis, "Defining Treaties" in The Oxford Guide to Treaties, edited by Duncan B. Hollis, (Oxford: Oxford University Press, 2012) 11-44.
142. Consultation Paper on "Treaty-Making Power under Our Constitution", National Commission to Review the Working of the Constitution, New Delhi January 8, 2001.
143. Constitution of India, published under the website of Ministry of Law and Justice, Government of India, http://lawmin.nic.in/olwing/coi/coi-english/Const.Pock%202Pg.Rom8Fsss%2835%29.pdf, (Apr. 10, 2013) .
144. *Ibid.*
145. Constitution of India, published by Ministry of Law, Government of India.
146. S. K. Verma, An Introduction To Public International Law, (New Delhi: PHI Learning, 2004) 64; and .
147. Naheed Murtaza (1998) 63-65.
148. MP Brinda Karat has introduced the private members bill at the Parliament which has turndown by the Parliament. For detail see at "Brinda Karat wants all international treaties ratified by Parliament" Times of India, Dec 20, 2008, At http://articles.timesofindia.indiatimes.com/2008-12-20/india/27929978_1_treaties-Parliament-agreements.
149. A.G. Noorani, Treaties & States, Frontline, Volume 29 - Issue 02 :: Jan. 28-Feb. 10, 2012 http://www.frontline.in/static/html/fl2902/stories/20120210290204300.htm

Chapter - 4

Parliament and the Making of India's China Policy during the Era of Friendship and Brotherhood 1947 to 1958

Relations between India China, the oldest living civilizations of the world, had been warm, friendly and cooperative long before their independence. India and China had established greater linkages through cultural exchanges and trade throughout the history. Ancient trade and religious pilgrimages had been flourishing through the ancient silk route for centuries. British expansionism after colonizing India searched for a new territory to expand its trade. As result the East India Company repeatedly attempted to inflate trade with Tibet, but never succeed till 1904.[1] Looking at the Soviet advance towards India, British authorities occupied Tibet and signed the Lhasa Convention with Tibetan government that restricted the entry of the governmental representative of other foreign states.[2] The expansionist British Empire later in 1914 signed Shimla accord with Tibetan government which extended the British authority over the Southern Tibet while the "Outer Tibet" remained as the independent state.[3] The boundary between the British India and Tibet *vis-a-vis* China has been clearly marked which later known as McMahon line. The Chinese government remained silent at that time but later refused to recognize the accord and the demarcation of boundary and termed the treaty as illegal.[4] The burden of the colonial legacy is still visible in the India-China relation even after over sixty years of independence, though both the nations try to resolve the issue.

While the British policies towards China had been critical, the attitude of Indian leadership had been pro-China during the pre-independence era. Though Indian leadership was not officially controlling the foreign policy of colonial India, the resolution of the Indian National Congress mostly encouraged the Chinese freedom movement and its stand against the colonial power.[5] After the independence, India tried to maintain friendly relation with China. In this background, the section one of the fifth chapter discuss the attitude of Indian parliament on India's China policy during the period of friendship and cooperation. Divided into further sub-sections, this section analyzes the attitude of various political parties and the attitude of Indian parliament as a whole on the important issues of India-China relations such as the Chinese freedom movement, China's gain of independence, the Korean crisis, China's admission into United Nations, and the Panchsheel agreement.

The attitude of Indian Parliament on China's freedom Struggle

After the independence, India was more concerned about its administrative settlement and resolving internal problems hence did not pay much attention towards the world environment. In the post-independent India, China was not figured for a short time in the debates and discussions of the Indian Parliament, the workshop of India's foreign policies. In December 4, 1947 participating in the parliamentary (Constituent Assembly (legislative) as it was called) debate, parliamentarian Brajeshwar Prasad of ruling congress party asked the government to work out for a joint plain to drive out imperialism from China as India and China shared ideological, cultural, religious, ethnical, philosophical and political similarity. He further stated" India and China are destined to be leaders of Asia. Joined together they will be a force to be reckoned with".[6] In reply External Affairs Minister and Prime Minister Jawaharlal Nehru clarified that China had not disclosed its position so far, hence India should not interfere in China's internal matters as it might have negative consequences on Sino-Indian relationship.[7]

Similarly the year 1948 had been of low profile for the Chinese issues in the Parliament. Though the number of debates had been limited, still some vibrant and important questions were raised at the constituent assembly (legislative) on China. H.V. Kamath (Congress) while arguing for greater alignment with USSR and China during parliamentary debates stated that ".... I think it is high time for an alliance of USSR, China and India, the three great countries of Asia which will lead us towards the goal of liberty, equality and fraternity for the whole world"[8] . But Nehru stating his disagreement with the argument vowed for India's non-involvement policy and argued to maintain the neutrality between the blocks for India's own growth.[9]

China's Gain of Independence and reaction of Indian Parliament

The year of 1949 was one of the most important periods in the India-China relations. China got independence in this year by defeating the Kuomintang (KMT) regime through armed revolution on October 1, 1949. During this period, China remained the most debatable topic in the Indian Parliament. India was the second non-communist country to recognize Peoples Republic of China (PRC) within two months of its independence on December 30, 1949.[10]

Referring to India's reorganization President Rajendra Prasad in his first address to the Indian Parliament on January 31, 1950 expressed greater cooperation with China by extending diplomatic exchanges. He also vowed for continuation of friendly relations between the two countries that had been maintained for centuries for the peaceful Asia.[11]

Debating on India's reorganization Prime Minister Jawaharlal Nehru stated in the Parliament on March 17, 1950 that:

> *"It was not a question of disproving or approving it was a question of reorganizing a major event in history, of appreciating it and dealing with it. When it was clear that the new Chinese government was in possession of practically the entire mainland of China, when it was quite clear there was no force which was likely to support it or push it away, we offered reorganization to this new government and suggested that we might exchange diplomatic missions."*[12]

He further explained

> *"It affects us because we are in Asia; it affects us because we are in a strategic part of Asia. Set in the centre of the Indian ocean with intimate connections.... with western Asia, with south East Asia and Far Eastern Asia. We could not ignore it even if we would and we do not want to ignore it."*[13]

Extending India's backing on China's recognition K.M. Panikkar was appointed as the first Indian Ambassador to China on April 1, 1950. It opened a new chapter on the India-China relations. However, a section of political leadership of India, especially Deputy Prime Minister Patel wanted to delay India's recognition proposal and requested Nehru to wait and study the attitude of the important powers before officially reorganize the PRC. But Nehru as well as the overall public opinion of India was in favor of early recognition.[14] Nehru believed that the early taken steps would certainly strengthen the India-China ties. Despite this Chinese leadership was not happy on India's non-aligned aspects of freedom movement and branded

India as the "stooge of western imperialism" and Nehru as the "imperialist running dog".[15] In his message to Communist Party of India (CPI) on 19 October 1949, Mao Zedong appealed to the Indian people to throw out the "yoke of imperialism" with the help of CPI.[16] This dynamic development also further erupted parliamentary debates and discussions.

Korean Crisis and India-China Relationship

When the India-China diplomatic relations was at its pick, the Korean crisis has broke out in the Korean Peninsula. Communist backed North Korea and attacked the South Korea on June 25, 1950 which forced the United Nations to send the international force to drive out North Korean occupation. China joined the war in October 1950 against UN force to protect North Korea which turned the course of Korean War.[17] At this juncture, an emergency session of the Parliament was convened to discuss on the crisis and decide India's stand on July 31, 1950. In his address to the special session, President Dr. Rajendra Prasad said that Indian had requested the Soviet and American authorities to disassociate themselves from the Korean crisis and nullify the international involvement over their bilateral disputes. He also appealed to the world communities to break the dead lock in the United Nations Security Council (UNSC) over the admission of the People's Republic of China (PRC), so that the present international tension might be eased and the way opened for a solution for the Korean problem by discussion in the UNSC.[18]

Later, answering to the parliamentary debate on Korean issues, on August 3, 1950, Nehru maintained that "after having recognized the new regime, it would have been exceedingly unreasonable not to accept the logical consequences thereof". He further added, "Ever since we recognized the new People's Government of China, it naturally followed the consequence of such recognition should come… It is none of our business to like or dislike governments, though we can do so of course…" briefing his views on China's admission into the United Nations he said, "… as a result of China not being admitted into the United Nations, and the representative of the old Kuomintang regime being there, the House knows that the USSR and some of their friendly countries, more or less walked out of various organs of the United Nations, more essentially from the Security Council."[19] The debate in the Parliament on China's entry into Security Council had been explanatory rather than critical. Largely the members of the Parliament were in support of the government stand on the issue and there was a feeling that China would have to be recognized by all nations sooner or later.

India's support to China's Admission into United Nations

Though India is struggling to obtain a permanent membership at the UNSC at present and the Chinese wall seems to be the biggest obstacle in its way, in past India was one of the front line advocates of the Chinese admission into UNSC. While most of the western countries including US opposed China's entry, India was one of the first Asian countries to sponsor the Soviet backed resolution in the Security Council to replace the Kumintang representative with China (PRC).[20] Both within and outside the Parliament most of the political parties and leaders supported the Government of India's stand with Chinese aspiration. When the Chinese aspiration was in pace, the Korean crisis also emerged at the same time. India believed that China's entry into the UN would bring stability to the region and promote world peace as the Soviet Union had been exceeding itself out of UNSC. India also rejected the American proposal to recognize Taiwan. At the beginning India openly branded North Korea as an aggressor, and at the same time criticized UN forces for the crossing of the 38th parallel and supported the Chinese involvement in the Korean war. [21]

Briefing the crisis on August 03, 1950 Prime Minister Nehru said in the Parliament that, India supported the admission of the China into the Security Council as it might bring some solution to the Korean crisis. In another parliamentary debate on December 06, 1950, Nehru again defended his government's stand to support China's admission into United Nation Security Council. Defending India's opposition to the UN resolution, he informed the house that China's stand against the UN forces was logical as he saw the crossing of the 38th parallel by US led UN forces was a threat to its national security.[22] Clarifying further he stated:

> *"We had perhaps rather special responsibility with regard to China, because we were one of the very few countries represented there, and we were the only country, apart from the countries of the Soviet bloc, which could find out... what the reactions of the Chinese Government were to developing events... I cannot conceive of a peaceful solution in the Far-East... even if there is war, any solution after the war, which does not take fully into consideration of this great country of China with regard to those, problems"*[23]

Answering to a parliamentary debate Nehru once again defended India's support to China's UNSC membership bid and said to the house that it might be an important factor to avoid the ongoing crisis. In his own words he said at the Parliament that:

"The House is aware that for over a year, we have been firmly of the opinion that the People's Government of China should be brought to the United Nations. This, according to us, was not only a recognition of a patent fact but was a necessary consequence of the whole scheme of the United Nations organization indeed, it may be said that if this unfortunate error of keeping out the new China from the UN had not been committed, much of the trouble that has subsequently occurred might have been avoided."[24]

Indian Parliament had been active on the Chinese issues during the Korean issues and China's UN membership. While there were some disagreements among the members, most of the members supported government of India's decision to support China's UN membership. India has been advocating China's admission into United Nations for years till October 25, 1971 when China was formally accepted by the UN, despite China's attack during 1962 India-China war. Indira Gandhi for example openly supported China's aspiration on April 12, 1967 when she told:

"As you know we have always stood for China's admission. And we did not change our policy even when China was against us and fought us and took some of our territory, because we believe that it is good for any large nation to be isolated or concerned. Again it was a question of facing the reality of the situation. The question was not, do we like or not, will China be friend to India or not. The fact was that China was there. And how can you just say it is not there. I think it is better for it to be in a position where it can act with people or listen to other people's view points, rather than form a remote corner which is cut-off from the rest of the world."[25]

Indian parliament on the Panchsheel Agreement

Four year after the Chinese incursion into Tibet, India and China signed the historic "Agreement on Trade and Intercourse between the Tibet Region of China and India", which, in its preamble enunciate five principles of peaceful coexistence, popularly known as *"Panchsheel"*. The treaty was signed by N. Raghavan, Indian Ambassador to China and Chang Han-fu, Deputy Foreign Minister of China on April 29, 1954. The preamble of the treaty comprised of five important principles that eventually became the corner stone of India's China policy.[26] The five principles are:

1. Mutual respect for each other's territorial integrity and sovereignty;
2. Mutual non-aggression;

3. Mutual non-interference in each other's internal affairs;
4. Equality and mutual benefit: and
5. Peaceful coexistence. [27]

Apart for the preamble the body of the treaty contains five articles that have been explained briefly below:

1. China to establish trade agencies at New Delhi, Calcutta and Kalimpong, on the other hand, India got rights to establish its trade agencies at Yatung, Gyantse, and Gartok. The trade agencies of both the countries are allowed to enjoy the traditional status, freedom and privileges to conduct their business and granted immunity from arrest and deportation. (Article 1)
2. Both the countries agree to allot three specified market places on each side for trade as per the customary practice. While China agrees to specify Yatung, Gyantse and Phari as markets for Indian traders, India allotted three markets at Kalimpong, Siliguri and Calcutta for trade of Chinese items. Both India and China also agree to identify the markets for common trade. (Article 2)
3. Both the Parties agree to allow pilgrimages to visit holy places of both the countries. While Indian pilgrimages are allowed to visit Kang Rimpoche (Kailash) and MavamTse (Mansarowar) in the Tibet region of China, Pilgrims from the Tibet region of China are allowed to visit Banaras, Sarnath, Gaya and Sanchi in India in accordance with custom. (Article 3)
4. India and China also agreed to open passes like Shipki La Pass, Mana Pass, Niti Pass, Kungri Bingri Pass, Dana Pass, and Lipu Lekh Pass for traders and pilgrimages. (Article 4)
5. Finally, Other than the traders and pilgrimages, all diplomatic personnel, officials and nations of the two countries shall hold passports issued by their own respective countries and visas by the other party to travel each other's territories.(Article 5) [28]

Though the agreement helped to improve India's bilateral relation with China, for many scholars it was a major setback for India's over all foreign and strategic policy. The treaty in no way had served India's interest on Tibet, rather surrendered India's traditional rights and interests on Tibet before China. In addition to this, mutual agreed notes had been exchanged that further abandoned India's decades long stand on Tibet. Some of the important provisions of the text of notes that hampered India's interests are:

1. India will withdraw its military escort entirely from Yatung and Gyantse in the Tibet region of China within six months. (Article 1)
2. Post, telegraph and public telephone services managed by India in Tibet will also be handed over to China at a reasonable price. (Article 2)
3. India will also hand over its twelve rest-houses at the Tibet China at a reasonable price. (Article 3)
4. Indian government has to lease the lands it holds at Tibet by its trade agencies from China. So do the Chinese traders in India. (Article 4)
5. India will return all the lands used or occupied at the Tibet other than the lands within its Trade Agency compound wall at Yatung to China. (Article 5) [29]

Some scholars believed that Nehru's decision to hand over its British inherited rights over Tibet was an attempt to get rid of the colonial legacy, including colonial occupation on foreign territories like Tibet. But, more than this, it shows India's reluctant attitude to strengthened bilateral relation with China.[30] As per the Nehru's argument, the colonial legacy and the 'irritation left by imperialism' may endanger regional peace and *Panchsheel* is "an effort to find a peaceful method of solving irritations directly between the two great neighbors."[31] However, for many it was the greatest blunder of post-independent India and was the primary cause of Chinese incursion of Aksai Chin on 1962.[32] This treaty directly acknowledged Chinese sovereignty over Tibet as the title of the agreement itself states Tibet as the "Tibet Region of China and India". By the treaty, India had withdrawn its military escorts and bases from the Tibet besides surrendering communication links and services.

Despite heavy sacrifices by India, China had not offered anything in return except betrayal during 1962 war. India had been already running the trade agencies at Yatung, Gyantse, and Gartok since decades, where as China had no such consulates in India. Therefore allowing India to establish the trade agencies in Tibet region did not make sense. Secondly, surrendering the communication services and other facilities restricted the possible means of communication with Tibet and the source of information about Chinese activities in Tibet. Thirdly, withdrawal of Indian armed escorts from Tibet raised the risk of Chinese incursion into India. Finally and most importantly, fixing the term of the "agreement of peaceful coexistence" for eight years and putting the condition for the renewal of the agreement with the will of the both side "if they needed". As a result the agreement got expired after eight years from the date of signing by 1962. These eight years were enough to settle the Tibet issue and China did not show its interest to renew the agreement. Since the agreement came to an end by 1962, the five principles of "peaceful coexistence" did not make any sense for Chinese authority when they attacked India in 1962.[33]

However, by signing the treaty and bringing China into the fold of the principle of "Panchsheel" India believed that it would permanently resolve the border disputes with China. Moreover Nehru assumed that the five principles of peaceful coexistence would automatically reduce most of the conflicts and promote world peace. Highlighting the significance of the agreement, Jawaharlal Nehru on May 15, 1954 stated in the Parliament that:

> *"the major thing about the agreement to which I would like to draw the attention of the house is the preamble, the principles which were to Sino-Indian relation were: Mutual respect for each other's territorial integrity and sovereignty; Mutual non-aggression; Mutual non-interference in each other's internal affairs; Equality and mutual benefit: and Peaceful coexistence".*[34]

Nehru believed that these principles, if applied, would eventually resolve all existing disputes between India and China would be the significant mile-stone in the Sino-Indian relationship. Hence, stating the wider implications of these five principles of peaceful coexistence he further explained:

> *"It is a matter of importance to us as well as to China that these two countries which have now about 1,800 miles of frontier, should live in terms of peace and friendliness and should respect each other's sovereignty and integrity, should agree not to interfere with each other in any way and, in fact, though it is not formally stated as such, but practically speaking, not committing aggression on each other. By this agreement, we ensure to a very large extent peace in a certain area of Asia. I would earnestly wish that the area of peace could be spread over the rest of Asia and indeed over the rest of the world"*[35].

In addition he stated that the treaty was merely a "reorganization of the existing situation in Tibet" which had been claimed by the Chinese authorities for decades. To defend India's reorganization of Tibet as "the Tibet region of China" Nehru said that no country had ever challenged the Chinese sovereignty or suzerainty over Tibet not even the Great Britain, though it had always stood for greater autonomy for the Himalayan region. In his own words:

> *"... so far as Tibet is concerned, it is a recognition of the existing situation there. In fact, that situation had been recognized by us two or three years ago. Some criticism has been made that this is a recognition of Chinese sovereignty over Tibet. Apart from that fact, I am not aware of any time during the last hundred years when Chinese sovereignty or if you like suzerainty was challenged by any outside country and all during this period whether China was weak or strong and whatever the Government of China was, China always maintained this claim to the sovereignty."*[36]

However, he acknowledged that, "Recent events made some........ factual changes because a strong Chinese state was against the practical evidence of exercising that sovereignty". He also clarified that India's attitude towards the Tibet issue vis-à-vis *Panchsheel* is based on the "historical and practical" policies and not recognized anything new.[37]

The overall attitude of the Parliament towards *Panchsheel* was favorable and supportive during and after Nehru's briefings, though the nation knew about the price of the treaty that India had paid to buy the peace and cooperation with China. The reason might be that, both the largest and dominant parties of the Parliament- the Indian National Congress (INC) and the Communist Party of China (CPI) had supported the treaty and the size of other parties were so small that it didn't make significant voice against the treaty during the parliamentary debate. However, members of the Praja Socialist Party (PSP) and Hindu Mahasabha (HM) along with some independent candidates had opposed Nehru's statement and the treaty.

Initiating the attack against the treaty, Acharya Kripalini (PSP) stated that signing the treaty was a great loss to the interest of India and was an attempt of blind friendship with China. Questioning the validity of the age old Chinese suzerainty over Tibet, he argued that the claim was antiquated and theoretical. The claim, he said, had never exercised or rarely exercised and that also hypothetically, hence not valid in the present scenario. He further argued that, culturally Tibet was more proximate with India than China, at least in the modern communist China and used to the buffer state between India and China. Highlighting the significance of buffer state in international politics he said, "In international politics, when a buffer state is abolished by a powerful nation, that nation is considered to have aggressive designs on its neighbors."[38] He also informed the Parliament about the

Chinese grand strategy towards its neighbors where China had shown large territories of Sikkim and Nepal as Chinese territories in its map.[39] Similarly, V.G. Deshpande (HM) termed Chinese aggression toward Tibet as an attempt to colonize it and criticized India's silence over the issue of Chinese colonization of its immediate neighbor Tibet.[40]

Some independent candidates also raised voice against the treaty during the subsequent Parliamentary debates. Independent candidate like Lanka Sundaram (Independent) for instance, criticized the government of India's attitude towards the Tibetan government. Referring to the earlier assurance to Dalai Lama by New Delhi, he heavily condemned the Indian government's silence during the annexation of Tibet by Chinese communist government, despite India's assurance to Dalai Lama for help.[41]

While the oppositions criticized the "Panchsheel Treaty" and congress government for its weak stand towards Tibet issue, the members of the ruling congress party largely supported the treaty. Joachim Alva (INC) for instance, hailed the treaty and assumed that this treaty would boost the India-China relationship and help to resolve the border issues. He also asked the government to initiate a mutual defense pact with China and Soviet Union for the greater pace of Asia.[42] Similarly, Prajeswar Prasad (INC) also praised the treaty and said "I regard this pact as a non-aggression pact in embryo".[43]

However, some of the congress members openly criticized the treaty and Nehru's foreign policies towards China. Members like S.N. Sinha (INC) criticizing India's Tibet policy stated that Tibet had been declared its independence since 1912 and broke its traditional alliance with China thereafter. He also opposed the "treaty of peaceful cooperation" and branded it as the "Chinese trap". He also warned the government about the future Chinese threat and asked the government to review its policy towards Tibet.[44] Similarly, Congress parliamentarian P.D. Tandon objected India's attitude towards Chinese aggression on Tibet and felt regretted about it.[45]

In reply, Prime Minister Nehru said that the treaty was a significant achievement of India in strengthening ties with China and it was the best thing that India had ever done since independence. The treaty, he predicted would bring peace to Asia and the world. In repldy to India's weakness in accepting China's sovereignty over Tibet he said, India could not follow the British policy of possessing extra-territorial rights over Tibet. Sooner or later it had to give up those rights. He also slammed the criticism over the withdrawal of Indian troops from Tibet. In its deference he argued that, India had no right to station its troops in another independent country.

The treaties and military agreements that British India had signed was a product of British imperialism that should not be continued with the changing environment.[46] But for many parliamentarians these justifications didn't satisfy. Time and again they stood against the treaty and raised voice against the treaty.

On May 21, 1954, the sixth session of the Parliament was adjourned and so did the debate on "Agreement on Trade and Intercourse between the Tibet Region of China and India". The general feeling about the treaty was quite positive and the voice of media was favorable to the treaty. The positive atmosphere after the treaty paved the way for the state visit of Chou En-Lai, the Prime Minister of China to India on June 1954. During his visit the China-India joint statement was published where both the countries expressed their desire to uphold peace and friendship with each other emphasizing peaceful development of both the countries.[47]

The monsoon session of the Parliament was started on August 23, 1954. From the very opening the focus of the debate was shifted to issues related to China. Briefing the Joint Agreement, Nehru expressed his satisfaction towards the statement in the Parliament. On August 25, 1954 he stated in the Parliament the commitment of both the countries to adhere to collective peace and avoid conflicts. While his view was welcomed by most of the parliamentarians, some of them objected to the Government of India's attitude towards the Tibet vis-à-vis Panchsheel agreement.

During the parliamentary debate on September 30, 1954, Acharya Kripalilani (PSP) criticized the government on its failure to contain the Chinese march up to the Indian borders and the demolition of the buffer state of Tibet. Similarly, another PSP leader Ashok Mehta regretted on the government of India's for its acceptance of Panchsheel which addressed Tibet as "Tibet region of China". He also warned the government about the consequences of this agreement.[48] N.C. Chatterjee of Akhil Bharatiya Hindu Mahasabha (ABHM) opposed the Panchsheel Agreement as he believed that China had dismissed the precondition for peaceful coexistence by occupying the Tibet. He also perceived that India was moving towards the Sino-Russia block by making a chain military base at North Korea, Sinkiang and Tibet, which he felt unfortunate.[49] P.N. Raj Bhoj of Scheduled Case Federation (SCF) in condemning India's China policy argued that the government's inaction against the Chinese aggression in Tibet might encourage China to invade Nepal and Kashmir in future.[50]

Apart for the opposition members, a section of the congress members also cautioned the government about the Chinese intension through the agreement. Ila Pal Chowdhury, for instance blamed the government for its weak approach towards the Tibet and Formosa issues.[51] Similarly, K. Raghuramaiah (INC) also requested the government to remain cautioned towards the Chinese aggression against the neighboring states.[52]

In reply Nehru stated that looking at the history of the Tibet, Tibet didn't have any affiliation with India before the arrival of British. Therefore India had no role to play in Tibet issue unless it adopted the aggressive policy and he believed that it would be foolish to stand against the "great countries like China". He also defended the agreement and emphasized for friendly relationship with China.[53]

On September 30, 1954 the Monsoon Session of the Parliament ended and Nehru made the return visit to China in October 1954. After the reassembling of the Parliament on November 16, issues related China and Nehru's state visit to China once again dominated major part of the parliamentary debates. Meanwhile the Formosa Strait Crisis emerged as the major international crisis and became the flashpoint of discussion in Parliament. The opposition members raised the issues and demanded government's response on the issue. Despite repeated assurance by the government, the oppositions continued to disrupt the Parliament at various occasions.

The visit of Chinese Prime Minister Zhou Enlai in November 1956 and Indian Vice-President S. Radhakrishan's state visit to China on September 1957 in many ways improved the India China relation and subsequently lowered down the state of suspiciousness over Chinese attitude. In the later stage The Parliament also seemed to have somewhat ignored the Chinese issues, though a section of the parliamentarians such as, P.N. Raj Bhoj (AISCF), Illa Pal Chowdhury (INC), Bhakta Darshan (INC), and Kripalini had been periodically raised their concern on Tibet and Panchsheel for quite long time.

Conclusion

Since centuries, relationship between India and China was warm and friendly. The cultural and economic exchanges between the two Asian giants date back to ancient times. Since Fourth Century, several Chinese pilgrims namely, Faxian and Xuanzang visited India to learn Buddhism through the ancient Silk Road which was the major trade route between India and China in the ancient time. Even during the period of colonialism, Indian leadership was critical towards the ill attitude of British towards China and encouraged the Chinese freedom struggle against the colonial power. After the independence, India openly supported the ongoing freedom movement of China and became the second non-communist state to recognize the People's Republic of China.

During this period, the political leadership across the party line supported the Chinese freedom movement and the attitude of the parliament was warm and sympathetic towards China, though comparably lesser number of debates had been raised in the Parliament on issues related to China. Even, some members of the Parliament asked the government to assist China in their freedom struggle with the help of Russia, which was rejected by the Indian government. During the Korean Crisis, the parliament and the government opposed the internalization of Korean Crisis and involvement of international troops which indirectly supported the Chinese stand on the crisis. India and the Indian parliament as a whole also backed the Chinese bid for United Nations, though a section of parliamentarians opposed the move in the latter period.

However, the 1954 'India China Agreement on Tibet' eventually became the center of debate in the parliament and came under strong attack by the opposition. The parliament for the first time also witnessed massive furor in the parliament on this issue. While Nehru was justifying his decision for the abandonment of India's rights over Tibet, which he believed as the product of colonial legacy, most of the opposition parties, such as Praja Socialist Party and Hindu Mahasabha took strong exception to this argument. However, the parliament as a whole supported the government of India's decision to have greater cooperation with China through the agreement. Therefore, by analyzing the debates and the discussions of the Indian parliament, it can be stated that, the India parliament was quite supportive towards the issue related to China during this period.

Notes

1. B.R. Deepak, India and China 1904-2004: A Century of Peace and Conflict (New Delhi: Manak Publication, 2005) 2-4.
2. Neville Maxwell, India's China War (Dehradun: Natraj Publishers, 2010) 41.
3. Neville Maxwell, "The Pre-history of the Sino-Indian Border Dispute: A Note", Mainstream, Vol. XLIX, No. 8, February 12, 2011.
4. Alastair I. Johnston, Robert S. Ross, New Directions in the Study of China's Foreign Policy, (Stanford: Stanford University Press, 2006) 104; also see, Byron N. Tzou, China and International Law: The Boundary Disputes (New York: Praeger Publishers, 1990) 106.
5. Bidanda M. Chengappa, India-China relations: Post Conflict Phase to Post Cold War Period (New Delhi: A.P.H. Pub. Corp., 2004) 1-2; also see, Tan Chung,

Across the Himalayan Gap: An Indian Quest for Understanding China (New Delhi: Gyan Publishing House, 1998) 20.

6. *Constituent Assembly (Legislative) Debate*, Vol. 2-3, 1947, p. 1255.
7. *Ibid.*, 1263.
8. *Ibid.*, Vol. 3, 1948, p. 1757.
9. *Ibid.*, p. 1769.
10. K.R. Gupta and Vatsala Shukla, Foreign Policy of India (New Delhi: Atlantic Publishers, 2009) 529.
11. See Parliamentary Debates, Vol. 1, 1950, p. 22.
12. *Parliamentary Debates*, Vol.3, Part-II, March 17, 1950, 1699.
13. *Ibid.*, 1696-97.
14. See Letter of Deputy Premier Patel to Nehru on November 3, 1949 printed at R.K. Jain(ed.), China South Asia Relations 1947-1980, Vol. 1, India (New Delhi: Radiant Publications, 1981) 13-14.
15. D. R. Sar Desai, Indian Foreign Policy in Cambodia, Laos, and Vietnam, 1947-1964 (Barkely: University of California Press, 1968) 22; also see, John Rowland, A History of Sino-Indian Relations: Hostile Coexistence (Princeton, NJ: D. Van Nostrand, 1967) 82.
16. Mao-Tse-tung Appeal Massage to Communist Party of India (CPI), as printed at R.K. Jain(ed.), China South Asia Relations 1947-1980, Vol. 1 (India) (New Delhi: Radiant Publications, 1981) 10.
17. Paul M. Edwards, The Korean War (Westport: Greenwood Publishing Group, 2006) xx.
18. Lok Sabha Debate, July 31, 1950, Col. 10.
19. Lok Sabha Debate, July 31, 1950, Cols. 225-226.
20. Shalendra D. Sharma, China and India in the Age of Globalization (Cambridge: Cambridge University Press, 2009) 182.
21. Arndt Michael, India's Foreign Policy and Regional Multilateralism (Hampshire: Palgrave Macmillan, 2013) 36-37 ; see also, N. Jayapalan, Foreign Policy In India (New Delhi: Atlantic Publishers, 2001) 154.
22. Lok Sabha Debate, August 03, 1950, cc. 218-228.
23. Lok Sabha Debate, December 06, 1950, Col. 1262.
24. Lok Sabha Debate, February 12, 1951, Col. 2699.
25. Speech at the Presentation to U Thant of the first Nehru award for International Understanding, New Delhi, April 12, 1967, as stated in S.K. Sethi, "India and the UN: the Indira Gandhi Era". In United Nations India And The New World Order, edited by Saroj K. Patnaik, Jaya KrushnaBaral, and Jagdish Prasad Sharma (New Delhi: Mittal Publications, 2004) 94-95.
26. Claude Arpi, Born in Sin: The Panchsheel Agreement: The Sacrifice of Tibet (New Delhi: Mittal Publications, 2004) 111.
27. *Ibid,* 115.
28. A copy of the agreement can be seen at, Swaran Singh, "Three Agreements and Five Principles between India and China", in Across the Himalayan Gap: A

Chinese Quest for Understanding India, edited by Tan Chung, Zhang Minqiu and Ravni Thakur (New Delhi:Gyan Publishing House,1998) 506-08.

29. Swaran Singh (1998) 506-08.
30. T.N. Kaul, Diplomacy in Peace and War (New Delhi: Vikas Publishers, 1978) 103-04.
31. As quoted in Claude Arpi, Born in Sin: The Panchsheel Agreement: The Sacrifice of Tibet (New Delhi: Mittal Publications, 2004) 113.
32. Many scholars, bureaucrats and oppositions and even the MP's of the ruling congress party have criticized Nehru's stand and Panchsheel. For instance see, Claude Arpi, Born in Sin: The Panchsheel Agreement: The Sacrifice of Tibet (New Delhi: Mittal Publications, 2004) 111-15; M. L. Sali, India-China Border Dispute: A Case Study of the Eastern Sector (New Delhi: APH Publishing, 1998) 77-78 ; Sankar Ghose , Jawaharlal Nehru: A Biography, Allied Publishers, 1993) 264; Arun Kumar Banerji, "Borders", in Jayanta Kumar Ray, Aspects of India's International Relations, 1700 to 2000: South Asia and the World (New Delhi: Pearson Education India, 2007) 222.

33 Claude Arpi, 1962 and the McMahon Line Saga (Atlanta: Lancer Publishers, 2013) 147.

34. Lok Sabha debates, Vol. 5, 1954 col. 1954.
35. *Ibid.*, Cols. 7496.
36. Lok Sabha Debate, Vol. 3, 1954, Col. 7609.
37. *Ibid.*, Vol. 5, Cols. 7497.
38. *Lok Sabha Debate*, Vol. 5, Col.7609.
39. *Ibid.*, Cols. 7547-48.
40. *Ibid.*, Cols. 7602-08.
41. *Ibid.*, Cols. 7569-70.
42. *Ibid.*, Col. 7623.
43. *Ibid.*, Col. 7609.
44. *Ibid.*, Cols. 7556-65.
45. *Ibid.*, Cols. 7631-34.

46 *Ibid.*, Cols. 7569-70.

47. Lok Sabha Debates, Vol. 6, 1954, Cols. 8.
48. Lok Sabha Debates, Vol. 7, 1954, Cols. 3835.
49. *Ibid.*, Cols. 3758-59.
50. *Ibid.*, Cols. 3792-93.
51. *Ibid.*, Col. 320.
52. *Ibid.*
53. *Ibid.*, Cols. 3881-83.

Chapter - 5

Parliament and the Making of India's China Policy during the Era of Direct Confrontation 1959 to 1962

India and China had been sharing friendly and cooperative relationship with each other since ancient time. The cultural and economic exchanges between the two Asian giants date back to ancient times. This relationship had developed further after the independence of both the countries during late 1950s. The period between post-independence to 1957, known as the "Period of Panchsheel" is perhaps the golden age of India China relationship. India's full support to China's freedom movement and its reorganisation, its unconditional support to China's admission into UN, support to China's stand on Korean crisis, annexation of Tibet and India's policies towards Formosa crisis are some of the events on which India and China shared similar thoughts. However, this momentum did not last long. The emergence of Tibetan uprising in 1959 and the Chinese allegation of Indian involvement in the armed struggle put these two neighbours apart. India's decision to grant political asylum to Tibetan spiritual leader Dalai Lama and its permission to run a 'Tibetan Governmental in Exile' in the Indian soil further increased the Chinese suspicion towards New Delhi. The century old friendly relation between India and China started detonating after Chinese claim of Indian territories and decline to recognise the McMahan line as the border between India and China. This unsettled frontier eventually led to series of armed clashes and subsequently resulted in to an all-out war between India and China in 1962.

In this background, this chapter discusses the attitude of Indian Parliament on India's China policy during the 'Era of Sino-Indian Confrontation (1959-75)', which is one of the important turning points of India-China relationship and Asian political order as a whole. Divided into further sections, this Chapter analyses the stand of various political parties and the attitude of Indian Parliament as a whole on the important issues of India-China relations between 1959 and 1975.

India-China Relations before Tibetan Crisis

Being the oldest civilizations, the bilateral relationship between India and China are believed to be dating back to ancient times. Even before the establishment of any kind of political relations, both the countries enjoyed wide range of economic and cultural relations. A trade relation between India and China was flourishing through the 'Silk Road' which eventually became the vital link of Sino-Indian cultural exchanges. Though the major contact between the ancient civilizations was initiated after the spread of Buddhism in China, historians believe that there was some kind of relation or the other between the two entities for centuries. Perhaps due to the historical links, the reference of China can be found in the Indian epic of the Mahabharata (3139 BC) and in Kautilya's Arthasastra.[1] However, the major contacts between India and China were established between first and tenth century mainly, due to the spread of Buddhism into China. During the Ming ti reign, two Indian Buddhist monks – Kasyapa Matanga and Dharmaratna arrived in China in 65 A.D and translated five Buddhist texts into Chinese.[2] Similarly, saint Batuo (464-495 AD)–the founder of the Shaolin Monastery and Bodhidharma founder of Chan/Zen Buddhism travelled to China to spread the message of Buddhism in China. On the other hand, many Chinese monks, such as Fa Xian (407 A.D.), Xuanzang (602-664AD), Hiuen-Tsiang (603-664 AD), Xuan Zang (633 to 643 A.D.), I Ching (635-713AD) and Yi Qing (673-695 A.D.) visited India to learn Buddhism and many of them studied at Nalanda University. This era of religious interaction, which is called as the golden period of Buddhist influence in China, lasted for eight centuries from the 5th Century to 12th Century A.D.[3]

Apart from the Silk Road Corridor, India and China also shared the maritime link for trade and commerce. General Zheng He from the Ming dynasty, for instance, sailed through Indian Ocean and arrived in Cochin and Calicut in the early Fifteenth Century AD.[4] In the Records of the Grand Historian, Zhang Qian (114 BC) and Sima Qian (145-90 BC) make references to "Shendu", which may have been referring to the Indus Valley (the Sindh province in modern Pakistan), originally known as "Sindhu" in Sanskrit. Fa xian, was the first one from China to visit India as a pilgrim in 407 AD, during the reign of Chandragupta II.[5]

Beginning of India–China Political Relations

Though India and China had been sharing centuries-old relationship, there was hardly any political contact between the two neighbours till the mid-eighteenth century, mostly, due to the physical barrier of high Himalayas on one hand and the far flung sea routes on the other. The earliest known appearance of political factor in Indo–China relations was the Sino-Sikh War of 1841. The Sikh Confederacy, which was basically confined to Punjab region started military expedition into adjourning states. The Sikh army invaded Tibet and overran parts of Western Tibet in 1841. Chinese forces retaliated and defeated the Sikh army in December 1841 forcing them to withdraw from Tibet, and in turn entered Ladakh and besieged Leh. The Sikh Army further attacked the Chinese force and defeated them. However, this process of retaliation and counter retaliation came to an end, as neither side wanted to continue the conflict due to their political compulsion. While the Sikhs embroiled with British that would lead up to the first Anglo-Sikh War, the Chinese was in the midst of the First Opium War with the British. Hence, the Sikhs and Chinese signed the 'Treaty of Chushul' in September 1842 agreeing to maintain the status quo and not to attack each other's frontiers. Thus, Indo-China relations in the modern period appear to have begun with an armed conflict even before proper political or diplomatic relations were established.[6]

India-China Relations during the Colonial Era

After colonizing India, British expansionism searched for a new territory to expand its trade into neighbouring states. As a result the East India Company repeatedly attempted to inflate trade with Tibet, but never succeeded till 1904.[7] Following the weakening of Chinese empire at the end of Eighteenth Century,[8] the British India invaded Tibet in 1904 to expand their trade activities in to Tibet and signed the 'Treaty of Lhasa' with Tibetan authorities on July 30, 1904, which barred the Tibetan authority to establish any bilateral relation with foreign countries and facilitate hassle free trade with British India.[9] The Anglo-Chinese Convention of 1906 has further extended British patronage towards Tibet.[10] With the extensive trade relation and indirect external administration, the British Indian government was enjoying an unparallel special relation with Lhasa, which continued till their departure from India.[11]

During the ant-colonial movement, the attitude of Indian leadership was largely sympathetic on Brutish India's negative attitude towards China. When the anti-imperialistic revolution was getting momentum, several

Indian leaders, such as Rabindranath Tagore (1924), Jawaharlal Nehru (1939) and Dr. S. Radhakrishnan (1941) visited China and highlighted the importance of Sino-Indian friendship. Nehru also stated India's solidarity towards the Chinese people during the Sino-Japanese War.[12]

During the Chinese freedom struggle, several rallies and agitations were conducted in India in support of Chinese freedom struggle, and Indian political leadership, media and Indian public at large supported and showed their solidarity towards the People's Liberation War.[13] Even before India independence, the Indian National Congress under the leadership of Nehru sent a medical team to China to assist the wounded soldiers of Chinese freedom struggle, and the heroic story of Dr. Kotnis and the Indian medical team had been admired by the Chinese leadership.[14] After a long struggle, the Mao Zedong Led People's Republic army defeated the Kuomintang regime and declared China an independent nation on October 1, 1949.

India-China Relations in the Post-Independence Era

The year of 1949 was one of the most important periods in the India-China relations. In this year, China got independence by defeating the Kuomintang (KMT) regime through armed revolution on October 1, 1949. India became the second non-communist country to recognise People's Republic of China (PRC) within two months of its independence on December 30, 1949[15] and established the diplomatic relation with PRC on April 1, 1950.

Following the Korean Crisis, India reversed its previous policy and supported China's stand and opposed the US led resolution to brand China as an aggressor. [16] India even went further and advocated UNSC membership to People's Republic of China[17] and refused to attend the San Francisco Conference as China was not invited to the meeting. [18] Furthermore, India always took modest stand to facilitate Chinese interest and introduced a resolution in UN General Assembly in 1953 to discuss the question on Prisoner of war to accommodate the Chinese viewpoints. The Chinese leaderships had also admired the Indian position and praised Nehru's statesmanship during the Korean crisis.[19]

India-China Relation during the Era of Panchsheel and Hindi-Chini-Bhai-Bhai

Four years after the Chinese incursion into Tibet, India and China signed the historic "Agreement on Trade and Intercourse between the Tibet Region of China and India", which, in its preamble enunciates five principles of peaceful coexistence, popularly known as *"Panchsheel"* on April 29, 1954. The preamble of the treaty comprised of five important principles that eventually became the corner stone of India's China policy.[20] This treaty directly acknowledged Chinese sovereignty over Tibet, as the title of the agreement itself states Tibet as the "Tibet Region of China and India". By the treaty, India had withdrawn its military escorts and bases from the Tibet besides surrendering communication links and services.

Though the agreement helped to improve India's bilateral relation with China, for many experts it was a major setback for India's overall foreign and strategic policy.[21] The treaty in no way had served India's interest on Tibet, rather surrendered India's traditional rights and interests on Tibet before China. In addition to this, mutual agreed notes had been exchanged that further abandoned India's decades long stand on Tibet.[22] For experts, Nehru's decision to hand over its British inherited rights over Tibet was an attempt to get rid of the colonial legacy, including colonial occupation on foreign territories like Tibet. But, more than this, it shows India's commitment to strengthen its bilateral relation with China.[23] However, by signing the treaty and bringing China into the fold of the principle of "Panchsheel" India believed that it would permanently resolve the border disputes with China.

As a symbol of growing Sino-Indian friendship, the Chinese Prime Minister Zhou Enlai visited India in June 1954 and Indian Prime Minister Nehru paid his counter visit to China later in the same year. While both the countries vowed their commitment to the five principles of Panchsheel, China published the map showing the NEFA region as the Chinese territory. During his state visit to China, Nehru raised India's concern towards the Chinese map, which was downplayed by Chinese authority. Zhou Enlai assured Nehru that, those were old maps of KMT Regime and needed to be revised. However, no joint communiqué was issued at the end of his visit, which might have addressed the map issue publicly.[24] India and China signed the Sino-Indian trade agreement in Beijing during Nehru's visit and decided to establish the "Sino-Indian Friendship Associations" in both the countries. During the successive high level diplomatic visits, India-China diplomatic relation touched a new mile stone and the spirit of *"Hindi-Chini-Bhai-Bhai"* (Indians and Chinese are brothers) was at peak. Both the countries vowed to maintain the spirit of friendship and brotherhood and committed to take the age old relationship to a new height.

India facilitated China's inclusion into the Geneva Conference (1954) as well as Afro-Asian Conference (1955), despite the stiff criticism from the third world countries.[25] Following the Bandung conference, Chinese Premiere Zhou Enlai paid a goodwill mission to India for the second time in Nov 1956 and expressed his commitment to strengthen the relationship further. Similarly, Indian Vice-President S. Radhakrishnan paid a counter visit to China in September 1957.[26] Besides these high level visits, India also took several constructive measures to deepen its relationship with China. As a gesture of friendship, India signed the Lhasa protocol on April 1, 1955 and handed over the existing communication services at Lhasa to Chinese government. Similarly, India extended her full support to China over the Formosa (Taiwan) issue and adhered to the 'one China policy'. During this period, which often called 'the era of friendship and brotherhood', both the countries remained committed to strengthen their relation further. However, the Sino-Indian honeymoon did not last long and started shrinking at the end of Bandung Conference, where Zhou did not like India's protagonist attitude and called Nehru an 'arrogant man'. Due to their asymmetrical ideological perceptions and increasing suspicion over the Tibetan crisis, the differences between India and China started widening and led to an all out war in the Himalayan frontiers in1962.

Indian Parliament on Tibetan Uprising of 1959

India China relation was seriously damaged by the incident of militant Tibetan uprising of 1959. The revolt once again brought the age long issue of Chinese sovereignty over Tibet into live. The uniqueness of the revolution was that it was mostly driven by armed militants and carried out by the people against the Chinese authority, while the previous revolutions were mostly unarmed and state sponsored.

Since the annexation, the Chinese government has successfully brought back Tibet into Chinese manifold by signing the "Agreement of the Central People's Government and the Local Government of Tibet on Measures for the Peaceful Liberation of Tibet" with Tibetan government on May 23, 1951.[27] It kept India at bay while signing the treaty, though Indian foot prints had been firmly visible in the Himalayan kingdom since British era. Later, it successfully convinced the Indian government on its sovereignty over Tibet and got its stamp approval by signing the "Panchsheel Agreement" on 1954 which clearly stated Tibet as the "Tibet region of China". While signing the treaty China promised to maintain the status quo of the position of the Dalai Lama and the autonomy of Tibet which was gradually curbed by the Chinese authority and tried to impose the Chinese policies over Tibet. In protest the anti-Chinese revolt erupted on March 10, 1959 on the capital of Tibet Lhasa.[28] The People's Liberation Army used subsequent forces to dismantle the revolution. The cruel and extensive crackdown of the Chinese army forced many Tibetans to cross Indian border and flee into India. Spiritual leader Dalai Lama was also forced to leave Lhasa following the Chinese armed operation. He entered into India on March 31, 1959 and the government of India granted asylum to Dalai Lama and 13,000 other Tibetan refugees.[29]

After the voluntary surrendering of all its traditional rights in Tibet and accepting Chinese suzerainty over Tibet, India hardly got interested to intervene in the so called "internal matters" of China and restricted its stand just as a spectator. On the other hand, Chinese authority was suspicious about India and was constantly alleging its involvement in the Tibetan uprising.[30] Chinese authority criticized India for extending its asylum to Dalai Lama and the other Tibetans and alleged Indian backing in the armed confrontation. However, India denied any involvement and made it clear that its asylum to Tibetan spiritual leader was based on humanitarian ground. Clarifying Chinese allegation on India's political interest and function of the government in exile of Tibet it stated that "Government of India...... did not recognize any separate government of Tibet and hence there is no question of Tibetan government under the Dalai Lama functioning in India".[31] However, this assurance and clarification did not satisfy the Chinese authority and premier Mao Zedong asked the *People's Delay* to criticize India. He himself drafted the article where he termed India as "expansionist" and alleged that India "wants ardently to grab Tibet".[32]

The public opinion in India was very much sympathetic towards the Tibetan people and critical on China's brutality with Tibetans. The Indian media carried out extensive reports on the Tibet and was equally critical against the Chinese army action. Demonstrations and rallies were organized against the Chinese action at various parts of India.

Similarly, in Parliament the Tibetan crisis dominated most of the Parliamentary debates during this time. The Parliament was furious and critical against Chinese policies towards Tibet at large. Most of the political parties except CPI were unanimous against the Chinese brutality and demanded for review of India's China policies vis-à-vis latest Tibetan crisis. On March 16, 1959 debating on foreign affairs matters, Asoka Meheta (PSP) pointed out that India's stand should not be different from the goal of Tibet as India was maintaining special relationship with Tibet for centuries and should be equally cautioned against the Chinese actions. He also criticized Chinese action in Tibet and accused China for the violation of the seven point agreement with China that included the autonomy of Tibet. He asked the Indian government to review its policies of India China friendship and viewed that it should not be achieved at the cost of suppression of Tibet.[33] The Communist Party leader Renu Chakravarti rose in between to reply and strongly condemned Mr. Mehta's words. In reply she stated that if India would interfere in the Tibetan issue, then China, in return might question the issue of Nagaland. She downplayed the international media reports on the situation of the Tibet and claimed that the report was far from reality and had been exaggerated.[34]

This statement created a new wave of criticism and strong furore in the floor of the Parliament. Several parties and members demanded a comprehensive debate on the Tibet crisis in the Parliament and sought urgent statement from the Prime Minister on India's stand over the issue. After a long hue and cry, Prime Minister Nehru presented his view on March 17, 1959 on the recent crisis in Tibet. Acknowledging the situation in Tibet as a difficult one, he stated in the Parliament that, almost all the countries recognized the Chinese suzerainty over Tibet and so did India. In fact, India had clearly recognized China's suzerainty over Tibet in its 1951 agreement with China. "But so far I know, no country had ever recognized the independence of Tibet. We certainly did not; and it was inevitable, therefore for us to recognize the suzerainty … call it sovereignty three things are fine distinctions, and they depend on the power of the state how far it goes." He also believed that the seventeen point agreement was just an agreement of autonomy to Tibet and the recent uprising was the product of "clash of will than, at present, A clash of arms or clash of physical bodies".[35]

During the end of March 1959 the Tibet issue had gone bad to worse, when the fighting between Chinese army shifted from southern regions of Kham and Amdo to Lhasa, the capital of Tibet. Amidst the Chinese attack and mortar shelling Dalai Lama fled to India on March 17, 1959. The massacre by the PLA was extensively covered by Indian Media. As the Tibetan story was published in Indian media, it resulted in strong people uproar in India against Chinese brutality. A similar type of echo also erupted in Indian Parliament following the news of Tibetan revolution. Most of the political parties, except CPI stood united against the Chinese brutality. Amidst the tension, PSP leader Nana Saheb Goray and Jan Sangh leader Atal Bihari Vajpayee presented two Adjournment Motions regarding the Tibetan crisis before the speaker on March 23, 1959. However, both the proposals were put down by speaker M. A. Ayyangar.[36] Still most of the Parliamentarians demanded an intensive debate on Tibet problems. Seeing the uproar, Prime Minister Nehru presented a detail report on the fate of Tibet in Lok Sabha on the same day. In his briefing to the Parliament he said that the situation in Tibet was a matter of concern. He also informed that large number of Tibetan people met the Indian Consulate general and appealed for its interference in the Tibetan matters which India rejected. Terming the recent conflicts as "new development" he stated in the Parliament that India had no intension to interfere in the internal matter of China and vowed for greater friendship with China. However he stated his deep sympathy towards the Tibetan people and the safety of Dalai Lama.[37]

The normal proceedings, of Parliament continued to paralyze due to the tough uproar of conflict in Tibet despite Nehru's statement in the Parliament. Members across the party line criticized the government's stand and demanded further detail discussion on Tibetan crisis. Members like M.R. Masani (Independent), Asoka Mehta (PSP), N.S. Goray (PSP), Frank Anthony (Independent) and C.D. Pande (INC), besides other members continued to clamor for a full discussion, whereas CPI members and some Congress members were in defensive position. Interfering in the discussion, Nehru cautioned the Parliament that: "a general discussion over the events which are happening in another country would be a bad precedent which may have far-reaching consequences".[38] Still the Parliament was continued to be disturbed due to the opposition's uproar.

China's Charges of Indian Involvement in Tibetan Conflict

So far, the debate in India was merely a reaction to the Tibet conflict and the sufferings of the Tibetan people due to the conflict. India did not come under any of the Chinese criticisms directly and China did not link India with the conflict. But, on March 28, 1959 Chinese government in its official communiqué termed the Tibetan uprising as the conflict against imperialism and alleged its base at the Kalimpong, the Indian consulate. By doing so, China indirectly alleged Indian involvement in the conflict. The communiqué also criticized the conduct of debate on Tibetan uprising in Indian Parliament and termed the debate as an attempt to interfere in China's internal matters.[39] After three days on March 31, 1959 another similar propaganda article was published in the state run *People's Daily* where the Indian consulate at Kalimpong was charged as the epicenter of Tibetan conflict.[40] These consecutive statements erupted strong uproar in Indian Parliament.

In Reaction, majority of the political parties, including the ruling Congress party openly criticized the Chinese allegation in the Parliament.

Reflecting the deep anger on the Chinese allegation, Hem Barua (PSP) and Atal Bihari Vajpayee (BJS) gave notice for adjournment motion on China's irresponsible statement about Kalimpong and India's involvement on March 30, 1959. Vajpayee in his argument emphasized for review of India China relations where Tibet could be revived into its past Indian friendly form.[41] Similarly, another Socialist leader Nath Pai (PSP) asked the government to maintain friendship with China but not at the cost of India's friendship with Tibet.[42] Parliamentarian Hem Barua(PSP) and Braj Raj Singh(PSP) and Frank Anthony (Independent) condemned China's criticism on Indian Parliament for discussing China's internal matters like Tibetan issue and called for greater protest against Chinese statement.[43]

The spate of adjournment motions on Chinese aggression on Tibet disappointed the Congress government especially Nehru, who vowed not to interfere in internal matters of China including Tibet. He made it clear that, the government of India's stand on Tibetan uprising was based on two broad objectives: geographical, cultural and religious ties with Tibet and its people; and non-interference in the affairs of Tibet. He also defended his government's decision to accept Chinese suzerainty over Tibet that many believed as a significant reason for the present conflict in Tibet and stated that, almost all the countries had recognized Chinese suzerainty over Tibet. Therefore it was in the interest of India to recognize the same. Explaining the fate of India's special privileges in Tibet Nehru stated that: the extra territorial rights of India over Tibet are "relics of British imperialism, which India did not seek to have in any country in the world, Tibet or any other. It was patent from the strictly practical point of view, even apart from sentiments, that we could not do anything in Tibet either in law, constitutionally or practically".

Answering the question of fixing the responsibility for the outbreak of the conflict, Nehru said: "I cannot say who began it, but it began. Normally, one would say that where it is a question of military might, the Chinese government is much stronger than some kind of local recruits from the Tibetan army". He also rejected the Chinese allegations which stated that 'Kalimpong is center of foreign reactionaries'. Clarifying further, Nehru stated that India had warned the Tibetan students and other activists in Kalimpong not to carry any propaganda or subversive activities from Indian soil and adequate forces had been deployed at each border check post for constant watch. He condemned the Chinese criticism of debating Tibetan issue at the Indian Parliament and firmly upheld the right of the Parliament. With regard to the criticism he stated in the Parliament that:

> *"It is I suppose a little difficult for the people trained in a difficult tradition for a long time to understand the normal ways in which a Parliamentary system of government functions and we should not be over-eager to find fault with somebody who does not agree with us..... it should be made perfectly clear to all concerned that this Parliament is not going to be limited in the exercise of its rights of discussion, saying or action of any thin, by ant extern al or internal authority, whomever it may be.... and whatever I may say, whatever the government may do, may have far reaching consequences".*[44]

Following the Chinese statement in People's Daily, Communist Party of India issued a statement on March 31, 1959 justifying the Chinese statement and emphasized that the Panchsheel guarantees each country to maintain complete neutrality and non-interference in each other's internal matters. Hence, India should not allow its territories to be used for any acts that meant to harm others.[45]

This statement by CPI had stormed another upheaval in the Parliament. Almost all the parties condemned the statement and criticized CPI for its pro-Chinese advocacy. Parliamentarian R.K. Khadilkar of Mazdoor Kisan Party (MKP) introduced an adjournment motion against the statement on April 1, 1959. In his introduction speech he pointed out that, "this statement by the communist party or the allegation of People's Daily, I think violate certain solemn agreements entered into by that great and friendly country with our country". He also believed that by criticizing the Indian Parliament following Nehru's statement at Parliament, China violated the diplomatic privileges. Hence the attitude of China should be condemned.[46] Parliamentarian Acharya Kripalini (PSP) reacted sharply to the CPI's statement and said that, the Communist Party was always ready to please the Chinese Government and the Communist Party of China and CPI would welcome the action if China would attack India in future.[47]

Replying to the criticism on CPI statement, Communist leader Hiren Mukherjee clarified that his party did not do anything wrong while referring to stop the undesirable activities that were flourishing in Kalimpong by the foreign elements. He also stressed that "it is our responsibility in regard to the maintenance of friendly relationship between India and China..."[48] Reacting to the Chinese criticism on Nehru's statement in Parliament, Home Minister G.B. Pant cautioned Chinese authority that if China would repeat the allegation in future, India would "deplore such an attitude".[49] Extending the debate, Deputy Minister External Affair Lakshmi Menon (INC) stated that the attitude of Chinese Embassy in reaction to Nehru's statement was improper. However, she informed the house that the criticism by the Chinese Embassy on the statement of Prime Minister of India was not the act of violation of the diplomatic privileges. Condemning the CPI's allegation on Prime Minister, she replied that "in this case, the Prime Minister's integrity, his honesty has been challenged. We take very strong exception (to it)".[50]

Prime Minister Nehru was absent for the next day in the house to comment on the Chinese criticism over his statement at Parliament, hence Deputy Foreign Minister was put in charge to reply on behalf of Nehru and his government on the issue. The very next day of the debate, Nehru himself was presented before the house for debate on the Chinese comment. Replying to the Chinese allegation on Kalimpong he admitted that, for the last few years the Kalimpong became the hotbed of spies and counter-spies of all shaded nationalities. However, he clarified that the Indian government had made a thorough inquiry in to the changes and found most of them baseless. He stated at the Parliament that: "I did repudiate and I do repudiate today that to say that Kalimpong has been the commanding center gives it a place in the matter which is, I think, completely untrue…"[51]

Counter-arguing to Nehru's statement CPI leader Hiren Mukherjee stood up to condemn, what he believed the "anti-Chinese stance of the Parliament". In his defence he said that, "even yesterday it was a frightful thought that in the absence of Prime Minister the mask put on by the Congress government was turn off and all kind of things were said by the Deputy Minister which he cannot possibly second."[52] The statement caused strong uproar in the house and was strongly objected by several members of the house including the Speaker.

India's Asylum to Dalai Lama and the Chinese Reaction

Following the outbreak of rebellion in Lhasa and subsequent attack of Chinese army on Norbulingka, the summer residence of Dalai Lama, there was a severe threat to the life of the Dalai Lama, especially after March 17, 1959,[53] when China ordered its army to crush the rebel and Tibetan authority. Looking at the situation Dalai Lama fled to India along with his mother, brother and other 80,000[54] fellow Tibetans and reached India on March 31, 1959.[55] The Indian public opinion was sympathetic towards the sufferings of the Tibetan people and there was increasing public pressure to grant political asylum to Dalai Lama and India granted the same to Dalai Lama subsequently.

The issue of Dalai Lama's protection and granting of asylum was raised for the first time by some members in the Parliament for debate on March

30, 1959 Raising the issue in Parliament, N.G. Goray stated his concern about the consequences granting of political asylum to Dalai Lama.[56] He feared that Chinese might put military pressure on Indian border to deprive India to grant political asylum. Nehru on the other hand declined to comment anything on the issue as he felt that it might complicate the issue further. He informed the house that "there has not been any slightest, vaguest approach to us of this kind or any fact indicating that such an approach, such a thing might happen."[57]

The very next day Nehru announced in Lok Sabha that Dalai Lama had entered into Indian Territory and would be given respectful treatment while being in the asylum in India. This announcement brought over all support of Parliament and majority of the members, except CPI lauded the decision to grant the asylum to Dalai Lama. He informed the house and all the check posts were informed to receive the spiritual leader and the other fellow Tibetans if they wanted to enter into India for asylum.[58]

The Chinese authority started criticizing India and accused for the violation of 1951 Panchsheel agreement by granting asylum to Dalai Lama. They also accused India for pressurizing and motivating Dalai Lama to leave Tibet. Clarifying the doubt over his exile, Dalai Lama declared on April 18, 1959 that he had fled into India "of his own will and not under duress". He also made it clear that "there was a strong desire for independence on the part of the people of Tibet" and the seventeen point Agreement had been concluded under the pressure from the Chinese government". He also showed his gratitude towards the Indian government and the public for their generosity and support towards the people of Tibet and charged China for the violation of the 1951 'Seventeen Point Agreement' and gradual withdrawal of autonomous status to Tibet.[59] However, as earlier, China claimed that the recent statement also was full of lies and was prepared under duress.[60] Defusing the charges, the spiritual leader issued another statement on April 22, 1959 where he clarified that "I wish to make it clear that the earlier statement issued by my authority and indicated my view and I stand by it"[61]. This statement also was followed up by Chinese criticism and anti-Indian propaganda back home.

The Indian public opinion was sympathetic towards Tibetan movement and largely critical to Chinese policy of army action in Tibet. Hence, granting of political asylum by Indian government was welcomed by all sections of people. Several rallies and demonstrations were arranged by the people and organisations in front of Chinese embassy at New Delhi. An Afro-Asian Conversion on Tibet was conducted on April 1960 under the chairmanship of renowned socialist leader Jayparakash Narayan to show international solidarity to the people of Tibet in their freedom struggle.[62] Several political parties also showed their support to the Tibetan movement and condemned the Chinese action in Tibet. For instance, Congress Working Committee passed a resolution on May 10, 1959 to show its sympathy towards the people of Tibet.[63] China reacted to Dalai Lama's claim and the overall Indian reaction sharply. Chinese authority also criticized most of political parties and news media for their anti-Chinese stand on Tibet crisis.

Following the constant demand from various political parties to declare government of India's policy towards Dalai Lama and Tibetan uprising as well as to clarify Chinese spuriousness on India's interest, Nehru presented a detailed statement in Indian Parliament on April 28, 1959. "I need not tell the house that Dalai Lama entered India entirely of his own volition. At no time had we suggested that he should come to India. We had naturally given thought to the possibility of his seeking asylum in India and when such a request came, we readily granted it." Pointing to the criticism of Panchan Lama and other Chinese authorities on Dalai Lama's arrival and subsequent statements he said that:

"All I can say is that I have been greatly distressed at the tone of the comments and the charges made against India by responsible people in China. They have used the language of cold war regardless of truth and propriety. This is peculiarly distressing in a great nation with thousands of years of culture behind it, noted for its restrained and polite behaviour. The charges made against India are so fantastic that I find it difficult to deal with them. There is the charge of our keeping the Dalai Lama under duress. The Chinese authorities should surely know how we function in this country and what our laws and Constitution are. Even if we were so inclined, we could not keep the Dalai Lama under some kind of detention against his will, and there can be no question of our wishing to do so. We can gain nothing by it expect the burden of difficult problems. In any event, this matter can be easily cleared. It is open to the Dalai Lama at any time to go back to Tibet or whatever he wants to."[64]

He also asked the Panchan Lama and other Chinese authorities including the Chinese ambassador to meet Dalai Lama and find some solution for Tibetan crisis. Countering the Chinese charges on "Indian expansionism" Nehru stated that:

"Another and an even stranger allegation has been made about "Indian expansionists" who, it is alleged, are inheritors of the British tradition of imperialism and expansion. .... Being entirely opposed to any such extraterritorial rights in another country, we did not wish to retain them. .... Soon after the Chinese armies entered Tibet, the question of these extraterritorial rights was raised and we readily agreed to give them up. .... We laid down the Five Principles of the PanchSheel and placed our relationship with the Tibet region on a new footing. ..... and that India had no political or ulterior ambitions in Tibet. Indeed, even from the narrowest practical point of view, any other policy would have been wrong and futile. Ever since then we have endeavoured not only to act up to the agreement we made, but to cultivate the friendship of the Chinese State and people."[65]

Condemning the Baseless criticism he said, "It is therefore a matter of the deepest regret and surprise to us that charges should be made which are both unbecoming and entirely void of substance. We have conveyed this deep feeling of regret to the Chinese Government, more especially at the speeches delivered recently in the current session of the National People's Congress in Peking".[66] Nehru also made it clear that the charges over the Indian involvement in the Tibetan rebellion and the charges of "Kalimpong as a centre of the Tibetan rebellion, is wholly unjustified".[67] He further clarified that Indian policy towards Tibet vis-à-vis India-China relation was broadly based on three factors: (1) the preservation of the security and integrity of India; (2) our desire to maintain friendly relations with China; (3) our deep sympathy for the people of Tibet. "That policy we shall continue to follow, because we think that a correct policy not only for the present but even more so for the future" he added.[68]

Emphasizing on the greater and long term cooperation between India and China Nehru stated: "It would be a tragedy if the two great countries of Asia, India and China, which have been peaceful neighbors of ages past, should develop feelings of hostility against each other. We for our part will follow this policy, but we hope that China also will do likewise and that nothing will be said or done which endangers the friendly relations of the two countries which are so important from the wider point of view of the peace of Asia and the World. The Five Principles have laid down, inter alia, mutual respect for each other. Such mutual respect is gravely impaired if unfounded charges are made and the language of cold war was used".[69]

Nehru's statement, which was intended to clarify Indian policies towards China and Tibet and improve India-China relation by dissolving Chinese speciousness towards India, was mistaken by most China and considered the other way around. The public opinion of China which was used to be soft on Nehru turned against it drastically after the statement. Criticizing Nehru's statement and India's Tibetan policy The *People's Daily* published a long editorial entitled "Tibet and Nehru's Philosophy" on May 6, 1959 questioning the intention and attitude of Nehru on Tibet. The article condemned Nehru's policy towards Tibet and alleged to bow down before the pressure of anti-political parties like Praja Socialist Party and Bharatiya Jan Sangh. It also charged Nehru for the violation of the Panchsheel agreement by interfering in the internal matter of the friendly china. China also made it clear that Nehru's assumption for the peace in Asia through India-China friendship is only possible after the non-interference in Tibet.[70]

Following the article, Communist Party of India on May 12, 1959 issued a resolution on Nehru's statement over Tibet and alleged Nehru for the violation of the principles of Panchsheel Agreement. It also criticized the opposition parties like PSP, BJS and Hindu Mahasabha for its anti-China stand in Parliament. These subsequent statements sparked another furore in the Parliament, though Nehru and the ruling party were reluctant to downplay any such demand due to the fear of further damage to the relations with Chinese.

R. K. Khadilkar of Mazdoor Kisan Party (MKP) by condemning China's constant criticism on Indian leadership and policies said that, India should resist these Chinese attempts to demoralize India with full efforts. He appealed to the Chinese authority to respect the public sentiment of India which wanted nothing more than the protection of the rights of the Tibetan people and honourable solution to the Tibetan crisis. Criticizing the Chinese charges on India's intention to annexation of Tibet he clarified that, "no section of responsible opinion, no party in the land has seriously advocated the independence of Tibet".[71] Extending the debate Acharya Kripalini (PSP) stated that, China's charges on Nehru's statement on Tibet were not right as, countries used to criticize each other in their internal and external policies. Mere criticism on each other's internal policies should not be treated as the interference into the internal matter of the other country. If so, China should be charged for interfering in the internal matters of Yugoslavia, as it had been constantly criticizing the international matters of Yugoslavia. He also warned that China would never be friendly with India even though India highly emphasized on "*Hindi-Chini-Bhai-Bahi*" (Indians and Chinese are brothers).[72] A.B. Vajpayee of Bharatiya Jan Sangh, repeated his demand for Indian assistance to Dalai Lama for the liberation of Tibet. Branding the Chinese action in Tibet as "yellow Imperialism" he claimed that the agreement of Panchsheel between India and China was meaningless as China had violated all its promises towards Tibet. He asked the government to review its China policy and withdraw all diplomatic relation with China.[73] Socialist leader Braj Raj Singh also criticized the "Chinese expansionism" into Tibet and asked the government to follow the hard decision for the re-establishment of Tibet's autonomy and bring to an end the sufferings of the Tibetan people.[74]

However, CPI leadership had a different and lenient feeling towards the Chinese criticism. They were very critical to the opposition led anti-Chinese debates and asked the government to show some kind of restraint in dealing with China. S.A. Dange (CPI), while condemning the opposition's charges said that, "if China is acknowledged by the Prime Minister also to have suzerainty over Tibet and if Tibet is acknowledged to be an autonomous region of the Chinese republic, then naturally, diplomatically or in terms of international politics, the question does not arise why we should discuss the Tibet problem in India or anywhere else…." He also criticized Kripalini and Vajpayee for their advocacy of Tibetan freedom and claimed that the Tibetan movement was a class struggle and not a national uprising. The communist leader asked the government not to bow down before the vested interest groups and political parties and deal with the issue in such way that it won't affect the India-China friendship. [75]

Prime Minister Nehru in reply stated that, the agreement of *Panchsheel* was still valid, though some of the provisions had been violated by China in recent time. Hence, there was no need to withdraw the agreement and interfere in the Tibetan matters. He disagreed to the argument of A.B. Vajpayee as he believed it almost led to "armed conflict" with China over the Tibetan issue. Nehru felt that, the matter should be resolved in a peaceful way. He also repeated his past argument that India and China should coexist peacefully and be friendly and should not be hostile to each other. Talking about the Chinese criticism he stated, the previous statement was just a reaction to the recent development in Tibet and should be taken in a positive way. However, he also warned that the fair language for Tibet would not serve any purpose rather would widen the existing differences with China.[76]

Looking at the debate, it is clear that the Indian public and the political parties are very critical to the Chinese aggression into Tibet. Most of the political parties, except Communist Party of India were sympathetic towards the suffering of people of Tibet and its spiritual leader Dalai Lama. They supported the Government of India's decision to give political asylum to Dalai Lama and other Tibetan refugees. Some of the political parties and interest groups also demanded for the military help to Dalai Lama for the freedom of Tibet. The Praja Socialist Party, for instance, always demanded for self-determination of the people of Tibet and issued resolution in its third annual conference in April 1959. Similarly, the Bharatiya Jana Sangh advocated for freedom for Tibetan people and constantly pressurized the government to offer military help to Dalai Lama for the liberation of the Tibet. The Swatrantra Party did not consider the Tibetan crisis as the internal affairs of China and asked the government to deal with China carefully. It also passed a resolution against the Chinese aggression into Tibet during the first national convention of the party. However, the Communist Party of India had been adopting pro-China policies and continually supported the Chinese actions towards Tibet and India. It also criticized the Indian government for its interference in the internal matters of Tibet. The party also criticized the parties and the leaders that argued pro-Tibetan policies for government.[77]

Tibet's Appeal to United Nations

Following the Chinese armed aggression into Tibet and deportation of Dalai Lama to India, there was a strong feeling among the Tibetans to internationalize the issue in order to mobilize international support. Dalai Lama also felt that if United Nations could come to rescue South Korea from North Korean and Chinese aggression, it could also send the peace keeping force into Tibet to push back China from Tibet. The Tibetan government in exile started a systemic campaign to approach the member states to raise the Tibet issue at United Nations. Dalai Lama wrote a letter to Dag Hammarskjold, the UN Secretary General on September 9, 1959 seeking the UN intervention in Tibetan crises by highlighting the traditional position of Tibetan sovereignty and violation of basic rights of Tibetan people.[78]

Much before Dalai Lama's approach to UN, opposition parties had been demanding the government to seek international support and referring the Tibetan crisis to United Nations. An All India Tibet Convention was organized in Calcutta between May 30 and 31, 1959 under the chairmanship of Jayprakash Narayan to pressurize the government to take the Tibetan issue into United Nations.[79] The matter was also brought into the Parliament for discussion. The Bhatatiya Jan Sangh Introduced a resolution on August 21, 1959 regarding raising the Tibetan issue in UN. Entitled with "this house is of the opinion that the government should refer the Tibetan issue to the United Nations" the resolution was moved to show the solidarity with the people of Tibet.[80] Initiating the debate Jan Sanghleader A.B. Vajpayee argued in the house that, the people of Tibet had been denied the basic rights and freedom in the hands of Chinese force. Therefore the world community, especially India could not remain silent over the suffering of Tibetan people and should raise the Tibetan issue at UN, no matter Tibet was a member of UN or not. He also disagreed over Nehru's argument that the Tibetan issue at UN would intensify cold war. He felt that if India would mobilize world support against the Chinese aggression, it would serve Indian interest in dealing with bilateral level China. Vajpayee also requested the Indian government not to support Chinese bid into United Nation.[81]

On line with Jan Sangh argument, Hem Barua of Praja Socialist Party also criticized the People Republic of China's military action in Tibet and violation of the fundamental principle of Universal Declaration of Human Rights (UDHR). He further argued that the Tibetan issue would no longer remain China's own internal problem but become an international problem, as China had forced the Tibetan authority to sign the 1951 accorded. Hence, he requested the government to raise the Tibetan question at the UN.[82] Braj Raj Singh (SP) felt that Indian frontiers were prone to threat with the demolition of the buffer states like Tibet. He warned the government to deal with China with ample care and appealed to the government to mobilize world opinion against the Chinese aggression into Tibet with the support of nonaligned counties.[83] Similarly, Granatrantra Parishad leader P.K. Deo stated that it was the morale duty of India to raise the Tibet issue at UN, as India barred the agenda of Tibetan autonomy at UN during 1950 just to please China.[84]

The members of ruling Congress, at large had backed the government of India's policy towards Tibet vis-à-vis. Narayan Das and Joachin Alva (Both belongs to INC), for instance vowed for friendly relations with China and asked the government to resolve the Tibetan problems through peaceful way.[85] Similarly, Brajeswar Prashad (INC) cautioned the government to handle the Tibetan issue with utmost care as any wrong move by India might lead to full-fledged war between India and China. If so, it might be converted into a nuclear war on a global scale.[86] However, a section of ruling party also raised their concerns over the Chinese aggression into Tibet. Dr. Deorao Yeshwantrao Gohokar (INC) asked the government to support the Tibetan issue if brought into United Nations. He also asked the government to review India's China policy, as the sovereign ruler (the Dalai Lama) was not the part of the Sino-Tibetan treaty of 1951.[87]

In reply to the demand of the resolution and subsequent opinion of the members, Prime Minister Nehru informed the house that India was fully concerned about the suffering of the Tibetan people and extended political asylum to Dalai Lama and other 13,000 Tibetans. But going beyond this, especially internationalizing the issue or taking to UN was not good for India. He disagreed with the opposition's demand to take the Tibetan issue into United Nations and clarified that, Tibet was not an independent state, though it enjoyed greater autonomy under the Chinese statehood. Thus it would create unnecessary problems for India. He further clarified that UN could take decision on Tibetan crisis on two issues, the violation of human rights and the Chinese aggression. In both the cases the result would be below the expectation because, China never signed the UDHR, thus was not bound to obey it by law and as Tibet was not an independent nation there was point of external aggression. There India should not do anything that does not make any sense under the international law and more importantly, it should remain out of the works that endanger to the peace of this region.[88]

Reflecting the wider sympathy, the motion served as the diagnosis report in defining the attitude of Indian Parliament and public opinion towards the Tibetan situation. The mounting pressure over Indian government to support the resolution if Tibetan crisis was brought into UN, encouraged Dalai Lama to file a formal appeal to United Nations. On 30 August 1959 the spiritual leader declared his decision to appeal to UN and by September 9, 1959 he finally took the case into UN.[89] The matter was discussed in the UN General Assembly on the recent crisis in Tibet on October 21, 1959 and adopted a resolution where it appealed to bring to an end the gross human right violation in Tibet without naming China as violator.[90] Dalai Lama's appeal to the UN started a new debate among the political communities of India where political parties were divided on the issues. While the government and the communist party opposed Indian involvement, the Socialist and the Jana Sangh approached the government to extend necessary supports.

China's Attack on Indian Nationals in Tibet and Reaction of Parliament

Amidst the crisis in Tibet, it had been reported that Indian traders and pilgrims were attacked and harassed by the Chinese army in Lhasa. There was also a news of unnecessary restrictions being put into practice and some Indians were arrested by the Chinese authorities to demoralize Indian traders. Subsequently, it became one of the hot topics for Parliamentary debate.

On August 6, 1959, Braj Raj Singh sought to move an adjunct motion about the attitude of Chinese authority towards the Indian communities at Tibet. In the motion he complained about the practices of flagrant discrimination by the Chinese officials towards the Indian traders and pilgrims living at Lhasa. He felt that it was the clear violation of the Sino-Indian trade agreement on Tibet, which allowed the traders and pilgrims to move to each other's country without any restriction.[91] The motion was not introduced in the Parliament for discussion. But Nehru stood up to clarify the government's perception towards the issue. He openly admitted the suffering and the harassment of Indian nationals in Tibet by the Chinese authorities and stated that it was against the spirit of 1954 agreement. He also informed the house that the government of India had been in touch with the Chinese authorities to resolve the issue and asked the Chinese government to extend possible security to Indian nationals.[92]

P.C. Barooah of Congress introduced a call attention notice entitled "The position of Indian nationals............. in Tibet" on August 11, 1959. Defending the motion he said that, the Indian communities in Tibet had been targeted by the Chinese authorities and the traders had been denied to do their business freely. He also claimed that the Indians are asked to register their names before the Chinese authorities without fail which was not made compulsory for Indian traders previously. [93] Similarly, on August 24 Jan Sangh leader A.B. Vajpayee raised the problems faced by Indian communities at Lhasa and sought the government's intervention to address the issue. Citing the example of Chinese warning towards the Indian consulate at Lhasa, he said that the Indians had been put into virtual house arrest and their movements had been restricted by the Chinese authorities. The traders were also facing enormous problems in their business and put under sharp scanning by the Chinese authorities, he further stated.

In reply, Jawaharlal Nehru stated that no Indian had been kept under house arrest so far, though the Indians at Lhasa faced Chinese harassment in their day to day life. He also informed the Parliament that the Chinese government never denied permission for Indian pilgrims rather advised to travel into Tibet at their own risk. This reply failed to satisfy the Parliamentarians, especially the members of opposition and the wave of furore was continued in the house. The continuous public and Parliamentary pressure to address the issue put the Indian government and Nehru to take undesirable steps in Tibet issue in future.

The Emergence of Sino-Indian Border Disputes

The theory of *"Hindi-Chini-Bhai-Bhai"* got a major setback during the late fifties of twentieth century due to the increasing scepticism between India and China over Tibet. While China was complaining on Indian involvement in Tibet and India's warm welcome to Dalai Lama, India, on other hand, was more worried about the Chinese claim of several areas of Indian Territory. China in addition, tried to get closer to India's arch rival Pakistan and gradually shifted its earlier stand by advocating self determination in Kashmir to please Pakistan leadership.[94] At the juncture of mistrust, India noticed repeated Chinese incursion at several Indian border sectors. It sparked huge public outrage in India and subsequently became an important issue during Parliamentary debates.

In the Parliament the issue of Chinese incursion into Indian territories had been raised as early as March 1959. To draw the attention of the house about the reported violation of border by Chinese forces, an adjournment motion was proposed to be introduced by Hem Barua (PSP), A.B. Vajpayee (BJS) and Braj Raj Singh (Socialist) on March 30, 1959. However, this proposal did not materialize. On the same day PSP leader Mohammed Imam also raised the issue in the Parliament and asked the government to take necessary steps to curb such attempts. Nehru however, was not convinced about the media reports and questioned the validity of the fact.[95]

Meanwhile, Chinese government published a map where several areas of India had been shown as the parts of China. It created furore in Indian Parliament. On April 22, 1959 several Parliamentarians across the party line raised the issue of Chinese claim of Indian Territory and wanted to know the government of India's measures to deal with the issue. Prime Minister Nehru as usual down played the issue and informed the house that the Chinese map was a older one and hence nothing to worry about it. He also informed that his government was in touch with the Chinese authorities to rectify the map for further use.[96] Braj Raj Singh (Socialist) and D.C. Sharma (INC) highlighted the Chinese claim of Indian territories and asked the government to be prepared to deal with any possible consequences. Nehru, however, replied that the Chinese authorities had never claimed any area of Indian territory and he had been in discussion with China to resolve the issue peacefully.[97]

Looking at the gravity of Chinese hostility and consecutive border violation, A.B. Vajpayee (BJS) moved an adjournment motion regarding "grave threat to India's security and territorial integrity" on August 13, 1959. He argued that, China was planning to liberate Ladakh, Sikkim and

Bhutan and hence Indian government need to be prepared to counter any future threat and protect India's national integrity.[98] Joining in the debate Braj Raj Singh (Socialist) wanted to know the government of India's reaction to the reports of Chinese planning for the formation of a Himalayan Federation extracting Ladakh, Tibet, Bhutan, Sikkim and some parts of NEFA regions which might pose greater security threats for India. However, Nehru down played the whole issue and informed the house that the government of India had no such communication from China and India was fully capable to handle any future threats from any corner of the world. Hem Barua was not satisfied with Nehru's answer and further wanted to know about any Chinese communication challenging the validity of the McMahon line. Nehru in reply said that, there was no such communication from China regarding the validity of the line and informed the house that McMahon line had been created through international treaty and even Chinese authority like En-lai had accepted the line as the international border in the past.[99]

The Pangong and Longju Border Incidents

As a consequence of the Tibetan Crisis and India's political asylum to Dalai Lama, China in many matters took a strong stand, including the issues of border disputes. While China had never raised the border issues during the 1954 agreement and perhaps, as Nehru said had accepted the McMahon line as the de facto border between India and China gradually denied to recognize the same after the Tibet crisis. First, it issued the map showing some eastern sectors of India as Chinese territory and subsequently raised its army's presence in these regions. India, on the other hand also increased its patrolling activities to protect its border, though both India and China had vowed for the peaceful settlement of the frontier line. As ground border forces of both the countries tried to maintain the perceived border line according to their own assumptions, often they came front to front during the patrolling and accused each other as the violator of border line. Sometimes the military activities led to the small intensity armed clashes between the forces like the incidents of Pangong, Migyitum and Longju.

In extension of its claim, Chinese forces intruded into the Indian Territory near to Pangong Lake on July 28, 1959 and arrested six Indian police men including an officer. India soon reacted sharply to the border violation act and demanded the immediate release of its policemen. However, China denied the allegation and accused Indian forces for their incursion into Chinese territories.[100] Similar incident occurred near Migyitun on August 25, 1959, where the Chinese forces attacked an Indian army post and killed one Indian soldier and injured another three. On the very next day, the Chinese force marched further into the Indian Territory and surround the small garrison of Indian army at Longju on August 26, 1959. In defence the Indian forces opened firing but did not sustain longer against the large Chinese force. The Indian forces abandoned the barrack after heavy losses from the Chinese army.[101] The Chinese version, however blamed the Indian troops for its firing on Chinese troops after crossing the Chinese border.[102] These incidents started a series of public uproar across India and the center of the Parliamentary debate.

Soon after the incidents, members of various political parties criticized the Chinese actions and the government of India's weak defence policy towards Chinese border violation. They wanted to know the detail account of the border incidents from Prime Minister Nehru. On August 28, 1959 Nehru in reply made a comment in the Indian Parliament about the incident. He stated that most of the eastern border regions were hilly and uninhabited for centuries. Despite this some military posts were setup near to the international border that came under the Chinese attack. He further revelled that such type of border violation was also repeated in the Khurnak, Spanggur and Khinzemane but subsequently chased out by Indian forces. Answering to India's stand against the Chinese claim of territorial area he clarified that, "there is no physical demarcation of the frontier in these mountain passes, although our maps are quite clear on this subject".[103]

Raising supplementary question, N.S. Goray (PSP) wanted to know more over the media report of the construction of a strategic roadway by Chinese government across Gartok and Yark of Tibetan region. In reply Nehru stated that the government of India came to know that such road really existed and passed through the inaccessible remote corner of north eastern region of Ladakh.[104] Congress leader Dr. Ram Subhag Singh put another supplementary question about the Chinese claim of annexing Bhutan and Sikkim into the motherland of China and government of India's stand against the claim. Nehru, in reply made it clear that the government of India was responsible to protect the sovereignty and integrity of the two Himalayan Kingdom and "any aggression against Bhutan and Sikkim would be considered as aggression against India".[105] However, these assurances did not satisfy the opposition leaders and the uproar continued to paralyze the business of the house.

An adjournment motion was introduced by Barua, Goray, Braj Raj Singh and Vajpayee on the same day regarding the grave threat to Indian frontiers from China. Initiating the debate Hem Barua stated that the Chinese forces had traced into Indian Territory at Kameng and hoisted the Chinese flag on Indian soil. It showed the rigid mind set of Chinese government towards the border disputes and the Indian government need to be ready to face any possible threat. Goray on other hand warned the government to read the Chinese strategy carefully as Chinese authority pursued a grand and strong policy towards Indian frontiers. Similarly, Vajpayee asked the government to be ready to handle any hard situation that might erupt out of the present situation.[106] Independent member B.C. Kamble criticized the government of India's inadequate policy towards the Chinese provocation.[107]

Prime Minister Nehru reacted to the motion sharply and termed it as baseless/ upside down and stated that border violation occurred due to the absence of land demarcation at the ground. As a result, he clarified, that each side was unable to recognize the actual border line. Chinese forces withdrew from the Indian side after strong protest of Indian government and the matter was closed there. Regarding August 7 incident, he repeated the Indian version of the story as stated in the government white paper and blamed Chinese force for the incident.[108]

However, Nehru's attempt to downplay the border incident did not satisfy majority of the house and the members continued to demand greater explanation on government of India's China policy and its present preparedness to tackle any possible Chinese threat in coming days. Looking at the immense pressure Nehru once again came up to explain India's stand towards Chinese hostile policy. In the house he stated that, "we have taken the line that minor border incidents and border differences should be settled by negotiations. We must distinguish between this and that broad approach of the Chinese maps which have a stroke of the brush coloured hundreds of miles of Indian Territory. That is totally and manifestly unacceptable and we have made it clear. We stick to the McMahon line." He further agreed to negotiate with the Chinese authorities for the settlement of the border disputes with little readjustment of frontier line. Nehru however, admitted that the situation was far more serious than the accidental violation and assured the house that he would take necessary measures to strengthen the border posts and surveillance system (such as bringing the border areas of NEFA under military authorities) so that to tackle future incidents.[109] These words of Nehru failed to satisfy the unconvinced opponents and many members demanded further clarification in this regard including issuing a detailed white paper.[110]

On September 4, 1959 while debating on Tibet opposition, members like Braj Raj Singh, P.K. Deo, Hem Barua and A.B. Vajpayee once again raised the issue of Chinese encroachment into Indian Territory. Terming the aggression as a major threat to India's sovereignty and integrity, they criticized the ruling Congress government for its weak stand to handle the issue. In reply to the criticism Nehru stated that, "it is hard to judge the incidents of border violation at this juncture. Whether it is just a local aggressiveness or just to show us our place, ... so that we may not get uppish or whether it is something deeper" he explained. He also objected to the Chinese map showing "half of north-eastern frontier agency, one third of Assam and one third of Bhutan" as the part of China. However, he was not in favour of taking any hard steps, by either side to decide for two miles of uninhabitable land. Explaining the government of India's stand on the border settlement he stated that, his government's policy was adhered to any settlement based on the McMahon line. However, he showed his willingness to settle the disputes through "any kind of conciliatory, mediatory process" or "arbitration of any authority agreed by the two parties" if necessary. If India and China had opted for the hard option and stood hostility to each other, it would be a tragedy for not only India and China but also for the whole Asia and the rest of the world.[111]

These clarifications did not satisfy the opposition members and the demand still went vocal for the presentation of the White Paper before the house for discussion. Bowing down to the demand and to clear out the smokes, Nehru tabled the first white paper in the Lok Sabha on September 7, 1959. The white paper comprised of all letters, communiqués and agreements between India and China clearly showed that there was serious rift, disparity of perceptions between the Asian giants. Each side claimed the unmarked area as their own and tried to convince the other with some evidence to make their case strong. India on one hand referred to British and other ancient records to show its legitimacy over the Eastern and western sector. On the other hand, China rejected the British map and the McMahon line terming it the product of British imperialistic encroach policy against Tibet region of China. No Chinese government had ever agreed to the agreements, therefore the boundary need to redrawn, said the Chinese. This bunch of confusion and controversy led to small armed clashes between the two armed forces. According to the white paper, each side blamed the other for the violation of border line and encroachment to each other's territory. Despite the series of border incidents, both sides agreed to deescalate the tensions and solve the border disputes through peaceful means. But one can analyse out of these documents that, the rift had grown up between the two neighbours and slowly moved towards the dangerous phase.[112]

Looking at the intensity of differences, Nehru wrote series of letters to Chinese counterpart Zhou En-Lai citing various historical records, ancient maps and provisions of agreements to reclaim the Indian stand. After a silence of about six months, Chinese premier En-Lai replied to Nehru's letter on September 8, 1959 where he raised a number of arguments in justifying Chinese claim over the border regions of India. En-Lai in his letter wrote that China was not party to the treaty of 1842 and did not approve it later. Therefore there was no question of recognizing the frontier line. He made it clear that the Chinese government was not recognizing the McMahon and illegally occupied the Longju Yaxier Shatze, Khinzemane and Tamaden regions of China. He also blamed the Indian forces for the Lonju incidents and argued that the deployment of Chinese border guard at the Indian border was just to threat India, but to prevent the Tibetan gorillas to inter into Tibet and make disturbances.[113]

The En-Lai letter to Nehru for the first time made a formal claim of 90,000 square Kilometer of the Indian Territory. It became headline for most of the Indian media and inflamed public opinion in India.

The Parliament also faced a storm of debates on this demand and the opposition members demanded the reply from the government on the new Chinese demand. Debating on the En-Lai's letter and his claim, P.K Deo criticized Nehru government's approach to deal with the Chinese question. He felt that the Prime Minister should have taken the house in to confidence and placed all its strategies in the Parliament while handling the Chinese issues. He also criticized the government for its failure to press for border resolution by using the 1954 Panchsheel Agreement. Chinese provocative approach and construction of strategic roadways in the border region clarified the Chinese claim much before the formal claim. He suggested the government to create an atmosphere for negotiations with China and not press the same at this uneasy situation.[114]

Praja Socialist Party leader Mohammed Imam moved an amendment in criticizing the government's weak stand against the Chinese provocations and asked the government to "take immediate and effective steps to make the Chinese withdraw from the regions forcibly occupied by them".[115] Acharya Kripalani attacked Nehru's China policy and acceptance of Chinese sovereignty over Tibet through 1954 agreement. He argued that India did a great blunder to recognize Chinese sovereignty over Tibet and subsequent demolition of a buffer state; and the recent boundary dispute was the product of the blunder. He took critical stand on the recent border incursion and the government's failure to restrict the Chinese expansionism. In his own words of criticism he said that:

> *"Our territories have been occupied, our people have been kidnapped, our guards have been fired at, taxes have been collected, roads have been built all leading towards India; check and observation posts established along our borders...but, whether aggressions have been there so far, I have regret to say that the country has been kept in ignorance of this aggression for a long period, between the two countries. The Parliament itself has been elicited through question about aggression in this...house. No information was ever given voluntarily. Even then it has been meager; and often, the acts of aggression have been minimized...Sometimes, it would appear that there has been special pleading for the Chinese."* [116]

Kripalani's last line perhaps was said against Nehru's statement about the construction of Chinese roads, where Nehru tried to down play the opposition's blame by stating that it was not a regular road, but a passage marked by stones and later revealed as motorable road. Criticizing Nehru's statement of "where not a blade of grass grew" to name captured frontier regions, he said that, "the Prime Minister's varying statements confuse the public minds".[117] Socialist leader Ram Sevak Yadav tabled an amendment asking the government to "make suitable amendments in its foreign policy in conformity with the policy followed by the Sociality Party of India" towards the Chinese aggression.[118] Braj Raj Singh of the same party criticized the government for its weak foreign policy towards China and its failure to clarify the border disputes during the signing of 1954 treaty. He argued not to tolerate any violation by the Chinese authority and the threat to India's integrity. Singh emphasized that, any negotiation with China should start, only after the withdrawal of Chinese troops.[119] Similarly, A.B. Vajpayee of Bharatiya Jan Sangh in his amendment asked the government to take appropriate steps to make the Indian case strong and to foil any Chinese aggression. He further asked the government to make sure that the Chinese forces vacate the occupied area within a certain period and make settlement of border disputes through negotiation according to the bases on McMahon line.[120]

While most of the opposition parties condemned Nehru's approach in dealing with the border and overall Chinese aggression, Communist Party of India however, supported the government's broad policy towards China. The broad stand of the party was to settle the border disputes peacefully and in a friendly manner. S.A. Dange, the party spokesperson stated that the "approach to the problem must be one of settlement and not of whipping up a war atmosphere". Clarifying his party's stand on McMahon line he said that "we as a whole so far had accepted the McMahon line as our frontier. Now the honourable Prime Minister himself says that it is not demarcated, it is not delineated but there is a general contour.... at the moment demarcation does not exist, disputes about villages, grasslands and all that which are in white paper are bound to arise".[121] In his long debate he stressed that the recent development of disputes is the product of India's Tibet policy and its sanctuary to the Tibetan rebels against China. He objected to the set up and function of "Tibetan government in exile" in the Indian soil and its appeal to the United Nation to liberate it from China. However, he predicted that, there would not be any invasion form the Chinese side, hence the government should not take any unpleased things under the political pressure that might deteriorate the relation further.[122]

While opposition parties were critical to the Government of India's China policy, some of the Congress members also remained upset over the new turn of the India – China relation and demanded tougher policy towards China. Congress leader Manabendra Shah (INC) for instance, asked the government to take strong and effective measures to counter the Chinese threat including the bringing of all border check posts under the supervision of Indian army and declaring all Himalayan districts as border areas.[123] Similarly, Nemi Chandra Kasliwal (INC) doubted the Chinese intention and criticized unnecessary delay by China to answer Nehru's letter. He felt that the six month delay was intentionally made by China for the favourable time to raise its disagreement.[124]

Though the Congress members at large showed their concern over the recent crisis, they were extremely careful while making comments. They did criticize Chinese aggression but, did not criticize Nehru's policy towards the border disputes. However, a small segment of Congress Parliamentarians openly criticized the government of India's Chinese policy. Initiating the criticism Bhakta Darshan stated that the government had ignored the importance of northern frontier in spite of repeated cautions form the members of the Parliament. He condemned the government's decision not to send army to the Bara Hoti during 1956 when it had been reported that Chinese forces had stayed for some days. He asked the government to hand over the security administration of the whole NRFA region to Indian army to foil any future Chinese incursion.[125] Similar criticism was also made by Ram Subhag Singh (INC) on the same day in the Lok Sabha. Criticizing the government of India's stand on the border crisis, he stated that thousand miles of Indian Territory had been captured by China. He also criticized India's decision to recognize Chinese sovereignty over Tibet through Panchsheel Agreement and the failure of the government to capitalize the agreement in settling the border. He felt that it was a blunder to withdraw Indian civil and military authorities from Bara Hoti, which was an Indian territory. Arguing for multiple vigilant mechanism in the border areas, he demanded for the reappraisal of the India's China policy and took a tough stand against any Chinese aggression not only into India, but also against Bhutan, Sikkim, and Nepal.[126] However some of the Congress members were not in favour of strong criticism against China. Joachim Alva (INC), for instance felt that it was wrong to offer asylum to Dalai Lama in India and encouraged to run the government of exile on Indian soil that eventually anguished Chinese authority. He argued that, "if Sheikh Abdullah is released from Kashmir tomorrow and entered in China we do not know what would be our feelings".[127]

Looking into the prolonged and critical question on Chinese Incursion, Prime Minister Nehru replied the important questions consecutively. Replying to the debate against the "surrendering even an inch of Indian Territory" Nehru said that, "it is not a question of an inch, or a yard or a mile; it is a question of submitting to compulsion, submitting to force and we will never submit to force whatever happens to our country". Clarifying the withholding information from Parliament he said, "it is not ideal to ask the government to bring each and every minor matter before the Parliament". However, he acknowledged the Chinese incursion in Aksai Chin under dark "It is only one thing I kept … when we were dealing with the Aksai Chin area and the road there". He clarified that, the government had not earlier wanted the situation to be worsened by bringing the matter into the public domain. Explaining about the Chinese claim of Indian Territory and Zhou Enlai's letter, Nehru stated that "there can be no mediation, conciliation or arbitration about these demands of the Chinese about large chunks of territory". Taking strong exception to the demand he clarified that "this is a claim which is quite impossible for India or almost every Indian ever to admit whether the consequences ….. this is a thing, whether India exists or does not exist, cannot be agreed to. There the matter ends."Replying to the question of seizure of Indian Territory by China, Nehru assured the house that no other territory except the Longju was under the Chinese control at this moment and his government was in the talk with China for its return. Referring to India's position with regard to Sikkim and Bhutan, Nehru clarified that, "we have publicly, rightly, undertaken certain responsibilities for the defence of Sikkim and Bhutan, if they are attacked…. If something happens on their borders, then it is the same thing as interference with the border of India".[128]

Kongka Pass Incident and Indian Parliament

Kongka pass, was one of the border regions of Aksai Chin area of Ladakh region. As per the White Paper II of Ministry of External Affairs, Government of India, a three member of Indian patrol party was detained by Chinese forces near Kongka Pass on October 20, 1959. When another patrolling team went for the search of the missing persons under the leadership of Deputy Superintendent of Police (DSP) Karam Singh, they came under the ruthless firing from Chinese side. Ten Indian soldiers were killed in the incident and the rest of the team, including DSP Singh were arrested and treated badly. One Chinese soldier was also killed during firing. However the Chinese version claimed that it was the Indians who passed into Chinese side and attacked the Chinese picket subsequently and they (Chinese forces) only retaliated to the attack.

Whatever the truth, the ruthless killing of the Indian soldiers created a wave of public outrage in India. Though the public reaction was at peak, the Parliament was not in session to debate with. As the house reassembled on November 16, 1959 the PSP leader moved an adjournment motion in the Lok Sabha regarding "the failure of government to take prompt and effective action against unabashed violation of India's sovereignty by China on 21 October 1959, when Chinese troops penetrated deep into Indian territory and ambushed our police patrols…."[129] Similarly, several opposition leaders like, Vajpayee, P.K. Deo, Braj Raj Singh and Frank Anthony also gave notice for the adjournment motion, but were not able to move that in the Parliament.

In reply to the adjournment motion and subsequent questions, Nehru stated that the recent incident came as a great surprise for India. He strongly condemned the killing of the martyrs and informed the house that, Chinese authorities had handed over ten Indian prisoners and nine bodies of the Indian soldiers. Nehru also assured the house that this kinds of incidents would not be repeated and the entire frontier regions would be put under the control of Indian army. He also informed the house that the government would take all kind of measures to prevent this kind of incidents and would discuss the matter with Chinese government. Replying to the question of security of the Bhutan and the Sikkim, Nehru clarified that, his government is stuck to the previous stand and that any attack to the border of these two countries would be considered as the attack to the border of India. But as of now India had no intention to send its army, unless the king of Bhutan asked for such assistance.[130]

The Diplomatic Communications between Nehru and Zhou Enlai

Amidst growing tensions in the border regions, Prime Minister Zhou Enlai wrote a letter to Nehru proposing to maintain status quo on the border and to ensure tranquillity at the border by withdrawing forces twenty kilometres away from both the sides of the McMahon line in the east and Line of Actual Control (LAC) in the West. He also proposed not to send patrol party into the evacuated region to avoid any conflict, while maintaining civil administrative personnel there. At last he suggested for a meeting between the two Prime Ministers at a convenient venue to discuss and resolve the border issues.[131]

Replying to Prime Minister En-Lai, Nehru wrote on November 16, 1959 that he ordered his personnel not to send any forward patrol in the eastern borders without Longju. He also suggested to suspend all border patrol in this region from both the sides and China to withdraw from occupied regions as India could not reoccupy those regions. On the Western region, Nehru proposed to withdraw Indian troops to the West of the line shown as the boundary in the 1956 Chinese map, whereas Chinese personnel should withdraw to the east of the international boundary as claimed by India. He felt that the risk of the border clashes would be minimal as the two lines are separated by a long distance. Replying to En-Lai's proposal meeting, Nehru suggested that, there should be pre-agreed agenda or an interim Plan on which two sides might discuss upon during the meeting.

Zhou Enlai in in his reply letter wrote to Nehru on December 17, 1959 that, China could not follow two different policies in border patrolling, rather would agree to stop forwards patrolling if the principals would extend to the whole border. He also disagreed to Nehru's proposal for the withdrawal of Chinese forces from Ladakh region of Western border what he believed from "her own territory" and asked if India would follow the same proposal to withdraw its forces from the Eastern sector also. Repeating his willingness to hold a meeting he proposed December 26 as the date for the meeting between the two Prime Ministers.[132]

In his quick reply, on December 21, 1959 Nehru wrote that he felt regretted for the rejection of his proposal and appeal to the Chinese to learn out of history and to avoid any direct confrontation between the traditionally friendly neighbours. He also blamed China for the recent tension as he believed that it was China that violated the border line. As there were clearly visible differences between the two counties towards the border disputes, Nehru suggested to wait for the suitable time for the high level meeting.[133]

Meanwhile, the Chinese reply to Nehru's letter of September 26 reached Prime Minister's office on December 26, 1959. In the long letter Zhou Enlai repeated the Chinese claim of the 33,000 square kilometres of territory in the Western sector and 90,000 square kilometre of area in the Eastern sector, stating that the entire Sino-Indian border had never been demarked earlier. He also suggested for withdrawal of the forces twenty kilometres of the present holding line from both sides and suspension of border patrolling by other the party until reaching any solution.[134]

Replying to Zhou Enlai's letter, Nehru wrote another letter on February 8, 1960. In the letter Nehru stated that, it was hard to reach any interim negotiation during the Prime Ministerial level meeting, as there was no common ground between their respective viewpoints. However, Nehru invited Zhou Enlai to visit New Delhi, which was a ground breaking decision of government of India not to hold meeting unless reaching to a pre-negotiated proposal.[135] The letter was handed over to Chinese authority along with a detail note on Sino-Indian boundary question on February12, where India rejected Chinese statement that the boundary had never been demarked.[136]

These series of diplomatic letters and communication exchanges further erupted consecutive Parliamentary debates in the Indian Parliament. While the opposition parties criticized Nehru's softness towards the border conflict and holding meeting without any preconditions, the CPI and ruling Congress party largely stood behind Nehru's decisions. Even Nehru had been criticized for his proposal to tranquilize the entire border. PSP leader Kripalani for instance by criticizing the proposal sated that, "in whatever words couched, our proposals amount to this that we tell the Chinese, 'we are leaving our territory provided you also leave our territory'. This is strange reciprocity and maintenance of status quo".[137] Similarly, A.B. Vajpayee of Bharatiya Jan Sangh also objected to the withdrawal of Indian troops from its own soil and alleged that the government was more eager to appease China, rather than strengthening its own security forces.[138] Another opposition party also took strong objection to Nehru's recent offer to China. Its leader Braj Raj Singh stated that the nation wanted peace but not at the cost of occupation of its territory by foreign powers.[139] The independent members also criticized the government for its weak stand against the expansionist China and advised the government not to fall on the great Chinese design by accepting their proposals.[140]

However, Communist Party of India and the Indian National Congress by and large supported Nehru's policy towards China and asked the government to take significant steps to maintain peace in the border. CPI leader Hiren Mukherjee by extending support to Nehru's policy stated that, "in this time of crisis… we stand by the Prime Minister, whether he relishes or not, and we say that we support him entirely…". Similarly, most of the Congress members also supported the government of Indian's offer to calm down the border. Nehru, however tried to defend his decision and his proposal for the withdrawal of forces from two side of the border. Clarifying further he stated that "when the proposals that we have sent have been accepted, there is some basis for meeting, tension become less or some other preparation made for it".[141] It did not satisfy the opposition members and the members also attacked Nehru's decision to hold a meeting with Zhou Enlai. Despite this, Nehru set the ground to hear formally the viewpoint of China face to face.

Nehru-Zhou Summit and the Reaction of Indian Parliament

Despite steep domestic pressure, Nehru decided to hold a meeting with Chinese premier Zhou Enlai on April 19, 1960 at New Delhi. Prime Minister Zhou Enlai with a huge Chinese delegation that included Foreign Minister, Chen Yi, Vice-Foreign Minister, Zhang Hanfu and Assistant Foreign Minister Zhang Qiaogun visited New Delhi to discuss and resolve the outstanding border conflict. Apart from Nehru, the Chinese Premier held discussion with various political leaders such as vice-President Radhakrishan, Defence Minister Krishna Menon, and Home Minister Pandit G.B. Pant separately. The talks went on up to six days between Indian and Chinese delegation to find some interim solution that was convenient to both the parties. After 20 hours of talks between Nehru and Zhou, no such significant result came out, except the joint communiqué. The communiqué read that, the officials of the two governments would meet from June to September alternatively at the two capitals and examine, check and study all historical documents, records, accounts, maps and other study materials relevant to the boundary question on which each side relied in support of its stand, and draw up a report for submission to the two governments". The two governments also agreed to take all possible and available mechanism to avoid the ongoing border clashes between the two armies[142] There is no doubt that the talks failed to resolve the issue, as there was huge differences between Indian and Chinese view points, besides lack of mutual trust.

Soon after the end summit, Nehru laid the joint communiqué on the table of Lok Sabha for discussion on April 26, 1960. Despite the failure of the talk, Nehru stated that it was an initial attempt to resolve the differences.

"In a state of affairs of this kind," he added "one naturally tries every method which might prove helpful". He also informed the house that the discussion did not progress because the Chinese side did not have much documents with them and both the sides agreed to explore and examine all related documents in the coming days.[143] But this remark was not sufficient to satisfy the overwhelming oppositions. Looking at the demand to hold a full debate on the issue by the opposition parties, especially Jan Sangh and Socilist Pary, the speaker fixed April 29 as the date for debate.

On the scheduled day, the speaker allowed the members to raise their concerns on the Sino-Indian border disputes and the recent Prime Ministerial level meeting. Initiating the debate while introducing an amendment to the government motion, S.N. Dwivedy (PSP) argued that "no useful purpose would be served by continuing the talks or by appointing a team of officers to consider the details of the Chinese claim".[144] He further stated that India wanted concrete steps to defy the Chinese aggression and restore the country's integrity. By questioning Zhou's intention, Dwivedy argued that the Chinese premier was not at all ready to lose an inch of land to India and India should be prepared to face any challenge from China. He also objected to the agreement regarding dispatch of patrol to the border regions and stated that "we have not only allowed ourselves to be equated with the aggressor, but have committed ourselves to a course of action which … might enable the enemy to consolidate their position in occupied territory". He also requested the government to take hard steps to get vacated the occupied land by using all sorts of means.[145]

Similar view was also possessed by Jan Sangh, one of the strong anti-Chinese opposition parties. Following the party line, A.B. Vajpayee also moved an amendment rejecting China's claim on the captured Indian Territory. Through the amendment he opposed the India-China talks and stated that, India was losing its rights to reoccupy its lost land by agreeing to withdraw its troops from the present line of control. The amendment mentioned that, "This house feels that it is imperative that avenues, other than negotiations must be exploited to secure early vacation of Chinese aggression." Vajpayee felt that, while the talk had not served any interest of India, it helped China in various angles. He also criticized the government for its failure to brand Chinese act on the border as the policy of "aggression" and not perceptional "differences" as it mentioned in the joint communiqué. He cautioned Nehru to think twice before "falling into the Chinese trap of prolonged talk" that, he believed was meant for buying time for greater preparation for future action.[146] Extending the debate Prof. Nayakulu G. Ranga (INC) stated that there was no doubt that the high level talks failed.

But it was more painful that India lost its right to patrol, while China continued to sit there. He also asked Nehru to mobilize opinion against Chinese aggression through the Non-aligned countries by using the Badung Declaration. Similar appeal was also made by Braj Raj Singh (socialist) to internationalize the Chinese aggression and suggested the government to organize Bandung Conference like "Afro-Asian Conferences", excluding China, to mobilise world opinion.[147] Another socialist leader Ramsevak Yadav moved an amendment criticizing government of India's weak foreign policy to deal with Chinese threat and termed it as "complete failure". He further asked the government to take all possible steps to drive out Chinese occupation.[148] Similar amendment was also moved by P.K. Deo of Gantantra Parishad pushing for a clear deadline to vacate the occupied Indian Territory and strengthening of India's frontier lines from Chinese aggression.[149] He also asked the government not to waste time in investigating documents and to adopt a proactive approach to regain the lost land, for which he believed, India must increase its military power.[150]

However Communist Party of India was very supportive towards the Nehru's China policy. Rejecting the allegation of the "talk as a failed show", H.N. Mukherjee stated that, it is unfortunate that no decision had been made to settle the boundary question it definitely opened the door for further discussion, besides proving the base to discuss and understand each other's perception. He also welcomed the agreement to neutralize the clashes and maintain tranquillity in the frontier. By criticizing the voice of anti-talk Parliamentarians, he moved an amendment in the Lok Sabha stating "certain vested interests in our country do not desire that there should be continuation of the talks … they are strongly backed by the reactionary section of the press."[151]

Prime Minister in his reply disapproved the criticism and condemned the attitude of the members towards the recent completed talks. He argued that, it was an attempt to know each other's stand and realize the situation. "I say any time even in the middle of a war, I think I will talk, at no time I shall refuse to talk" Nehru emphasised. Attacking the baseless argument of oppositions he stated that, he and his government might be wrong in dealing Chinese aggression but, merely shouting loudly about the courage, about thronging out the aggressor would not show the realist i.e understanding of the situation. He felt, the members of the opposition had shown "themselves amazingly incompetent to even understand the situation, far less to face". Replying to the question of mobilization of non-aligned countries against the Chinese aggression, he said it was not right for India to seek other's support in order to protect its territory, it showed a "sense of weakness, a sense of non-reliance on ourselves..."[152]

As usual, the reply of Nehru did not convince the house and the opposition members continued to shout in the house. The opposition at large, except CPI stood together in criticizing the government's weak foreign and defence policy against the aggressive China, whereas, Communist leaders mostly supported Nehru's China policy. Though majority of the Congress leaders followed the party line, some of the leaders were not happy with Nehru's present approach towards the border disputes.

Increasing Infiltration in NEFA and Parliament's Reaction

Though both the Prime Ministers agreed not to send its patrol party to the border region, the agreement seemed failed within a few weeks. According to the official reports, Chinese troops intruded into NEFA region of Indian Territory on June 3, 1960.[153] More than two months later on August 13, Nehru informed the house about the incident briefly. But he presented the real picture of the story only on August 31, 1960. During the Parliamentary debate he explained that India lodged a strong protest to the incursion on which China admitted that only nine woodcutters and not Chinese army had entered into the Indian Territory and returned later.[154]

This deliberate attempt to hide the incident evoked sharp outrage from all sections of the house. Vajpayee (BJS) moved an amendment criticizing the delayed information stated that "the country was not immediately informed of the violation of Indian border in the NEFA area by Chinese soldiers on 3 June 1960". By criticizing the present condition of strategic management, Congress leader Ram Subhag Singhstated that the present situation in NEFA region only showed "the effectiveness of our administration there in NEFA" and need to be strengthened further. He also objected to Nehru's statement that declared Shipki Village as part of Chinese territory, whereas, he believed, it was established by Indians long ago.[155]

India further complained for repeated air space violation by Chinese air force during the second half of 1960. In a note handed over to Chinese Embassy on October 24, 1960 stated that, as much as 52 air violations had been made by Chinese side. India Also complained for the imposition of unnecessary restrictions to its traders and pilgrims in western Tibet. [156] In reply, China also complained about the Chinese air space violation by Indian air force and expulsion of representative of Hsinhna News Agency (HNA) by Indian officials.[157]

Failure of Sino-Indian Talks and Reaction of Indian Parliament

Similarly, most of opposition parties (Except CPI) criticized the ongoing talks and negotiation process between Indian and Chinese official. They believed that it was only beneficial to China as it was going to get a chunk of the Indian Territory during negotiation. Praja Socialist Party for example, argued that China had proposed for negotiation only after grabbing what it wanted and successfully termed border aggression into border disputes during meeting.[158] Correspondingly, Swantra party leader Prof. N.G. Ranga doubted the successiveness of the talks, which he felt was unnecessarily extended up to all sectors, rather than being limited to disputed frontiers.[159] On the other hand, Surendra Mohanty of Ganatrantra Parishad strongly opposed to the appointment of the Indian officials to discussion on the boundary questions, where India had declared earlier that its borders with China had been demarcated and settled.[160] A.B. Vajpayee, presenting Jan Sangh's stand said that, China was only baying time through unnecessary talks to explore its legal stands. He also wanted to know the government's strategy if the talk would fail.[161]

However, Communist Party opposed any criticism to the ongoing negotiation talk. Its leader H.N. Mukherjee warned the house that, this kind of criticism may 'queer the pitch of settlement particularly when the discussions are now proceeding…"[162] Nehru on the other hand informed the house that, the talk was going at the right direction, though it had been enlarged.[163]

Meanwhile, the report of the ongoing Sino-Indian border talks was published on February 14, 1961. As expected by most of the non-communist opposition parties, it failed to resolve the outstanding disputes. Instead of one unanimously accepted report, the whole bunch consisted of two different independent reports, each narrating the arguments of one side, followed by a short three page joint declaration. And the Indian version of the report was totally contrasted with the Chinese version. The fundamental difference was surrounded to the demarcation of the frontier line. While India argued that it had been demarcated previously, China said, it had never been delimited earlier. China also refused to have discussion on Sino-Bhutanese and Sino-Sikkim boundaries stating that they were beyond the scope of present discussion. On the other hand India argued that, it was treaty bound to protect Bhutan's boundary, hence should be discussed in the ongoing talks. Even the short joint report lacked any concrete mechanism to settle the border, hence the talk could be considered as a failed attempt. The Only thing both the parties gained out of the talks was perhaps an attempt to understand each other's stand.[164]

The Government presented the report of the Sino-Indian Border Talks in the Lok Sabha on February 14, 1961. The reaction of the opposition parties, except CPI, was strong. They criticized the government for its weak policy (policy of appeasement as some of them argued) and its failure to defend Indian borders. Ashoka Mehta (PSP) for instance criticized the government for its failure to maintain the Police Check Posts along the border of Akashi Chin which was, as mentioned in the report, established by rulers of Kashmir as early as 1865.[165] Prof. Ranga (INC) stated that, the report clearly states that Tibet was enjoying autonomy to attend international conferences and sign any treaty regarding its border settlement with India. Hence, he believed that the government was paying the price for its failure to protect Tibet that might have saved the border of India.[166] Similarly, Jan Sangh leader A.B. Vajpayee stated that, it was a grave mistake to accept Chinese sovereignty over Tibet, whereas China was deliberately questioning India's special relations with Sikkim and Bhutan, as well as the legal rights over Kashmir.[167] Achraya Kripalani (PSP) stated that India would have prepared this kind of report just after the Chinese aggression in Tibet to educate and mobilize international support. As the report states Tibet's was an independent and autonomous kingdom and before Chinese annexation, the government should revise its policy towards Tibet.[168] However, the stand of the Communist Party was entirely different on the report of the border talks. Following the party line, S.A. Dange argued that the successful completion of talks and the production of report were major advancements towards resolving Sino-Indian border disputes. The report, as he believed, was a sincere attempt to seek the historical positions of both the sides in the context of present differences and understand each other's positions.

The discussion did not end there and once again was raised on April 1, 1961 in Lok Sabha. During the debate on foreign affairs, the issue of Sino-Indian talks was raised in the Lok Sabha. Initiating the debate, Nehru stated that, the talks did not fail; rather it offered an opportunity to place Indian argument before the Chinese authority. He stated that the documents that India presented were apparently strong and might be able to convince the Chinese official and make them realize their faults one day. Responding to the question regarding strong action against China, Nehru stated, "… one takes strong action, when other actions are all precluded, and when one is prepared for the strong action. It would not be wise to take strong action when one cannot take it with any effect."[169] He believed that as India's case was very strong, there was no need for the strong action and the matter could be solved peacefully by talks.

However, Kripalini did not subscribe to the argument and pressed for the strong military action as he felt that expecting any solution from strong

Chinese leadership was a vain hope.[170] Similarly, Nath Pai also attacked Nehru's hypothetical aspirations of realization of faults by Chinese authority. Critiquing Nehru's "only option" remark to solve the disputes, he put a provocative question, "are there no other methods to us? (to drive out Chinese aggression)". Swatrantra Party leader Mohammad Imam regretted about Nehru's one sided peace approach whereas, he believed, China was opting for stronger actions. Criticizing Nehru's policy towards the Chinese aggression he further stated, "... so far as China is concerned, our Prime Minister's policy has been a failure. It has been a failure from the very beginning'. He sought for revision of the present policy towards China.[171] Parliamentarian Ram Sevak Yadav of Socialist Party, however, condemned the weak Indian policy and felt that China would take advantage of this and continue to expand its territory deep into Indian borders. He asked the government to take special efforts to establish greater relationship with the Nepal, Bhutan and Sikkim to defeat all kinds of Chinese aggression.[172] However, the Communist Party of India favoured the ongoing negations and other efforts to resolve the disputes peacefully. Its leader, Renu Chakravarti stated that, "if political settlement is a process which we advocate for all areas of disputes and conflicts, surely this must be a method of settlement of our dispute with China..."[173]

Prime Minister Nehru in reply stated that, he was very optimistic towards the peaceful settlement of the border disputes and hoped that China would change its policy because of "the logic or circumstances, facts and pressures". Answering the question regarding seeking support from neighboring states and other world powers Nehru observed that, India's stand became weaker, thought most of the states were against the Chinese aggression. He also refused Kripalani's "war is the only option" argument and stated that his government would continue to bank on the peaceful approach. At the same time, he said, India must be ready to face any unexpected challenge.[174] The opposition members were not satisfied and took every opportunity to attack government and its policy. The members also attacked Defence Minister Menon. They mostly criticized Menon for his failure to protect India's frontier line and weak defence policy. The constant criticism forced Menon to clarify the subject that was largely rejected by the opposition parties.[175]

Indian Parliament on Visit of the Secretary General of MEA to China

Amidst the growing differences and difficult times, Secretary-General of the Ministry of External Affairs, R.K. Nehru visited China in July 1961 on his return journey from the Mongolia, representing India at the 40th

Anniversary of the Mongolian independence. He had meeting with President, and Prime Minister of China and other imminent officials and discussed various issues with them including the ongoing boundary problems.[176] This visit drove sharp criticism from the non-communist opposition parties, as they felt it was not right time to visit China while Chinese troops continued to occupy vast areas of Indian Territory. Reacting to the increasing criticism on the Secretary-General's China visit Nehru informed the house on August 16, 1961 that, R.K Nehru had chosen the shortest route to Mongolia and hence, decided to stay and meet some of the important Chinese officials. Denying the meeting as negotiations Nehru said, "Talking does not mean negotiating anything" and further clarified that he (Secretary-General) had no power to negotiate, nor could he do so." However, Nehru informed the house that, the recent talk with Chinese officials was not productive and concluded without any agreement. "In some small matters here and there, there was some slight variation, but basically it was a repetition. So the position regard to border situation remains, more or less, what it was", he added. The Prime Minister also informed the house that no further incursion had been taken place by the Chinese forces, at the same time the Chinese did not withdraw its troops from the occupied territories, except Longju.[177]

However, Nehru's Clarification and arguments did not satisfy the opposition members, especially members of Non-Communist parties. Jan Sangh Leader A.B. Vajpayee reacted strongly to the Secretary-General's visit and stated that it was inappropriate to pay a high level official visit by Secretary-General just to know China's reaction to the joint report of the delegate level Sino-Indian Border talks. He argued that Chinese reaction could be estimated by its decision not to publish the report. Hence, the recent diplomatic visit was a waste of resources and openly showed India's weakness to handle the Chinese aggression.[178] Similarly, Mohammad Imam of Swantra Party condemned the visit and termed it as another act of appeasement.[179] P.K. Deo of Gantantra Parishad criticizing the unproductive talks stated that, China only understood the "the language of strength". Asking the government to transfer the charges from diplomatic leadership to military leadership to drive out Chinese occupation, he said, "I think it is high time that the entire job should be entrusted to our gallant *jawans* and they should be asked to push out the Chinese intruders from the Indian soil and give them a destructive blow". [180]

Nehru in reply said that, it was not correct to oppose the Secretary-General's China visit and talk to the Chinese official, especially when there were differences widely visible. He made it clear that, talk does not mean "giving up something that is vital to us or subordinating our interests through fear or otherwise". The visit was normal and "something necessary" and should not be seen through bad light. Justifying the purpose of the visit, Nehru also informed the house that there was no case of recent incursion from the Chinese side.[181]

The assurance of Nehru was soon proved negative as new report of border violation by Chinese forces was coming from the border regions. The opposition parties, except Communist Party of India attacked the government for its deliberate attempt to hide the incidents, though the government had lodged an official complaint before China on October 31, 1961.[182] Many opposition members across the party line attacked the Prime Minister and Defence Minister and demanded a separate debate of the recent incursion and criticized Nehru's China policy. The constant demand forced the government to place White Paper-V on the floor of house for discussion. But the repeated assurance by the government to take all possible steps to protect India's frontiers did not satisfy the oppositions and the house remained under fire quite often on Sino-Indian relations.

India's Forward Policy and Reaction of Parliament

Despite all possible attempts to convince the Chinese leadership, China continued to occupy a large chunk of Indian Territory and refuse to withdraw its troops back. The peaceful options such as talks and negotiations also failed to resolve the issue and there was a report of Chinese military buildups along the borders. At this juncture, India opted to use hard power to push back Chinese occupation from the occupied Indian territories, assuming that China was unlikely to launch a major operation to counter Indian move. Popularly, known as India's "Forward Policy", the plan intended to deter further Chinese aggression and reoccupy the lost territories that India assumed to fall within its territorial jurisdiction. For the realization of the plan, Indian government decided to create additional forward posts and cover unreachable areas along the Chinese border. In addition to this, the strength of the Indian posts was increased with the deployment of additional forces and the soldiers were asked to drive out the Chinese incursion.[183] Though the operation gained success initially, it led to full-fledged war and cost heavy casualties subsequently due to improper planning and lack of logistics. The Forward Policy also became a point of Justification for China to lunch a massive attack against India that ended with loss of large chunk of Indian Territory to China.

The Forward Policy, though succeeded a lot to restore the government's image in the Indian Parliament (which have been blamed for its soft policies towards China), it did not silent the opposition parties. While the non-communist opposition parties criticized the government for its delay to use force against Chinese aggression, the Communist Parties attacked the government for the violation of *Panchsheel* agreement and initiating war like situation with China. In addition, the opposition members also attacked the government whenever the border incidents used to occur. But the government came under heavy criticism by the opposition Parties, both Communist and Non-Communist, when the *White Paper-V* on Sino-Indian Relations was placed in the Parliament for discussion on December 4, 1961. The general argument of the non-communist opposition parties was, the government must meet the Chinese threat with equal force, as China had been using force from the beginning. Parliamentarian A.B. Vajpayee of Jan Sangh for example, condemned the government for its failure to prevent the Chinese aggression and restricting the armed forces from attacking the Chinese soldiers at the beginning stages, which, he believed could have prevented the situation to escalate to present stage. He also criticized the government's deliberate attempt to suppress information related to Chinese aggression to the nation for such a long time. Vajpayee regretted that, Nehru would even surrender Ladakh to China, if similar kind of appeasement policy continued. He asked the government to be proactive with aggressive policies to deter Chinese aggression by supporting Tibetan movement, building roads and communication facilities in Ladakh and increasing the force strength in the frontier posts.[184] Similarly, PSP leader Ashok Mehtaaccused Nehru for his weak Chinese policy which, he felt, is based on "Miasma of Misunderstanding". Blaming Nehru for his directionless China policy he stated: "I do not know if the Prime Minister in his mind as to the nature of the threat that China holds out to us and the manner in which that threat has to be countered". He felt that, it was only the soft policy adopted by India that resulted into the Chinese encroachment in Ladakh. Mehta sought for peruse of strong policies towards the Chinese aggression and drove out Chinese occupation by using force and adoption of aggressive diplomatic strategy to own international support without taking the issue into United Nations.[185] Prof. N.G. Ranga also followed the hard-line in criticizing Nehru's China policy and Government's failure to defend Indian borders. He appealed the people of the country to "enlist themselves in the new cadres of army … and defend the frontiers of our country". He regretted for the state of affairs of Sino-India border disputes where government of India had failed to release Longju form Chinese occupation since 1956. In criticizing Nehru's foreign policy Prof. Ranga stated that, "if this is the manner our foreign policy has been adopted so far as China is concerned, then I can only say, God alone can look after this country, if this is not able to vacate this party from power". Like Ashok Mehta he also called for the withdrawal of all diplomatic ties with China and asked the government not to support the membership of China at the United Nations.[186] Similarly, Socialist leader Braj Raj Singh and Acharaya Kripalini (PSP) condemned the government for its failure over the Chinese aggression and the overall situation of India's defence scenario. Both Kripalani and Singh attacked the government and the present political leadership for its overall failure to protest India's frontiers and its inaction to overthrow the Chinese occupations. Kripalini also attacked the Defence Minister for the present state of affairs at Longju and other frontier posts and objected to its statement in UN where he (Defence Minister) stated that there was no real threat from China. Kripalani also called the government to face the challenge posed by China and deal the situation with equal force and power.[187]

While the Con-communist parties were demanding strong action against Chinese incursion, leftist parties were advocating tranquillity in the border to resolve the issue peacefully. CPI leader Hiren Mukherjee for instance, appealed the government not to listen to the extremist views of the oppositions and to peruse the cooperative approach with China to resolve the differences on frontier regions. Criticizing the BJS and PSP and other opposition parties demands, Mukherjee stated that some parties tried to pull the country into a warlike situation by misleading the nation and putting pressure over the government. Denying any possible Chinese attack, he asked the government to deal with the Chinese government patently during all difficult times without seeking weaponry from Western powers.[188]

The voice inside the ruling Congress party also went vocal against Nehru's weak policy towards China and his inaction to liberate India lost territories from the Chinese occupation. Members of the ruling Congress Party such as Ram Subhag Singh and Sushila Nayar for instance, strongly criticized the government for its failure to protect India's frontiers and inaction to overthrow the Chinese occupation. They also questioned Nehru's Tibet policy and asked Nehru to deal with Chinese aggression strongly.[189]

Replying to the allegations of the oppositions Nehru stated that, security arrangement of the frontier regions of India had improved a lot with the setup of new border posts and increment of force strength all along the Chinese border. He also assured the Parliament that the government was determined to get back the occupied land and would not hesitate to take hard steps if required. "We hope...., he added "that we shall be able to succeed in getting this land vacated through pressures, through other things, whatever they may be, and without engulfing the whole world in a major war". Besides exploring peaceful means, Nehru further explained, that the government was also actively engaged in "administratively, militarily building it (the frontiers) up, preparing the ground for advance….. (by) putting up our posts, administrative centres and others (along the Chinese borders)". He also denied the charges of restricting the Indian army to fire upon the Chinese soldiers and stated that, "our military posts ….. obviously….. are there to defend, to attack or to do whatever the position may demand". Replying to the opposition's charges of not paying enough importance to the national frontiers, Nehru stated that, "... I would beg the house at least to accept this statement of mine that we attach the greatest importance to it and it is not a party matter, it is obviously; it is a matter of national importance….." Replying to the question of Tibet, Nehru justified India's stand and stated that it was the best policy that government of India had adopted towards Tibet issue.[190] But these replies of Nehru did not serve any cause and the Lok Sabha continued to be pessimistic towards the government's China policies.

By this time the Chinese authority began to object India's forward posts and military buildups along the border regions. They also issued protest notes and ultimatums to India asking it to be prepared to face the consequences if it won't withdraw its troops from the Chinese borders. Such kind of protest note, for the first time was received by India on November 30, 1961. In this note, China suggested to call back Indian forward posts and to maintain the earlier line.[191] Another similar note was presented to India on March 1, 1962 accusing India for refusing to hold talks with China while continuing to march towards the Chinese territories.[192] These consecutive Chinese ultimatums drove strong voices in the Parliament. The opposition parties made huge noise in the house, while some of the members sought to bring adjournment motions. Nath Pai for instance, on May 3, 1962, proposed to move an adjournment motion regarding the Chinese ultimatum to India demanding the withdrawal of Indian forces from some of the frontier posts or else they would push back Indian military by action.[193] Replying to the motion and declaring government's stand to the Chinese notice Nehru stated that, China was complaining because of its worry over the growing Indian military strength." I do not think" he further added, "that any serious situation has arisen by their sending this note … but we propose to remain where we are, and not to move because of any Chinese threats."[194]

Nehru's this bold statement and the growing Chinese worry due to India's "forward policy" presented Nehru in a complete different light and resulted huge applause from all sections of the house. The oppositions that used to be critical towards Nehru's China policies praised the changed stand of the government. Nathpai, one of the biggest critiques of Nehru's China policies, for instance welcomed the changed approach to deal with the Chinese aggression. Complementing government's new face he stated, "I think that the new kind of firming of the will is the true policy of the government of India. These new notes exchange between the two governments are gradually reflecting the policy".[195] Similarly, Swatantra party leader Nersimha Reddy also applauded the government for its changing policies towards Chinese invention and asked the Prime Minister to follow the same in future. He believed that the transformation of the attitude of the Prime Minister occurred due to the constant public pressure through democratic machinery like the Parliament.[196] Another critic of Nehru's China policies, Frank Anthony (Independent)also welcomed government's 'u' turn policy in dealing with Chinese aggression. "Today our government has come to a long overdue realization that in China we are dealing with a country whose rules are not only militant but intransigent too..." he stated.[197]

Thus the new avatar of the government was mostly welcomed by the opposition parties and Congress members. However, Communist party of India was not happy and reacted sharply to the government's new policies towards China. Its leader Inderjeet Gupta refused to subscribe the government's new policy and asked the government to follow the earlier approach of dialogue and negations and to bring down the differences.[198]

Nehru, in reply to the debate stated that, he had proposed to the Chinese authority for the mutual withdrawal of forces from both the sides of the border shown in the Chinese map. But he made it clear that the proposal of mutual withdrawal was only applicable to Ladakh regions and not to eastern regions. Repeating his policies he declared that, his government was committed to explore all peaceful means and also agree to allow Chinese to use the Aksai chin road for civilian purpose, besides holding negotiations for the settlement of the boundary.[199]

Despite Nehru's clarifications and assurance to treat the Chinese aggression with equal force, the opposition parties, including a section of ruling party remained critical because of the looming tension between the two countries. Number of diplomatic notes had been exchanged between the nations during this disturbing situation and the tension was escalating between the two governments regarding the border disputes. The government machinery, especially the Indian Parliament remained vigilant to the situation and the opposition parties exploited the situation to criticize the government, hence the atmosphere of the Parliament was hot during this time. The consecutive diplomatic and warning notes were made public and presented in the Parliament. Every time the opposition members rose into their toes to criticize the government for its inaction against China. Members of Jan Sangh, Socialist, PSP and other rightwing parties often asked the government to review their Chinese policy and deal China with iron hand. They were constantly pressuring and insisting the government to follow a realistic foreign policy towards China as it had continued to violate the basic norms of Panchsheel and forcefully occupied a large chunk of Indian Territory. Therefore the Parliament remained critical to Nehru's China policy.

Chinese Proposal for the Renewal of Panchsheel

While the heated argument was being exchanged and the situation of the frontiers was intense, China proposed India to negotiate for a new agreement on trade and intercourse (as popularly known as Panchsheel earlier) on December 3, 1961. On December 15 government of India, in reply wrote a letter to the Chinese government showing little interest mentioning the collapse of the previous agreement due to China's unnecessary restrictions on Indian businessman and pilgrims.[200]

Soon after receiving the Chinese proposal, Nehru briefed the house about the Chinese intention on December 5, 1961. The Parliament, especially the members of the opposition party reacted sharply to the proposal and warned the government against any such negotiation. Swatantra Party leader M.R. Masani, while initiating the debate asked the government not to enter into any negotiation with China unless and until China withdrew its forces from the Indian Territory.[201] Similarly, Nath Pai of PSP also appealed to the government not to fall into the Chinese trap for a second time by signing the treaty while China continued to occupy large chunk of Indian territory.[202] Following the party line Jan Sangh leader Balraj Madhko moved one step ahead and requested the government to rectify its mistake of 1954 treaty and recognize Tibet as an independent country. He also asked the government to stay away from any such negotiations that endanger Indian security.[203]

During the address to the Parliament, President Rajendra Prashad mentioned about the new proposal and it led another round of debate on the renewal of the Panchsheel agreement.[204] Balraj Madhok (Swantantra) moved an amendment to explore the opportunities to rectify its mistakes and reorganize India's Tibet policy. He also objected to the reply note that failed to mention to vacate the occupied territories of India categorically.[205] Similarly, debating on India's reply note S.N. Dwivedy also objected to

India's demand for "reversal Policy" and demanded clarification on the special term on the present contest.[206] P.K. Deo of Swatantra also asked the government not to have any agreement with China as the 1954 agreement had been repeatedly violated by China while inventing Indian territories.[207]

A few consecutive notes were exchanged between India and China. After a long exchange of notes, India, on April 11, 1962 informed that it had no objection to the proposed negotiation for a new agreement, but China had to withdraw its troops from the Indian soil. In other words, it put the condition of vacation of occupied frontiers before any negotiation, on which China never agreed. Hence the proposed negotiation never happened and the old treaty of trade and intercourse lapsed on its due date of June 3, 1962.

The Increasing Tension on the Border

As India showed little interest to renew the 1954 treaty of trade and intercourse, China informed India to recall its trade agencies from Calcutta and Kalimpong on May 23, 1962. In return India also decided to shut down its trade agencies at Gyantse, Yatung and Gartok. The decision to close down the trade agencies finally brought all trade relationship to an end on June 3, 1962, on the date of expiry of the existing agreement.[208] Due to the expiry of Panchsheel agreement, the breakup of trade relationship and the rising tension at the frontiers, the India- China relationship gradually started declining and led the border tensions further high. By July 10, 1962, the situation led to the massive military movement from both the sides and the Indian and the Chinese soldiers stood face to face within a few hundred yards. Chinese forces moved back when India informed that it would use force if Chinese army marched further. In a different incident, two Indian patrols came under the heavy fire from the Chinese army in the Chip Chap Valley and in the vicinity of Pongong Lake. Both the countries blamed each other for the incidents. To ease the tension, India repeated its willingness to hold talks after the normalization of current tensions on the basis of official reports, on which Penking did not agree upon and the situation remained intense.[209]

Nehru briefed the incidents in the Parliament and presented the White Paper VI for discussion. He also informed the house that his government was committed to defend the frontiers by establishing several border posts to prevent the Chinese aggression. As a result Chinese forces were compelled to move back. Refereeing to the Galwan Valley he stated that no untoward incidents took place though, both the forces continued to face each other.

About the Chip Chap valley he clarified that Indian patrols came under fire from Chinese troops and only opened fire in self-defence after Chinese attack, hence the Chinese accusations were baseless. He further blamed China for the recent increment of tensions and stated that the situation excelled due to the heavy Chinese military activities and buildups along the borders. Nehru also informed the house about the government of India's desire to negotiate with China if the situation improved to normalcy and he would present everything before the house in detail, if the negotiation took place.[210]

Though the Indian decision to use force against the Chinese aggression was welcomed by opposition parties, they opposed to hold any talks with Chinese government about the border disputes and demanded for a separate discussion on the recent development of the Sino-Indian Border disputes. Members like Frank Anthony and S.N. Dwivedy came to the front and asked for a special discussion on the issue.[211]

Initiating the debate S.N. Dwivedy argued "I don't think there is any further room for any peaceful discussion (with China) ......" Looking at the growing voice for the debate, the government moved a motion calling the attention of the house about the grave situation along the India China borders, more particularly in the Ladakh regions. Presenting the motion Nehru stated that the situation of the frontier regions remained hostile due to the military standoffs. Referering to his decision to hold talks, he clarified that, India did not recognize Chinese line of 1956 and 1960 and it stood by the international frontiers that had been shown in our maps. Nehru also informed the house that, any discussion with China would start only after the restoration of the line prior to1959.[212] However, in his talks, he never denied to hold talks with China to dismantle the tense.

Absence of any assurance regarding not to hold talks with China drove huge criticism from all corners of the house, especially from the members of Non-Communist opposition parties. Members like, UM Trivedi (Jan Sangh), S.N Dwivedy (PSP), P.K. Deo (Swantantra) and Frank Anthony moved individual amendment motions against possibility of holding any talks and reaching to any negations with China, while China continued to occupy large areas in Indian territories.[213] Several other members from the opposition parties also supported the motions and supplemented further debates against the governmental decision to negotiate with China.[214]

However, members of the Communist and ruling Congress party advocated the initiation of talks with Chinese authority to normalize the situation. CPI leader H.N. Mukherjee for instance, asked Nehru to hold talks with China for the peaceful negotiation of border disputes. He also lashed out the Non-Communist oppositions for their constant opposition to talks and advocacy for the India-China war. He believed that China was determined to resolve the boundary problem through peaceful means, as it settled the border disputes with Nepal, Burma and Indonesia. He further urged the government not to miss the opportunity by bowing down to the pressure of opposition parties.[215] Similarly, majority of the members of the ruling Congress Party also blamed the opposition members for advocating war with China without thinking of the consequences. Congress leader R.K. Khadilkar for instance criticized the oppositions for its unrealistic stand on the India China border disputes and blamed the opposition for misleading the country for the political mileage.[216] Bakar Ali Mirza (INC) while advocating for the bilateral talks with China stated, "if you want negotiations you must give freedom of manoeuvre to the negotiator. You have to see who the negotiator opposite is. He has not got to take account to any Parliament. He is not to satisfy any important daily or the press. … if you want to take back all the territory from China, before the start of the negotiations then what is there to negotiate?"[217] Similarly, Brajeswar Prashad also asked the government to start negotiating with China without any pre-conditions. Presenting his unconditional support to the Sino-Indian Border negotiation he said, "I stand by peace at any price; for the alternative to peace is global destruction of the world".[218]

Replying to the opposition's sharp objection to any future negotiation with China and their advocacy for war, Nehru stated that he would not base himself from holding any talks if China was interested to negotiate. Branding the opposition's childish argument he said, "it is childish nonsense, if I may say so, it is absurd for the government if it is to be carried on in this way; do not talk; do not have tea with him; do not have launch with him! Is this the way to carry on this great debate, this great argument, in this great conflict with another country?" Justifying government of India's decision Nehru further explained "First of all there is a difference between negotiations and talks …. One should always talk, whatever happens, whatever the position, and whatever the chances. If I have the chance to talk I will talk to them". However, Nehru informed the house that, he would not agree to anything out of the negotiations, that "sullies the honour of India. (But) for rest, I want free hand". Nehru also requested the opposition to withdraw the amendment motions. In response to Nehru's appeal the opposition members withdrew their amendment motions, but disagreed to approve the government's motion.[219]

While the two countries were deciding to hold a negotiation, it had been reported that, on September 8, 1962, Chinese forces had crossed the McMahon Line in the Khemang Division of NEFA region. After the investigation on ground, the government of India confirmed the report of border violation and protested sharply.[220] However, China denied any border violation and proposed the mutual withdrawal of forces 20 kilometres back from the present line all along the border. China also formally proposed October 15 as the date of Sino-Indian Discussion on the basis of official reports without setting any preconditions. India confirmed its willingness for the discussion on the particular day.

After a few days, on September 20, Chinese forces crossed the McMahon line and attacked a remote forward post at the Dhola region. Similar Chinese attack was reported on September 29 in the same region of NEFA and war like situation erupted all along the frontier lines of eastern sector. India objected to the ruthless attack on Indian forces and refused to discuss on eastern sector, on which China never agreed. Hence, no discussion took place in this time to bring down the tension between the two countries, and gradually, the situation had gone bad to worse.

China's All Out Invention and the Indian Parliament

Looking at the intensified Chinese aggression and heavy military buildups, a high level meeting was organized on September 9, 1962 under the Presidentship of Defence Minister, Krishna Menon. In the meeting it was decided that the Chinese forces had to push back from the Thang La Ridge immediately at any cost and by any means.[221] This decision was reflected on Prime Minister Nehru's statement. While leaving for Sri Lanka on October 12, Nehru informed the press that he had ordered the army to "clear Indian territory in the NEFA".[222] Government of India decided to raise a new army crops, named IV Crop, under the Eastern Command on October 12, 1962 and General B.M. Kaul was appointed its Commander to evict the Chinese occupation in NEFA. A Code named as "Operation Leghorn" an offensive military operation, for the first time from the Indian side, was launched in Thang La Ridge and the other regions of NEFA on October 10, 1962.[223] There was a general assumption among the Indian leaderships that, China would not involve in large-scale offence against India, which proved wrong later. Proving Indian calculation wrong, China reacted to the Indian movement and attacked back the Indian troops on October 10, 1962. After the Indian offensive attack and loss of 77 soldiers during the military clash, China decided to punish India and lodged a massive attack in NEFA and Ladakh simultaneously on October 20, 1962.[224] With the large scale Chinese attack, an undeclared war between India and China started in the high Himalayas. The overwhelming Chinese troops easily chased out Indian attackers and within 48 hours most of the Indian posts fell down in Ladakh and NEFA. Following the catastrophic casualties, Nehru, in a broadcast to the nation on October 22, 1962 appealed the people "to be united in this great enterprise and put aside the controversies and arguments, and present a solid united front before all those who see to endanger our freedom and integrity".[225]

Following the Mao Zedong's "*da da, tan tan* (fight fight, talk talk)." strategy,[226] China offered three point ceasefire proposal to India on October 24, 1962. The three proposals include:

1. Both parties affirmed that the Sino-Indian boundary question must be settled peacefully through negotiations. Pending a peaceful settlement, the Chinese Government hoped that the Indian Government would agree that both the parties should respect the line of actual control between the two sides along the entire Sino-Indian border, and the armed forces of each side withdraw 20 kilometres from this line and disengage.
2. Provided that the Indian Government agreed to the above proposal, the Chinese Government was willing, through consultation between the two parties, to withdraw its frontier guards in the Eastern Sector of the border to the north of the line of actual control; at the same time, both China and India undertook not to cross the line of actual control, i.e., the traditional, customary line, in the Middle and Western sectors of the border. Matters relating to the disengagement of the armed forces of the two parties and the cessation of armed conflict should be negotiated by officials designated by the Chinese and Indian Governments respectively.
3. In order to seek a friendly settlement of the Sino-Indian boundary question, talks should be held once again by the Prime Ministers of China and India at a time considered appropriate by both the parties. The Chinese Government would welcome the Indian Prime Minister to Peking; if this should be inconvenient to the Indian Government, the Chinese Premier would be ready to go to Delhi for talks.[227]

However, on October 27, Nehru refused to accept the proposal that attempted to compel India to follow Chinese plan of boundary settlement by taking the advantage of India's weak position in war. He replied to China that, India had no objection to any further peaceful negotiation on border disputes, provided China would pull its army back to the pre September 8 line.[228] Few consecutive notes were exchanged between India and China but it failed to reach any conclusion. Following India's refusal to Chinese designed ceasefire proposal, China marched ahead deep into the Indian Territory and continued its brutal attack on Indian defend lines. Looking at the increased Chinese attack, a state of national emergency, for the first time in the history of India was declared by the President of India, and the emergency session of the Parliament was called on November 8 to discuss the grave situation of the country.

Before the start of Parliament, Nehru announced the resignation of Defence Minister Krishna Menon on October 31, 1962. However, Menon was allowed to hold the portfolio of Defence Production. He did not even follow the customary duty of making statement in the Parliament following Nehru's advice. When the Parliament reassembled on November 8, 1962, Nehru moved a resolution affirming the support of people of India to overthrow the Chinese aggression. The resolution was gratefully acknowledged by the "moral and material support" received from the friendly countries.[229]

While presenting the motion, Nehru stated with great regret that, China, the champion of anti-imperialism, had been adopting an imperialist policy towards India since 1959 and constantly inching Indian territories by force. China's non-membership to United Nations facilitated its policy of aggression and misbehaviour. Its constant use of force for each and every problem indicated its dangerous state of affairs not only for India, but for the rest of the world, he added. Nehru also stated that, India, being the true friend of China stood behind her for all its difficult times and extended its unconditional support for its inclusion into United Nations, but in return received bullets and bombs from China. Challenging the Chinese aggression Nehru stated, "No self-respecting country, which loves its freedom and integrity can possibly submit to this challenge. Certainly, India this dear land of ours, will never submit to it, whatever the consequences. We accept the challenge in all consequences, whatever they may be."

Nehru, however, agreed to the view that, India was unprepared to the large scale Chinese attack and did not shape its defence strategy and facilities to meet the aggression. But he refused to accept the criticism of non-availability of winter clothes, blankets and shoes, and stated that the government provided every possible facilities and instruments that were available, to the soldiers. India had not imported and stocked sufficient foreign defence equipment, as it might weaken the economic development, he explained. Nehru further clarified that, China's large military buildups and available infrastructure for logistic supply which had been created following the Tibetan uprising, gave China upmost advantage during the present war. Refereeing to Chinese intension behind the recent border attack, he said, the nation need to be prepared to face the challenges of any type. He also asked the Parliament to "stand united in this great venture and demonstrate to the world that free India which has stood for peace will always stand for peace .... Never tolerate aggression and invasion". Nehru also presented India's grateful gratitude to the countries that supported India in these difficult times and extended their moral and material support.[230] Nehru's speech, presented in the state of the India's military debacle was moreover his compassioned regret before the Parliament and seemed helpless while making comments on India's security arrangements.

Opposition parties, especially non-communist members were not impressed by Nehru's regretful speech and charged him for the recent military disaster. Swatantra leader N.G. Ranga, by initiating the debate moved an amendment criticizing the "unpreparedness of the government to defend the frontiers of India against the aggression and invasion". He further blamed the government for its failure to provide adequate supplies to the soldiers. Objecting to the Chinese proposal of September 8 line, he stated "for the time being they say 8th September (1962) line. Where is it guaranteed that it is not likely to be 20th October and sometimes later 8th November?" India should, he added, approach the Western block for assistance and should not merely adhere to the policy of Non-alignment. Refereeing to Nehru's requisition of supports from all sections of Parliament, Prof. Ranga declared that his party would extend unconditional support to government to overthrow the Chinese aggression.[231]

Jan Sangh leader U.M. Trivedi moved another amendment against any possible talks with China and asked the government to refuse to negotiate any term or proposal until it vacated the captured areas.[232] He also condemned the government's unpreparedness to face the Chinese incursion despite increasing Chinese activities in the frontier regions. In spite of repeated warnings by the opposition parties the government did nothing other than criticizing the oppositions. However, he promised to extend all cooperation from his party to the government to fight with the aggressor as one nation.[233] Similarly, Parliamentarian Lahri Singh of the same party further argued with the government that India should review its Non-Aligned policy and should reach to the western blocks for military assistance in order to meet the Chinese challenge.[234]

Praja Socialist Party, another Non-Communist opposition party exploited the opportunity and attacked the government for its inactive actions. Its leader S.N. Dwivedy blamed the government for this military debacle due to its unpreparedness to meet the challenge and for hiding the fact to the nation about the Chinese aggression.[235] Similarly, V.M. Kamath of the same party, appealed the government to learn out of its mistakes and take immediate steps to make India capable enough to meet any future threats. By rejecting China's proposal of September 8 line, he stated that India should not trust the Communist conspiracy, which believed nothing other than expansionism.[236] Another prominent leader Hem Barua extended Kamath's arguments and condemned the attitude of expansionist Communism and the silence of Soviet Union, India's trusted friend and the leader of Communism on the Chinese attack. He suggested the government to approach the Western blocks to defeat the Communist aggression.[237]

The Socialist Party also condemned the government's failure to tackle Chinese aggression. Senior Socialist leader Ram Sevak Yadav moved an amendment to register his party's frustration to government's "unprincipled policy of appeasement". In the motion he asked the government to keep its policy open to secure arms and ammunitions from both Western and communist blocks and continue the "holy war" till the recovery of the last inch of the lost Indian territory.[238]

Little known independent members, alike the oppositions also attacked the government for its catastrophic failure to protect the frontlines. Independent members like Frank Anthony, Karni Singhjee and L.M. Singhvi openly criticized Nehru's ignorance to earlier warnings and government's unpreparedness to face the Chinese challenge. Anthony moved an amendment motion stating, the government should prepare the nation to face a "total war against the Chinese with immediate massive aid from the democracies". He argued that the policy of Non-alignment had no meaning at that time as no Afro-Asian country had come out to show open support to India, except Malaya. Hence, India should seek assistantee from Western countries.[239] Similarly, Singhjee suggested the government to think about developing nuclear weapons to beat any future foreign aggression.[240] Another independent leader Singhvi advocated for large scale attack against China with the help of Western powers.[241]

The Communist Party of India, which had been advocating for peaceful and cooperative relation with China, on other hand, was fixed in a dilemma to clarify its stand during the border clash. But, for the first time it argued to treat China as an aggressor and advocated to take strong action against the aggressor. Condemning the Chinese attack, its prominent leader Hiren Mukherjee stated that, China had "openly violated our borders and invaded our territory", hence need to be punished. Extending his party's full support he stated that "we join hands with all those who are behind the Prime Minister and we give support to the policies that he is pursuing at this juncture of our history". He also declared his unconditional support to the government's November 8 line stand and asked China to come to the agreement. However, he objected to beg before the Western block and argued to uphold the policy of Non-Alignment.[242]

The ruling Congress party at large supported the government's policy against the aggressive China. But a section of the Congress Party also criticized Nehru and his strategies. Its leader U.N. Dhebar, while supporting Nehru's strategy stated that, it was not possible to maintain the frontier when powerful country like China was determined to invade.[243] Similarly, A.P. Jain argued that, the attack was legacy of cold war strategy, where democracy had been considered as the greatest enemy of communism.[244] M. Thirumala Rao however, moved an amendment suggesting the government to be prepared to face prolonged and all-out war with China.[245] Similarly, Bibhuti Mishra also moved another amendment asking the government not to be trapped by the Chinese conspiracy by entering into any negotiation with Chinese authorities.[246]

A large section of Congress party, however, criticized the government for its repeated blunder that led to the recent military destruction. Seth Govind Das, for instance blamed the government for its recognition of Tibet as the part of China, that later resulted into the present Chinese border aggression.[247] Hare Krishna Mahtab, on other hand, asked the government to take this case of Chinese aggression into international community and seek international guaranty against future Chinese attack.[248] Some of the members objected to the government's September 8 line stand. Criticizing government's September 8 stand, P.C. Deshmukh asked the government not to enter into any interim arrangement. Mahavir Tyagi, repeating the same demand stated, "I must tell him (Nehru) that people are not happy with any idea of negotiations now". K. Hanumanthaiya had gone further in criticizing Nehru and directly attacked Nehru for his wrong policy against China. Fixing the responsibility on Nehru he stated, Nehru's arrogance and dictatorship in policy making led the country into the recent military disaster. He suggested the government to approach the United Nations against China's invasion.[249] Another Congress leader, Rajeshwara Patel defended Mr. Hanumanthaiya when he was attacked by the Congress members and stated that the party should stand by truth rather than false praising to leadership.

"We" he added, "should fearlessly place the facts before the Prime Minister who is responsible for the sad state of affairs in the country"[250].

Prime Minister Nehru in reply regretted for the emotional criticisms of the honourable Parliamentarians and stated that, he had planned the strategy as per the inputs from the military and defence experts. Based on the inputs, he ordered to drive out the Chinese aggression expecting that China would not go for such type of all-out war. Defending his idea he stated that, it was not good for the country to ignore the aggression and "walking back in our own territory". He also rejected the criticism of under equipment of the armed forces and argued that the soldiers had been provided with minimum equipment and clothing except the semi-automatic rifles which most of the developing countries did not possess. Referring to the role of Soviet Union, Nehru stated that, China had been the important ally of Soviet Union and it was difficult for Soviet Union to be aggressive against China. However, Soviet Union had been the old friend of India and "we have had their good-will and good wishes all along, even very recently, and that is a consolation to us and we recently hope to have that in future". Clarifying the confusion regarding the Chinese proposal of November 1951 position, Nehru stated that, China for the first time officially claimed the line on November 1959. Indian soldiers, he further clarified, "Pushed them back little" and setup several border posts ahead of the claimed line, which would help them to open access to Indian Territory through Thang La Pass. Therefore India rejected the proposal and advocated to maintain November 8 line, which, if applied would force China to go back and facilitate India to occupy the lost posts. Nehru also regretted for the opposition's objection to any negotiation with China and their unrealistic demand for the liberation of Tibet.[251]

This session witnessed several uneven debates. The whole Parliament, for the first time stood united against the Chinese aggression. In addition to the oppositions, members of independent parties, ruling Congress and more importantly, the Communist leaders also echoed in the same voice in denouncing the forceful invasion. The DMK party also suspended its pro-separation agitation until the end of war. The CPI, for the first time criticized Chinese aggression and vowed to stand to protect the unity and integrity of India at any cost.

With the request of the government, some of the amendment motions were withdrawn and rest of the motions were voted down by the Lok Sabha. The Lok Sabha then, passed two unanimous resolutions in regard to the recent Chinese aggression. Firstly, the proclamation of National Emergency by the President due to the Chinese led external attacks and condemning the Chinese aggression despite India's continuous goodwill gesture to the government and people of China. Finally the resolution also acknowledged the moral and material supports extended by friendly countries during the grim hours.[252]

During this time, China attacked the Eastern Sector and captured Tawang and Walong on November 16. Nehru, on November 19 (next sitting of the session, as November 17 and 18 was weekend holiday) informed the house about the grave situation of Eastern Sector and the fall of Tawang and Walong. He also vowed to take all possible steps to fight back and throw them out of the region.[253]

The house was shocked by the news. The opposition members further blamed the government for the recent aggression. PSP leader Hem Barua wanted to know the government's next move to counter the aggression. i.e. whether the government was thinking to go for a total war, with the help of foreign military assistance or opt for a negotiation with China irrespective of the cost.[254] Parliamentarian V.M. Kamath (PSP) and N.G. Ranga (Swatantra) expressed their concern about the present situations and asked the government to inform each and every bit of the fact to the house.[255]

The very next day (on November 20, 1962), Nehru informed the house about the loss of Bomdila into the Chinese hand and the fall of Chushul Post.[256] The news further drove strong reaction in the house. PSP leader V.M. Kamath alleged that, while the Indian posts were falling down one after another, the government had no plan to tackle the situation. He suggested a Parliamentary Committee to review the state of affairs of the war and the Prime Minister to discuss the situation with the committee on the daily basis.[257] N.G. Ranga (PSP) and U.M. Trivedi (BJS) requested the government to organize a secret session to discuss all aspects of the border conflicts.[258] Congress leader, Mahavir Tyagi criticized the government for not taking adequate steps to stop the Chinese march.[259]

Replying to the debates Nehru stated that it was not possible for the government to share everything in the Parliament, as the decisions were taken by the military authorities deployed at the ground. However, he informed the house that the government would approach the friendly nations and would continue its fight with the Chinese forces till the recuperation of last inch of the captured territory.[260] Convinced by Ranga and Trivedi's suggestion, on the same day Nehru also called a Non-Parliamentary meeting of important leaders of the Parliament cutting across the party line and discussed the state of the affairs of the Eastern and Western sector. He made it clear in the meeting that, India would not accept any ceasefire proposal until the vacation of the captured Indian Territory by China.[261]

China's Ceasefire Declaration and the Reactions of the Parliament

While the Chinese attack was at its peak during the late November and Indian posts were falling down consecutively, China declared the unilateral ceasefire in Eastern, Western and Middle sector. It also declared to withdraw its troops twenty kilometres back from the line of actual control that was maintained on November 7, 1959. The note further asked the Indian government to re-establish the consultative activities and negotiation in future to discuss the delimitation of the ceasefire line and demilitarized zones.[262]

Nehru briefed the Parliament about the Chinese ceasefire declaration and unilateral withdrawal of twenty kilometres from the line of actual control. However, he refused to comment anything on the declaration as no official communicated to India in this regard. He also repeated India's earlier stand that said, India would not go for any negotiation until China pulled back its army to the pre September 8 line. Nehru also declared that, India would continue to acquire military equipment from friendly countries, as China reserved the right to fight even after the deceleration of ceasefire.

The Parliament, however, remained concerned about the unilateral ceasefire declaration and China's right to fight back strategy. V.M. Kamath (PSP), Mahavir Tyagi (INC) and Hem Barua (PSP) suggested the government to continue the weapon procurement programme from friendly countries and their suggestions should be well taken care before reaching to any negations.[263] Some of the opposition leaders also warned the government to be alert and not to remove soldiers from the border as they believed it might be a Chinese strategy of buying time for next round of attack.[264]

Nehru in reply stated that, his government would look into every aspect of the unilateral ceasefire declaration and all the suggestions given by members would be taken care before reaching into any conclusion. However, he refused to discuss the government of India's reply against China's ceasefire declaration, he argued, "I am afraid, this is a very novel produce. General principles are discussed here and we are guided by whatever the house may decide. But to discuss these communications between one government and another would be a very extraordinary thing; and it is a very undesirable and harmful thing". While showing his desire for negotiation, the ultimate aim of the negotiation was to vacate the Chinese aggression from every inch of Indian Territory. But he added, the negotiation would be conducted through several stages and the first stage would be to create the environment to reach the ultimate goal. Reacting to the demand of the oppositions he also agreed to extend the period of the Parliament session for a few more days.[265] Nehru moved a motion regarding the recent development of the Chinese aggression and the China's unilateral ceasefire declaration on December 10, 1962.[266] Most of the Non-Communist political parties and independent members advocated the rejection of the ceasefire proposal and asked the government to continue its military strategy until the complete eviction of the Chinese troops.[267] Similarly, opposition leaders like P.K. Deo, S.N. Dwivedy, and Ram Sevak Yadav moved several amendments against the Chinese ceasefire proposal and any future negotiations with China, which later got rejected by Lok Sabha.[268] Hence, the house adopted the government motion in approving the government's measures and policies against the Chinese aggression.

This session of Lok Sabha was one of the most debated sessions, though it was comparatively short. By and large, this session was very fruitful in pressuring the government to remove Defence Minister Krishna Menon and shaping the government's policies. The Lok Sabha also moulded the voice of Communist Party of India for the first time and not only the oppositions, all members of the house made full use of the session to express their opinions on the recent Chinese aggression and the fate of Indian reaction.

Conclusion

The period of Sino-Indian confrontation from 1958 to 1968 was one of the important chapters of India China relationship and one of the defining moments of Asian politics. The century old Sino-Indian relationship started sinking/ took a u-turn after the Tibetan uprising of 1958. After the voluntary abandonment of all British inherited traditional rights by signing the 'agreement of trade and intercourse', popularly known as Panchsheel Agreement, India expected the end of issues with China, including the border disputes. India also recognized Tibet as the integral part of China and mentioned silence during the Chinese invention into Tibet and Tibetan uprising, which she believed as internal matters of China. However, China accused Indian involvement in the Tibetan uprising and condemned India's decision to grant political asylum to Dalai Lama.

Indian Parliament, which used to be supportive towards the matters related to China, took strong acceptation to the Chinese allegation and members across the party line denounced the Chinese allegation. Opposition parties such as PSP, BJS and MKP strongly criticized the government of India's silence towards the Tibetan uprising and asked the government to help the rebel for their fight to self-determination. However, Nehru led Congress as well as CPI rejected the opposition's demand and backed the government's decision to maintain neutrality.

Short after the fall of the Tibetan uprising and the successful Tibetan annexation, Chinese troops initiated the long range border patrolling along the Indo-Tibetan border and came face to face with Indian troops, which led to several border clashes, in which India allegedly lost large chunk of its territory to China. Each of the party accused each other for the border violation, before deciding to hold formal discussion for the demarcation of inhabited frontiers. However, no result was achieved in the negations and left the situation unsolved, even without any interim mechanism. As a result, India decided to use force to drive out Chinese occupation by lunching massive military operation. China reacted to the Indian action strongly with greater force which led to the breakup of the Sino-Indian border war in 1962. India received major defeat and China forces forced back Indian troops in Aksai Chin and occupied around 37,244 square kilometres (14,380 sq. mi.) of Indian Territory, which they believed belonging to China. On November 19, 1962 China declared unilateral ceasefire and decided to pull back its troops 20 kilometres back from the ceasefire line.

The whole political spectrum and the Indian Parliament at large condemned the Chinese attack. Members from opposition parties and even from the ruling party targeted Prime Minister Nehru and the government as a whole for the failed Chinese policy and the military disaster. Defence Minister Krishna Menon also came under strong attack by the oppositions in the Parliament. The Jan Sangh, Socialists and the Swatrantra Party made accountable to the government for the defeat and moved several motions including no confidence motion against the government. They also demanded immediate resignation of the Defence Minister and the Prime Minister. Interestingly, a section of ruling Congress Party also criticized government's China policy and blamed Nehru for the military defeat of India. Communist Party of India, which had been adopting pro-Chinese stand on several occasions, also openly condemned the Chinese attack, which was a rare phenomenon in the Indian Parliament.

Notes

1. Dinesh Lal, Indo-Tibet-China Conflict (New Delhi: Gyan Publishing House, 2008) p. 10.
2. Prabodh Chandra Bagchi, India and China : Interactions through Buddhism and Diplomacy (New Delhi: Anthem Press, 2011) pp. 13-14.
3. Dinesh Lal, Indo-Tibet-China Conflict, 15-17, also see, P. S. Deodhar, Cinasthana Today: Viewing China from India (New Delhi: Tata McGraw-Hill Education, 2013) p. 48.
4. Tan Chung, "A Sino-Indian Perspective For India-China Understanding", in Across The Himalayan Gap: An Indian Quest for Understanding China, Edited by Tan Chung (New Delhi: Gyan Publishing House, 1998) pp. 135-34.
5. Lal, Indo-Tibet-China Conflict, p. 10.
6. Lal, Indo-Tibet-China Conflict, p. 19.
7. B.R. Deepak, India and China 1904-2004: A Century of Peace and Conflict (New Delhi: Manak Publication, 2005) pp. 2-4.
8. Arun Kumar Benerji, "Borders" in Aspects of India's International Relations, 1700 to 2000: South Asia and the World edited by Jayanta Kumar Ray (New Delhi: Pearson Education India, 2007), p. 186 .
9. Alex McKay, Tibet and the British Raj: The Frontier Cadre, 1904-1947 (London: Curzon Press, 1997) pp. 10-12.
10. A Copy of the Convention can be seen at the Melvyn C. Goldstein, A History of Modern Tibet, 1913-1951: The Demise of the Lamaist State (Los Angeles: University of California Press, 1991) pp. 827-828.
11. Neville Maxwell, India's China War (Dehradun: Natraj Publishers, 2010) p. 41.
12. Shri Ram Sharma, India-China Relations, 1947-1971: Friendship Goes with Power, Part 1 (New Delhi: Discovery Publishing House, 1999) pp. 12-13.
13. B. R. Deepak, India China Relation (New Delhi: APH Publishing, 2001) pp. 155-57.
14. Vice President K.R. Narayan at Fudan University, October 27, 1994. As stated in Tan Chung, Across the Himalayan Gap, pp. 20-21.
15. K.R. Gupta and Vatsala Shukla, Foreign Policy of India (New Delhi: Atlantic Publishers, 2009) p. 529.
16. Quoted in Prakash Nanda, Rediscovering Asia: Evolution of India's Look-east Policy (New Delhi: Lancer Publishers, 2003) p. 130.
17. *Ibid.* pp 131-32.
18. Sharma, India-China Relations, p. 19.
19. M. L. Sali, India-China Border Dispute: A Case Study of the Eastern Sector (New Delhi: APH Publishing, 1998) 79-80, also see, Shri Ram Sharma, India-China Relations, 1947-1971: Friendship Goes with Power, Part 1 (New Delhi: Discovery Publishing House, 1999) pp. 14-15.
20. Claude Arpi, Born in Sin: The Panchsheel Agreement: The Sacrifice of Tibet (New Delhi: Mittal Publications, 2004) p. 111.
21. See, Brahma Chellaney, Asian Juggernaut: The Rise of China, India, and Japan (New Delhi: Harper Collins Publishers, 2012) 158, Claude Arpi, "The Famous

Five That Broke India's Back", The Pioneer, Thursday, 24 April 2014,http://www.dailypioneer.com/columnists/edit/the-famous-five-that-broke-indias-back.html, Subhash Kapila "India-China Panchsheel Agreement: Hanging on to a Moth-Eaten Rag" Research Paper No. 5735, South Asia Analysis Group, dated Jun 30, 2014, http://www.southasiaanalysis.org/node/1557, Sanat Kaul, "Panchsheel is not in India's Interests"Daily Mail, September 11, 2014, http://www.dailymail. co.uk/indiahome/indianews/article-2752720/Panchsheel-not-India-s-interests.html, RN Ravi, "60 years on: Unforgiving legacy of the Panchsheel Agreement", radiff.com http://www.rediff.com/news/column/60-years-on-unforgiving-legacy-of-the-panchsheel-agreement/20140429.htm.

22. Singh, "Three Agreements and Five Principles", pp.506-08.
23. T.N. Kaul, Diplomacy in Peace and War (New Delhi: Vikas Publishers, 1978) pp. 103-04.
24. Dennis Kux, India and the United States: Estranged Democracies, 1941-1991 (Washington DC: National Defence University Press, 1992) p. 122.
25. Amitav Acharya, Itty Abraham, "Bandung and State Formation in Post-colonial Asia", in Bandung Revisited: The Legacy of the 1955 Asian-African Conference for International Order (Singapore; NUS Press, 2008) 63-64.
26. Jayapalan, Foreign Policy of India, p. 205.
27. Dinesh Lal, Indo-Tibet-China Conflict, (New Delhi: Kalpaz Publications, 2008) 145.
28. Chen Jian, "The Tibetan Rebellion of 1959 and China's Changing Relations with India and the Soviet Union," Journal of Cold War Studies, 8:3 (Summer, 2006): 54 –101.
29. Warren W. Smith, Tibet's Last Stand: The Tibetan Uprising of 2008 and China's Response (Lanham, Mary land: Rowman& Littlefield, 2010) 240.
30. Srinath Raghavan, War and Peace in Modern India, (New York: Palgrave Macmillan, 2010) 249.
31. As quoted in M. L. Sali, India-China Border Dispute: A Case Study of the Eastern Sector (New Delhi: APH Publishing, 1998) 78.
32. John Garver, "China's Decision for War With India in 1962", New Directions in The Study of China's Foreign Policy, ed. Alastair J. Johnston and Robert S. Ross, (Stanford: Stanford University Press) 93-4.
33. Lok Sabha Debates, Vol. 27, 1959, Cols. 6457-60.
34. *Ibid.,* Cols. 6440-43.
35. *Ibid.,* Cols. 6683-84.
36. Lok Sabha Debates, Vol.27, 1959, Cols. 6457-60.
37. *Ibid.*
38. *Ibid,* Col. 7709.
39. As stated in Girilal Jain, Panchsheel and after: A Re-Appraisal of Sino-Indian Relations in the Context of the Tibetan Insurrection (Bombay: Asia Pub. House, 1960) 85.
40. As stated in n. 20 p. 310.
41. Lok Sabha Debates, Vol. 28, 1959, Col. 8511.

42. *Ibid.* Col. 8527.
43. *Ibid,* Col. 8510.
44. Lok Sabha Debates, Vol. 28, 1959, Col. 8520.
45. Chanakya Sen, Tibet Disappears (Bombay: Asia Publishing House, 1960) 306.
46. Lok Sabha Debates, Vol. 28, 1959, Cols. 9011-13.
47. *Ibid,* col. 9014.
48. *Ibid.,* Col. 9020.
49. *Ibid.,* Col. 9022.
50. *Ibid.,* Cols. 9034-35.
51. *Ibid.,* Cols. 9274-76.
52. *Ibid.,* Cols. 9283-84.
53. 1959: Dalai Lama Escapes to India, on this day, March 31, BBC Online Archive, available online at, http://news.bbc.co.uk/onthisday/hi/dates/stories/march/31/newsid_2788000/2788343.stm.
54. Thomas Laird, The Story of Tibet: Conversations with the Dalai Lama (New York: Grove Press, 2007) 341;Also see, Dalai Lama, My Spiritual Autobiography (Noida: Random House, 2011) 179.
55. Steven A. Hoffmann, India and the China Crisis (Berkeley: University of California Press, 1990) 63; see also, Rollie Lal, Understanding China and India: Security Implications for the United States and the World (Westport, US: Greenwood Publishing, 2006) 134.; Thomas Laird, The Story of Tibet: Conversations with the Dalai Lama (New York: Grove Press, 2007) 341.
56. Lok Sabha Debate Vol. 28, 1959, Col. 8464.
57. Lok Sabha Debate Vol. 28, 1959, Col. 8464.
58. *Ibid.,* Cols. 9559-61.
59. As quoted in B.R Deepak (2005) 207.
60. Deepak (2005) 207-8.
61. *Ibid.,* 210.
62. Sali (1998) 78-79.
63. Nancy Jetly, Indian China relations, 1947-77: A Study of Parliament's Role in the Making of Foreign Policy (New Delhi: Radiant Publishers, 1979) 65.
64. *Lok Sabha Debates*, Vol. 30, 1959, Cols. 13495-96.
65. *Ibid.,* 13597-98.
66. *Ibid.,* 135001.
67. *Ibid.,* 135000.
68. *Ibid.,* Col. 13499-01.
69. *Ibid.,* Cols. 13502.
70. Steven A. Hoffmann (1990) 60-61 (a copy of the article is available at the personal website of the Claude Arpi,expertise on Tibet at http://www.claudearpi.net/maintenance/uploaded_pics/Nehru_Philosophy1.pdf.
71. Lok Sabha Debates, Vol. 31, 1959, Cols. 15871-77.
72. *Ibid.,* Cols. 15878-83.

73. *Ibid.,* Cols. 15921-24.
74. *Ibid.,* Cols. 15909-18.
75. *Ibid.,* Cols. 15892-905.
76. *Ibid.,* Cols. 15925-35.
77. Nancy Jetly (1979) 71-72.
78. Michael Lempert, Discipline and Debate: The Language of Violence in a Tibetan Buddhist Monastery (Berkeley: University of California Press, 2012)131. A full copy of the letter can be seen at the personal website of the Claude Arpi,expertise on Tibet. Available at http://www.claudearpi.net/maintenance/ uploaded_pics/ 5909DalaiLama_appeal_UN.pdf.
79. Nancy Jetly (1979) 72.
80. Lok Sabha Debates, Vol. 33, 1959, Col. 3682.
81. *Ibid.,* Cols. 3685-87.
82. Lok Sabha Debates, Vol. 34, 1959, Cols. 6531-32.
83. *Ibid.,* Cols. 6496—503.
84. *Ibid.,* Cols. 6506-8.
85. *Ibid.,* Cols. 6511-18; 6521-28.
86. *Ibid.,* Cols. 6535.
87. *Ibid.,* Cols. 6519-21.
88. *Ibid.,* Cols. 6536-54.
89. Deepak (2005) 214.
90. United Nations General Assembly Resolution 1353 (XIV), Session 14, 1959, Plenary Meeting 834, 519-21, a copy of the resolution can also be seen at official website of Claude Arpi, available at http://www.claudearpi.net/maintenance/ uploaded_pics/1959UNGeneral AssemblyResolution.pdf.
91. Lok Sabha Debates, Vol. 32, 1959, Col. 930.
92. *Ibid.,* Cols. 932-33.
93. Lok Sabha debates, Vol. 32, 1959, Cols. 1724-27.
94. Deepak (2005) 215.
95. Lok Sabha Debates, Vol. 28, 1959, Col. 8515.
96. *Ibid.,* Vol. 30, 1959, Col. 12716.
97. *Ibid.,* Vol. 30, Col. 12721.
98. *Ibid.,* Vol. 32, 1959, Col. 2246.
99. *Ibid.,* Vol. 32, 1959, Col. 2246.
100. White Paper I, 1954- 1959, Ministry of External Affairs , Government of India, 38-40, a copy of the white paper can be seen at official website of the Claude Arpi, at http://www.claudearpi.net/maintenance/ uploaded_pics/ White Paper1.pd.
101. White Paper II(New Delhi: Ministry of External Affairs, Government of India) 6; also see, Deepak (2005) 216.
102. Deepak (2005) 216-18.
103 Lok Sabha Debates, Vol. 33, 1959, Col. 4793.

104. *Ibid.,* Col. 4801.
105. *Ibid.*
106. *Lok Sabha Debate*, Vol. 33, Cols. 4860-62.
107. *Ibid.,* Col. 4861.
108. *Ibid.,* Cols. 4862-71.
109. *Ibid.,* cols. 4865 and 4869-70.
110. While members demanded further detail account of the August 7 border incidents and the India China relation, A.B. Vajpayee argued the government to issue a white paper on this issue. For detail see, Lok Sabha Debates, Vol. 33, 1959, col. 4871.
111. *Lok Sabha Debates*, Vol.34, 1959, Cols. 6546-52.
112. White Paper I, Ministry of External Affairs, Government of India, New Delhi, 1959.
113. The latter published in the second White Paper , detail can be seen, White Paper II, Ministry of External Affairs, Government of India, New Delhi, 1959.
114. Lok Sabha debates, vol. 34, 1959, cols. 7990-97.
115. *Ibid.,* col. 7999.
116. *Ibid,* cols. 8006-13.
117. *Ibid,* cols.8013-17.
118. *Ibid,* Col. 8003.
119. *Ibid,* Cols. 8062-75.
120. *Ibid,* Cols. 8001.
121. *Ibid,* Cols. 8023-37.
122. *Ibid.,* Cols. 8023-37.
123. *Ibid,* Col. 8079.
124. *Ibid,* Col. 8081.
125. *Ibid.,* Cols. 8038-47.
126. *Ibid.* Cols. 8018-22.
127. *Ibid,* cols. 8106-7.
128. *Ibid,* 8109-25.
129. Lok Sabha Debates, Vol. 35, 1959, Col. 83.
130. *Ibid,* Cols. 87-93.
131. As stated on White Paper III, (New Delhi: Ministry of External Affairs, Government of India, 1960) 46.
132. The entire letter can be seen at the, White Paper III, (Ministry of External Affairs, Government of India, New Delhi, 1960) 52-57.
133. Detail can be seen at White Paper III, 58.
134. *Ibid,* 60-82.
135. *Ibid,* 83.
136. For details see, White Paper III, 85-98.
137. Lok Sabha Debates, Vol. 35, 1959, Cols. 1680-1700.

138. *Ibid*, Cols. 2040-49.
139. *Ibid*, Cols. 2030-39.
140. Masani for instance appeal Nehru not to follow the Chinese design. For Details see, ibid, cols, 1749-62s.
141. Lok Sabha Debates, Vol. 33, 1959, Cols. 3685-87.
142. Official Report of the Summit, Ministry of External Affairs, Government of India, Vol. 6, 1960, 107-08.
143. Lok Sabha Debates, Vol. 43, 1960, Cols. 13795-800.
144. *Ibid*, col. 14786.
145. *Ibid*, cols. 14795-807.
146. *Ibid*, cols. 14820-24.
147. *Ibid*, cols. 14828.
148. *Ibid*, cols. 14787.
149. *Ibid*, cols. 14786.
150. *Ibid*, cols. 14824-27.
151. *Ibid*, cols. 14789-95.
152. *Ibid.*, Cols. 14828-42.
153. *White Paper IV* (Ministry of External Affairs, Government of India, 1960) 3.
154. *Lok Sabha Debates*, Vol. 46, 1960, Cols. 5943-44.
155. *Ibid.*, Cols. 5961.
156. See White Paper IV, Ministry of External Affairs, Government of India, 1960, 39-40.
157. *Ibid.* 43-45.
158. PSP leader NathPai raised the question in the Lok Sabha. See, Lok Sabha Debates, Vol. 46, 1960, Cols. 5961.
159. *Lok Sabha Debates*, Vol. 46, 1960, Cols. 5997.
160. *Ibid.*, Cols. 6028-29.
161. *Ibid.*, Cols. 6042-44.
162. *Ibid.*, col. 5950.
163. *Ibid.*, Cols. 6211.
164. See official report of the Government of "India and China on Boundary Question" (New Delhi: Ministry of External Affairs, Government of India) 1-11 .
165. *Lok Sabha Debates*, Vol. 50, 1961, Cols. 918-20.
166. *Ibid*, 1124-27.
167. *Ibid*, cols. 1110-13.
168. *Ibid*, Cols. 1207-10.
169. Lok Sabha Debates, Vol. 53, 1961, Cols. 8577-79.
170. *Ibid.*, cols. 8757-61.
171. *Ibid*, cols. 8150-53.
172. *Ibid.*, Cols. 8821-23.
173. *Ibid.*, Cols. 8776-77.

174. *Ibid.*, Cols. 8914-20.
175. The Long Debate can be seen in the Different Columns of Lok Sabha Dates, Vol. 54, 1961. See for Example Cols. 10514-590.
176. Steven A. Hoffmann, India and the China Crisis (Barkley: University of California Press, 1990) 90-91.
177. Lok Sabha Debates, Vol. 56, 1961, Cols. 2424-27.
178. *Ibid*, Cols. 2552.
179. *Ibid*, Cols. 2499.
180. *Ibid*, Cols. 2502-04.
181. *Ibid*, Cols. 2779-81.
182. See White Paper V, Ministry of External Affairs, Government of India, 1961, 51-54.
183. S.N. Prasad, ed., History of the Conflict with China, 1962 (Unpublished Report), (New Delhi: History Division, Ministry of Defence, Government of India) 65; see also, SrinathRaghavan, War and Peace in Modern India: A Strategic History of the Nehru Years (Ranikhet, India: Permanent Black, 2010) 273-75.
184. Lok Sabha Debates, Vol. 60, 1961, Cols. 2954-67.
185. *Ibid.*, Cols. 3015-21.
186. *Ibid*, Cols. 2983-94.
187. *Ibid*, Cols. 2995-3013.
188. *Ibid.*, 2967-76.
189. *Ibid.*, cols. 2976-83.
190. Lok Sabha Debates, Vol. 1, 1962, Cols. 1207, 1216, 1219.
191. See White Paper VI (New Delhi: Ministry of External Affairs, Government of India, 1962) 3-5 & 15.
192. *Ibid*, 18.
193. Lok Sabha Debates Vol. 2, 1962, Cols. 2458-59.
194. *Ibid.*, Vol.3, 1962, Cols. 4263.
195. *Ibid.*, Cols. 4456-57.
196. *Ibid.*, Cols. 4438.
197. *Ibid.*, Cols. 4434-35.
198. *Ibid.*, Cols., 4564-66.
199. Lok Sabha Debates, Vol. 3, 1962, Cols. 5870-73.
200. For details see White Paper VI, Ministry of External Affairs, Government of India, New Deli .
201. Lok Sabha Debates, Vol. 60, 1961, cols. 3879.
202. *Ibid.*, Cols. 3892.
203. *Ibid.*, Cols. 3917.
204. See Lok Sabha Debates, Vol. 61, 1962, Col. 21.
205. *Ibid.*, Cols. 492.
206. *Ibid.*, Cols. 586.

207. *Ibid.*, Cols. 780.
208. Lok Sabha Debates, Vol. 4, 1962, Cols. 9165-67.
209. White Paper VII, (New Delhi: Ministry of External Affairs, Government of India, 1962) 3-8.
210. Lok Sabha Debates Vol. 6, 1962, Cols. 121-24.
211. *Ibid.*, Cols. 126-28.
212. *Ibid.*, Cols. 1479-81.
213. For Detail see, Lok Sabha Debates, Vol. 6, 1962, Cols. 1482-1506, 1527-40, 1570-81.
214. *Ibid.*
215. Lok Sabha Debates, Vol. 6, 1962, Cols.1507-14.
216. *Ibid.*, Cols. 1520.
217. *Ibid.*, Cols. 15998-99.
218. *Ibid.*, Cols. 1612.
219. *Ibid.*, Cols. 1751-78.
220. White paper VII (New Delhi: Ministry of External Affairs, Government of India, 1962) 71-78.
221. Prasad (1992) 94-95.
222. As stated in, Anna Orton, India's Borderland Disputes: China, Pakistan, Bangladesh, and Nepal (New Delhi: Epitome Books, 2010) 50; also stated in Jetly (1979) 171.
223. Brij Mohan Kaul, The Untold Story (New Delhi: Allied Publishers, 1967) 355-56.
224. Deepak (2005) 250.
225. Ministry of External Affairs, Prime Minister on Chinese Aggression, (New Delhi: Ministry of External Affairs, Government of India, 1963) 1-20.
226. The aim of the strategy is to the opponent leaders not to make them agree to the compromise solutions, "but to buy time, colour his opponent's views, and influence third parties. The ultimate goal never changed,whatever the negotiating positions". For detail see, Cheng, Dean. "Fight Fight, Talk Talk": China's Model for Military-to-Military Relations," 2011, July 27. http://blog.heritage.org/2011/07/27/fight-fight-talk-talk-Chinas-model-for-military-to-military-relations/ (November 26, 2013).
227. White Paper VIII (New Delhi: Ministry of external Affairs,1962) 1.
228. *Ibid.* 4-5.
229. Lok Sabha debates, Vol. 9, 1962. Cols. 109-10.
230. *Ibid.*, Cols. 110-33.
231. *Ibid.*, Cols. 153-63.
232. *Ibid.*, Cols. 139.
233. *Ibid.*, Cols. 177-90.
234. *Ibid.*, Cols. 65-67.
235. *Ibid.*, Cols. 138.

236. *Ibid.*, Cols.186-99.
237. *Ibid.*, Cols. 728-30.
238. *Ibid.*, Cols. 139-40.
239. *Ibid.*, Cols. 139.
240. *Ibid.*, Cols. 666.
241. *Ibid.*, Cols. 1026.
242 *Ibid.*, Cols. 143-52.
243. *Ibid.*, Cols. 164-66.
244. *Ibid.*, Col. 410.
245. *Ibid.*, Col. 141.
246. *Ibid.*, Cols.141-42.
247. *Ibid.*, Cols. 173-77.
248. *Ibid.*, Col. 404.
249. *Ibid.*, Cols. 433-40.
250. *Ibid.*, Cols. 680-87.
251. *Ibid.*, Cols. 1644-70.
252. Lok Sabha Debates, Vol. 9, 1962, Cols. 1672-77 .
253. *Ibid.*, Cols. 2230-32.
254. *Ibid.*, Col.2234.
255. *Ibid.*, Col. 2240.
256. *Ibid.*, Cols. 2453-54.
257. *Ibid.*, Col. 2454.
258. *Ibid.*, Col. 2468.
259. *Ibid.*, Cols. 2456-57.
260. *Ibid.*, Cols. 2464-67.
261. Lok Sabha Debates, Vol. 10-11, 1962, Cols. 2689-90.
262. A. Appadorai, Select Documents on India's Foreign Policy and Relations (New Delhi: Oxford University Press, 1982) 676-77; also see, White Paper VIII, Ministry of External Affairs, Government of India, New Delhi, 1963, 17-21 .
263. Lok Sabha Debates, Vol. 10-11, 1962, Col. 2693.
264. Ram SevakYadav and Frank Anthony argued the government to be careful about China's bye time strategy. See, Lok Sabha Debates, Vol. 10-11, 1962, Col. 2694-2700.
265. *Ibid.*, Cols. 2700-2.
266. See White Paper VIII, Ministry of External Affairs, 1963, 24-31.
267. Most of the Non-communist Political Parties, including PSP, BJS, Socialist Party, Swantantra, Republican Party, etc. have suggested the government not to accept the Chinese ceasefire offer. For details see, Lok Sabha Debates, Vol. 10-11, 1962, cols. 5101-95. (at different pages).
268. Sabha Debates, Vol. 10-11, 1962, Cols. 5196-99

Chapter - 6

Parliament and the Making of India's China Policy during the Era of Hostile Coexistence 1963 to 1975

At the high tide of cold war during 1960s another undeclared Berlin wall was developed over India and China relationship, baring the two Asian giants from regular engagement, when both the countries decided to break all diplomatic ties with each other after the end of Sino-Indian Border war. The efforts of a group of Non-Aligned frontiers to engage New Delhi and Beijing through Colombo Proposal also failed to break the wall of estrangement. Hence, both the counties continued to maintain freezing relationship and were living under hostile coexistence until the restoration of regular relationship in 1975. Indian Parliament and the Indian political entity posed a critical stand against Chinese policies and its activities. Hence, it is important to explore the attitude of Indian Parliament towards China during these difficult times. In this background, this chapter discusses the reaction of the Indian Parliament and its political components towards the important issues of India-China relationship between 1963 and 1975, which often known as the period of estrangement and hostile coexistence. In this section, issues like Colombo proposal, China's nuclear explosion, Chinese premier Zhou Enlai's warning to India, Sino-Pak Boundary agreement, Indira Gandhi's initiatives to normalize Sino-Indian relationship, Chinese reaction towards Bangladesh Crisis and the merger of Sikkim into Indian union have been thoroughly discussed and an account of the attitude of India Indian Parliament and various political parties towards these issues have been elicited to measure the Parliamentary influence of the Indian Parliament on India's China policy.

The Reaction of Indian Parliament towards the Colombo Proposal

Though both India and China agreed to adhere to maintain ceasefire, neither side was able to fix the ceasefire line and demilitarization zone due to perceptional differences. Meanwhile, some Afro-Asian countries came forward to facilitate the ceasefire formula. With the prime initiative of the Ceylonese (Sri Lankan) Prime Minister, Mrs. Bandaranaike, Six Afro-Asian Countries such as, Burma, Cambodia, Ceylon (Sri Lanka), Ghana, Indonesia and United Arab Republic (Egypt) met in Colombo between December 10 to 12, 1962 to finalize a workable agreement between India and China to resolve the border disputes. At the end of the conference, a suggestive document was produced which prescribed a way out formula for all the three disputed frontier regions. In the Western sector, the document suggested, China had to withdraw its troops 20 kilometres from the ceasefire line as per the declaration, whereas, India could hold the present ceasefire line and need not withdraw its troops anyway. After the Chinese vacation, this 20 kilometre frontier region would be a demilitarized zone and would be "administrated by civilian posts of both sides to be agreed upon, without prejudice to the rights of the previous presence of both India and China in that area." In the Eastern Sector, both the countries had maintained the "Line of actual control" as the *de-facto* border, whereas, status quo had to be maintained in the Middle sectors. A delegation led by Prime Minister Bandaranaike visited India and China to convince the countries to accept the Colombo proposal. India, first did not accept the proposal and informed the Bandaranaike delegation that, it could give its reply to the proposal only after consultation with Parliament.[1]

The Parliament, although, was not in session, political parties at large appreciated government's decision to refer the Colombo proposal to the Parliament. However, most of the Non-Communist political parties disapproved the proposal in the present form. In a joint statement, Jan Sangh, PSP, Swatantra and the Akali Dal rejected the Colombo proposal and warned the government against compromise in accepting the proposal.[2] On January 21, 1963 the Parliament was recalled and on the very first day Nehru placed the proposal on the floor of Lok Sabha for debate.[3]

Placing the proposal before the Lok Sabha, Nehru said that, his government was committed to India's November 8 line stand and would not compromise to any other proposal. As accepted by the Parliament the November 8 line had to be maintained by China in order to start any bilateral negotiation. At the same time he was not against the Colombo proposal, as it was more favourable towards India and bore almost all the provisions of 'India's November 8 line stand'. Going into details, Nehru stated that, as per the proposal, Indian troops could patrol up to the McMahon Line, except Longju and Thagla Ridge in Eastern sector, which was almost similar to the government's previous stand. In the Western sector too, India was in advantage as China had to withdraw its troops 20 kilometres back and allowed Indian civilian posts, whereas in Middle the proposal recommended to maintain status quo. Hence, the proposal in many ways bring China near to India's November 8 line demand, Nehru added.[4]

Nehru's argument towards the acceptance of Colombo proposal came under sharp criticism from the opposition parties. Members of Jan Sangh, PSP and Swatantra attacked the government for its policy of peaceful surrender. Jan Sangh leader, U.M Trivedi for instance condemned the government for its weak policy against the China and warned the government not to continue the policy of appeasement by surrendering the whole area of Qiziljilga to China and leaving Thangla ridge and Longju under Chinese preview. [5] Similarly, Socialist leader Ram Sevak Yadhav stated that, there was no similarity between the Colombo proposal and the September 8, 1962 line, as argued by Prime Minister, Nehru and the proposal appeared more close to the Chinese demanded line of November 7, 1959. He also insisted the Parliament to oppose the proposal as it was arguing to surrender thousand miles of Indian Territory.[6] Kisan Patnaik, went further and demanded the resignation of Prime Minister if he could not treat China as the prime aggressor and the number-one enemy of India. He also rejected the Colombo proposal and stated that, agreeing to the proposal would mean accepting the Chinese plan of border settlement.[7] Bishan Chandra Seth of Hindu Mahasabha warned the government not to accept the proposal as it had no right to do so due to mass anti-proposal public reaction. He also asked the government to pay respect to the Parliamentary decision which unanimously approved the restoration of September 8 line.[8] Similarly, republican leader B.P. Maurya and Muslim League leader Mohammad Ismail criticized the government for misguiding the Parliament by presenting unauthentic facts to show the similarity between September 8, 1962 and the line proposed by Colombo proposal. They also called the Parliament to reject the proposal.[9] Some of the independent members also opposed the Chinese proposal and criticized the government for its blind argument in favour of the proposal. Independent members like Frank Anthony, Prakash Vir Shastry and Bhanu Prakash Singh for instance, attacked the government for ignoring the Parliament's November resolution in accepting the proposal. They also appealed to the government to show a minimum level of resistance towards the Chinese policies.[10]

However, a section of the Independent leaders like S.M. Banerjee asked the Parliament to accept the proposal as it involved the efforts of the Afro-Asian Countries and the rejection of the proposal would send a wrong message to the world.[11] Similarly, some of the opposition parties such as

DMK and MGJP also backed the proposal and appealed the house to accept the proposal.[12]

The Congress Party on the other hand, was confused and a section of the party membership put their reservations in accepting the proposal. Renuka Roy, for instance suggested the government not to be in a hurry to accept the proposal and to wait for the Chinese response. India, he argued, should accept the proposal, if the Chinese government accepts the final version of the proposal without any pre-conditions. Similarly, C.K. Bhattacharya and Mahavir Tyagi, also asked the government to accept the proposal, only after attaining necessary military preparedness to implement the principles of Colombo proposal.[13] Another Congress leader Joachim Alva appealed to the government not to believe any verbal assurance to accept the proposal and to accept the proposal if China would give its approval in writing.[14]

Replying to the opposition's arguments, Nehru stated that, his government would not accept any amendment to the present proposals and strictly adhered to the present form of proposal only. He regretted the confusing nature of the House, which failed to reach any conclusion despite high voltage debate and stated, "I have to take some action and not merely deliver a speech here…." Arguing in favour of the proposal, he stated that the Parliament had approved the November 8, 1962 line resolution, hence should not remain confused towards the Colombo proposal, which is almost similar to the earlier Parliamentary resolution. "… it is the proposition", Nehru further declared, "of the government that we should tell them definitely and precisely that we are prepared to accept these Colombo proposals subject to the amplifications and elucidation. Whether they will come into effect or not depends up on the other party accepting them." Nehru also reminded the House not to press any motion against the recent resolution of Colombo proposal in respect to the earlier unanimous agreement.[15]

Despite Nehru's repeated requests, Socialist leader Ram Sevak Yadhav substituted motion against the Colombo proposal, which infuriated Nehru. Clarifying the government's stance against any substitute motion, he stated, "I did not wish to create precedents for the future that every matter is voted upon by Parliament. It is not a good precedent. It is not followed by other Parliaments….. Secondly, because the Chinese had given their final reply, I thought it was on the whole desirable for this matter to be left by the house to the government to pursue within the line of the general policy."[16] The opposition members did not subscribe to Nehru's argument and called for a comprehensive debate on the legislative and executive superiority in foreign policy decision making. Members like Ranga, and Frank Anthony criticized Nehru's argument and his decisions to bar all motion against the resolution.

Countering the criticism, Nehru argued that, neither the government is bound to take vote on each and every policy decision, nor practically possible to approach the Parliament to decide the fate of the government policies. Despite this, the government had introduced a resolution in Parliament to decide India's demand of November 8 line and took decision only after the approval of the Parliament, he clarified. He also argued to accept the present form of Colombo proposal as it bore all the qualities of India's November 8 stand which had been approved by the Parliament earlier.[17]

Nehru's answer, however, did not silent the opposition and at various occasions they criticized the loop holes of government's weak Chinese policies. They also attacked Prime Minister Nehru directly for India's military failure and asked the government to step aside the Non-Alignment policies and rebuild India's defence infrastructures.

China's Refusal to Accept Certain Points of Colombo Proposal

On April 20, 1963 Zhou Enlai informed the government of India that, China would not accept the added provisions (which included the clarification wanted by India) of the Colombo Proposal as it was not part of the official report. India strongly objected to China's decision and made it clear that there should not be half acceptance of the proposal suggested by Colombo Powers.[18] Zhou's letter in rejecting Colombo proposal drove another huge anti-Chinese public opinion. While intimating the Chinese decision to Lok Sabha on May 7, 1963 Nehru once again repeated that, no further negotiation was possible, if China would not accept the Colombo proposal in total.[19] While answering to the question on Chinese border violation on August 16, 1963, Nehru acknowledged that, China had setup twenty-six civilian posts in the declared demilitarized zone. He also argued that, China had repeatedly violated India's air space boundaries and increasing military presence in the Tibet regions to maintain the tension alive in the border. He was afraid that, China might have a greater design just to maintain tension and might in a process to invade India once again. But, he assured, India was fully prepared to handle the situation better than the past.

The rejection of Colombo proposal and increasing alarming tension at border, resulted into a strong furore in the Indian Parliament. The Non-Communist opposition parties moved a no-confidence motion against the government's repeated failure to defend Indian border and its failed Chinese policy on August 19, 1963. It was the first ever no confidence motion faced by Nehru government since it came to power.

Initiating the opposition's attack, Independent leader Acharya Kripalani regretted for the government's weak policy towards China, which he felt was based on the policy of appeasement and far from reality. He also criticized the government for its failure to prevent Chinese aggression despite repeated assurance from the government. He also questioned the government's decision to proclaim National Emergency without declaring war against China. "Today," he stated, "the emergency exists not for the government but for the opposition so that if they raise the voice of the people they are considered traitors .... Those who have been urging stringent measures against the Chinese have repeatedly been accused of hampering war effort, because they have spotlighted the grievances of the people." He further asked the government to rectify its mistake by taking strong action against Chinese aggression and recapturing the lost Indian territories.[20]

M.R. Masani (Swatantra) demanded the resignation from the Prime Minister and stated that the government was no longer eligible to rule the country which failed to protect India's borders and handed over large areas of Indian territories in the hands of Chinese aggression.[21] Similarly, PSP leader S.N. Dwivedy in attacking the government stated that the government had failed miserably to defend the country, hence should be removed from power. Demanding the resignation of the Prime Minister, he stated, "I don't think that in a matter like this when the nation's security is in danger, any Parliament would ever excuse a government like this." He also appealed to the government to rectify the old mistakes and bring out the truth in public by placing the NEFA inquiry report in Parliament.[22] Jana Sangh leader, U.M. Trivedi on other hand, asked the government to reoccupy the Chinese held territories and said, " ...the time is ripe for us to make a march. I do not say these are mere brave words. No. it is a question of taking a decision and acting according to that decision without any vacillation"[23] Ram Monohar Lohia (Socialist) demanded the resignation of the Prime Minister and criticized India's continuous support to China's United Nation bid, despite recent Chinese betrayal.[24] Similarly, Republican Party, the Muslim League, Hindu Mahasabha and the DMK voted in favour of the no-confidence motion and demanded for a fresh election.

However, some independent members, such as Prakash Vir Shastri and Frank Anthony opposed the motion, though they were unhappy with Nehru government. The CPI, as expected also backed the government and opposed the motion. While, presenting CPI's stand, its leader Hiren Mukharjee stated that, the government was right in practicing the policy of non-alignment, as it was the best alternative for India at this moment. He also opposed the opposition's demand as he believed that they wanted to push India's foreign policy further right.[25] The Congress members, as always stood behind Nehru and rejected the no-confidence motion. At the end the motion was rejected by 346 votes to 61, which indicated the weak numerical strength of opposition parties in Parliament.[26] However, the opposition parties were not discouraged by their strength in Parliament and continued to attack the government in various occasions demanding the publication of NEFA inquiry report before Parliament.

China's Nuclear Explosion and Reaction of Indian Parliament

Two years after the Sino-Indian border war, on October 16, 1964 China conducted a nuclear test at the Lop Nor nuclear testing site in the Xinjiang province and became the fifth nuclear power state on the planet. India, the fore runner of nuclear Disarmament programme, reacted strongly to the Chinese. Newly elected Prime Minister, approached the super powers to guaranty security for India, but failed to get positive response.[27]

The nuclear test by aggressive China resulted in a huge uproar in the Indian Parliament. The oppositions, especially the Non-Communists strongly condemned the Chinese action. M.R. Masan representing Swatantra party criticized the Chinese nuclear test and stated that, the recent Chinese test was the biggest security threat for India, as any conflict in the subcontinent might lead to a nuclear war. However, he suggested the government not to go for any weapon hunting programme and asked the government to negotiate with the superpowers for a Mutual security agreement guaranteeing total security for India against the Chinese nuclear attacks.[28]

However, Jan Sangh leader R.V. Bade moved a substitute motion criticizing the government for its complete failure in assessing Chinese threat and tracking the Chinese nuclear development programme. He also asked the government to take immediate steps for the return of Indian territories forcefully occupied by China.[29] U.M. Tivedy of the same party asked the government to review its policy of disarmament and reply to the Chinese by developing same and equal weapons. He argued, if India would not acquire the nuclear weapon then, it might not have the same in future.[30] Similarly, Nath Pai (PSP) proposed the government to keep open the nuclear options and not to bow down under the Chinese pressure.[31] Frank Anthony (Independent) also appealed to the government to pursue a nuclear development programme with the help of Asian countries such as Japan, in order to meet the Chinese nuclear threats.[32] Some of the Congress members, such as Vidya Charan Shukla and Bibhiti Mishra also asked the government to initiate its own nuclear programme and development for the nuclear weapon.[33]

On the other hand, Socialist leader Ram Monohar Lohia asked the government to breakup all diplomatic and cultural relations with China and stay away from advocating China's UN bid. J.B. Kripalini suggested the government to approach the West for help and seek for a guaranty over Indian security by facilitating US military base in India.

In reply, Shastri stated in the house that, it was not possible for India to acquire the nuclear weapon all of a sudden by sacrificing large amount of public expenditure. Defending the existing nuclear policy of India, he argued that, India's present nuclear policy was highly beneficial for India and heartily welcomed by world powers. He also made it clear that India was not in a hurry to develop any nuclear weapon and would take appropriate decision to match the Chinese threat. On December 24, while clarifying the government's stand in separate debate Shastri said that, it was not possible to negotiate with China if this kind of activities would continue, though the government of India was determined to resolve the existing border disputes peacefully.[34]

Shastri's cooling down remark, however did not satisfy, which was strong by advocating the development of own nuclear weapons rather than approaching the superpowers for help. The huge public pressure, Inside and outside the Parliament pushed the government to think about India's own nuclear programme. Additionally, the outbreak of war between India and Pakistan in 1965 and 1971, and China's unconditional support to Pakistan in both the occasions led the Indian leadership to pursue up the nuclear option. With the help of the scientist, India successfully tested its first nuclear weapon on 18 May 1974 under the leadership of Prime Minister Indira Gandhi.[35]

Zhou Enlai's Warning to India over NEFA and the Indian Parliament

With the nuclear weapons in hand, Chinese leadership started threatening India over the unsettled frontier regions. Warning India, Chinese Prime Minister, Zohu Enlai stated that, China had never relinquished its sovereignty over the 90000 square kilometres of territory south of McMahon line and condemned India's demand of dismantling of Chinese civilian posts across the frontier line.[36] This new Chinese claim created strong reaction in the Indian Parliament. All Non-Communist oppositions condemned the recent Chinese claim and wanted further clarification from the Prime Minister, to deal with the Chinese claim. Members like, Kamath, Hem Barua, and Yashpal Singh demanded detail statement from the Prime Minister on Zhou's recent remarks. Mrs. Lakshmi Menon, Minister of State for External Affairs, while replying on behalf of the government stated that, Zhou's recent statement had "put the facts upside down and reflected an attitude of total intransigence". While rejecting the Chinese claim, she further stated that, China had already occupied 14,500 square miles of Indian Territory in the Ladakh region and still aiming towards the Eastern sector. He also declared, India would not be cowed down by these aggressive demands which she categorically rejected. The Government of India was, however, willing to talk with China, at any time when the Chinese gave up their obstinate stand and agreed to talk on the basis of the Colombo proposal." She also assured the house, that the government was fully capable to meet any Chinese aggression towards the recent claimed Western sector.[37] This assurance of Deputy External Affairs Minister however, did not silence the oppositions and the oppositions continued to demand greater security arrangements for the Eastern sector.

Sino-Pak Boundary Agreement and China's Support to Pakistani Aggression

Based on the old dialect of "enemy's enemy is friend", China and Pakistan decided to built-up their relationship after the Sino-Indian border war. Both the countries found a common national interest based on 'anti-India outlook' to get closer. Hence, to improve the ties and for the settlement of the unsettled frontier line with China, Pakistan agreed to handover a large area of about 5,309 square kilometres (2,050 sq. Miles) to China out of its Pakistani Administrative Kashmir (PAK) region. The final boundary protocol was signed in Rawalpindi on March, 26, 1965.[38] India strongly condemned the Sino-Pakistan Boundary Protocol and called it illegal. After a few days, on April 8, 1965, Pakistan launched a massive attack on Indian frontiers at Rann of Kutch.[39] China, surprisingly, supported Pakistan and blamed India for the violation of Pakistan frontiers. It also issued a warning note to India, cautioning to face exemplary consequences for its "criminal and Extended aggression", if the conflict escalated to war.[40] This new dimension to Sino-Indian rivalry put India in worry, where for the first time China had supported Pakistan in the war against India and posed a serious security threat to India, which now faces threats from both the sides simultaneously.

Reacting to the Chinese warning, Ministry of External Affairs issued a statement condemning Chinese backing to Pakistan on May 7, 1965. Criticizing China's support to Islamabad's aggression in Rann of Kutch, MEA stated, "The Chinese government's stand on Pakistan's aggression in the Rann of Kutch is a reflection of its familiar technique of trying to change the established frontiers of states through the use of military force …." Naming China as the main antagonist to Asian peace, the statement further states, "China has emerged as the greatest disruptive force in Asia, a chauvinistic and imperialist power which has made a mockery of principles of peaceful coexistence and is trying to bully and intimidate its neighbours and other Asian countries."[41]

The Chinese support to Pakistan did not end here. In fact, the Chinese state owned media run a series of anti-India propaganda and supported Pakistan in its confrontation against India. China also alleged India for violating Chinese border near Sikkim and kidnapped Tibetan nationals along with their livestock. On September 2, 1965, a day after the Indo-Pak war turned into a major war, China issued a warning statement against India, followed by another warning note. Justifying her reaction, China argued that, "India's aggression against any one of its neighbours concerns all of its neighbours" and hence China had every right to condemn to it. China further stated that, as India attacked Pakistan first, it could not "evade responsibility for the chain of consequences arising there from". In putting pressure on Indian government, when it was fighting a major war at its Western border, China accused India for violating Chinese borders in the Western sector and demanded to dismantle all military infrastructures constructed in that region.[42]

India, in the reply note rejected all Chinese allegations and agreed to allow any natural observer to analyse the validity of the Chinese claim. India also condemned the Chinese intention, which wanted to take advantage by connecting the Kashmir issue with alleged Sino-Sikkim border violation.[43] In reply, China refused the Indian proposal of investigation by neutral observer and gave an ultimatum to India that, India had to dismantle all the military facilities at the border within three days or be ready to face the consequences. Condemning India's oppressive movement against the people of Kashmir, China clarified that, the people of Kashmir have every right to decide the fate of their own destination and declared China's full support to the Kashmir movement.[44]

Placing the Chinese notes in Parliament on September 17, 1965, Prime Minister Lal Bahadur Shastri stated that, Indian note to China had rejected China's claim of border violation and made it clear that, Indian soldiers had not "transgressed the international boundary and the line of actual control in the Western sector at any time at any place." He also regretted on Chinese objection to 'Indian offer of investigation by neutral observer'. However, he agreed to the Chinese demand for joint inception and stated that, the inception would be held "as early as possible, at an appropriate level, on a mutually convenient date". Stating the recent Chinese reaction in the difficult times as "nothing but interference on the part of China" Shastri hoped that, "China would not take advantage of the present situation and attack."[45]

Meantime, China issued another diplomatic note, demanding to dismantle the existing military infrastructure within next three days, as well as return of kidnapped Tibetans along with their livestock. Laying the second Chinese note in the Parliament, Shastri mentioned that, China only wanted to maintain tension in the border by either attacking Indian soldiers or putting verbal warnings. Now the aggressive intention of China was exposed, when it opened fire to Indian posts at Ladakh and Sikkim sector. Pointing to Sino-Pak nexus, he mentioned that, China wanted to dictate India by putting pressure from both side and "start its aggressive activities again, this time acting in collusion with its ally, Pakistan." Shastri also denounced Chinese claim of Indian aggression in Tibet and stated that, the Chinese claim lacked fact. China, he argued, is "pretending to be the guardian of Asian countries who according to China, are being bullied by India". Reacting to China's argument on Kashmir, he stated "we reject China's claim to tell us anything about what we should or should not do about Kashmir which is an integral part of India." Shastri announced that, India was fully capable enough to deal any challenge posed by China and would not go down by Chinese dictation.[46]

On September 22, 1965, a ceasefire was declared between India and Pakistan and thus brought the Indo-Pak war an end. However, the tension remained tense at the Sino-Indian borders. On September 23, Chinese forces opened fire to Indian posts in the Sikkim and Ladakh region. Chinese forces also intruded into Sikkim borders and killed three civilians of the Indian patrol party. Following the series of ceasefire violation, India protested strongly and asked to stay away from the "willful provocation". India also objected to the massive military movement and subsequent deployment of large forces along the Sino-Sikkim border. This type of military movement and provocative firing happened for the first time after the Chinese ceasefire declaration of 1962.[47]

The subsequent development along the Sino-Indian borders resulted in massive public outrage within and outside Indian Parliament. Opposition parties, especially, Non-Communist members attacked the government for the lack of any strong action against the recent Chinese aggression. On November 15, Ram Sevak Yadav demanded a statement from the Defence Minister regarding the recent Chinese firing. Following the large demand, Defence Minister stated that, it was unfortunate that China was continuing to engage in unprovoked firing to Indian border posts and making unnecessary tensions in the border regions. Chavan's statement was strongly criticized by most of the Non-Communist members, such as, Kishan Patnaik, S.N. Dwivedy, Nath Pai, and Ram Monohar Lohia as they believed, was soft on Chinese incursion and lacked strong condemnation.[48] Looking at the opposition's criticism, Minister of External Affairs, Swaran Singh, strongly condemned the Sino-Pakistan joint strategy to dismantle India and stated that supporting Pakistan to invade India had become the very principle of Chinese foreign policy. The Chinese ultimatum, he added, during the difficult time of war was a signal that, China was trying to help Pakistan to achieve its goal in Kashmir.[49]

Non-Communist oppositions like, Surendranath Dwivedy (PSP), Bade (JS) and Masani (Swantantra) moved different individual substitute motions against the recent Chinese provocation and criticized the government for not taking strong action against Chinese incursion which was happening time and again. While, Dwivedy condemned Sino-Pakistan nexus against India, Bade asked the government to withdraw its support to China's UN bid. Swantantra leader Masani, on the other hand asked the government to extend moral and material help to the Tibetan movement and to establish diplomatic relation with the Republic of China.[50] Some of the Congress members also suggested the government to withdraw its support from the Chinese entry to United Nations and for the revival of India's Tibet policy.[51] However, CPI condemned the opposition's argument to recognize Taiwan and establish diplomatic relations with the government of Taiwan.[52]

Replying to the opposition's argument, Shastri rejected the opposition's argument to recognize Taiwan and revive India's Tibet policy. It was not appropriate, he argued, to raise these issues at this difficult times and it might pose a serious security threat for India, especially, when the Sino-Pak alliance was aiming to attack simultaneously. Instead of emphasis on these issues, India should focus to improve its strength with the help of friendly countries.[53]

On January 10, 1966, India and Pakistan signed the 'Tashkent Declaration', a peace agreement in Taskent, with the mediation of Soviet Union. The treaty was backed by both United Sates and the Soviet Union and under the supervision of United Nation. China rejected the declaration and called it the joint Soviet-American conspiracy to humiliate China. China's disapproval was, what Swaran Singh, stated an assurance to Pakistan that, China was always there to help and was the sole protector of troubled Pakistan.[54] It was also a set back to China, which wanted to mention the level of tension at the Indo-Pak Border to take advantage out of the situation by pressurizing India.[55]

Amidst the disturbed situation, China tested the thermo nuclear bomb on May 9, 1966. The third nuclear test with a period of three years clearly posed serious security threats to India. Again the timing of the explosion happened, when the situation in the Sino-Indian border was tensed. It produced another high tide in Lok Sabha, where the opposition members demanded a detail statement from the government. Replying to the Call Attention Motion of H.V. Kamath, External Affair Minister, Swaran Singh condemned the explosion and termed the explosion "contrary to the interests of humanity at large". Arguing for complete elimination of nuclear weapons from the world, he stated that such a nuclear test was a threat, not only for India but for the whole world. He also assured the House that, the government was determined to protect the frontiers of the country and China could not blackmail India by acquiring the nuclear devices.[56] However, the house remained critical to the recent Chinese nuclear explosion in the subsequent sittings.

Indira Gandhi's Initiatives to Normalize Relationship with China

The landslide victory of Mrs. Indira Gandhi in the 1966 general election brought a new turn in the troubled relationship between India and China. Mrs. Gandhi, after becoming the third Prime Minister decided to follow his father's foot prints and argued for a peaceful relation with China. On January 1, 1969, she declared at a press conference to re-establish the normal diplomatic relation with China which had been curtailed since June 1966. (Following the expulsion of two Indian diplomats by Government of China)[57] President Zakir Hussain while addressing the Parliament also repeated government of India's policy to improve relation with China and stated, "government has expressed more than once with frankness and sincerity its desire to have friendship of relation with (China) …..consistent with our sovereignty, territorial integrity and on the basis of absolute non-interference in each other's internal affairs".[58]

However, Non-Communist oppositions did not subscribe to government's initiatives to have friendly relation with China. Following a debate on India's external relation on April 3, 1969, opposition leader Balraj Madhok (JS), Mahant Digvijai Nath (HM) S.N. Dwivedy (PSP) and Rabi Ray (SP) moved different individual cut motions, in criticizing government's policy to normalize relation with China, which they believed won't serve any cause rather than surrendering Indian rights in the hands of China. They asked the government to take bold steps to liberate the occupied Indian territories from China.[59] Similarly, after the President's address, which repeated government's intention to improve relation with China, Non-Communist oppositions also opposed any policy shift to normalize relation with China.[60] In another occasion, while debating on India's external relations on April 7, 1970, opposition members stormed the house against the normalization of relation with China. Opposition members like, Beni Prasad Shanker Sharma (JS), Om Prakash Tyagi, M.L. Sondhi (JS), R.K. Amin (Swatantra), Ashoka Mehta (Congress –O) and Hem Barua (PSP) condemned the government for its appeasement policy towards China. China, they argued, had been illegally possessing 14500 square miles of Indian Territory and always tried to dismantle Indian integrity by joining hands with its ally Pakistan. They also stated that, instead of taking strong action, was bowing down its head before China.[61]

However, Communist Party of India welcomed the government's initiatives to extend friendly relation with China. CPI leader Hiren Mukherjee, for instance, asked the House to realize the present situation where most of the Chinese neighbors had settled their problems with China. Hence, he argued, it was high time for India to resolve all its outstanding disputes with China peacefully.[62] Similarly, C.K. Chakrapani (CPM) asked the government to go ahead with its peace agenda and redefine the relationship with China, which, he believed was more important for the development of the country.[63] Utkala Congress leader Surendra Mohanty also appealed to the government to continue its efforts to initiate a friendly relationship with China.[64] Tridip Chouhdari of RSP regretted for the government's earlier decision to shut down all doors of negotiation with China and allowed the situation to remain unsettled for years. Appreciating the government's decision he stated that, India had to initiate a negotiation with China, if she wanted to resolve the outstanding issues.[65] Some Congress leaders also asked the government to normalize its relation with China. Congress leader Unni Krishnan, Dinesh Singh and Priya Ranjan Dasmunshi asked the government not to miss the opportunity and the goodwill gesture by China with the restoration of Ambassador level diplomatic relation and Mao's personal greetings to Indian leaders to restore normal relationship with China.[66] To summarize it, almost all the sections of the House, except the major Non-Communist oppositions, backed the government's efforts to normalize relation with China.

Chinese Reaction to Indo-Pak War and Indian Involvement in Bangladesh Crisis

Mrs. Gandhi's landslide victory in the March 1971 General Election opened up further opportunities for the Indian Prime Minister to continue her efforts for the establishment of normal relationship with China. Meanwhile, an anti-Pakistan revolt was started in East Pakistan (the present Bangladesh). Pakistan launched massive crackdown to dismantle the revolution, which resulted in a bloody civil war. In this difficult times Pakistan President Yahya Khan Requested for Chinese help. In reply, Chinese premier, Zhou Enlai wrote a personal letter to Pakistani president on April 12 declaring Beijing's unconditional support to government of Pakistan and warned India not to interfere in internal matters of Pakistan by initiating any military aggression.[67]

India however, ignored the Chinese criticism, in order to maintain the momentum of increasing friendship. Going further, Prime Minister Gandhi wrote two successive personnel letters to Chinese premier Zhou Enlai in July and November regarding India's concerns and position towards East Pakistan (Bangladesh) crisis.[68] When the war cloud was looming above India and Pakistan, China suggested for resolving the issue peacefully and by mutual consultation.[69]

The Non-Communist parties like Jan Sangh, Congress-O and Socialist Party, however, criticized Chinese statement stating it pro-Pakistani and absent of sympathy to the people of East Pakistan. Sadiq Ali of Congress–O while taking exception to Chinese statement asked the government to be alert to the Chinese actions and be prepared to face any unwanted challenges by China. Similarly, Socialist leader Surendra Mohan also asked the government to be prepared to deal with Pakistan, as he believed it might attack India with the support of China.[70]

Playing down the question, Swaran Singh stated in the Lok Sabha on November 18 that, China had not issued any warning to India officially and vowed to improve relation with India. He further clarified that India had been in touch with China regarding the East Pakistan issue and had informed its stand to China. External Affairs Minister Singh also mentioned in the house that, China was responding well to India's goodwill gestures and had been less critical to India nowadays.[71]

On November 23, 1971 Yahya Khan proclaimed a state of emergency in Pakistan and ordered to military crackdown which led to a large scale massacre in East Pakistan. A large number of refugees poured into the Indian Territory, which caused huge domestic pressure in India to resolve the East Pakistan crisis. India started assisting the anti-Pakistan Insurgent Movement, led by Sheikh Mujibur Rahman and ordered its army to drive out Pakistani soldiers. On December 3, 1971 another war broke out between India and Pakistan simultaneously on Eastern and Western borders. After a bloody war, on December 16, 1971 Pakistan forces surrendered before India in Dhaka. A ceasefire was declared by India on the very next day, on which Pakistan readily agreed upon.[72]

China, though, initially warned India not to interfere in the internal affairs of Pakistan (Bangladesh crisis), it did not physically involve into the crisis, except verbal condemnation of Indian involvement and extending political backing to Pakistan. China, did not also try to aggravate the situation by sending any ultimatum to India, as it did during 1965 war. Surprisingly, it only issued three protest notes against India, out of which none of the notes directly condemned Indian involvement in Bangladesh crisis, except objecting organized public protest in front of Chinese embassy for its support to Pakistan. But, the consequences of Bangladesh Crisis and the subsequent Indo-Pak war did affect the process of normalizing relationship between India and China. The Sino-India relation suffered a major setback, when China recalled its *Chargé d'affaires* by October 1971 and let the mission run by a junior officer. As a result, there was less or almost no contact between the two Asian giants for years until the restoration of ambassadorial level diplomatic relations in 1976.[73]

Debating on India's sincere efforts to normalize relation with China on April 25, 1972, CPM leader Dasaratha Deb and Jyotirmy Basu appreciated the government of India's efforts and asked the government to go extra mile to improve relation with China and to resolve the existing disputes. [74] Similarly, Dinesh Singh of Congress also appealed to the government not to wait for China's call to normalize relation and continue to hunt for all possible opportunities to have a friendly neighbour like China, stating the importance of China for Asian power balance.[75]

However, some of the Congress members criticized the government's unilateral attempts to extend friendly relation with China. Congress leaders Unni Krishan and H.P. Sharma for instance, condemned the government's current Chinese policy and stated that it was inappropriate to bow down before Chinese arrogance and begging for friendship. They also suggested the government not to surrender before China as Soviet Union was treaty bound to help India in case of any Chinese attack.[76]

In reply, External Affairs Minister Swaran Singh stated that, the government was always concerned for the greater relation with China and had taken necessary action to improve, whenever there were opportunities. He also stated that, India had carefully avoided the provocative situation and played down the Chinese criticism during recent Indo-Pak war in order to improve its troubled relation with China. The Indo-Soviet treaty, he clarified, was not an obstacle between India-China friendships, as it directed against China.[77]

The Non-Communist members, however, did not subscribe to Government's policy to normalize relation with China and asked the government to take strong steps to reoccupy the captured Indian territories. Jan Sangh leader H.C, Kachwai and P. C. Varma, for instance criticized the government for its policy of unilateral friendship, while China still continued to hold large chunk of Indian territories at Aksai Chin and NEFA. They also wanted to know the government's strategy and the dead line by which the Indian territories could be recovered. Minister of External Affairs, in reply stated that, it was important to have a good and friendly relation with China, but not at the cost of other interests. The government determined to negotiate with China about all existing disputes. However, he refused to draw any timeline at this moment.[78]

Meanwhile, the Shimla Agreement was signed between India and Pakistan on July 2, 1972, which cleared the path for the release of surrendered forces of Pakistan. China supported the agreement and requested India to release all Pakistani soldiers as well as the withdrawal of Indian force from Bangladesh. However, China opposed the Indian sponsored resolution at the United Nation Security Council for the entry of the Bangladesh and used its veto power for the first time, claiming an Indian conspiracy to blackmail Pakistan.[79] The Indian attempt had gone waste and Bangladesh referred to the General Assembly, which later cleared the entry of Bangladesh by accepting the resolution on September 17, 1974.[80]

Despite government's repeated attempts to play down the situation, the Chinese veto against Indian sponsored resolution became another subject of Parliamentary debate. Some political parties, especially Non-Communists used the issue to criticize the government. But, a section of the Parliament, Besides CPI and CPM, requested the government not to read more out of the issue and suggested the government to move ahead for better relation with China. Samar Guha of Socialist party for instance, asked the government not to be disappointed by the recent attitude of China in United Nations and carry on its attempt to improve relationship with Beijing.[81] The House, however, remained divided on the issue of normalization of relation with China. While Communists advocated for greater relation with China, the Right Wing political parties stood critical to the government's unilateral friendship policy and demanded to take appropriate action to bring back the occupied Indian territories.

China's Condemnation to the Merger of Sikkim

When the Sino-Indian relation was getting positive momentum, the political uncertainty broke down in the Himalayan Kingdom of Sikkim, which pushed India and China into an era of hostility once again. The Kingdom of Sikkim used to enjoy special relationship with India because of the Indo-Sikkim Treaty of 1950, which allowed Sikkim to be a protectorate of India. But following the general election in January 1973, a struggle erupted between the leaders of the democratic fronts and the ruler of Sikkim, known as "Chogyal" (The Divine Ruler) which resulted in the breakdown of law and order in the Kingdom. When the kingdom was in skirmish, the ruler of Sikkim requested for India's help. After the written request, India sent its armed forces to bring the situation under control. Following the April 10, 1975 resolution passed by Sikkim General Assembly, a referendum was conducted throughout Sikkim where, the people of Sikkim opted to merge with Indian Union. On April 23, 1975, after the thirty eighth constitutional amendment Sikkim became a part of Indian Union.[82]

China, which always opposed India's special relation with Sikkim, reacted strongly to the Indian moves towards the political transformation of Sikkim. The Chinese media condemned Indian government for, what believed, the use of force to trample the sovereignty of Sikkim. It also rejected the, so called referendum, which it alleged was a farce enacted at the point of Indian bayonets"[83] and stated that, "Chinese government solemnly states once again that it absolutely does not recognize India's illegal annexation of Sikkim and firmly supports the people of Sikkim in their struggle for national independence and defence of state sovereignty against Indian expansionism".[84] Except verbal condemnation, the Chinese Government had hardly any scope to do any disruption in Sikkim, due to the overwhelming Indian presence.

The Chinese criticism towards the merger of Sikkim created another furore in the Indian Parliament. Jan Sangh leader Atal Bihari Vajpayee Condemned the Chinese reaction to the merger of Sikkim and stated that, the Chinese objection was adverse to the will of the Sikkim people. Appreciating the government's timely measures, he stated that, by sending the army, India was only performing its duty (i.e. the protection of the Sikkimese people) and the merger was conducted only after the popular referendum and not by use of force.[85] Similarly, Frank Anthony (Independence), while debating on India's foreign Affairs stated that, China might retaliate to Indian Sikkim move and might create problems at the frontiers by alleging Indian violation of LAC. Asking to take precautionary measures, he warned the government that, China wanted to mention its influence in the subcontinent and would not miss any opportunity to embrace India.[86]

However, Communist leaders remained divided to the amalgamation of Sikkim. While, CPM opposed India's action, CPI backed the government. Denouncing India's army mission to Sikkim CPM leader Saroj Mukherjee stated that, it was inappropriate to send the army to protect the Chogayal regime, which was unpopular and intolerable, despite India's commitment to protect the Sikkim from internal and external threats. According to him, Sikkim should be allowed to remain as an "independent sovereign state" as it was used to be for decades and the merging of Sikkim into the Indian union was against the spirit of international law.[87] But, unlike, CPM, CPI has justified India's role in Sikkim. Its prominent leader clarifying his party's stand stated that, the government's decision to send force and successive merger of Sikkim was only initiated after the due request of the ruler and people of Sikkim.[88]

External Affair Minister, Swaran Singh however, played down the Chinese attitude towards Sikkim crisis and vowed to normalize the relation with China. He further stated that, there was a significant improvement in the Chinese attitude towards India. Despite India's decision to send army to Sikkim, the propaganda campaign was reduced to the lowest ever, he added. Singh hoped that China's positive gesture would continue and the relation would improve gradually.[89] Looking at the Swaran Singh's statement and the absent of any anti-Chinese remarks by any Congress leadership, it was clear that, the government was desperate to improve relation with China and for that they did not highlight the Chinese attitude. On the other hand, China also did not involve physically in the Sikkim crisis and continued to maintain its romance with India by sending the Vice-Premier and Chinese Table Tennis team to India in order to record goodwill gestures. The opposition parties, especially Non-Communist oppositions asked the government to break all relations with China, but it was not ready to accept anything other than its own agenda.

End of Hostility and Emergence of Sino-Indian Détente

Amidst the Sikkim Crisis, in January 1975, Chinese Vice-Minister paid a goodwill visit to India along with the Chinese Table Tennis team to deescalate the situation and bring normalcy in the relationship. On February 22, while addressing the Indian media during his brief halt at Calcutta (Now Kolkata) on his way to Beijing, Chinese Vice-Premier conveyed China's wish to improve relations with India and bring an end to the decades long hostilities.[90] Meanwhile, Chinese Premier Zhou Enlai died of Cancer on January 8, 1976. Following the death of Zhou, Mrs. Indira Gandhi called up Chinese Vice-Premier Deng Xiaoping and expressed her sympathy for the people of China. In addition, along with External Affairs Minister Chavan, she visited the Chinese embassy and expressed her condolences.[91] As the Sino-Indian empathy was at its peak, Chinese Vice Foreign Minister conveyed the Chinese intention to *chargé d'affaires* of India for the establishment of normal diplomatic relation with India and stated, "China would welcome India's initiative of sending an ambassador to China, and it is my personal thing that the Chinese government respond positively". [92] To extend the growing friendship, Indian government announced to appoint Indian Ambassador to China, in April 1976 and send K.R. Narayan as the Indian ambassador to China on July 7, 1976.[93] In reply, China sent Chen Zhayuan as the Chinese ambassador to India on September 10, 1976. Hence, both the countries restored the ambassadorial level diplomatic relation after a gap of 15 years. With the normal diplomatic relation, the era of 'Sino-Indian confrontation' came to end and the new 'era of Sino-Indian reengagement' started.

Following the 1977 General Election, the Janata Party formed the government, defeating the Indira Gandhi led Congress Party. This election result was significant, because for the first time a non-Congress government voted to power. It was also highly significant for India-China relationship, as the founding partners of Janta Party, the Swatantra, Sociality, and Jan Sangh, used to remain critical towards China earlier. As the so-called Anti-China parties were in power, there was a sense of concern among the Chinese leadership regarding the fate of relationship with India. However, beating all worries, Foreign Minister, Atal Bihari Vajpayee informed in the Parliament that his government would continue the process of normalization of relationship with China, which was essential for the betterment of both the countries and for the region as a whole.[94] Extending the goodwill gesture, a Chinese delegation headed by Wang Binnan, visited India on March 7, 1978. During their extensive 16 days visit to different parts of India, Wang invited External Affair Minister, Vajpayee to visit China.[95]

Responding to Chinese invitation, Minister of External Affairs A. B. Vajpayee visited China on February 12, 1979 and laid the foundation for Sino-Indian talks. [96]

Chinese Vice Premier and Foreign Minister Huang Hua paid his return trip to India on June 25, 1981. It was the first visit by any Chinese Foreign Minister ever. During the visit, the Chinese Foreign Minister invited Mrs. Gandhi to visit China. Speaking to the reporter, Huang stated that the boundary problems should be resolved through peaceful negotiation.[97] During the visit of Huang, both the countries agreed to resume talks in order to resolve the long pending border problems. The first round of proposed series of talks was held between 10 to 14 December 1981in Beijing, where India remained adhered to the implementation of the Colombo proposal, whereas China proposed for "mutual understanding and accommodation" and "package deal". The talk ended with no conclusive decision or agreement. There were altogether eight similar talks held between December 1981 and November 1987. Due to subsequent rejection of each other's proposal, the series of talks eventually ended without any workable solution, though both the countries were determined to resolve the issue. However, these series of negotiations opened up several new doors for both the governments to understand each other's concerns.[98]

While the series of negotiations was going on, both the countries decided to take the century old India-China relation into new a stage with the normalization of trade and economic relations. After a series of discussion between Indian and Chinese trade delegations, New Delhi and Beijing signed a trade agreement giving Most Favoured Nation (MNF) status to each other on August 15, 1984.[99] Hence, the normal trade relationship between the countries, which had been derailed after the expiry of the 1954 trade agreement, was re-established with the signing of the agreement. The new agreement also helped to boost confidence between India and China and showed a new path to the Sino-Indian friendship. To improve the relation further, Prime Minister Rajiv Gandhi made his historic five day visit to China on December 19, 1988 along with External Affairs Minister, Narasimha Rao and several other high level Indian delegates. It was the first visit by an Indian Prime Minister to visit China after a gap of thirty years. During the visit, several agreements were signed on civil aviation, science and technology, and cultural exchanges. Both the sides also agreed to setup a Joint working Group (JWG) at the level of Vice Ministers to negotiate on the border disputes. The joint communiqué declared that both the countries had determined to resolve the boundary dispute through peaceful negotiation based on mutual acceptance. The communiqué also stated that India and China would not leave the fate of the relationship to the boundary disputes and efforts would be made to extend the relationship into other possible areas. To summarize, Rajiv Gandhi's China visit, as most of the Indian and Chinese scholars described, was one of the mile stones in the Sino-Indian relationship and took the relationship into a new stage.[100]

Conclusion

Being one of the important episodes of India-China relationship and one of the defining moments of Asian politics, the period of Sino-Indian Confrontation, from 1958 to 1975 had witnessed several significant developments in the bilateral relationship between India and China. The century old Sino-Indian relationship started sinking after the Tibetan uprising of 1958. After the voluntary abandonment of all British inherited traditional rights by signing the 'agreement of trade and intercourse', popularly known as *Panchsheel* Agreement, India expected the end of issues with China, including the border disputes. India also recognized Tibet as the integral part of China and mentioned silence during the Chinese invention into Tibet and Tibetan uprising, which she believed as internal matters of China. However, China accused Indian involvement in the Tibetan uprising and condemned India's decision to grant political asylum to Dalai Lama.

Indian Parliament, which used to be supportive towards matters related to China, took strong acceptation to the Chinese allegation and members across the party line denounced the Chinese allegation. Opposition parties such as PSP, BJS and MKP strongly criticized government of India's silence towards the Tibetan uprising and argued the government to help the rebel for their fight to self-determination. However, Nehru led Congress as well as CPI rejected the opposition's demand and backed the government's decision to maintain neutrality.

Short after the fall of the Tibetan uprising and the successful Tibetan annexation, Chinese troops initiated the long range border patrolling along the Indo-Tibetan border and came face to face with Indian troops, which led to several border clashes, in which India allegedly lost large chunk of its territory to China. Each of the party accused each other for the border violation, before deciding to hold formal discussion for the demarcation of inhabited frontiers. However, no result was achieved in the negations and left the situation unsolved, even without any interim mechanism. As a result, India decided to use force to drive out Chinese occupation by lunching massive military operation. China reacted to the Indian action strongly with greater force which led to the breakup of the Sino-Indian border war in 1962. India received major defeat and Chinese forces forced back Indian troops in Aksai Chin and occupied around 37,244 square kilometres (14,380 sq. mi.) of Indian Territory, which they believed belonging to China. On November 19, 1962 China declared unilateral ceasefire and decided to pull back its troops 20 kilometres back from the ceasefire line.

The whole political spectrum and the Indian Parliament at large condemned the Chinese attack. Members from opposition parties and even from the ruling party targeted Prime Minister Nehru and the government as a whole for the failed Chinese policy and the military disaster. Defence Minister Krishna Menon also came under strong attack by the oppositions in the Parliament. The Jan Sangh, Socialists and the Swatrantra party made accountable to the government for the defeat and moved several motions including no confidence motion against the government. They also demanded immediate resignation from the Defence Minister and the Prime Minister. Interestingly, a section of ruling Congress party also criticized government's China policy and blamed Nehru for the military defeat of India. Communist Party of India, which used to back Nehru's Chinese Foreign Policy on several occasions and had been adopting pro-Chinese stand also openly condemned the Chinese attack, which was a rare phenomenon in the Indian Parliament.

Though China declared the unilateral ceasefire on November 21, 1962 and pulled back its forces 20 kilometres back from the ceasefire line, both the states failed to decide the ceasefire line proposed zone of demilitarization. Looking at the looming danger, some Afro-Asian countries gathered at Colombo, the capital of Cylone (present Sri Lanka) to facilitate the negotiation and prepared a ceasefire formula, known as Colombo proposal. India agreed to accept the formula, but China objected to certain points and accepted a part of the proposal. As a result the proposal failed to achieve its purpose.

On October 16, 1964 China conducted its first nuclear test and emerged as the fifth nuclear state of the world. India reacted strongly to the Chinese nuclear programme. After attaining the nuclear weapon, Chinese Prime Minister Zohu Enlai stated that China never relinquished its sovereignty over the 90000 square km of territory in NEFA region, the present Arunachal Pradesh. China also tried to get closer to India's traditional enemy, Pakistan and signed a boundary protocol with Pakistan on Mar 26, 1965. By signing the protocol, Pakistan handed over nearly 5309 sq km of area out of its administrative region of Kashmir. Following the breakup of Indo-Pak war in April 1956, China supported Pakistan and labeled India as the aggressor. China also supported the Kashmir movement and demanded the right to self-determination for the people of Kashmir. China also condemned the "Tashkent declaration" signed between India and Pakistan on January 1966 and called it as the Soviet-American conspiracy to humiliate China.

Following the land slide victory in the 1966 general election, Mrs. Indira Gandhi decided to follow the footprints of her father and vowed to normalize relation with China by re-establishing diplomatic ties. But most of the Non-Communist opposition parties criticized the Government of India's unilateral initiatives to improve relation with China. However, CPI and CPM supported the government's decision and asked the government to take necessary steps to re-establish full diplomatic relation with China. Prime Minister Indira Gandhi also supported China's bid to United Nation in 1971.

Meanwhile, an anti-Pakistani revolt was developed in the East Pakistan, the present Bangladesh in 1971 and Pakistan lunched massive army operation to dismantle the revolution. During this difficult time, Pakistan requested for Chinese assistance/ support. China readily extended its unconditional support to Pakistan and warned India to stay away from the internal matters of Pakistan. India maintained silence at the initial periods for the sake of its normalization of relationship process with China. But, after the breakdown of large scale massacre and following the flowing of large scale refugees into India, the Indian Government ordered its army to drive out Pakistani army from East Pakistan. China, however, did not intervene physically in the conflict. But the consequence of Indian involvement in the Bangladesh crisis did affect the process of normalization of relation with China. China extended its support to the Shimla Agreement and indicated to improve relation with India.

When the Sino-Indian relation was getting positive momentum, a political crisis broke down in the Himalayan kingdom of Sikkim. The leaders of the democratic fronts revolted against the king and demanded for the end of kingship. Following the request of the ruler of Sikkim, India sent its army to bring the situation under control. A referendum was conducted following the resolution passed by the Sikkimese General Assembly, in which the people of Sikkim voted to merge with Indian union. On April 23, 1975, Sikkim became the 22nd state of Indian union after the 38th Constitutional Amendment. China, which recognized Sikkim as an independent kingdom, condemned the merger of Sikkim and termed India the aggressor. Chinese leadership also accused India for forcefully occupying the Himalayan kingdom and refused to recognize Sikkim as the state of India.

However, after the end of Sikkim crisis both India and China decided to move ahead to develop normal relationship. The process of Sino-Indian détente started getting momentum after the non-intervention of China in the Sikkim crisis. The goodwill visit of the Chinese Table Tennis team led by the Chinese Vice-Minister Wang Bingnan helped to break the deadlock in the years of estrangement. As the first step towards Sino-Indian rapprochement, India sent K.R. Narayanana as the Indian Ambassador to China and Beijing sent Chen Zhayuan as the Chinese ambassador to India in 1976 and the two Asian giants once again re-established their ambassador level diplomatic relations after a gap of 15 years. Similarly, Foreign Minister Vajpayee visited Beinjing on February 12, 1979. India and China granted the status of Most Favoured Nation (MNF) to each other on 15 August 1984. Prime Minister Rajiv Gandhi paid his historic visit to China on December 19, 1988. And the Chinese Prime Minister Li peng visited India in December 1991followed by Narshimarao's China visit in December 1993. During 1976 to 1997 several high-level visits and diplomatic exchanges occurred, which further stringed the age old relation between India and China and put the relationship on track.

Notes

1. Hoffmann (1990) 226-28.
2. Jetly (1997) 201-02.
3. Lok Sabha Debates, Vol. 12, 1963, Col. 5978.
4. *Ibid.*, Cols. 5983-6002.
5. *Ibid.*, Cols. 6035-45.
6. *Ibid.*, Cols. 6385-93.
7. *Ibid.*, Cols. 6108-15.
8. *Ibid.*, Cols.6331-40.
9. *Ibid.*, Cols. 6349-57, 6369-74.
10. *Ibid.*, Cols. 6070-80.
11. *Ibid.*, Cols. 6127-32.
12. *Ibid.*, Cols. 6301-07.
13. *Ibid.*, Cols. 6304-12.
14. *Ibid.*, Cols. 6363-09.
15. *Ibid.*, Cols. 6511-50.
16. *Ibid.*, Cols. 6537-43.
17. *Ibid.*, Cols. 6535.
18. *White Paper IX* (New Delhi: Ministry of External Affairs, 1963) 10-20.

19. Lok Sabha Debates, Vol. 18, 1963, Cols. 14195-96.
20. Lok Sabha Debates, Vol. 19, 1963, Cols. 1219-37.
21. *Ibid.*, Cols. 1281-1305.
22. *Ibid.*, Cols. 1315-24.
23. *Ibid.*, Cols. 1546-60.
24. *Ibid.*, Cols. 1830-60.
25. Lok Sabha Debates, Vol. 55, 1966, Cols. 15712-13.
26. *Ibid.*, Cols. 5067-70.
27. Itty Abraham, The Making of the Indian Atomic Bomb: Science, Secrecy and the Postcolonial State (London: Zed Books, 1998) 125.
28. Lok Sabha debates, Vol. 34, 1964, Cols. 1240-55.
29. *Ibid.*, Cols. 1258-0-59.
30. *Ibid.*, Cols.1512-18.
31. *Ibid.*, Cols.1300.
32. *Ibid.*, Cols.1315-20.
33. *Ibid.*, Cols.1659-63.
34. *Ibid.*, Cols. 1564-73, & Lok Sabha Debates, Vol. 37, 1964, Cols. 6702-11.
35. Abraham (1998) 126, 141-145.
36. The Hindustan Times (New Delhi), January 1, 196537*Lok Sabha Debates*, Vol. 28, 1965, Cols. 664-65.
38. Byron N. Tzou, China and International Law: The Boundary Disputes (New York: Praeger Publishers, 1990) 70; also see, Vidya Nadkarni, Strategic Partnerships in Asia: Balancing Without Alliances (New York: Routledge Publication, 2010) 116-17.
39. Michael Brecher and Jonathan Wilkenfeld, A Study of Crisis (Michigan: University of Michigan Press, 1997) 170-71.
40. Xinhua News Agency, May 4, 1965.
41. Foreign Affairs Record, Ministry of External Affairs, Government of India 1965, 100-01.
42. White Paper XII (New Delhi: Ministry of External Affairs, Government of India,) 39.
43. *Ibid.*, 40-41.
44. *Ibid.*, 43.
45. Lok Sabha Debates, Vol. 46, 1965, Cols. 6332-5.
46. *Ibid.*, Cols. 6570-71.
47. Foreign Affairs Record, 1965, 134-35.
48. Lok Sabha Debates, Vol. 47, 1965, Cols. 1868.
49. *Ibid.*, Cols. 1893-94.
50. *Ibid.*, Cols. 1966-7, 1981, 1901-3.
51. *Ibid.*, cols. 1913-15.
52. *Ibid.*, Cols. 1936.

53. *Ibid.*, Cols. 2291.
54. Swaran Singh (1966) 58.
55. Shri Ram Sharma, India-China Relations, 1947-1971: Friendship Goes with Power, Part 1 (New Delhi: Discovery Publishing House, 1999) 84.
56. Lok Sabha debates, vol. 55, 1966, Cols. 15712-13.
57. See Times of India (Bombay) January 2, 1969.
58. Lok Sabha Debates, Vol. 27, 199, Cols. 23.
59. *Ibid.*, Cols. 224-25, 242, 301-312, 327.
60. Lok Sabha Debates, Vol. 36, 1970, Col. 12.
61. *Ibid.*, Vol. 39, 1970, Cols. 219-275 (Scatteredly Located).
62. *Ibid.*, Cols. 312.
63. *Ibid.*, Cols. 321-2.
64. Lok Sabha Debates, Vol. 6, 1971, Col. 274.
65. *Ibid.*, Cols. 187.
66. *Ibid.*, Cols. 201, 250, 237-8.
67. Richard Sisson, Leo E. Rose, War and Secession: Pakistan, India, and the Creation of Bangladesh (Berkeley: University of California Press, 1999) 246-153; also see, Jetly (1979) 267.
68. *Ibid.*
69. Detail can be seen at, The Statesman, November 24, 1974. 70 *Lok Sabha Debates*, Vol. 6, 1971, Cols. 236-43.
71. *Ibid.*, Col. 258-59.
72. Richard Sisson (1991) 265-66.
73. *Ibid.*, 252-53.
74. *Lok Sabha Debates,* Vol. 14, 1972, Col. 218, 228..
75. *Ibid.*, Col. 270.
76. *Ibid.*, Cols. 223-4, 295-6.
77. *Ibid.*, Cols. 216-17.
78. *Ibid.* Cols. 357-64.
79. Alan Lawrance, China's Foreign Relations Since 1949 (Oxen: Routledge, 2007) 225-27; also see, EyalBenvenisti, The International Law of Occupation(Oxford: Oxford University Press, 2012) 190.
80. Benvenisti (2012) 190.
81. Lok Sabha Debates, Vol. 18, , 1972, Cols. 410-12.
82. G. S. Bajpai, China's Shadow Over Sikkim: The Politics of Intimidation(New Delhi: Lancer Publishers, 1999) 209-11.
83. *Ibid.* 212.
84. As stated in Bajpai (1999) 212.
85. *Lok Sabha Debates*, Vol. 27, 1973, Cols. 257-8.
86. *Ibid.*, Cols. 342-43.
87. *Ibid.*, Cols. 257-28.

88. *Ibid.*, Col. 274.
89. *Ibid.*, Cols. 263-64.
90. As stated in Shri Ram Sharma (300) 52.
91. Swaran Singh, "Building Confidence with China" in Tan Chung, Across the Himalayan Gap: An Indian Quest for Understanding China (New Delhi: Gyan Publishing House, 1998) 521.
92. Deepak (2005) 298-99.
93. Lok Sabha Debates, Vol. 9, 1967, Cols. 9326-28.
94. Lok Sabha Debates, Vol. 3, 1977.
95. *Ibid.*
96. Satya Bhusan Jain, India's Foreign Policy and Non-alignment (New Delhi: Anamika Publishers, 2000) 229.
97. Beijing Review, July 13, 1891, 7.
98. Lal (2008) 24; also see, Pobzeb Vang, Five Principles of Chinese Foreign Policies (Bloomington: Author House, 2008) 174.
99. Tan Chung (1998) 524-25; also see, Bibek Debroy and Amitendu Palit, "China and India: Growth Outcomes and Economic Change", in A Resurgent China: South Asian Perspectives, edited by S.D. Muni, Tan Tai Yong (New Delhi: Routledge, 2011) 137-38.
100. Deepak (2005) 327-33; also see, C.V. Ranganathan, "Memories of an Indian Ambassador: 1987-1991", in Across the Himalayan Gap: An Indian Quest for Understanding China, edited by Tan Chung (New Delhi: Gyan Publishing House, 1998) 443-45; and, Chung Tan, Rise of the Asian Giants: The Dragon-Elephant Tango (New Delhi: Anthem Press, 2009) 232.

Chapter - 7

Parliament and the Making of India's China Policy during the Era of Reengagement 1976-1999

With the collapse of the great wall of Sino-Indian hostility at the end of Sikkim crisis, both India and China decided to move ahead to develop normal relationship. The process of Sino-Indian détente was started getting momentum after the non-intervention of China in the Sikkim crisis. The goodwill visit of the Chinese Table Tennis team led by the Chinese Vice-Minister Wang Bingnan helped to break the deadlock in the years of estrangement. Chinese leaderships showed her interest to re-establish the normal diplomatic relationship with India. On the other hand, Foreign minister Chavan declared to send K.R. Narayan as the Indian ambassador to China. Subsequently, Chen Zhayuan was sent as the Chinese ambassador to India in September 1976 and the two Asian giants once again reestablished their ambassador level diplomatic relation. Following the invitation of Wang Bingnan, foreign minister Vajpayee visited Beinjing on February 12, 1979. India and China granted the status of Most Favored Nation (MNF) to each other on 15 August 1984. Prime Minister Rajiv Gandhi paid his historic visit to China on December 19, 1988. And Chinese Prime Minister Li peng visited India in December 1991 followed by Narshimarao's China visit in December 1993. During 1976 to 1997 several high-level visits and diplomatic exchanges occurred, which further stringed the age old relation between India and China and put the relationship on track. This chapter discusses the attitude of Indian parliament during the important period of reengagement. The chapter is dived into several chronological subtitles such as, the process of normalization of relationship, the diplomatic and political exchanges between India and China, India's nuclear programs, Chinese attitude towards Kargil war and the Karmapa Crisis and each section has analyzed the outlook of different political parties as well as the attitude of the parliament as a whole towards these issues.

Restoration of Ambassadorial Level Diplomatic Relations

Amidst the Sikkim Crisis, in January 1975, Chinese Vice-Minister paid a goodwill visit to India along with the Chinese Table Tennis team to deescalate the situation and bring normalcy in the relationship. On February 22, while addressing the Indian media during his brief halt at Calcutta (Now Kolkata) on his way to Beijing, Chinese vice-premier stated that, the Chinese government is reluctant to improve relations with India and bring an end to the decades long hostilities.[1] Following the death of Zhou Enlai, Mrs. Indira Gandhi called up Chinese Vice-Premier Deng Xiaoping and expressed her sympathy for the people of China. In addition, along with External Affairs Minister Chavan, she visited the Chinese embassy and expressed their condolences. As the Sino-Indian empathy was at its peak, Chinese Vice Foreign Minister conveyed the Chinese intension to *chargé d'affaires* of India for the establishment of normal diplomatic relation with India and stated, "China would welcome India's initiative of sending an ambassador to China, and it is my personal thing that the Chinese government respond positively".[2] To extend the growing friendship, Indian government announced to appoint Indian Ambassador to China, in April 1976.

Informing the government's decision to restore normal diplomatic relation with China, Foreign Minister Chavan , on April 15, 1976, stated in the Lok Sabha that, "it is proposed to appoint Shri K.R. Narayanan ...... as our ambassador to the people's republic of China". He also announced that, Chinese government had agreed to this appointment and reluctant to restore ambassadorial level relation in India.[3] The Parliament at large supported the government's decision, though the non-communist oppositions stayed unconvinced. Replying the opposition's queries on the discussion of the question of Chinese occupied territories with Chinese government, Chavan mentioned that, it was not too early to discuss the much complicated boundary question as the normal diplomatic relations was just going to resume.[4] K.R. Narayanan, met the Chinese officials and took charge of his duty as the new Ambassador to China on July 7, 1976. In reply, China sent Chen Zhayuan as the Chinese ambassador to India on September 10, 1976. Hence, both the countries restored the ambassadorial level diplomatic relation after a gap of 15 years. With the normal diplomatic relation, the Sino-Indian relation entered into a new stage of friendly relationship.

While the normalization of relationship was at its pace, there was sudden change in the Indian political scenario. In the 1977 general election, the Janata party formed the government, defeating the Indira Gandhi led congress party. This election result was significant, because for the first time a non-congress government voted to power. It was also highly significant for India-China relationship, as the founding partners of Janta Party, the Swatantra, Sociality, and Jan Sangh, used to remain critical towards China earlier. As the so-called Anti-China parties were in power, there was a sense of concern among the Chinese leadership regarding the fate of relationship with India. Beating all worries, foreign minister, Atal Bihari Vajpayee informed in the Parliament, while debating on foreign affairs that, his government would continue the process of normalization of relationship with China and clarified that, it was then up to China to enhance the relation into the next level. He also informed the house that, the present government had determined to improve the relation with China, which was essential for the betterment of both the countries and for the region as a whole.[5]

Some of the members of the ruling Janata Party, however, still remained critical to the government's decision to continue the effort to normalize relation with China, and asked the government to wait for further steps to improve the relationship. Requesting the government not to go single handedly to the improve relation with China, Janata leader, H.V. Kamath for instance, argued not to take further move, until China took the next call.[6] Similarly, Sushila Nayar of the same party, while welcoming the normalization of relations stated that, India should develop friendly relation with China, but not at the cost of its own dignity. He argued to raise the issue of occupied Indian territories and stated that, India should continue to fight for its right.[7]

On the other hand, opposition parties like Congress and Communists suggested the government should go beyond quantifying their efforts and take further steps to improve the relationship. Congress leader Henry Austin and CPM leader Diren Bhattacharya for instance expressed their full support to the government policies that meant to strengthen Sino-Indian cooperation. While, Austin asked the government to name a notable personality as the Indian Ambassador to China[8], Bhattacharya suggested the government to extend the level of cooperation into new areas such as trade and commerce and not just the diplomatic relation.[9]

But, as noticed, the government of India was not in a hurry and, perhaps wanted to perceive slowly regarding the normalization of relation with China. It was clarified after foreign minister Vajpayee's statement at a press conference, where he stated that, India had taken enough steps to normalize relation and the ball was then at the Chinese court. He also made it clear that, the government's next step in this direction would purely depend on Chinese actions.[10]

Meanwhile, on August 4, 1977, Chinese *Chargé d'affaires* put a critical allegation against India that, India was helping the anti-Chinese activities carried out by Dalai Lama and Tibetan refugees and openly supporting the Tibetan sassiest movement. In addition, China reacted to the meeting with Dalai Lama. Chinese media also reportedly run an anti-Indian propaganda against the alleged Indian involvement. This Chinese attitude raised sharp public reaction inside and outside the Parliament and some members of the ruling party moved a call attention motion against the Chinese allegation and subsequent propaganda.

In reply to the motion, foreign minister Vajpayee stated that, it was regretful that the Chinese media was still practicing the propaganda campaigning which was "factually incorrect and needlessly provocative". He also informed the house that, the government of India's stand on the Sino-Indian border disputes remained unchanged and the present governments would firmly adhere to the 1961 official reports. Denying to any future aggression against China, he further clarified that, "we should remain firm on our territorial claim but at the same time, try to normalize relations with China."[11] Further clarifying, Morarji Desai in a statement mentioned that, India did not want to spoil the improving relations with China, but, there could not be lasting friendship between India and China as long as the border dispute remained unsolved. Denying any plan of recapturing the lost Indian territories, he further stated, "it is our land how can we give it up? But we won't go to war about it. We shall follow the path of negotiations, but they must also be ready for negotiations".[12]

Similar views to resolve the existing disputes and normalization of relation with India also came out from the other side of the border. Chinese Premier Hua Guofeng, while presenting the report of the government's performance to the National People's Congress (NPC) stated that, "Chinese people have always harbored friendship for the people of India. People of both the countries wish to improve friendly exchanges and improvement in the bilateral relations. Although there still exist some unsolved problems between the two countries, however, so long as there are sincere efforts from both the countries, bilateral relations could be further improved." [13] Extending the goodwill gesture, a Chinese delegation headed by Wang Binnan, visited India on March 7, 1978. During their extensive 16 days visit to different parts of India, Wang invited External Affair Minister, Vajpayee to visit China.[14]

External Affair Minister Vajpayee's Visit to China

While addressing the press in 1977, Vajpayee expressed his desire and stated that he would be glad to visit Beijing, if Chinese government would extend their official invitation to him. Following Vajpayee's remarks, Wang Binnan during his visit to India formally invited the Indian foreign minister to visit China. Responding to Chinese invitation, Minister of External Affairs A. B. Vajpayee visited China on February 12, 1979.Though border issue was the main agenda of Vajpayee's visit, there was no clear-cut matter for discussion with the Chinese government. He called the trip as "exploratory" and "probing".[15] It was proven true following the Chinese invasion into Vietnam during the Vajpayee's visit, leaving the Indian foreign minister in blind in presenting India's stand, as neither the Chinese government, nor the Indian intelligence officers had briefed him about the incidents.[16] Vajpayee, however, did not adhere to the sole issue rather, agreed to press for normalization of relation with China.

Raising a call attention notice on March 16, 1979, Janata party leader H.V. Kamath wanted to know about the stand of government of India over the border disputes. In reply, Prime MinisterMorarji Desai stated that, his government had already clarified the Indian stand and only adhered to the 1962 parliamentary resolution. However, rather over driving the Chinese occupation, they would ask the Chinese government to vacate the land through peaceful negotiation. Repeating his previous statement, he again informed the house that, unless the core issues of border disputes remained unsolved, the lasting friendship was unachievable. However, the government of India would continue the efforts to normalize the relation.

Huang Hua's Visit to India and Eight Rounds of Border Talks

Chinese vice premier and foreign minister Huang Hua paid his return trip to India on June 25, 1981. It was the first visit by any Chinese foreign minister ever. Though Huang's India trip was scheduled in late 1980, India's reorganization to Heng Samrin government in Cambodia made China fury and led to the cancelation of Huang's India visit. However, the visit was later rescheduled to June 1981. During the visit, the Chinese foreign minister held talks with foreign minister Narashimha Rao, Prime Minister Indira Gandhi, and President Neelam Sanjeeva Ready, as well as other important personalities. He also invited Mrs. Gandhi to visit to China.

Speaking to the reporter, Huang stated that the boundary problems should be resolved through peaceful negotiation. He also stated that, both the sides had to develop an "attitude of treating each other on an equal footing, mutual understanding and mutual accommodation and seek through negotiations a fair and reasonable overall statement of the problem , taking into consideration the historical background and the present actualities as well as the national feelings of the people of both countries." He however asked both the sides to maintain status quo and tranquility in the border and bring immediate solution to the small irritations, in order to facilitate strong Sino-Indian friendship.[17]

During the visit of Huang, both the countries agreed to resume talks in order to resolve the long pending border problems. The first round of proposed series of talks was held between 10 to 14 December 1981in Beijing, where India remained adhered to the implementation of the Colombo proposal, whereas China proposed for "mutual understanding and accommodation" and "package deal". The talk ended with no conclusive decision or agreement. There were altogether eight similar talks held between December 1981toNovember 1987. Due to subsequent rejection of each other's proposal, the series of talks eventually ended without any workable solution, though both the countries were determined to resolve the issue. However, these series of negotiations opened up several new doors for both the governments to understand each other's concerns.[18]

The attitude of Indian Parliament was very cordial towards the Chinese foreign minister's visit and the growing Sino-Indian friendship. There was undeclared consensus among the Indian political leadership to the normalization of bilateral relationship with China. However, the opposition parties remained cautious over Chinese attitude. Even before the visit of the Chinese Foreign Minister, Devi Lal (Janata Secular) raised a question regarding India's position to discuss the border disputes with China during the foreign minister level talks. He wanted to know whether, India was going to raise the border disputes with the Chinese foreign minister or move beyond the controversial debates and focus on other areas. In reply, External Affairs Minister Narasimha Rao stated that, the government was ready to discuss on any matter with the China, including the border disputes and equally opened to extend the bilateral cooperation to other fields.[19] Another Janata party Leader George Fernandez asked the government to initiate talks for the reopening of border passes and ancient routes of pilgrims.[20] Janata leader Subramanian Swamy wanted to know the prospects of the meeting of different political leaders with the Chinese Foreign Minister and objected to the mass meeting of the Indian communist leaders with the Chinese leader. He believed that, the Chinese guest had ignored most of the important political leaders and scheduled his meeting with the large CPI leaders and it showed the hidden connection between Indian communist leadership and the CPC.[21] Apart from these small objections, the Parliament at large remained positive and the members across the party line welcomed the changing Chinese attitude towards India.

Similarly, the issue of ongoing border talks was also repeatedly raised during the parliamentary debates in India. Chandra Sekhar of Janata Party, while raising a question on India-China border talks, asked the government to pose strong stand on China India border talks and not to accept any Chinese proposal that went against Indian security.[22] R.P. Verma also posed a question related to Sino-Indian talks and wanted to know the details of the officers who were participating in the talks and argued the government to appointed efficient and experienced officers to hold a meaningful dialogue.[23] BJP leader K.K Goyal wanted to know India's position in the ongoing border talks.[24] A.B. Vajpayee of the same party asked the government to table Indian arguments on the floor of parliament and questioned the progress of the talks. According to him, China was not pursuable and India was only wasting its efforts in participating in the talks.[25] Charan Singh of Janata (Secular) requested the government to raise the Menser issue at the Sino-Indian Border talks, stating that it had been traditionally under Indian control before the Chinese incursion.[26]

However, the communist leaders and the members of the ruling party supported the ongoing border talks with China. Uploading the government's efforts, CPM leader Samar Mukherjee stated that, India China friendship was important for the sake of mutual growth and development of that region. He asked the government to resolve the long standing hostilities with China and extend the negotiation into other areas.[27] Another communist leader Indrajit Gupta also asked the government to seeped up the talks and resolve the disputes with China on prioritize basis.[28] As the talk went several rounds the parliament remained vibrant with related debates. But overall, the parliament remained positive and cooperative during Sino-Indian border talks.

Most Favoured Nation (MFN) Status to China

While the series of negotiations was going on, both the countries decided to take the century old India-China relation into new a stage with the normalization of trade and economic relations. A team of FICCI officials visited China in 1984 and recommended for the reestablishment of greater economic relation with China. Another trade delegation was also dispatched to China in order to analyze the fusibilities to implement the recommendation. After a series of discussions, India-China signed a trade agreement giving Most Favored Nation (MNF) status to each other on August 15, 1984.[29] Hence, the normal trade relationship between the countries, which had been derailed after the expiry of the 1954 trade agreement, was reestablished with the signing of the agreement. The new agreement also helped to boost confidence between India and China and showed new path to the Sino-Indian friendship.

The granting of MFN status to China and resume of Sino-Indian trade relations however evoked mixed reaction in India. While the communists and the members of the ruling party supported the agreement, the oppositions, especially, Janata and Bharatiya Janata Party (BJP) objected to the government's decision. While the signing of the MFN was on the card, CPI leader Indrajit Gupta suggested the government to sign the agreement that, he believed, would open a new chapter in India China economic relation, where, both the countries would be benefited by the agreement. [30] However, BJP and other right wing parties remained suspicious against the Chinese attitude and opposed the decision. Raising a question on India's Most Favored Nation status to China, BJP leader, K.K. Goyal stated that, the extinction of MNF status was not the interest of Indian economy, as the inflow of Chinese products would paralyze the Indian industries. He believed that, India in no way would be benefitted by the return MNF status granted by China. He requested for the review of the decision and withdrawal of MFN status from China.[31]

Apart from the debate on MFN status, a section of the members from both the opposition and Congress members questioned the relevance and outcome of ongoing Sino-Indian talks. Janata (S) member B.S. Rao asked the government to table the outcome of bilateral border talks.[32] Similarly, criticizing government's China policy, he also asked the government to seek other options for recovery of Aksai Chin area. He felt that China didn't want to handover the Indian territories and the ongoing talk was just an act of eyewash. Sudarsan Das of Congress (S) and V. Sreenivasa Prasad of Janata demanded to table the detailed report of the Sino-Indian talks.[33]

The granting of MFN status was welcomed by majority of the parliamentarians, though hardline opposition parties such as Janata, socialist and congress (S) often criticized it. It was also backed by communist parties and other opposition members. This move was also considered as one of the mile stones in India China relationship and helped to build confidence between the two Asian giants for future negotiation.

The Sumdorung Chu Crisis

While the normalization of relations with China and the series of border talks were in full swing, an unexpected border clash started up at the Sumdorung Chu area of Arunachal Pradesh. It is important to state that, Sumdorung Chu falls north to the McMahon line, which has been under Indian control after the unilateral withdrawal of Chinese troops after the 1962 war. China considered the area as theirs, as China did not recognize McMahon line, if they had the Sumdorung Chu area would clearly fall into the north of the line.

During 1884, India's intelligence bureau constructed a forward post in the Sumdorung Chu area to monitor Chinese activities. When the Indian troops left the post to collect their salaries and groceries, the Chinese army reoccupied the post with heavy weaponry and aerial support. India protested against the Chinese action and openly condemned it on July 15, 1986. China in reply stated that, Chinese troops were well inside its own territories and it was India that violated the line. When the Indian appeal failed to serve any purpose, India deployed sizable troops at the Sumdorung Chu and all along the McMahon line to stop further Chinese incursion and to avoid 1962 like territorial lose. However, the situation did not escalate further, and the situation was put on for discussion during the seventh round of talks. Finally, China pulled back its troops during the Rajiv Gandhi's China visit as a symbolic gesture.

This Chinese intrusion drove huge furor in the Indian parliament. Almost all sections of the house condemned the Chinese incursion and demanded for strong action against China. Raising a debate on recent Chinese intrusion in Sumdorong Chu valley, Janata leader V. S. Krishna Iyer condemned the Chinese aggression and stated that China had been a security threat to India. He asked the government to review its policy of appeasement against China and take tough stand against the recent Chinese invention in the Arunachal Pradesh.[34] Similarly, S. M. Guraddi of Janata Party moved a Calling Attention Motion on Chinese aggression in the Arunachal Pradesh. Raising the issue at the Lok Sabha he stated that, the recent goodwill gesture by the Chinese government was a farce to divert the Indian attention from its war preparation against China and India had to reconsider its romance with china. He also asked the government to mobilize adequate force to the Chinese border to avoid 1962 like situation.[35] Extending the debate, TDP leader M. Subba Reddy attacked the government for its failure to protect the frontiers and demanded for a strong action against china.[36] A.K. Patel (BJP) also criticized the government's soft policy towards china and its alleged attempts to downplay the incidents. Arguing to throw out the Chinese aggression, he stated that the government should send clear message to the Chinese leadership that India would not tolerate any foreign aggression.[37]

CPI and CPM however, took a different stand and argued for peaceful resolution of the issue through talks and negotiations. CPI leader Indrajit Gupta for instance, asked the government to utilize the well established channel of border talks to sort out the disputes.[38] Somnath Chatterjee of CPI-M asked the government to maintain maximum caution at the border while mobilizing the troops and requested to avoid any direct clash with Chinese force, as he believed it would not serve any purpose rather raising tension at frontier. He further asked the government to reach to the Chinese authority and resolve the issue.[39]

In reply, Minister for External Affairs P. Shiv Shankar condemned the Chinese aggression and stated that the government was looking at the matter at every angle. He revealed that, the soldiers of the frontiers were asked to remain alert and adequate measures had been taken to avoid any further Chinese aggression. However, he informed the house that India would be happy to resolve the issue through negotiation and the government of India had channelized the diplomatic talks in this regard. He further denied the argument of the oppositions of the repeat of 1962 situation and assured the parliament that the situation was under control.[40]

As assured by Indian foreign minister India promptly moved adequate troops to Sumdorung Chu valley and stationed further sizable army as backup force to nullify the Chinese aggression. This timely strategic movement helped to stop the Chinese army from further aggression. India also raised the issue at the seventh round of border talks and asked the Chinese to vacate the area. Though the Chinese forces were restricted from further aggression, it maintained its position till Rajiv Gandhi's China visit, when china finally pulled back its troops as the gesture of friendship.

Rajiv Gandhi's China Visit and the Setup of Joint Working Group

After the eight rounds of talks on border disputes which ended without any conclusion, it was clear that the bureaucrats alone could not resolve the issue and the political leaders had to reach to each. Secondly, the world politics also turned positive for better Sino-Indian relation, as the Soviet Union sought for the Sino-Indian friendship following Sino-Soviet rapprochement in 1988.[41] During his trip to India, Soviet president

Gorbachev emphasized on friendly relation between India and China and stated that "we are glad to see the signs of improved Indian-Chinese relations'.[42] In this background the young Prime Minister of India made his historic five day visit to China on December 19, 1988 along with External Affairs Minister, Narasimha Rao and several other high level Indian delegates. It was the first visit by an Indian Prime Minister to visit China after a gap of thirty years.

During his visit, Prime Minister Gandhi met Chinese president Yang Shangkum, Prime Minister Li Peng, CPC leader Deng Xiaoping and other Chinese leaders and asked for the everlasting friendship between China and India. External Affairs Minister Narasimha Rao also held talks with his Chinese counterpart, Qian Qichen regarding issues related to boundary disputes and other international matters. In the press conferences both the countries showed their desire to cooperate with each other to resolve the long standing issues, though there were differences of opinions. During Rajiv Gandhi's visit, several agreements were signed on civil aviation, science and technology, and cultural exchanges. Both the sides also agreed to setup a Joint working Group (JWG) at the level of Vice Ministers to negotiate on the border disputes. The joint communiqué declared that both the countries had determined to resolve the boundary dispute through peaceful negotiation based on mutual acceptance. The communiqué also stated that India and China would not leave the fate of the relationship to the boundary disputes and efforts would be made to extend the relationship into other possible areas. To summarize, Rajiv Gandhi's China visit, as most of the Indian and Chinese scholars described, was one of the mile stones in the Sino-Indian relationship and took the relationship into a new stage. [43]

Indian public opinion as well as the Indian parliament remained critical to Prime Minister Gandhi's China visit. Most of the non-communist oppositions, including Janata and BJP, as well as a section of the ruling Congress (I) members stood against the visit due to, what they believed a dare attempt to ignore the Chinese occupation. Janata Leader S.M. Guraddi in criticizing Prime Minister's state visit to China argued that, it was inappropriate to visit the land of aggressor, while thousands miles of Indian lands were under the Chinese occupation. He also asked the government to clarify its China policy and its strategy to regain the occupied Indian territories.[44] Similarly, K.P Unnikrishnan of Congress (S) also condemned Prime Minister's Rajiv Gandhi's China visit in parliament. Objecting to the visit he argued that none of the outstanding issues with China had been resolved so far, and China was not ready to withdraw its troops from Indian territories. He, however stated that it was not against friendship with China, but not at the cost of sovereignty and integrity of India.[45] Janata leader Sambhajirao Kakade also questioned the relevance of the visit of Indian delegations to China, especially at time when Chinese forces were reportedly at constant war with Indian soldiers in Arunachal Pradesh.[46] Another Janata leader H.M. Patel raised a question with reference to Chinese missiles during Prime Minister‘s talks with Chinese leaders. Objecting to the absence of direct indication to transfer of Chinese missile system to Pakistan in the Prime Ministers talk, he stated that China's policy of the peaceful coexistence and passing of deadly weapons to enemy states would not go together. [47]

Apart from the oppositions, some of the members of the ruling congress party also remained opposed to the prime minister's visit to China. Congress (I) leader Chandra Shekhar Tripathi for instance, objecting to Rajiv Gandhi's visit questioned the purpose of the visit. While raising question on Indo-China Agreement in Science and Technology on March 27, 1989 he stated that the agreement was just an eyewash tactics of China to divert Indian attention from the recent Chinese aggression in Arunachal Pradesh and would not serve any purpose for India.

Communist fronts however, backed the government's efforts and the Prime Minister's historic visit and hoped that, it would create a new chapter in indo-China friendship and would further open new doors for peaceful resolution of bilateral disputes. CPI leader Amal Datta following his party's stand initiated a debate under rule 377 regarding "initiating action to promote permanent friendship and lasting peace with the people and government of China". In his argument he stated that, the lasting peace with China was not only essential for the people of India, also necessary for the peace and prosperity of the whole region. He also argued that, both the nations should sit and settle down the outstanding disputes and should move ahead towards the path of mutual development. Welcoming the state visit of Prime Minister of India to China, he added the visit would facilitate the process of normalizing the relation with China and peaceful settlement of disputes.[48] Some of the Congress members also supported Prime Minister Gandhi's state visit to China. Apart from the differences in the political spectrum, Rajiv Gandhi's historic visit undoubtedly opened a new path for India China relationship which further improved during the successive leaders from both sides.

Visit of Prime Minister Li Peng's to India and Prime Minister Narasimha Rao to China

Following Rajiv Gandhi's invitation during his China trip, Chinese Prime Minister Li Peng visited India during December 11 to 16, 1991. This visit was one of the mile stones in the Sino-Indian relation, as it was the first visit by any Chinese Prime Minister in 31 years since Zhou Enlai's India visit of 1960.Li hold meeting with Indian President, Prime Minister and several other Indian leaders sought for greeter partnership between India and China. During his meeting with Indian Prime Minister Rao, both the leaders agreed to look beyond the border issues and to extend the Sino-Indian partnership to other spheres. On border disputes, both the sides agreed to resolve the issue based on "mutual understanding", until both the leaders decided to maintain peace and tranquility in the border. India and China also applauded the efforts of Joint Working Groups and asked to intensify their efforts for the early resolution of the border disputes. Replying to Chinese concern over anti-China activities by Tibetans, India assured that New Delhi always adhered to "one China policy" and considered Tibet as part of China and would not allow its land to be used for any anti-Chinese activities. During Li Peng's visit, India and China signed five different agreements on extension of consular service and trade related issues. Undoubtedly Prime Minister Li's visit to India was one of the landmark visits on the India-China relation. It break the ice and helped to normalize relation further.

In order to take the relationship to further heights, Prime Minister Narasimha Rao visited China during December 6 to 9, 1993. It is important to note that, Rao was the first Indian Prime Minister who chose to visit China prior to Soviet Union and United States. It shows India's appetency to improve relation with China. Narasimha Rao discussed with various senior leaders of China, including Chinese president Jiang Zemin, CCP General Secretary and foreign minister Li Peng and discussed on various bilateral and international issues. During his China visit, Prime Minister Rao signed four individual agreements including agreement on peace and tranquility on the border and cross border trade in Shipki La.[49] Under the agreement of Border issues, both parties agreed to resolve the issue through peaceful means and, "neither side should use force or threaten to use force against the other".[50] Both the countries also agreed to undertake Confidence Building Measures (CBM) along the borders and maintain minimum force at frontier lines to avoid any military escalation. Scholars, experts and media houses of the countries applauded the visit as an important border agreement and described the developments as the beginning of a new era of Sino-Indian friendship.

Unlike Rajiv Gandhi's China visit, Chinese Premier Li Peng's visit was highly applauded by Indian media, strategic analysts and above all by the Indian Parliament as whole. The first state visit by the Chinese Prime Minister after the 1962 border clash was welcomed by all political parties and was termed as historic. While the visit of Chinese Prime Minister was welcomed by most of the political parties, some of the opposition parties still stood critical to the Li Peng's visit and the growing Sino-Indian relationship. BJP leader Ram Kapse for instance raised a question seeking the details of the discussion between Foreign Secretary and the Prime Minister of China. In raising a question he stated that China is half hearted to resolve the border disputes, hence India should remain cautioned while dealing with China.[51] Similarly, Sanat Kumar Mandal of Revolutionary Socialist Party(RSP) also objected talks with Chinese Prime Minister and stated that it was fruitless to talk to the Chinese leadership as no result would be achieved through negations. He also asked the government to review its China policy and take strong action against Chinese aggression.[52] BJP leader Madan Lal Khurana while raising question on the Indian delegation meeting with Prime Minister of China stated that, his party was not against the talk with China but there should be friendship between an aggressor and a victim. At least the Chinese government had to vacate the occupied territories of India in order to normalize the relation between New Delhi and Beijing.[53]

Majority of the ruling Congress Party however stood supportive on India China growing friendship. While raising questions on Indo-China relations Congress (I) leader Subhash Chandra Nayak for instance, asked the government to go ahead with a friendly approach towards China and resolve the issues through dialogue and negation.[54] Similarly, Surendra Reddy of the same party supported the government's revised China policy. However, he raised some objection on the recently concluded Border Trade Agreement with China. According to him, the agreement was only serving Chinese interests and not helping Indian exports, hence need to be revised.[55] The communist party of India also backed the government's China policy and applauded Chinese Prime Minister's historic visit to India. To summarize we can state that, every section of Parliament except a few non-communist oppositions, remained positive towards Prime Minister Li Peng's historic visit and the government of India's approach to improve relation with China.

Similarly, Prime Minister Narasimha Rao's China visit to strengthen the century old relation and the signing of bilateral agreements was also commended by the members across the party line in parliament. K.P. Singhdeo of Congress (I) while raising questions on "the visit of Prime Minister to China" stated that this visit would help to improve the relationship further. He also appreciated the government's efforts to normalize relation with China and the agreements signed by Prime Minister Rao.[56] Another congress member Arvind Tulshiram Kamble also supported the ongoing effort to normalize relationship. Arguing for greater Indo-China cooperation he stated that, it was a win-win game for both the parties to extend their trade and economic cooperation would help to restructure the economic status of both the regions.[57] Raising a question on "Reduction of strength of armed forces from Indo-China border" the recently finalized agreement during Prime Minister Rao China visit, Vilas Baburao Muttemwar argued that it would help ease the tension between the two countries and would facilitate friendly relation between New Delhi and Beijing.[58]

Undoubtedly, the consecutive bilateral visit of Chinese and Indian Prime Minister to each other's country was a remarkable step in indo-China relationship. This helped to normalize and strengthen the roller coaster relationship between India and China. These bilateral visits were highly appreciated by all sections of people from both the sides. Indian parliament as a whole also backed the state visit of Chinese Prime Minister and the visit of Indian Prime Minister to China. But the non-communist oppositions, especially the right wing frontiers like PJP, Janata, and socialists remained critical to the changing Chinese approach and cautioned the government to study the Chinese attitude before making decision. But the efforts to extend cooperation were supported by Congress and Communist blocks as well as a large section of other parties.

The JWG Meetings and Settlement of the Sumdorong Chu Crisis

The Joint Working Group (JWG) on border disputes that were set up by the mutual agreement during Prime Minister Rajiv Gandhi's China visit, became an effective tool in the subsequent years to reduce tension at the border and promoting peace and tranquility at the border. The specialist group went through ten rounds of intensive negations during 1989 to 1997in New Delhi and Beijing alternatively. Just after a few months of formation, the first meeting of the JWG was convened at Beijing in between June 30 to July 4, 1989.Subsequent meetings of the JWG were conducted to resolve the boundary disputes and maintain peace at the frontiers. The meetings also offered the platform to understand each other's perceptions and arguments and worked as the mechanism to avoid the direct confrontation for both the militaries. As a result, in the eighth round of meeting in August 1995, both the countries agreed to withdraw their troops back from the Sumdorung Chu Valley to end the nine yearlong military standups. In order to avoid such kind of standups in future, both India and China decided to set up a meeting point for military officers at the Nathu La. More importantly, the 'pockets of disputes' were identified and it was decided to take utmost care to avoid any armed confrontation while patrolling. The subsequent meetings also helped to adopt the policy to boost the Confidence Building Measures (CBM) between both the armed forces and other normalization initiatives to deescalate the tensions.[59]

The Indian parliament remained cautious towards the Meeting of China-India Joint Working Group on the Boundary Question (ICJWGBQ), though a large section of the Parliament supported the process to normalize relation with China. Mainly, the BJP, Janata and socialists feared that this negotiation, like the previous attempts would not serve any purpose and would fail to find a way out formula on boundary disputes. Since the very beginning these parties posed a critical stand on the series of negotiation meeting of the Joint Working Group. Following the party line, Janata Dal (JD) leader Harish Pal raised objection to the function and the meeting of the joint working group. He stated that, the negotiation would not produce any result as China was not ready to accept the official documents produced by China. Hence he advised that, India should not believe on the eyewash tactics of China.[60] Looking at the unproductive result of the meeting after a few rounds of talks, another Janata Dal leader Rajnath S. Shastri asked the Indian government to take strong action to reacquire the occupied Indian territories from China and Pakistan.[61] Similarly, BJP leader Ram Naik while demanding for the tabulation of the meeting report of India-China Joint Working Group on Border Question, asked the government not to look only towards the joint working group as it failed to reach any solution, and should think other option for the reclaim of the lost territories.[62]

Majority of Congress and Communist fronts however, backed the negotiation meetings of India-China Joint Working Group on Border Question and the process of normalization relation between India and China. For instance, Congress leader Basava Rajeswari while seeking the outcomes of the Indo-China Joint Working Group appreciated the government for the formation of specialized body to resolve the boundary disputes.[63] Similarly, another congress member Syed Shahabuddin also asked the government to resolve the outstanding problems with China through peaceful negotiations.

He also argued to intensify the Negotiations with China on boundary question to reach early results.[64] V. Sreenivasa Prasad of the same party appreciated the government for its stand to extend good relation with China and its efforts to solve the boundary disputes through talks. However, he asked the government to maintain extra care while negotiating with china through India-China Joint Working Groups and see things going properly in the negotiation table.[65]

The decision to pull back troops from the frontier however, was objected by some of the congress members. Congress (I) leader Vilas Baburao Muttemwar for instance, raised concern on government's decision to reduce troops from the Indo-China border. While posing a question he wanted to know the strategy of the government to deal with situation after the reduction of troops.[66] However, CPI (M) leader Sudhir Kumar Giri, while raising questions on troops reduction from China border appreciated the government for such decision which further facilitated to build trust between India and China.[67] Congress leader Dr. Krupasindhu Bhoi, also backed the decision and stated that it would help to resolve the issue peacefully.[68] While showing his happiness after the resolve of Sumdorong Chu valley crisis, J. Chokka Rao (Congress – I) asked the government to proceed with caution while reducing troops along the china border.[69] Sultan Salahuddin Owaisi, leader of All India Majlis-E-Ittehadul Muslimeen (AIMIM) Party asked the government to open up new trade posts along the India china border and facilitate greater border trade.[70]

By looking at the debates we may conclude that, majority of the members supported the Meeting of China-India Joint Working Group on the Boundary Question and argued for the peaceful settlement of border disputes. Out of the debates, it can be summarized that, there is a growing demand for the normalization of Sino-Indian relation and permanent peace along the borders. Top of Form Bottom of Form.

President Jiang Zemin's India Visit and Agreement on CBM

To strengthen the bilateral ties further, Chinese President Jiang Zemin paid an official visit to India during November 28 to December 1, 1996. It was a South Asian tour of the Chinese President and India was the first destination in the Chinese preference. President Jiang's India visit was the first ever visit by any Chinese Head of the State in the history of nearly fifty years of diplomatic relations and further facilitated close relationship between India and China. During his four day visit, the Chinese President held cordial talks with his Indian counterpart, S.D. Sharma, Vice President,

K.R. Narayan, Prime Minister H. D. Devgauda and External Affairs Minister, I.K. Gujral and other Indian dignitaries and both the sides agreed to strengthen the century old relation further.[71] To extend the bilateral cooperation, India and China signed four important agreements on military and non-military sectors, including agreement on Confidence Building Measures (CBMs) in the military field along the India China frontiers. This agreement was highly important because, it not only ensured peace and tranquility in the border regions, also improved better understanding among the on ground forces to each other's positions through CBMs. For many defense analysts it was actually a "Partial no-war pact" that meant to deescalate and avoid direct conflict.[72] China also denied the allegation of passage of Chinese nuclear weapon technology or M-II missiles to Pakistan and clarified that it would not sale any of its advanced nuclear technologies to any of its neighbors.[73] On the Kashmir disputes, China ruled out any third party mediation and stated that India and Pakistan had to resolve the issue bilaterally. That means, as Perkovich believed, Kashmir for China is no longer an international problem, rather a bilateral dispute between India and Pakistan now.[74] Overall, President Jiang's visit to India was one of the important mile stones in the Sino-Indian relationship and in many ways strengthened the bilateral relationship. The agreements, especially the agreement on CBM actually nullified the future conflict and helped to understand each other's concerns and positions.

Chinese Reaction to George Fernandes's Number-one Threat Remarks and the Pokhran II Nuclear Detonation

After the 12th General Election of 1998, the Bharatiya Janata Party (BJP) emerged as the single largest party in Lok Sabha and formed a coalition government with the support of 14 political parties. Atal Bihari Vajpayee became the 12th Prime Minister of India in March19, 1998. BJP which had been criticizing the current defense and strategic policy of Government, promised in its election manifesto that, if voted for power it would bring major reforms in India's national security structures and transform India as a nuclear power state. Soon after voted to power, BJP led NDA government enacted a "National Agenda for Governance" by which they vowed to setup a National Security Council (NSC).[75] After the election George Fernandes, who had been called as the 'boss of Tibetan independence'[76] became the new Defense Minister of India. Less than six week of assuming power, Fernandes extended its attack on Chinese leadership and accused that Chinese patrol team had intruded into the Arunachal Pradesh by violating the McMahon line. Calling China as "the mother of (Pakistan's) Ghauri missile", further charged China for the proliferation of missile and nuclear technology to Pakistan. While giving interview to a private television, he termed China as the "potential threat number one" and stated that "reluctance to face the reality that China's intentions need to be questioned".[77] These remarks by the Indian Defense minister led a huge public outrage not only in China, but also in India. Chinese leadership reacted sharply to the statement and stated that "remarks by Fernandes have seriously sabotaged the favorable atmosphere for improving bilateral relations".[78] Even the Indian Political Leadership and media criticized Fernandes's remarks. As a result, Prime Minister Vajpayee stepped into and denied such allegations. The MEA spokesperson stated that, India was vowed to improve its relationship with China.[79] Looking at the positive reaction of the Indian leadership, China sent chief of the People's Liberation Army (PLA) to India for a goodwill visit. General Fu Quanyou along with five high level military delegation visited India during April 27 to 30, 1998.[80] Furnandes's careless statement led to a massive furor in Indian parliament. Members across the party line denounced the remarks of the Defense Minister. Opposition parties demanded resignation of the Indian defense minister and criticized his statement openly. However, Prime Minister Vajpayee stepped in and denounced the statement of Furnandes and clerified that the government did not subscribe these statements including the argument of growing Chinese threat on India.

When all was going well in the India China relationship despite the remarks of Defense Minister Furnandes and less than a fortnight after PLA chief's departure from India, India tested its second nuclear test at Pokhran, code named with 'Bhudha Smile Again'on13 May 1998. But, the news of the nuclear exploration had every reason to wipe-out the smile from the face of the Chinese leadership, especially, when Prime Minister Vajpayee (while writing to US president) cited Chinese threat as the reason behind India's nuclear explosion.[81] China condemned Indian nuclear test and asked the international community to come together to deprive India from further tests. They also asked India to sign the NPT and CTBT. India hit back China with equal attack stating:

"If China, with a large nuclear arsenal built with the experience of over 44 tests, felt compelled to test again in July 1996(when the CTBT was in the final stages) for its own security, then it should be possible to understand the rational of India conducting a limited number of tests after a 24-year-long period of voluntary restraint."[82] Chinese public opinion also turned against India's nuclear development programme and the Chinese daily claimed that about 89 percent of the Chinese people strongly condemned Indian nuclear test and about 80 percent sought UN sanction against India.[83] China, by taking the advantage as the chairman of the United Nations Security Council meeting in June 1998 asked both India and Pakistan to put down their nuclear programme and stay away from the further nuclear tests.[84]

Prime Minister Vajpayee presented his statement on India's nuclear test in the parliament on May 27, 1998. After expressing his gratitude to the scientists and engineers, he stated that "our leaders took the crucial decision to opt for self reliance and freedom of though and action. We reject the cold war paradigm and choose the more difficult path of non-alignment. Our leaders also realized that a nuclear weapon free world would enhance not only India's security but also the security of all nations. That is why disarmament was continued to be a major plank of our foreign policy."[85] He also highlighted that, the nuclear weapon was meant in the defense of the nation. Citing security concerns as the reason of the recent test he expressed that, ...in our neighborhood, nuclear weapons had increased and more sophisticated delivery systems inducted. In addition, India has also been the victim of externally aided and abetted terrorism, military and clandestine war. At the global level, we see no evidence on the part of the nuclear weapon states to take decisive and irreversible steps in moving towards a nuclear-weapons-free world. Instead, we have seen that the NPT has been extended indefinitely and unconditionally, perpetuating the existence of nuclear weapons in the hands of five countries.

Stating the purpose of the India's nuclear programme, Vajpayee further stated, "Our strength capability adds to our sense of responsibility. We do not intended to use these weapons for aggression or for mounting threats against any country, these are weapons of self-defense, to ensure that India is not subjected to nuclear threats or coercion. We do not intend to engage in an arms race".[86]

The government also laid the report of "Evolution of India's Nuclear Policy" in the parliament for debate. This was the first time in the history of Indian parliament that any such report on India's nuclear policy was laid on the table for debate.

Initiating the debate, Indrajit Gupta of CPI criticizing the government wanted to know the prime reason behind the nuclear detonation. He also asked more clarification how all of sudden China became an adversary to be deterred only with nuclear weapons and stated, "...

The Prime Minister has attributed this sudden testing to what he called the deteriorating security environment of India. And he makes it quite clear that he is referring to a threat from China and this appears to be in tune with the anti-Chinese fulminations of the defense minister made a few days earlier. In fact, the Defense Minister's aggressive remarks, I think were meant obviously to prepare the ground for official explanation which has been made available in the prime minister's letter to the U.S. President."[87]

The CPI leader also asked the government to clarify its stand on the "No first use policy" and the signing of the CTBT. Similarly, congress leader Natwar Singh raised similar questions and stated, "The reason given by the government in a letter to President Clinton ... (the government states) that there is a threat from China. Now, we are entitled to know from the honorable Prime Minister when did that threat begin?"[88] Another Congress leader Susil Kumar Shinde and Madhavrao Scindia, in another occasion asked the government to clarify India's no first use policy and wanted to know the stand of other countries on India's nuclear policy.[89]

Jagmohan Malhotra of BJP however, rejected the opposition's allegation and stated that national security was the prime duty of the government and all these tests were meant for India's defense purpose only. Regarding the Chinese threat remarks, he stated that, though they didn't have any severe problem with China at that moment, India should be prepared to face any challenge in future.[90]

In reply to the 'Chinese threat remarks' in the parliament, Defense Minister George Furnades cited the Annual Report of the Ministry of Defense to justify his controversial statement. In defending his statement, he stated

First I am mentioning three documents which the people should see and read. Do go through page no. 3 of the Annual Report for 1994-1995 of the Ministry of Defense, government of India..... Secondly, do go through page nos.2,3 and 4 of the Annual Report for 1995-1996 of the Ministry of Defense, Government of India. Thirdly, do go through the page nos. 2,3, and 6, of the Annual Report for 1996-1997 of the Ministry of Defense, Government of India. I would like to refer to three more reports – the fifth report of the standing committee on defense 1995, tenth Lok Sabha, talked in August 1995 and seventh and eighth report of March 1996. ... the standing committee of the Lok Sabha had warned the country about the challenges it will have to ace. It also recommended the steps to be taken to counter these challenges.[91]

The minister further stated that, India's nuclear test was for the defensive purpose only and it was not directed towards any country. CPI members, however, continued to criticize the minister and asked to take back his word. Congress leader Prof. P.J. Kurien also took exception of the Defense Minister's statement and demanded the resignation of the minister for his irresponsible statement. He also argued that these types of baseless statement would endanger the diplomatic relation of the county. [92] Shankar Pannu of the same party also demanded more clarification on Prime Minister Vajpayee's statement in denying the Chinese as the potential threat number one for India, the allegation, where as Defense Minister categorically declared so in an earlier interview.[93]

Tariq Anwar (INC) wanted know India's future relation with nuclear Pakistan and China and asked government's strategy to deal with these nuclear states with whom India had fought several wars.[94] Similarly, T. Subbarami Reddy of the same party objected to label China as the potential threat number one, especially when several CBMs agreements were under practice. He also requested the government to clarify its position regarding the signing of any CBM with China to avoid any future nuclear confrontation.[95]

However, a section of the Congress members criticized China over its reaction on India's nuclear explosion. They also condemned the big brother attitude of China, which, most of the members believed as the mother of Pakistan's nuclear programme. Sonaram Choudhary of congress for instance, raised concern over China's accusation against India over the nuclear test. He wanted to know the government's reaction towards China's objection and the future course of India-China relations.[96] Similarly, Samajwadi Party leader Jangbahadur Singh Patel also condemned Chinese allegation and stated that, China not only assisted Pakistan's nuclear programme, but also played active role in developing Pakistan's nuclear weapons. Hence its accusation against India was baseless.[97] V. Gopalsamy (popularly Known as Vaikeo) of Marumalarchi Dravida Munnetra Kazhagam (MDMK) in criticizing the Chinese allegation stated that, China had transferred the missile technology to Pakistan. Hence, India was rightful to conduct the nuclear test for its defense.[98] Braj Mohan Ram of BJP asked the government to negotiate with the Chinese leadership for a mutual agreement on non-use of nuclear weapons in future.[99] Therefore, it can be concluded that, Indian Parliament was often critical towards its own leadership rather defending its decision to go for nuclear explosion. The house also did not react much against Chinese condemnation. Even, the Congress and the Communist blocs attacked the Defense Minister's statement. However, a small section of the Parliament, supported the government for its efforts to revive India's national surety policy and the detonation of nuclear weapons for the defense of the country.

Chinese position during Krgil War

Since the Pokhran II nuclear explosion in May 1998, India and China had estranged relationship for a period of nine months until the reestablishment of official relationship in February 1999.Though India tried to down play the 'Chinese threat' perception, Chinese side continued to blame the Indian leadership for the irresponsible and illogical statement. On July 9, 1998 Chinese Ambassador Zhou Gang while giving interview to Indian media stated that, China was determined to "develop constructive partnership with India oriented towards the 21st Century".[100] In the sideline of Association of Southeast Asian Nations (ASEAN) regional forum meeting in July 1998, India's External Affair Minister, Jaswant Singh had a lengthy discussion with his Chinese counterpart Tang Jiaxuan and expressed that, India's nuclear explosion was meant for its own defense and denounced Chinese threat perception. Similarly, President K.R. Narayan expressed in his address to the parliament stated that, India desperately wanted to initiate dialogue with China to resolve the outstanding issues.[101] Following the continues desire from both the sides to improve the tainted relationship, India, on February 24, 1999 sent a strong official delegation to China led by the Joint Secretary (East Asia) of MEA to initiate the dialogue.[102] Looking at the positive response from the Chinese leadership, Indian External Affair Minister Jaswant Singh visited China during April 14 to 16, 1999. This historic visit brought the disturbed relationship into track. [103]

While the rapprochement process was on track, another crisis emerged in the Indian sub-continent. A war broke out between the two traditional rivalries, India and Pakistan in Kargil Sector of the state of Jammu and Kashmir (J&K).Pakistani army along with militants crossed the Line of Control (LoC) and intruded into Indian Territory and lunched massive attack on Indian army. The prime intension behind the attack was to block the National Highway Number one, the prime supply line between Dras and Kargil sector, cut off Leh from Srinagar, trap the Indian forces on the Siachin, raise the militants' banner of revolt in the valley, question the sanctity of the Line of Control and bring the Kashmir issue firmly back to the forefront of international agenda.[104] India lunched Operation Vijay to drive out Pakistani infiltration. After a three months ling limited conventional war, India successfully pushed back the infiltrates behind the LoC by July 26, 1999.

International public opinion was apparently harsh against the Pakistani infiltration and asked for its immediate withdrawal. The United States refused to extend its support to Pakistan and suggested to respect the LoC by pulling back its troops. China, the all-weather friend of Pakistan, also did not back her in the Kargil crisis, despite Pakistani Foreign Minister Sartaj Aziz's attempts to convince the Chinese leadership during his Chinese trip at the mid of the war. Looking to the job unfinished, Prime Minister Nawaz Sharif personally took flight to Beijing to convince the Chinese leadership. He met Chinese President Ziang Zemin and Premier Zhou Rongji and presented Pakistan stand in Kargil war. However, China seemed to remain unconvinced and persued the neutral path vis-à-vis Kargil Crisis. "Without slightest partiality to any side" Chinese leadership suggested Pakistan to resolve the issue peacefully.[105] For Swaran Singh, China's decision to maintain complete neutrality was the result of its changing role in post-soviet world order, but for India, it was apparently the fruit of the year long normalization process.[106]

Indian political leadership and the Indian parliament at a large were apparently appreciative towards the Chinese neutrality. Majority of the members of the parliament longed for greater cooperation and constructive engagement with Chinese leadership, though there was no formal session in debating Chinese neutrality in the Kargil war. Congress leader C. Naresh Kumar Puglia, while raising a question on Sino-Indian border issues, asked the government to explore the opportunity produced out of the Chinese neutrality to settle down the border disputes between India and China.[107] Similarly, P. Shiv Shankar of the same party asked the government to resolve the boundary disputes with China peacefully and establish lasting peace between India and China.[108] Another congress leader Vilas Baburao Muttemwar asked the government to sign a tripartite strategic treaty with Russia and China to enhance security of India.[109]

Though Chinese leadership maintained neutrality during the Kargil war, the attitude of the Chinese civil society and media was apparently anti-Indian. A section of parliament questioned the Chinese intension and termed it Chinese dualism. T. Subba Rami Reddy for instance criticized the Chinese attitude and stated that, China's neutrality was an act of eyewash, while it continued to assist the Pakistani army by selling huge quantity of military weapons to Pakistan.[110] Similarly, AIADMK leader T.M. Selvaganpathi while seeking government's attention towards Chinese military activities in borders of Arunachal Pradesh suggested the government to set up the security arrangement in the border regions and to observe Chinese activities in these regions.[111]

In another occasion, Congress leader Mrs. Sonia Gandhi presented a no-confidence motion against the government citing the government's failure to prevent the Kargil war. While presenting the motion in the Lok Sabha she stated:

> *The Prime Minister went to Lahore. His hosts were preparing for Kargil while he was there. The Prime Minister went to Beijing. While he was there, there was an intrusion of Chinese troops into Indian territory in Arunachal Pradesh. We have extended broad support to the Government on its policy in regard to both China and Pakistan. But, Sir, I must say - I am forced, compelled to say - that this Government's policy has lacked clarity and continuity. The stance of the Government has swung from one extreme to another.*[112]

Similarly, K. Natwar Singh (INC) criticized government's diplomatic failure in handling the Chinese attitude towards Kashmir issue. While raising concern regarding the reported Chinese involvement in any negotiation between India and Pakistan on Kashmir stated that,

> *A very profound and disturbing event has taken place yesterday. The President of the United States of America, Mr. Bill Clinton, while addressing the National Geographic Society said, ...because of its history with both the countries, China must be a part of any ultimate resolution of this matter which is Kashmir'. He said, 'if any discussion takes place between India and Pakistan, China must sit on the table'.*[113]

The Karmapa's Flight to India and the Chinese Reaction

As Chinese neutrality during the Kargil Crisis produced a promising ground for Sino-Indian relationship, another crisis emerged between New Delhi and Beijing, when Ugyen Trinley Dorje, the 17th Karmapa reached India after the dramatic escape from Tibet on January 5, 2000. It was an embarrassing situation for China, who recognized the boy Ugyen as the 17th Karmapa and his escape from Lhasa showed the lack of religious freedom for Tibetan people. To avoid the controversy, Beijing clarified that, the Karma left a letter stating that he was going to collect religious artifacts and he had not intended to "betray the state, the nation, the monastery or the leadership."[114] Karmapa's reaching at McLeodganj was quite a surprise for India and for the Tibetan government-in-exile as well.[115] India was put in difficult situation when the Karmapa Lama approached India for political asylum. Indian leadership was in a dilemma on the proposal of political asylum, as the situation might escalate to any level alike that of the last episode of India's asylum to Dalai Lama back in 1959.

On the other hand, India was also in worry of another 1962 like situation in Sikkim for various reasons. First China might attack Sikkim to seize the "musical instruments of Buddhist mass" and the "Black Hat" that were preserved at the Rumtek Monestry of Sikkim, as China had put the Tibetan clergy under strict Chinese authority after the Karmapa incident. Secondly, as China had refused to recognize Sikkim as the part of India and termed the voluntary annexation as the Indian policy of expansionism, it might attack Sikkim to teach another lesson to India. Third, China was reportedly unhappy on India's nuclear test and the Kargil crisis, it would design a draconian strategy to counter down Indian weight in the region. In addition, the spoke person of the Chinese foreign ministry indicated that, the grant of political asylum to the 17th Karmapa would go against the spirit of the Panchsheel, which in its core stated that, no country should interfere in other's internal matters.[116]

The issue did not escalate further, as both China and India decided to play down the situation and the several high level exchanges put the issue in to the back seat. India decided to grant political asylum to the 17th Karmapa with extreme caution. India assured Beijing that, it would not allow any anti-Chinese activity by any sect in its territory and would not allow the spiritual leader to be used by any foreign power to sabotage China. On the other hand, China did not raise the issue further and hoped that India would keep its promise.[117]

Due to the risk involvement, the issue related to the grant of political asylum to 17th Karmapa was given a low profile in the Indian Parliament. However, an overwhelming sympathy and support in favor of extending refugee status was quite visible in the parliament. Looking at the sensitivity of the issue, no full-fledged debate was under taken under the matters of unguent and Matters Under Rule-377. However, some members raised the questions related to government of India's stand on Karmapa issue. Amar Roy Pradhan of All India Forward Block (AIFB) instance, wanted to know the government's stand in giving political asylum to the Boy Karmapa, while raising questions on foreign affairs.[118] Similarly, Congress leader Smt. Shyama Singh also asked the government to clarify its position in extending refugee status to spiritual leader.[119] Replying to both the questions, Minister of External Affair Jaswant Singh stated in lip locked manner, that the government had received no such formal request from the Karmapa, and if received the government would take appropriate decision. He did not reveal much about the issue or the government's stand. Ramesh Chennithala of Congress Party appealed to the government to allow the spiritual leader to stay in India, while trying to attract government's attention towards the statement of the Chief Secretary of Sikkim, where he declared that the boy Karmapa was born in India.[120] Another congress leader Amar Roy Pradhan while posing a question wanted to know the state of security cover to the 17th Karmapa. Like earlier statement, External Affair Jaswant Singh played it safely and stated that, no such request came to the notice of government. However, the government of India had taken necessary steps to ensure the safety of the spiritual leader.[121] On the other hand, Raghunandan Lal Bhatia and Ramesh Chennithala (both from Congress) seeking government's clarification asked whether the government had discussed the Karmapa issue with China and wanted know the detail of the discussion, if it happened. Replying to the questions, External Affair Jaswant Singh stated that, Chinese government had discussed the issue with India and wanted to know the circumstance and root of the escape of the Karmapa. They also, he added, were against the granting of the political asylum to the spiritual leader.[122]

The flight of the 17th Karmapa and its approach to the Indian government for political asylum put India in a difficult situation, especially it had the experience of the hard consequences following extending such status to the 14th Dalai Lama back in 1959. The government of India, this time tried to give low profile to the incident both in public sphere as well as inside the Indian parliament. Hence, comparatively less debates and discussion were held in the floor of parliament on the Karmapa issue. In this occasion, the government tried to play it safe and gave careful answer to the questions to avoid in necessary controversy. Surprisingly, there was complete absence of any anti-Chinese statement and provocative statement on Karmapa issue in the Indian political sphere, which was quite common during the Dalai Lama's flight during 1959.

Conclusion

The uneasy relation between India and China started improving at the end of Sikkim Crisis. Apart for the verbal condemnation, there was no physical involvement of China in the Sikkim Crisis which was a positive development the India-China leadership. Secondly, both the nations behaved maturely to the emerging global order and were desperate to improve their troubled relationship. Looking at the growing interests from both the sides, China sent its Vice-Minister Wang Bingnan along with the Chinese Table Tennis team for a goodwill visit to India. Apart from this, Chinese leadership on several occasions indicated to improve relation with India. On the other hand, India also decided to establish the ambassadorial level relationship and sent K.R. Narayan as the next Ambassador to China. Subsequently, China sent Chen Zhayuan as the Chinese Ambassador to New Delhi. With the reestablishment of the Ambassador level relationship, the period of estrangement came to an end and Sino-Indian relationship entered into the golden era of reengagement where both the nations reached one another and discussed various issues on board. In August 1984, India and China offered each other the Most Favor Nations (MNF) status and intensified their trade relationship, which later became the important pillar of India-China relationship. Prime Minister Rajiv Gandhi paid his historic visit to China on December 1988. Similarly, Chinese Prime Minister Li Peng visited India in December 1991 and Narshimha Rao visited China in December 1993. Several high-level visits and diplomatic exchanges occurred between 1976 and 1999, which further stringed the age old relationship. The process of greater engagement led to the resolution of the Sumdorong Chu Crisis.

The Sino-India relationship got a major setback after the controversial 'potential threat number one' remarks of Indian Defense Minister George Fernandes and the Pokhran II nuclear test. China Reacted sharply in both the occasions. However, China never threatened to freeze the diplomatic relations with India, which was in practice earlier. India reached out to the Chinese leadership and discussed the issues for normalcy. Though Beijing was not fully convinced with the Indian clarifications, still decide to engage with New Delhi. During the Kargil war, China maintained complete neutrality, which was the unconventional development in Sino-Pak-India triangular relationship. It was again one of the significant factors in normalizing relationship between India and China. Indian public opinion, media and Parliament highly obliged to the Chinese neutrality. When India and China narrowly avoided the Kargil crisis, another disturbing matter erupted in Tibet. The spiritual leader, 17th Karmapa escaped from Tibet and sought for political asylum in India. China asked India to stay away from interfering into the internal matters of China. India reached out to Beijing and discussed the issue with Chinese leadership. India also did not let the issue to escalate and played down the issue within and outside the parliament. As a result, the issue was resolved within the diplomatic fronts without damaging the relationship further.

The Indian parliament as a whole was apparently in favor of pro-talks and constructive relation with China during the period of reengagement. There was not much objection in the parliament from the opposition parties towards the government's decision to reestablish ambassadorial level diplomatic relation. All sections of the house apparently supported this development, though there was some objection in the parliament from Jan Sangh and Socialist party. There was a visible consensus among all the sections of the Parliament towards improvement of relationship with China and the government's efforts to normalize relationship with China were supported by majority of parties. Hence, the high level visit from both the sides was welcomed by majority of the members of the Parliament. However, there used to be pressure over the government for the settlement of outstanding disputes. The process of normalization of relationship got another set beck when, Deference Minister George Furnades termed China as the potential threat number one and the government of India conducted nuclear test citing Chinese threat as the prime reason. In 12th General Election of 1998, BJP led NDA government came into power through the national security reform manifesto and George Furnades became the Defense Minister of India. George Furnades, one of the front line leaders who openly criticized by Chinese leadership for Tibetan human right violation on many occasions, labeled China as the threat number one in a media interview. It sparked another debate in the Indian parliament, despite Vajpayee's rejection to this irresponsible remark. Furnades's statement was condemned by various political leaderships and the opposition parties such as Congress, CPI and CPI-M demanded his resignation for this statement. Government of India soon came into action in rejecting the statement and sought friendly relation with China. Looking at the large scale opposition to Fernandez's statement and Vajpayee's commitment to improve the bilateral relationship, China sent the PLA chief for a bilateral visit to India. But the goodwill did not last for a long time. India tested the nuclear weapons on May 13, 1998. In his letters to US President, Prime Minister Vajpayee tried to justify India's nuclear programme by citing the increasing Chinese threat for the recent test. China reacted strongly to this statement and all those efforts to improve the relationship had gone in vain. In the Parliament, the opposition parties, especially CPI, CPI-M and Congress party criticized the nuclear test and government's China policy. They also criticized the government for its no first use policy and its decision for the partial acceptance of the CTBT and NPT. The relation between India and China remained in freeze for nine months, since the reestablishment of official dialogue in February 1999. While the official dialogue was in process to normalize relationship, the war between India and Pakistan broke out in the Kargil region of the state of Jammu and Kashmir. International community condemned Pakistan's draconian strategy for violating the line of Control. China remained neutral in this war, though the Chinese civil society and media apparently supported Pakistan. Indian Parliament appreciated the Chinese neutrality and there was wide feeling among the members to resolve the outstanding border issues peacefully with China. While the relationship between India and China was in the process of improvement, another crisis emerged in Tibet.

The 17th Karmapa fled from the Tibet and reached India on January 5, 2000. He approached India for political asylum, which put India in difficult situation. India could not have another confrontation with China, which seemed like looking at the past episode of Dalai Lama incident. But, India kept the issue low profiled and reached Chinese authority for discussion. The timely discussion to resolve the differences did not let the issue escalate. In the parliament the matter was also given a low profile and was ignored by most of the Parliamentarians, including the communists block. However, some questions were raised for the safety and security of the spiritual leader and the government of India's decision towards the political asylum issue. The government gave limited information in the Parliament in lip locked manner, with the intension to play down the situation.

Therefore, the period between 1976 and 1999 was one of the important episodes of India China relationship. During this period both the nations reestablished their diplomatic relationship and took enormous steps to normalize the relationship. This period also witnessed the major difficult times of the India China relation and major incidents such as the India's nuclear tests, Kargil war the issue of Karmapa crisis. Except for some occasions, the attitude of the Parliament was constructive, supportive and it supplemented to government's normalization efforts. However, during time of nuclear test it criticized the government. To conclude, it can be stated that, the Parliament was most favorable towards India's China policy during this period.

Notes

1. As stated in Shri Ram Sharma (300) 52.
2. Deepak (2005) 298-99.
3. Lok Sabha Debates, Vol.9, 1967, Cols. 9326-28.
4. *Ibid.*, Col. 9607.
5. Lok Sabha Debates, Vol. 3, 1977.
6. *Ibid.*, Cols. 252-54.
7. *Ibid.*, Col. 241.
8. *Ibid.*, Col. 241.
9. *Ibid.*, Cols. 314-15.
10. The Indian Express (New Delhi), August 17, 1977.
11. Lok Sabha Debates, Vol. 3, 1977, Col. 344.
12. The Hindustan Times, February 3, 1978.
13. As quoted in Deepak (2005) 301.
14. *Ibid.*
15. Satya Bhusan Jain, India's Foreign Policy and Non-alignment (New Delhi: Anamika Publishers, 2000) 229.

16. George Perkovich, India's Nuclear Bomb: The Impact on Global Proliferation (Berkeley: University of California Press, 1999).
17. Beijing Review, July 13, 1891, 7.
18. Lal (2008) 24; also see, Pobzeb Vang, Five Principles of Chinese Foreign Policies (Bloomington: Author House, 2008) 174.
19. *Lok Sabha Debates*, Vol. 12, (19-2-81) cols. 309-10.
20. *Ibid.* Vol. 17 (7.5.81) Cols. 27-30.
21. Lok Sabha Debates, Vol. 19, (3.9.81)Col. 88.
22. Lok Sabha Debates, Vol. 29 ,(15.7.82) Col. 42.
23. Lok Sabha Debates, Vol. 34, (24.2.83) Col. 64.
24. Lok Sabha Debates, Vol. 34, (24.2.83)Col. 84.
25. Lok Sabha Debates, Vol. 36, (24.3.83) Cols. 283-284.
26. Lok Sabha Debates, Vol. 40, (18.8.83) Cols. 260-61.
27. Lok Sabha Debates, Vol. 42, (17.11.83) Cols. 12-18.
28. Lok Sabha Debates, Vol. 45, (8.3.84) 131-32.
29. Tan Chung (1998) 524-25; also see, Bibek Debroy and Amitendu Palit, " China and India: Growth Outcomes and Economic Change", in A Resurgent China: South Asian Perspectives, edited by S. D. Muni, Tan Tai Yong (New Delhi: Routledge, 2011)137-38.
30. Lok Sabha Debates, Vol. 44, (2.3.84) Col. 182.
31. Lok Sabha Debates, Vol. 49, (27.7.84) Col. 276.
32. *Ibid.*, Vol. 10 (20.11.85) Cols. 33-34.
33. *Ibid.*, Vol. 12 (18.12.85) Col. 127 and Vol. 33,(2.12.87) Cols. 200.01.
34. Lok Sabha Debates Vol. 19, (8.8.1986) Cols. 278-81.
35. *Ibid.*, Vol. 19, (1.8.1986) Cols. 283-85.
36. *Ibid.*, Cols. 285-87.
37. *Ibid.* Cols. 292-94.
38. Lok Sabha Debates Vol. 19, (8.8.1986), Cols. 294-95.
39. Lok Sabha Debates Vol. 19, (8.8.1986) Cols. 296-98.
40. Lok Sabha Debates Vol. 19, (8.8.1986) Cols. 299-302.
41. Sali (1998) 113.
42. As quoted in Keshav Mishra, Rapprochement Across the Himalayas: Emerging India-China Relations Post Cold War Period (1947-2003) (New Delhi: Gyan Publishing House, 2004) 144.
43. Deepak (2005) 327-33; also see, C.V. Ranganathan, ''Memories of an Indian Ambassador: 1987-1991", in Across the Himalayan Gap: An Indian Quest for Understanding China, edited by Tan Chung (New Delhi: Gyan Publishing House, 1998) 443-45; and, Chung Tan, Rise of the Asian Giants: The Dragon-Elephant Tango (New Delhi: Anthem Press, 2009) 232.
44. Lok Sabha Debates, Vol. 35, (2.3.1988) Cols. 245-46.
45. *Ibid.*, Vol. 45, (February 23,1989) 179-86.
46. *Ibid.*, Vol. 40, (August 10, 1988) cols. 55-57.

4. *Ibid.*, Vol. 48,Question No. *419 (March 30, 1989)273-34.
48. *Ibid.*, Vol. 44, (December 12, 1988) 411-12.
49. A deal copy of the agreements can be seen at, Nimmi Kurian, Emerging China and India's Policy Options (New Delhi: Lancer Publishers, 2001) 163-64.
50. As quoted in Deepak (2005) 343.
51. Lok Sabha Question No. 2259 (Unstarred) raised on August 8, 1991. Collected from official website of Lok Sabha (here after the researcher has switched over to the online debate portal of Lok Sabha from manual document search and all the parliamentary debates and question that will be discussed here after, has collected from Official website of Lok Sabha).
52. See Lok Sabha Question No. 4694 Dated December 19, 1991.
53. See Lok Sabha Question No. 3325 Dated July 29,1992.
54. See Lok Sabha Question No. 247 Dated November 25, 1992.
55. See Lok Sabha Question No. *63, Dated February 26, 1993.
56. See Lok Sabha Question No. *49 Dated December 06, 1993.
57. See Lok Sabha Question No. *343, Dated August 20, 1993.
58. Lok Sabha Question No. 1730 Dated December 13, 1993.
59. Deepak (2005) 349-350.
60. See Lok Sabha Question No. *110 Dated 03/01/1991.
61. See Lok Sabha Question No. 1156 Dated 01/08/1994.
62. See Lok Sabha Question No. 2955 Dated 24/04/1995.
63. See Lok Sabha Question No. 1527 Dated 05/03/1992.
64. See Lok Sabha Question No. 6654 Dated 26/04/1993.
65. Lok Sabha Question No. 161 Dated 25/07/1994.
66. Lok Sabha Question No. 1730 Dated 13/12/1993.
67. Lok Sabha Question No. 1794 Dated 07/03/1994.
68. See Lok Sabha Question No.1827 Dated 14/08/1995.
69. Lok Sabha Question No. 6703 Dated 22/05/1995.
70. Lok Sabha Question No. 4786 Dated 08/05/1995.
71. Deepak (2005) 151-53.
72. Sali (1998) 129.
73. George Perkovich, India's Nuclear Bomb: The Impact on Global Proliferation (Berkeley: University of California Press, 1999) 387.
74. *Ibid.*
75. See the Election Manifesto of BJP 1998.
76. Deepak (2005) 357.
77. "George in the China shop: China is the potential threat No. 1, says George Fernandes", India Today, May 18, 1998, http://indiatoday.intoday.in/story/china-is-the-potential-threat-no.-1-says-george-fernandes/ 1/264241.html ; also see, Shalendra D. Sharma, China and India in the Age of Globalization (New York: Cambridge University Press, 2009) 177.
78. *Ibid.*

79. India Today, May 18, 1998.
80. Waheguru Pal Singh Sidhu and Jing Dong Yuan (2003) 30.
81. Ajai K. Rai, India's Nuclear Diplomacy After Pokhran II (New Delhi: Pearson Education India, 2009) 112.
82. As quoted in Rai (2009) 213.
83. Deepak (2005) 371-72.
84. Rai (2009) 213.
85. Lok Sabha Debates, May 27, 1998, Cols. 278-87.
86. Lok Sabha Debates (Discussion Under Rule 193), May 27, 1998, Cols. 278-87.
87. Lok Sabha debates (Discussion under Rule 193), May 27, 1998, cols.291-340.
88. Lok Sabha debates (Discussion under Rule 193), May 27, 1998, Cols. 291-340.
89. Lok Sabha Debates, Question No. 3210, Dated July 07, 1998 and Question No. 3280, Dated March 17, 1999.
90. Lok Sabha debates (Discussion under Rule 193), May 27, 1998, Cols. 291-340.
91. Lok Sabha debates (Discussion under Rule 193), May 27, 1998, Cols. 291-340.
92. Lok Sabha Debates, Question No. : 367, Dated May 28, 1998.
93. Lok Sabha Debates, Question No. 3508, Dated April 15, 1999.
94. Lok Sabha Debates, Question No. 3103, Dated July 07, 1998.
95. Lok Sabha Debates, Question No. 1367, Dated Mar 4, 1999.
96. Lok Sabha Debates, Question No. 4314, Dated July 16, 1998.
97. Lok Sabha Debates, Question No. 3209, Dated July 7, 1998.
98. Lok Sabha Debates, Question No. 3182 Dated July 7, 1998.
99. Lok Sabha Debates, Question No. 508, Dated Dec. 01, 1999.
100. As quoted in Deepak (2005) 382.
101. Deepak (2005) 383.
102. Swaran Singh, "India and China: Confidence Building Through Crisis" in Living with China: Regional States and China through Crises and Turning Points, edited by Shiping Tang, Mingjiang Li, Amitav Acharya (New York: Palgrave Macmillan, 2009) 74-75.
103. *Ibid.*
104. Navnita Chadha Behera, Demystifying Kashmir (Delhi: Pearson Education, 2007)84.
105. Deepak (2005) 386-87.
106. For detail see, Swaran Singh, "The Kargil Conflict: Why and how of China's Neutrality?", Strategic Analysis, 23:7 (1999)1083-1094.
107. Lok Sabha, Question No. 302, Dated 24/02/1999.
108. Lok Sabha, Question No. 5228, Dated 23/07/1998.
109. Lok Sabha, Question No. 562, Dated 01/12/1999.
110. Lok Sabha Debates, Question No. 3481, Dated 18/03/1999.
111. Lok Sabha, Question No. 604, Dated 02/12/1999.
112. No Confidence Motion, Lok Sabha Debates, August 19, 2003.

113. Lok Sabha Debates, June 12, 1998.
114. "Tibetan Lama flees to India", BBC, January 7, 2000.
115. "Tibetan Lama Meets Spiritual Leader", BBC, January 8, 2000; also see, Karmapa's Arrival in Dharamsala Embroils India in Bitter Feuding of Tibetan Clergy", India Today, January 24, 2000.
116. As stated in Mahendra Gaur, Foreign Policy Annual, 2001: Events And Documents (New Delhi: Gyan Publishing House, 2005) 33.
117. Deepak (2005) 394-95.
118. Lok Sabha Debates, Question No. 2013, Dated March 8, 2000.
119. Lok Sabha Debates, Question No. 7943, Dated May 17, 2000.
120. Lok Sabha Debates, Question No. 1050, Dated March 1, 2000.
121. Lok Sabha Debates, Question No. 1039, dated March 1, 2000.
122. Lok Sabha Debates, Question No. 1011, dated March 1, 2000 and Question No. 6843, May 10, 2000.

Chapter – 8

Parliament and the Making of India's China Policy during the Era of Cooperation and Competition 2000 to 2010

With the beginning of the 21st century the India-China relationship has entered into a new phase of cooperation and competition. After a short episode of disturbance following the Pokhran-II Nuclear explosion, the Kargil war and the Karmapa incident, the roller coaster relationship between India and China started improving after the visit of Indian President K.R. Narayanan to China. India's timely negotiation regarding these issues did not let the thing go wrong. China also realized the importance of friendship with India in order to attain its global stature and maintained constructive dialogue with Indian leadership to resolve the outstanding issues. In addition to this, the growing interdependency and trade relation also played significant role to promote Sino-Indian cooperation. As result, a number of agreements have been signed between the two countries to improve the state of relationship, trade and commerce. New Delhi and Beijing also decided to extend their area of cooperation in other non-explored areas including energy section. However, this honeymoon last apparently for a short period. Due to the rapid global transformation and emergence of new economic world order, both the countries found themselves just oppose to each other in many areas and knowingly or unknowingly, they indulged into the zone of competition soon. In this background the present chapter discusses the course of India-China relation in the twenty-first century and the outstanding issues of this defining relationship. Divided into several subsections, this chapter also analyzes the attitude of Indian parliament towards as well as the attitude of various political parties towards the changing Sino-Indian engagement in detail.

Opening of a New Chapter: President K.R. Narayanan's China Visit

The rise of Asian Economy and the growing attention towards economic reform India and China increased the level of dependency and forced the two Asian giants to adopt a normal relation. China and India opened up their economy in 1978 and 1991 respectively and signed the Most Favoured Nation (MFN) Agreement in 1984. The bilateral trade between India and China, which was as low as US$ 264 million in 1991 increased drastically and touched the US$ 2.92 billion mark in 2000.[1] As the economic relation was growing high, both Beijing and New Delhi showed their interest to move ahead from the recent problems of nuclear turmoil and apparently agreed to improve their uneasy relationship. It is important to mention that, this year was the 50th anniversary of the establishment of the diplomatic relations between India and China. To celebrate that, both the governments organized various ceremonial programmes jointly on April 1, 2000 and wished each other in this occasion. At this juncture, Indian president, K.R. Narayanan paid a week long official visit to China on May 28, 2000. The state visit of the Indian president attracted great importance among the political spectrums and termed it "as a big event". The members of the central committee of the CCP and Minister for International Department, Dai Bingguo called President Narayanan as the "a friend of China".[2] During his week-long visit, president Narayanan held a series of meetings with Chinese leadership including President Jiang Zemin and Premier Zhu Rongji. During the visit, China offered the four point formula for improvement of bilateral relation and establishment of friendly relation between India and China. These are:

- To facilitate and intensify the bilateral exchanges for greater mutual understanding,
- To expand the economic and trade cooperation,
- To strengthen the bilateral cooperation and cooperation on international affairs.
- To strive hard for the establishment of a new international political and economic order.
- To look to the future, and seek commonalities while reserving one's differences and reach an appropriate solution to the problems left over by history.[3]

President Narayanan's historic visit and the Chinese attitude towards this visit was one of the highest points of India- China relations. This visit helped to minimize the gap that was created after the Pokhran–II nuclear test and the subsequent Karmapa crisis. President Narayanan's visit also offered a platform where the two nations could sit together and discuss to resolve the outstanding issues.

President K.R. Narayanan's visit opened up a new chapter in India China relation and helped to resume several high level bilateral exchanges. As a result, Chinese Foreign Minister, Tang Jiaxuan and Chairman of the Standing Committee of the National People's Congress (NPC) Li Peng visited India on July 21, 2000 and on January 9, 2001 respectively. These two high profile visits further brought the two countries closer and supplemented for India-China friendship.[4] During the visit of the Foreign Minister Tang Jiaxuan, India and China signed the agreement to explore the ways for the demarcation and resolution of the LAC. Similarly, Chairman Li mentioned categorically that, India and China did "not pose any threat to each other" during his official visit.[5]

The overall attitude of the Indian parliament was quite positive towards the state visit of President K.R. Narayanan. Most of the political parties supported the historic visit, including the opposition parties and raised no concern in the parliament. As a result, there were only few questions raised in the floor of parliament on the visit of Indian president to China. Congress leader Sushil Kumar Shinde and Shri Madhavrao Scindia, for instance, raised a question in the Lok Sabha on the recent visit of President Narayanan and wanted to know whether India sought the support of China for India's permanent membership in United Nations. Answering to the question, External Affairs Minister Jaswant Singh stated that, the Indian president discussed the expansion of UN Security Council and the Chinese authority also expressed similar view during their discussion. He also stated to the parliament that, China was in favor of the expansion of the UNSC and ready to discuss the matter with India at the appropriate time.[6]

Chinese Reaction to the Indian Parliament Attack and the Indo-Pak Military Standups

Within three months of the horrific September 11 terror attack in the United States, five terrorist with heavy weaponry entered into the parliament compound and started indiscriminate firing. Though the loss of lives and properties in any way could not be compared to the September 11 attack, its impact was much larger, as it was an attack on the parliament of a country. The investigation revealed the involvement of Pakistan based terrorist organizations Jaish-e-Mohammed (JeM) and Lashkar-e-Taiba (LeT).[7] Indian Government demanded strong action against these organizations and the dismantlement of their training camp operating in the Pakistan soil. India also broke all links with Pakistan including the bus, train and air services to Pakistan. The tension between the two countries emerged gradually, and both India and Pakistan mobilized their troops into their border. The world community condemned the terrorist attack and asked Pakistan to take action against the accused organization. The world leaders also requested the two nuclear states to maintain self-restraint.[8]

The Parliament attack and the India–Pakistan military standup put China in difficult situation. For India it was the time to measure the Chinese attitude vis-à-vis the growing Sino-Indian cooperation. However, China condemned the terrorist attack on Indian Parliament and perhaps, for the first time acknowledged that it was also a victim of terrorism in Xinjiang.[9] Like the Kargil crisis, this time also China maintained equal distance from the crisis and asked both the countries to uphold calm in the border. Answering to a question during his official visit to India, Chairman Li Peng stated that, like India, China views international terrorism a big threat to its national security and offer China's cooperation to tackle the menace of international terrorism.[10] This was a new development in India-China relations, as China was a little hesitant to support India in its war on terrorism.

Similarly, Chinese Premier Zhu Rongli during his visit to New Delhi also condemned the parliament attack and assured China's full cooperation to combat terrorism. Even, both the countries agreed to establish an anti-terrorist dialogue mechanism to reduce the menace of terrorism in the region.[11] However, the state run China Institute of contemporary International Relations, the terror attack on Indian parliament was inside job and was carried out by the Indian outfits. Similarly, state run Institute of Strategic Studies warned that, if the war broke out China would support Pakistan.[12] In addition, China was the only country that opposed to the blacklisting of the Pakistan linked terrorist originations.[13].

The public opinion in India and the attitude of Indian parliament was positive towards the Chinese solidarity towards the terror attack on Indian parliament. Sushil Kumar Shinde and Shri Madhavrao Scindia of Indian National Congress raised a question in Lok Sabha regarding India China counter terror cooperation. In answering the question, External Affairs Minister Jaswant Singh stated that, India briefed about the growing terrorist incidence in the region to Chinese president Jiang during the state visit of President Narayanan to China and the Chinese president assured all possible assistant to root out terrorism in this region.[14]

On another occasion on May 8, 2002, Sushil Kumar Shinde raised another question and wanted to know about the formation and achievements of the Indo-Chinese Anti-terrorism Consultation Group (ATCG). In reply, External Affairs Minister Jaswant Singh stated that the ATCG had been setup to discuss the issues of terrorism between India and China and it has conducted its first meeting in New Delhi on April 23, 2002. He also informed the house that:

> *"Both sides shared their national experiences on dealing with terrorism, exchanged views on the international counter terrorism situation including developments in the region, cooperation at the United Nations and possibilities of bilateral cooperation. Both sides agreed that the first meeting of the dialogue mechanism was useful in enhancing mutual understanding. The next round is expected to be held in Beijing early next year."*[15]

The Indian parliament and the attitude of major political parties, in general, were positive towards Chinese response on the parliament attack and India's fight against terrorism in general. China's neutrality during India-Pakistan military standup and its efforts to cool down the tension were also hailed by most of the political parties in India. Similarly, the establishment of Indo-Chinese Anti-terrorism Consultation Group and China's assurance to cooperate India in combating terrorism was also complemented by most of the political parties.

Indian Objection to SAARC Observer Status to China and the Beginning of India China Great Game

The roller- coaster relation between India and China was gradually growing upwards since the official visit of the Indian president K.R. Narayanan. Since then, many high level visits were conducted from both the sides' periodically. Tang Jiaxuan and Chairman of the Standing Committee of the National People's Congress (NPC) Li Peng visited India on July 21, 2000 and on January 9, 2001 respectively. Similarly, Chinese Premier Zhu Rongli, visited India on January 2002 to strengthen the age old relationship. From Indian side, Foreign Minister Jaswant Singh and Defense Minister George Fernades visited Beijing on March 29, 2002 and April 21, 20002 respectively. Prime Minister Vajpayee paid his maiden China trip as the Prime Minister of India on June 2003 and his Chinese counterpart Wen Jiabao visited India on April 9, 2005. Meanwhile, for the first time, the total trade between New Delhi and Beijing crossed the US $ 10 billion mark in April 2005.[16]

This honeymoon, however, did not last long. The growing relationship took a new turn when India decided to oppose China's inclusion into South

Asian Association for Regional Cooperation (SAARC) as an observer. Clarifying its position Indian External Affair Ministry stated that, "India's position is that China's request along with others can be considered once the criteria and modalities for such association have been worked out."[17] Moreover, for India, China's entry into the SAARC, which is mostly dominated by India would curtail its influence.[18]

However, with the help of its alliance partner Pakistan and the backing of Nepal and Bangladesh, China managed to get the observer status. India on the other hand agreed to the Chinese bid when other SAARC members agreed to grant observer status to Japan. Furthermore, China had been blocking the Russian proposal to grant observed status to India in Shanghais Cooperation Organization (SCO). Beijing proposed the name of Pakistan as an observer and only allowed India when, Russia agreed to allow Pakistan into the SCO. Similarly, China also opposed the inclusion of India into ASEAN Regional Forum (ARF) as a full dialogue partner.[19] For many this was the beginning of a "New Great Game" and the Sini- competition.[20]

The issue regarding the extension of SAARC observer status to China was raised in the Indian parliament at various sessions on which the members across party line showed their concern. CPI leader P.K. Vasudevan Nair and C.K. Chandrappan and BJP leader Harisingh Nasaru Rathod in participating a question session sought government of India's clarification on its decision to abstain from the 13th SAARC Summit to be held in Dhaka, where China had been proposed to be shown as an observer. Answering to the question minister of state for external affairs, E. Ahamed cited the security reason and other reason for India's decision to stay away from the SAAC summit.[21] Similarly, All India Majlis-e-Ittehad-ul Muslimeen (AIMIM) leader Asaduddin Owaisi while raising the question on the grant of observer status to SAARC in Lok Sabha wanted to know the government of India's position and its future course of action towards this issue. In reply, minister of states for external affairs, E. Ahamed stated, "the decisions in the SAARC Summit are taken by consensus. The recently held SAARC Summit in Dhaka welcomed and agreed the principle with the desire of the People`s Republic of China to be included as `Observer`. The Summit further decided that the SAARC Council of Ministers will decide modalities in this regard in their Twenty Seventh Meeting in July 2006."[22] However, the parliament was more cautioned about China's role in SAARC and showed displeasure towards the recent development.

India-China energy Cooperation Agreement

The year 2006 was one of the important years of India-China relationship. The year 2005 was celebrated as the 55th anniversary of the establishment of India-China diplomatic relationship. In this event Premier Wen Jiabao visited India and signed the agreement on Political Parameters and Guiding Principles for the Special Representatives Talks. India and China also congratulated each other for the successful conclusion of the first phase of the talks. Besides, both the countries decided to observe the year 2006, as the "China-India Friendship Year". Throughout the year, more than 50 high level delegates exchanged and a large number of political, business and military activities were conducted to celebrate the moments of Sino-Indian friendship.[23] In this high moment of India-China friendship, Chinese President Hu Jintao visited India in November 2006 along with a high level delegation including Foreign Minister Yang Jiechi, State Councillor Dai Bingguo. During his visit, India China issued a Joint Declaration containing a ten-pronged strategy to intensify cooperation.[24] More importantly, India and China signed the "Memorandum for Enhancing Cooperation in the Field of Oil and Natural Gas" in January 12, 2006 and agreed to cooperate with each other in energy sector, especially, during the time of oil exploration and marketing in the foreign land.[25] Article 9 of the Joint Declaration issued during the state visit of President Hu also states that India and China will cooperate in energy section, including the joint exploration of petroleum production.On December 16, 2006 a multinational initiatives were taken to discuss the emerging issues of energy security. The energy ministers of China, the United States, Japan, Korea, and India met in Beijing to form a joint mechanism to maintain the stability in the international energy market and to promote cooperation to avoid unnecessary competing.[26]

However, the promises were apparently week in reality. The competition was quite visible when, China successfully persuaded the Myanmar government to own the bid for the exploration of natural gas at cost of the India's bid that failed to reach the negotiation.[27] Apart from this both the states were competing with each other in Africa, Middle East and Central Asia in energy exploration.[28]

This issue of India-China energy cooperation had debates and discussion in the floor of Indian parliament on several occasions. While most of the members welcomed the initiatives, a section of members, especially opposing parties remained cautioned about the implementation of the agreement. While asking a question, TDP leader Sambasiva Rayapati Rao wanted to know whether the government had signed any such agreement with China for joint exploration and sought government's statement regarding the step to implement the agreement on ground. In reply, Minister of Mines, Sis Ram Ola stated that, both the governments had signed the agreement to exchange information on mining investment, legislation and exploration, promote cooperation in research, policies and regulations, technical assistance, training programmes and joint ventures in third countries." He further stated that, "it has been agreed that the subordinate organizations like Geological Survey of India, Indian Bureau of Mines and Public Sector Undertakings under the administrative control of the Ministry of Mines shall identify the projects of mutual interest with their Chinese counterparts to implement the MOU"[29] Similarly, Eknath Mahadeo Gaikwad G.V. Harsha Kumar, Adhir Ranjan Chowdhury and Uday Singh raised questions on the nature of the energy cooperation and the proposed time of implementation of the joint venture. While disclosing the features of the Sino-Indian agreement, Minister of State for Petroleum and Natural Gas Dinsha Patel stated that both the governments were in discussion to initiate the process and the government would make public of the details if it came to force.[30]

While asking a question in the Lok Sabha H.G. Ahir wanted government's comments on the extension of Indo-Iran gas pipe line to China of BJP and asked details regarding this project. Petroleum and Natural Gas Minister, while answering to the question stated that, 'There is no formal proposal at present to extend the Iran – Pakistan- India natural gas pipeline to China, but the thought has been thrown up for public discussion. As such no bilateral negotiations have been held between India and China on this project."[31] Similarly, replying to the question raised by Anna Saheb M.K. Patil, Ratilal Kalidas Varma, Kiran Maheshwari, Minister of Information & Broadcasting, P.R. Dasmunsi informed the house that, China and India had signed the agreement to cooperate with each other on the field of energy exploration and a taskforce had been sent to negotiate the outstanding issues on this regard.[32]

Bilateral Trade Agreements and Reopening of Nathu La Pass

Despite the flip-flop relation, the bilateral trade between India and China had grown drastically since the grant of MFN status to each other and their economic liberalization. The bilateral trade between India and China, which was as low as US$ 264 million in 1991, had grown to US$ 2.92 billion in the year 2000.[33] During the historic visit of the Indian Prime Minister Vajpayee to China in 2004, both the nations promised to take further initiative to improve the relationship and to strengthen the bilateral trade by re-opening the Nathu La and the Jelepla Pass of Sikkim for border trade. After the series of negotiation, on 2006 the Nathu La pass re-opened for trade after 44 years of blockade following the 1962 war.[34] Though the contribution of the border trade through the Nathu La pass had been small, it was a significance step in the India-China relationship. Often described as the "routes of promises", the opening of the border pass was a symbolic gesture for a emerging relationship between New Delhi and Beijing.[35]

The Indian public opinion and the attitude of Indian parliament were mixed towards the opening of the Nathu La pass and the growing bilateral trade between India and China. Raising a question on the India China trade through Nathu La Pass, a group of parliamentarians, Kishanbhai Vestabhai Patel, Mohan Rawale, Jyotiraditya Madhavrao Scindia, Dushyant Singh, Ramakrishna Badiga, Asaduddin Owaisi, Sugrib Singh, Rewati Raman Singh and Mekapati Rajamohan Reddy asked for movements? Statement regarding the opening of the Nathu La passes for border trade with China and the government of India's actions to address the problem faced by the Indian traders through these trade route. In replying the question, the two countries signed the agreement to open the Nathu La pass for border trade. Regarding the strengthening of trade relation with China, he stated that both India and China had appointed a Joint Study Group (JSG) composed of officials and economists to explore the areas for further cooperation on trade and commerce.[36] Similarly, answering to the question raised by parliamentarian N. Janardhana Reddy regarding the difficulties faced by Indian trader in Lathu La pass, Minister of State for Commerce and Industry Shri Jairam Ramesh informed the house that, there was some report of difficulties in trading trough the Nathu La pass and the government issued a guide line to avoid these difficulties. He also stated that, the overall trade between India and China had improved after the opening of the trade route and both the countries have benefited by that.[37]

However, the debate of India China trade was not limited to the Nathu La pass and spared into other issues also. While some parliamentarians pitched for greater trade relation with China, others warned the government for the growing disparity between the import and exports. Congress Party leader K. Sudhakaran for instance, while stating concern for the widening gap between import and export wanted to know government of India's efforts to minimize the gap. In answering to the question, Minister of State for Commerce and Industry Jyotiraditya Scindia stated that, the government was aware of those issues and had been in negotiation with the Chinese government to resolve the issues. Regarding the difficulties and restrictions imposed by China he said,

"There are various factors which restrict export from India to China. China's macroeconomic policies, exchange rate policy and other

specific non-tariff measures make exports to China uneconomic and cumbersome. During the eighth session of India-China Joint Group on Economic Relations, Trade, Science and Technology (JEG) held on 19th January, 2010, the Commerce & Industry Minister raised the issue of growing trade deficit with his Chinese counterpart. As an outcome of 8th JEG, an MoU on Expansion of trade and Economic Cooperation was signed between India and China. The MoU recognizes that a balanced trade is conducive to long term, sustainable and harmonious development of economic cooperation between India and China. As per the MoU, the Chinese side shall strive to import as much of its requirement of value added goods from India as possible."[38]

While answering the question raised by Iqbal Ahmed Saradgi regarding the features of the Bilateral Investment Promotion and Protection Agreement (BIPA), Jairam Ramesh informed the hose that, the BIPA is an attempt to promote the bilateral trade between India and China as well as will be a protect wall to safeguard our own national interest while trading with China.[39]

The growing disparity between the trade volume between India and China was a matter of concern for most of the political parties. While some parliamentarians requested for strong action to minimize the gap, others sought for greater discussion with Chinese authority to resolve the issues. But, overall the parliament was in favor of greater bilateral trade and economic engagement with China. At the same time it remained concerned about the growing gap between import and export on the bilateral trade with China.

The Attitude of Indian Parliament towards China India Visa Row

Amidst the growing bilateral engagement, another disturbing incident occurred over the grant of visa to a young administrative officer of Arunachal Pradesh. The Chinese authority denied visa to Mr. Ganesh Koyu, the Indian Administrative Service officer of Arunachal Pradesh who was selected as member of a official delegation to visit China for a study trip. Giving clarification, Beijing stated that Arunachal Pradesh is a part of China and the people of this region need no visa to visit their own country.[40] Following this, India cancelled the official study trip and lodged strong objection over this incident. But, this was not the first time that, an Indian national from Arunachal Pradesh had been denied the Chinese visa. According to Times of India, Chinese officials had canceled the visa application of several Arunachalees, including ministers on the bases of their native identities and only after the negations a staple visa was issued to them since 1981.[41]

However, with the strong Indian criticism, China agreed to grant visa to Marpe Sora, the lecturer of the Arunachal Pradesh based Rajiv Gandhi Central University to visit China as a part of Indian delegation in November 2007.[42] Since then, China has been inconsistent in issuing visa to Indian nationals belonging to Kashmir and Arunachal Pradesh and the visa row still remains one of the outstanding issues to be resolved between India and China.

This issue of denial of visa to the Indian national of Jammu and Kashmir, and Arunachal Pradesh soon became the center of debate in Indian parliament. Members of all sections of the Indian parliament condemned the incident and criticized the Chinese attitude towards the Indian nationals. Congress leader R. Dhruvanarayana, Mekapati Rajamohan Reddy, Milind Murli Deora, Kishanbhai Vestabhai Patel and Anantha Venkatarami Reddy raised the issues at the Lok Sabha and wanted to know the government's stand to resolve the issue.[43] Similarly, BJP the principal opposition party also criticized government for its inaction to address the issue. Its leader D.B. Chandre Gowda for instance raised the parliamentary question on the Chinese visa issue in the floor of Lok Sabha on November 25, 2009.[44] Raising his concern about the denial of visa to Indian nationals, NCP leader Anand Prakash Paranjpe also wanted know the attitude of government towards this issue.[45]

In reply to these questions, Minister of The State Shashi Tharoor acknowledged that, Kashmir, according to China is a disputed territory and Arunachal Pradesh is a part of China. Hence, it is issuing the staple visa for the Indian citizens of these regions. However, the government of India has issued a travel advisory in this regard and raised the issue at the highest level.[46] During another question hour session, Samajwadi Party (SP) leader Shri Mithilesh raised a question regarding the denial of visa by the Chinese authority to Indians born in Jammu and Kashmir. S.M. Krishna, the Minister of State of MEA stated that, the Indian government has been condemning these discriminatory attitudes of China and perusing the issued with the Chinese authorities at the appropriate level.[47] Despite the assurance of the government, the issue still remains the fore front of parliamentary debate for several occasions and has been the most deeming factor of India China relations for quite long time.

Indian Parliament on China-Pakistan Nuclear Deal

Following the finalization of Indo-US nuclear deal and the subsequent denial of similar line of nuclear privilege by United States administration,

Pakistan approached its all weather friend China to its nuclear programme. Pakistan's President Asif Ali Zardari traveled China extensively and discussed the matters with the Chinese authorities. After finalizing the covert deal, China confirmed on April 29, 2010 that Islamabad and Beijing had signed an agreement to construct two nuclear reactors in Pakistan with the help of a Chinese firm. China further clarified that the deal, like the Indo-US deal was in conformity with the international standards set by the International Atomic Energy Agency (IAEA). China, as per the deal, will construct two nuclear reactors with a capacity of 300 MWS each to meet the power crisis of Pakistan with a future explanation plan.[48]

This Sino-Pak Nuclear nexus, however, is not the development of 21st Century. In 1986, China concluded a comprehensive nuclear cooperation agreement with Pakistan and had been actively assisting Pakistan's nuclear programme.[49] Since then, China has supplied Pakistan with a variety of nuclear products and services, ranging from uranium enrichment technology to research and power reactors. China also allegedly involved Pakistani scientists in a nuclear test at its Lop Nur test site in 1989. Apart for various technical assistant, China has helped Pakistan to design and setup a 50 MW Heavy–Water nuclear reactor near Khushab, and the PARR-2 research reactor in Rawalpindi. In their long history of nuclear cooperation, China also provided material assistant to Pakistan including the pressurized water reactor for Pakistan's Chesma Reactor and 5000 ring magnets to facilitate its nuclear programme.[50]

For India, it was a complete surprise and a matter of concern, due to Pakistan's past record of nuclear proliferation. Following the 1998 nuclear test, many scholars believed that, China had been actively assisting and closely guiding the Pakistani nuclear weapon programme at the very beginning.[51] However, China denied assistance to Pakistan's nuclear programme in strong word. The Chinese Ambassador to India rejected any Chinese hand behind Pakistan's nuclear programme and stated that China had no intention to harm India.[52]

However, these assurances had little support to convince the public opinion of India and the attitude of India parliament, given the fact that China had been closely associated with Pakistan's Nuclearization programme for long time. In fact, the Sino-Pak nuclear deal led to mass public outrage both inside and outside the Indian parliament. Members, across the party line condemned the agreement and asked China to review its policy. Raising a question on Sino-Pak nuclear agreement AIADMK leader C. Rajendran wanted to know government's position to safeguard

Indian interest vis-à-vis the agreement. Answering to the question, External Affair Minister S.M. Krishna stated that, the mater had been raised at the highest level and China had assured to bring these plants under the IAEA safeguards and supervisions. Regarding the India's initiatives to meet the possible challenges, he stated that the government was closely monitoring the issues and committed to take all necessary steps to safeguard India's national interest at any cost.[53] Similarly, Manish Tewari of Indian National Congress while raising a question sought government's clarification on the nature of the nuclear agreement between China and Pakistan and government of India's action in this regard. In reply, External Affair Minister S.M. Krishna stated that the proposed agreement was coming under the IAEA supervision and government of India was discussing the development with all NSG members.[54] On November 10, 2010 Vilas Baburao Muttemwar while raising a question on Sino-Pak nuclear deal wanted to know the detail of the Chinese assistant on Pakistan's nuclear programme. External Affair Minister S.M. Krishna in reply stated that, the Indian government had conveyed its concern to the Chinese authority and had been in dialogue with China to resolve the issue.[55]

Conclusion

The relationship between India and China during the first decade of 21st century witnessed several ups and downs. The Indian president visited China to ease the tension that erupted following India's nuclear detonation and the Karmapa incident. Since then, both the countries have taken several measures to improve their relation and several high level visits have exchanged. Few important agreements also have been signed between New Delhi and Beijing to facilitate the growing bilateral trade, including the agreement to open the Nathu La pass. The India-China cooperation also reached a new high when both the countries decided to go for the joint bidding and to co-operate each other in international oil exploration. However, the promises deemed low as the two countries slowly entered into competition in many areas.

During this period the attitude of Indian parliament towards India's China policy was mostly cooperative as well as cautious. While most of the constructive initiatives, such as the improvement of relationship and promotion of trade between India and China were appreciated by the members of the parliament. But matter that affects India's national interest, including the Sino-Pakistan Nuclear cooperation and the visa issues with China has been opposed by parliament as whole. The Indian parliament, at large has been encouraging greater Sino-Indian trade and economic engagement and also encouraged the opening of the Nathu La pass for border trade. However, there was a little hesitation among the members of the parliament about the attitude of China towards India and the growing gap between volume of importing and exporting in the bilateral trade with China. There was overall consensus among all sections of the parliament for greater relation with China and no political party, whether ruling party or oppositions have opposed to improve relation with China.

Notes

1. Data taken from the website of The Indian Embassy, Beijing and The Economic Times, September 19, 2005.
2. See, Deepak (2005) 399.
3. As stated in Deepak (2005) 400.
4. Swaran singh, "India China: Confidence Building through Crisis" in Living with China: Regional States and China through Crises and Turning Points, ed. Shiping Tang, Mingjiang Li, Amitav Acharya (New York: Palgrave Macmillan, 2009) 77.
5. Deepak (2005) 401-02.
6. Lok Sabha Question No. 154 (STARRED) Dated Aug 8, 2000.
7. Ramesh Chandra, Global Terrorism (New Delhi: Kalpaz Publication, 2003) 173-77.
8. Praveen Swamy, "The Roots of Crisis: The Post Kargil Conflict in Kahshmir and the 2001-2002 New War" in The India-Pakistan Military Standoff: Crisis and Escalation in South Asia, edited by Zachary S. Davis (New York: Palgrave Macmillan, 2011) 23-26.
9. The Renmin Ribao, November 14, 2001.
10. "China to Join India in Fighting Terrorism", The Hindu January 14, 2001.http://www.hindu.com/2001/01 /14/stories/01140001.htm
11. John Cherian, "Zhu Rongji in India", Frontline, Volume 19, Issue 03, Feb. 02 - 15, 2002. http://www.frontline.in/ static/html/fl1903/19031220.htm
12. As stated in Rajat Gupta, "Where are India-China relations heading? A Futuristic Outlook", in Emerging China: Prospects of Partnership in Asia New, Edited by Sudhir T. Devare, Swaran Singh, Reena Marwah (Delhi: Routledge, 2014) 383.
13. Daniel S. Markey, No Exit from Pakistan: America's Tortured Relationship with Islamabad (New York: Cambridge University Press, 2013) 183.
14. Lok Sabha Question No. 154 (STARRED) Dated Aug 8, 2000.
15. Lok Sabha Question No 612 (Starred), Dated 08.05.2002.
16. India-China Relations, Ministry of External Affairs, Government of India. http://www.mea.gov.in/Portal/ForeignRelation/China_Brief.pdf
17. Abanti Bhattacharya, China's 'Observer' Status: Implications for SAARC, Institute of Peace and Conflict Studies, New Delhi, Research Article, #1891, 21 November 2005. http://www.ipcs.org/article/south-asia/chinas-observer-status-implications-for-saarc-1891.html
18. Rajat Gupta (2014) 383-85.

19. Ibid. also see, Vidya Nadkarni, Strategic Partnerships in Asia: Balancing Without Alliances (Oxon: Routledge, 2010) 188; Gunther Hauser, Franz Kernic, China: The Rising Power (Frankfurt: Peter Lang, 2009) 116; Amaia Sánchez-Cacicedo, Building States, Building Peace: Global and Regional Involvement in Sri Lanka and Myanmar (London: Palgrave Macmillan, 2014) 169-70.
20. Marléne Laruelle, Jean-François Huchet, Sébastien Peyrouse, China and India in Central Asia: A New "Great Game"? (New York: Palgrave Macmillan, 2010); Bertil Lintner, Great Game East: India, China and the Struggle for Asia's Most Volatile Frontier (New Delhi: HarperCollins Publishers India, 2012); Anna Orton, India's Borderland Disputes: China, Pakistan, Bangladesh, and Nepal (New Delhi: Epitome Books, 2010) ; R. K. Bhonsle, India- Security Scope 2006: The New Great Game (New Delhi: Gyan Publishing House, 01-Jan-2006; Thant Myint-U, Where China Meets India: Burma and the New Crossroads of Asia (New York: Farrar, Straus and Giroux, 13-Sep-2011; David Scott, The Great Power "Great Game' between India and China: 'The Logic of Geography", Geopolitics, Volume 13, Issue 1, (2008) 1-26; C. Raja Mohan, The great Game Folio: China's railroads, the Indian Express, April 2, 2014; Balaji Chandramohan, India-China Great Power Rivalry starts, World Security Network, 03-May-10.
21. See Lok Sabha Question Number 262, dated March 2, 2005.
22. See Lok Sabha Question Number 2195, Dated December 7, 2005.
23. Amardeep Athwal, China-India Relations: Contemporary Dynamics (Oxon: Routledge, 2007) 112-13.
24. India-China bilateral Relation, Embassy of India, Beijing. http://www.indian embassy.org.cn/Dynamic Content. aspx?Menuld=2&SubMenuld=0; also see, Rajshree Jetly, The Visit of Chinese President, Hu Jintao, To India, ISAS Insights, No. 16 – Date: 28 November 2006. http://www.isn.ethz.ch/Digital-Library/Publications/Detail/?ots591= 0c54e3b3-1e9c-be1e-2c24-a6a8c7060233&lng= en&id=26966.
25. China, India Sign Energy Agreement, The China Daily, January 13, 2006.
26. Ma Jiali, The Energy Cooperation between China and India in the Post-crisis Era, Contemporary International Relations, Vol. 20, No. 2 Mar./Apr. 2010. http://www.cicir.ac.cn/english/ArticleView.aspx?nid=1923.
27. Hong Zhao, China and India: The Quest for Energy Resources in the 21st Century (Oxon: Routledge, 2012) 119-131; also see, Namrata Panwar, "India and China competing over Myanmar Energy Resources", working draft for BISA Conference 2009, http://bisa.ac.uk/index.php?option=com_bisa&task=view_public_ papers_ author_char_search & char_search=P
28. For detail Details see, Chietigj Bajpaee, India, China locked in Energy Game, Asia Times, Mar 17, 2005. http://www.atimes.com/atimes/Asian_Economy/GC17Dk01.html
29. See Lok Sabha Question No. 455, Dated December 23, 2005.
30. See Lok Sabha Question No. 3201, Dated December 14, 2006 and Question No. 521 dated July 27, 2006.
31. See Lok Sabha Question No. 379, dated November 27, 2005.
32. See Lok Sabha Question No. 2526, dated dec. 9, 2005.

33. Data taken from the website of Indian Embassy, Beijing and the Economic Times, September 19, 2005.
34. Dinesh Lal(2008) 28-29.
35. Kalyan Choudhury. Routes of promise, Frontline, Volume 20 (14) 2003-07-04; also see, Pema Wangchuk, India, China and the Nathu La Converting Symbolism into Reality, Issue Brief, No. 202, Institute of Peace and Conflict Studies, January 2013, http://www.ipcs.org/pdf_file/issue/IB202-CRP-Pema-NathuLa.pdf
36. See Lok Sabha Question No. 193, Dated July 25, 2006.
37. See Lok Sabha Question No.1738, Dated August 8, 2006.
38. See Lok Sabha Question No.1198, Dated August 2, 2010.
39. See Lok Sabha Question No.205, Dated July 25, 2006.
40. Jeff M. Smith, Cold Peace: China–India Rivalry in the Twenty-First Century (Lanham: Lexington Books, 2013) 43-45; also see, Saurabh Shukla, Beijing Turns Truant Again, India Today, June 11, 2007, http://indiatoday.intoday.in/story/china-denied-the-visa-to-ganesh-koyu/1/155630.html
41. China grants visa to Arunachal Pradesh academician, Times of India, 6 December 2007. http://timesofindia.indiatimes.com/India/China_grants_visa_to_Arunachal_Pradesh_academician_/rssarticleshow/2601877.cms
42. China U-turn: visa for lecturer from Arunachal, The Indian Express, December 6, 2007, http://archive.indianexpress.com/news/china-uturn-visa-for-lecturer-from-arunachal/247484/ also see, Edward N. Luttwak, The Rise of China vs The Logic of Strategy (London: The Belknap Press of Harvard Univeristy, 2012) 78-79.
43. Lok Sabha Question No. 1112, dated November 25, 2009.
44. Ibid.
45. Ibid.
46. See Answer to the Question No. 1112, ibid.
47. See Lok Sabha Question No. 2815, Dated August 11, 2010.
48. Siddharth Ramana, China-Pakistan Nuclear Alliance, IPCS Special Report, No. 109, Institute of Peace and Conflict Studies, August 2011. http://www.ipcs.org/pdf_file/issue/SR109.pdf; also see Syed Shahid Hussain Bukhari and Attiq-ur-Rehman, "Pakistan-China Nuclear Deal & International Fictions", Berkeley Journal of Social Sciences , Vol. 1, Issue 3, March 2011.
49. Mohammad Jamil, Sino-Pak nuclear collaboration, Pakistan Observer, April 30, 2014. http://pakobserver.net/ detailnews.asp?id=57684
50. Hooman Peimani, Nuclear Proliferation in the Indian Subcontinent: The Self-exhausting "Superpowers" and Emerging Alliances (Westport : Praeger Publishers, 2000) 14-17.
51. China's Nuclear Exports and Assistance to Pakistan, Research Articles, James Martin Center for Nonproliferation Studies, The Monterey Institute of International Studies, Monterey. http://cns.miis.edu/archive/country_india/china/npakpos.htm
52. "Chinese Envoy: China Not 'Threat' to India," *Deccan Herald*, 27 February 1999.

53. See Lok Sabha Question No. 50, Dated July 28, 2010.
54. See Lok Sabha Question No. 1780, Dated August 4, 2010.
55. See Lok Sabha Question No. 322, Dated November 10, 2010.

Chapter - 9

Theorisation and Conclusion

In any democratic setup, Parliament is the foremost institution to formulate all kinds of policies for a state, including matters of foreign affairs. Being the representative of people's voice, the Parliament is also the highest decision making body to take decision on any matters of statecraft. The constitution of India gives immense power to Parliament to formulate any policy or modify the existing policies on matters listed under the union list, including the matter related to foreign affairs. Apart from ensuring the executive answerability, the Parliament also enjoys several provisions, such as policy legislation, budgetary control, Parliamentary debates and discussion etc. to influence the process of Foreign Policy decision making of India. However, Indian parliament in practical the

In this regard, the present study attempts to understand the role and influence of Indian Parliament on shaping India's Foreign Policy towards China. Though significant amount of research has been conducted to study the role of Parliament and other legislative bodies in the formulation of foreign policy of major Western democratic setups, the theory seems inappropriate in the Indian context, mostly due to the nature and structure of Indian Parliamentary democracy. While legislative bodies of United States, United Kingdom, Canada and Australia play decisive role in determining the important external engagements, Indian Parliament does not have power to approve India's foreign policy, and its involvement in foreign policy decision making is limited to post-policy analysis. Similarly, under the Indian Parliamentary system, Parliamentary approval is not mandatory on crucial decision of the foreign policy and the rectification of international treaties and agreements, the standard procedure that has been practiced even some of the least developing countries of the world as a matter of minimum democratic norms. Hence, the gap between the democratic norms and its unusual practice in Indian Parliamentary system needs to be analysed to theorize the role of Indian Parliament in the making of India's foreign policy. It has been noticed that, during the early years of Indian Parliamentary experiment, the attention of the Parliament was mostly vested on domestic issues, and the Parliamentary involvement in foreign policy decision making was negligible. However, the scenario have drastically changed during the period of India-China confrontation, where the Parliament shoed enormous interest on the various issues of India's foreign policy and questioned, debated and discusses India's China policy substantially. Hence, the study of the role of Indian Parliament in making India's foreign policy on China is essential in this context.

The prime objective of the present work is to study the role of Indian Parliament and its level of influence on India's foreign policy decision making process in general and on India's China policy in particular. It also aims to analyse the attitude of different political parties towards China and their attitudinal difference on towards India's engagement with China. The analytical, descriptive and case study technique has been applied to the present research and try to theorise the Parliamentary role in foreign policy decision making by studying the 'attitude of Indian Parliament towards China' as a case study. The theoretical framework and main argument of the research is spread across ten different chapters and summary of the study discussed as follows.

A modern state needs a comprehensive and proactive Foreign Policy to attain its national objectives and for the all-round development of the nation. Similarly, the successful management of one's external relations largely depends upon the effectiveness of the Foreign Policy making decision unit that consists of different actors, agencies and institutions. It takes various information and necessary inputs from multiple resources and analyses the received data to make appropriate decision. The decision making unit is same in all kind of states and administrative structures. According to Graham Allison the decision making could be categorized into three broad models – the Rational Actor Model, the Organizational Process Model and the Bureaucratic Politics Model. While the Rational Actor model and Organizational Process Model prescribed the decision making based on rational choice and structural organisational outcome respectively, the Bureaucratic Politics model tends to consensus making rather than logical assessment. Under this model of decision making, several actors of the decision making unit compete among themselves for maximum benefit and often settled to a concessions based mediocre policies. In all these three models, the process of Foreign Policy decision making is multi-level and multi-dimensional in character and subject to internal and external influences. Various factors, such as the leadership, political setup, social and cultural affiliations, the economic and military strength and the geographical and international environment do play a role in influencing the decision making. A successful decision should have the quality to reduce these influences while making decision.

While most of the third world countries have been suffering due to lack of proper institutional setups for foreign policy management, India has been in advantage with well-established Foreign Policy setups. Even before independence, the western educated leadership of the Indian National Congress (INC), the principal organization of Indian freedom movement has largely been acquainted with the art of external affairs. Until India's independence, the INC had been successfully propagating its stand for India's freedom and the atrocity of the British government on various multilateral forums. Many of its leaders had attended the regional and international conferences and successfully conducted meetings with important delegates of different states. After independence the legacy of the Foreign Policy management has been successfully carried out by the congress led Indian government. As a result, India has been at the fore front of the third world movements including the Non Alignment Movement (NAM).

Foreign Policy Decision Making in India had been largely centred on the personality of the Prime Ministers during the early years of independence. During his tenure Nehru, the chief architect of India's Foreign Policy used to be the centre of the Decision making process. He used to be the fore front decision maker of India's foreign affairs. Being in charge of both External Affairs and Prime Minister during most of his tenure, he used to take most of the important decisions himself and the role of cabinet and advisors was limited. The Nehruvian style of decision making still seems in practice in the Indian Foreign Policy decision making units. Though all the stake holders of the decision making body express their view, it is the Prime Minister whose decision generally prevails.

Secondly, the process of Foreign Policy decision making in Indian context is the end product of bargaining and consensus, rather than rational. The bureaucrats, governmental institutions and other stake holders of the decision making unit try to dominate over others by prevailing their views on certain issues of foreign affairs. As a result most of the time the decision making process remains complex and tensed. Now, with the emergence of coalition politics, the regional parties also try to play larger role in foreign affairs which make the process even further complex. Therefore the decision outcomes used to be out of consensus and balanced. However, the government sometimes takes hard steps to takes rational decision during crisis.

Like most of the democratic countries, the inter-departmental conflicts often jeopardize the decision making process. In order to maintain the departmental supremacy, some organizations have been seen in hiding some of the information that is supposed to be passed to the other departments. The JIC, PPRD and other such organizations apparently hesitate to share the information and are reluctant to cooperate with others in most of the cases. As a result the decision making in India has been under performance for decades.

Bureaucrats are the dominant forces of the whole process decision making. Because of the pivotal role of bureaucracy in formulating and implementing of the Foreign Policy for the country, they often try to influence the decision making process for their own benefits. Both in civil and military branches, the bureaucrats enjoy some sort of monopoly and the drive force of the policy making, as most of the political leadership lacks experience and knowledge in issues of Foreign affairs. The lobby of the bureaucrats often influence the policy decision and bar the political leadership from taking right steps. For instance, the idea of establishing the NSC was first proposed in 1962. But the constant bureaucratic pressure barred the government to setup the same for decades, as the bureaucrats feared that they would lose their hold if the neutral experts and military bosses were brought into the decision making process through NSC. Though many factions have tried to influence the course of Foreign Policy decision making process to suit their personal interest, the counter actions and impartial measures put the process balanced and effective. Many times the government takes bold, surprising and unusual steps to maximize national interest, and the ideological driven decision making process is transformed into pragmatic at the time of need.

Being the highest institution and the ultimate voice of the people, Parliament, in a democratic state like India plays an important role in the formulation and implementation of foreign policies in a variety of ways. It can legislate on any matters that come under union list, including matters related to foreign affairs. The Parliament also influences the course of the Foreign Policy by approving or rejecting any government proposal related to Foreign Policy and can create any specialized agency and government institution to deal with the matter related to foreign affairs like Foreign Service Institute and National Security Council; or merge or modify the function of the existing machinery or create new posts like National Security Advisor. Using its power of budgetary allocation, the Parliament also influences India's Foreign Policy behaviour. In addition, Parliamentary debates and discussions are also considered one of the prime instruments to influence the process of foreign policy decision making in India. The opposition and the members of the Parliament find out the government lacunas and give necessary suggestions for better policies during the Parliamentary debates. The Parliament poses unparallel power to withhold, pass or reject any bill or resolution that is directly or indirectly related to India's external policy. Members of Parliament also move adjournment, no-confident or cut-motion, raise short or half-an hour discussion on any specific or an overall issue of Foreign Policy. Similarly, the Consultative Committees of Parliament, especially Standing Committee on Foreign Affairs has been playing a significant role in shaping India's Foreign Policy behaviour by scrutinising the government policy and give necessary recommendation to government. After all, the Parliament is considered as the face of the government and its behaviour and activities always have paid significant attention among the world communities.

But in practice, the Parliament despite all its powers and privileges has never been considered as one of the core actors of Foreign Policy decision making in India and involvement limited to a peripheral actor. Government always bypasses the Parliament while making decision on any important issue on foreign affairs. Though, the Parliament is empowered to legislate on any matter on foreign affairs, not many issues on foreign and defence policies have been referred to the Parliament for legislation. Unlike United States or Australia, it is not mandatory for international conventions, treaties and agreements to get approved by the Parliament before come into practice. In Indian context, it is supposed to be the document of secrecy for optimum result and the open discussion in the Parliament before actualization might endanger the entire goal of the treaty. Therefore, many of the treaties, such as the India–China Agreement of 1954, the Tashkent Agreement of 1965, the India-Soviet Agreement of 1971 and the Simla Agreement of 1972 have never been referred to the Parliament for debate before the conclusion of the treaty. Even the Parliament had deliberately hid a number of such important facts and policies from Parliamentary disclosure. The Parliament committees, which are supposed to guide the course of Foreign Policy, are often divided by the party affiliations and personnel ideologies. Due to this divisive character, the decisions of the committee become the by-product of negotiation rather than the result of rational choice. For this reason, M.C. Chagla, the ex-Foreign Minister under Indira Gandhi government termed Consultative Committee on external affairs as "more of an agency for getting policies accepted and muting criticism than for influencing Foreign Policy".

In spite of the limitations, on many occasions the Parliament has significantly influenced the Foreign Policy of India. For instance, Nehru's Foreign Policy towards China in the early periods used to be soft despite several border violations due to the overwhelming support of the Parliament. But, following the constant pressure in the Parliament, Nehru was forced to restructure his policies during late 1950s. The Parliament also successfully pressurized the Nehru government to disclose every single document on China, which was tabled in the Parliament in the form of White Papers for discussion. Similarly, during the Hungarian Crisis of 1965, Nehru initially turned towards Soviet line, but after the stiff pressure from the opposition in the Parliament, he changed his stand subsequently. Prime Minister Indira Gandhi also changed her stand from separation to united Czechoslovakia during the 1968 Czechoslovak crisis by the influence of strong opposition in the Parliament. To conclude we can say that, the Parliament played very minimal role in India's Foreign Policy decision making until 1960, but with the emergence of strong opposition and other national parties, the influence of the Parliament has multiplied significantly.

The period of Sino-Indian confrontation from 1958 to 1968 was one of the important chapters of India China relationship and one of the defining moments of Asian politics. India and China, the two old civilizations of the world had been sharing warm and friendly relationship since centuries. The cultural and economic ties between the two neighbours date back to First Century AD. This ancient tie was thriving during the middle, modern and colonial era. During the Chinese freedom struggle, India offered its full support. After the independence of China, India was the second non-communist country to recognize the People's Republic of China and established diplomatic relations with China in early 1950. The Sino-Indian relationship continued to thrive in the post-independence era and many politico-cultural exchanges have been conducted regularly. However, these friendly moments did not last long and the century old Sino-Indian relationship started sinking after the Tibetan uprising of 1958. After the voluntary abandonment of all British inherited traditional rights by signing the 'agreement of trade and intercourse', popularly known as Panchsheel Agreement, India expected the end of bilateral issues with China, including the border disputes. India also recognized Tibet as the integral part of China and maintained neutrality during the Chinese invention into Tibet and Tibetan uprising. However, China accused Indian involvement in the

Tibetan uprising and condemned India's decision to grant political asylum to Dalai Lama.

Indian Parliament, which used to be supportive towards the matters related to China, strongly denounced the Chinese allegation and members across the party line denounced the Chinese allegation. Opposition parties such as PSP, BJS and MKP strongly criticized the government's silence towards the Tibetan uprising and asked the government to help the Tibetan rebels in their struggle for self-determination. However, Nehru led congress as well as CPI rejected the opposition's demand and backed the government's decision to maintain neutrality.

Short after the fall of the Tibetan uprising and the successful Tibetan annexation, Chinese troops initiated the long range border patrolling along the Indo-Tibetan border and came face to face with the Indian troops, which led to several border clashes, in which India allegedly lost large chunk of its territory to China. Each of the party accused each other for the border violation, before deciding to hold formal discussion for the demarcation of inhabited frontiers. However, no result was achieved in the negations and left the situation unsolved, even without any interim mechanism. As a result, India decided to use force to drive out Chinese occupation by launching massive military operation. China reacted to the Indian action strongly with greater force which led to the breakup of the Sino-Indian border war in 1962. India received major defeat and Chinese army pushed back Indian troops in Aksai Chin and occupied around 37,244 square kilometres (14,380 sq. mi.) of Indian Territory, which they believed belonging to China. On November 19, 1962 China declared unilateral ceasefire and decided to pull back its troops 20 kilometres from the ceasefire line.

The whole political spectrum and the Indian Parliament at large condemned the Chinese attack. Members from opposition parties and even from the ruling party targeted Prime Minister Nehru and the government as a whole for the failed Chinese policy and the military disaster. Defence Minister Krishna Menon also came under strong attack by the oppositions in the Parliament. The Jan Sangh, Socialists and the Swatrantra Party made the government accountable for the defeat and moved several motions including, no confidence motion against the government. They also demanded immediate resignation of the Defence Minister and the Prime Minister. Interestingly, a section of ruling Congress Party also criticized the government's China policy and blamed Nehru for the military defeat of India. Communist Party of India, which used to back Nehru's Chinese foreign policy on several occasions and had been adopting pro-Chinese stand, also openly condemned the Chinese attack, which was a rare phenomenon in the Indian Parliament.

At the end of the India – China war, India lost about 38 km of territory to China. Though China declared the unilateral ceasefire on November 21, 1962 and pulled back its force 20 kilometres from the ceasefire line, both the states failed to decide the ceasefire line proposed zone of demilitarization. Looking at the looming danger, some Afro-Asian countries gathered at Colombo, the capital of Cyclone (present Sri Lanka) to facilitate the negotiation and prepared a ceasefire formula, known as Colombo proposal. India agreed to accept the formula, but China objected to certain points and accepted a part of the proposal. As a result the proposal failed to achieve its purpose.

On October 16, 1964 China conducted its first nuclear test and emerged as the fifth nuclear state of the world. India reacted strongly to the Chinese nuclear programme. After attaining the nuclear weapon, Chinese Prime Minister Zohu Enlai stated that China never relinquished its sovereignty over the 90000 square milometer of territory in NEFA region, the present Arunachal Pradesh. China also tried to get closer to India's traditional enemy, Pakistan and signed a boundary protocol with Pakistan on Mar 26, 1965. By signing the protocol, Pakistan handed over nearly 5309 km of area out of its administrative region of Kashmir. Following the breakup of Indo-Pak war in April 1956, China supported Pakistan and labelled India as the aggressor. China also supported the Kashmir movement and demanded the right to self-determination for the people of Kashmir. China also condemned the "Tashkent declaration" signed between India and Pakistan on January 1966 and called it as the Soviet-American conspiracy to humiliate China.

Following the land slide victory in the 1966 general election, Mrs. Indira Gandhi decided to follow the footprints of his father and vowed to normalize relation with China by re-establishing diplomatic ties. But most of the non-communist opposition parties criticized the Government of India's unilateral initiatives to improve relation with China. However, CPI and CPM supported the government's decision and asked the government to take necessary steps to re-establish full diplomatic relation with China. Prime Minister Indira Gandhi also supported China's bid to United Nation in 1971.

Meanwhile, an anti-Pakistani revolt was developed in the East Pakistan, the present Bangladesh in 1971 and Pakistan lunched massive army operation to dismantle the revolution. During this difficult time Pakistan requested for Chinese assistance/ support. China was ready to extend its unconditional support to Pakistan and warned India to stay away from the internal matters of Pakistan. India maintained silence at the initial periods for the sake of its normalization of relationship process with China. But, after the breakdown of large scale massacre and the following flowing of large scale refugees into India, the Indian Government ordered its army to drive out Pakistani army from East Pakistan. China, however, did not intervene physically in the conflict. But the consequence of Indian involvement in the Bangladesh crisis did affect the process of normalization of relation with China. China extended its support to the Shimla Agreement and indicated to improve relation with India.

When the Sino-Indian relation was getting positive momentum, a political crisis broke down in the Himalayan kingdom of Sikkim. The leaders of the democratic fronts revolted against the king and demanded for the end of kingship. Following the request of the ruler of Sikkim, India sent its army to bring the situation under control. A referendum was conducted following the resolution passed by the Sikkimese General Assembly, in which the people of Sikkim voted to merge with Indian union. On April 23, 1975, Sikkim became the 22nd state of Indian union after the 38th Constitutional Amendment. China, which recognized Sikkim as an independent kingdom, condemned the merger of Sikkim and termed India the aggressor. Chinese leadership also accused India for forcefully occupying the Himalayan kingdom and refused to recognize Sikkim as the state of India.

However, after the end of Sikkim crisis both India and China decided to move ahead to develop normal relationship with each other. The process of Sino-Indian détente started getting momentum after the non-intervention of China in the Sikkim crisis. The goodwill visit of the Chinese Table Tennis team led by the Chinese Vice-Minister Wang Bingnan helped to break the deadlock in the years of estrangement. As the first step towards Sino-Indian rapprochement, India sent K.R. Narayanana as the Indian Ambassador to China and Beijing sent Chen Zhayuan as the Chinese ambassador to India in 1976 and the two Asian giants once again re-established their ambassador level diplomatic relations after a gap of 15 years. Similarly, Foreign Minister Vajpayee visited Beinjing on February 12, 1979. India and China granted the status of Most Favoured Nation (MNF) to each other on 15 August 1984. Prime Minister Rajiv Gandhi paid his historic visit to China on December 19, 1988 and the Chinese Prime Minister Li Peng visited India in December 1991 followed by Narshimarao's China visit in December 1993. During 1976 to 1997 several high-level visits and diplomatic exchanges occurred, which further strengthened the age old relationship between India and China and put the difficult relationship on track.

The uneasy relation between India and China started improving at the end of Sikkim Crisis. Apart for the verbal condemnation, there was no physical involvement of China in the Sikkim Crisis which was a positive development the India-China leadership. Secondly, both the nations behaved maturely to the emerging global order and were desperate to improve their troubled relationship. Looking at the growing interests from both the sides, China sent its Vice-Minister Wang Bingnan along with the Chinese Table Tennis team for a goodwill visit to India. Apart from this, Chinese leadership on several occasions indicated to improve relation with India. On the other hand, India also decided to establish the ambassadorial level relationship and sent K.R. Narayan as the next Ambassador to China. Subsequently, China sent Chen Zhayuan as the Chinese Ambassador to New Delhi. With the reestablishment of the Ambassador level relationship, the period of estrangement came to an end and Sino-Indian relationship entered into the golden era of reengagement where both the nations reached one another and discussed various issues on board. In August 1984, India and China offered each other the Most Favor Nations (MNF) status and intensified their trade relationship, which later became the important pillar of India-China relationship. Prime Minister Rajiv Gandhi paid his historic visit to China on December 1988. Similarly, Chinese Prime Minister Li Peng visited India in December 1991 and Narshimha Rao visited China in December 1993. Several high-level visits and diplomatic exchanges occurred between 1976 and 1999, which further stringed the age old relationship. The process of greater engagement led to the resolution of the Sumdorong Chu Crisis.

The Sino-India relationship got a major setback after the controversial 'potential threat number one' remarks of Indian Defense Minister George Fernandes and the Pokhran II nuclear test. China Reacted sharply in both the occasions. However, China never threatened to freeze the diplomatic relations with India, which was in practice earlier. India reached out to the Chinese leadership and discussed the issues for normalcy. Though Beijing was not fully convinced with the Indian clarifications, still decide to engage with New Delhi. During the Kargil was China maintained complete neutrality, which was the unconventional development in Sino-Pak-India triangular relationship. It was again one of the significant factors in normalizing relationship between India and China. Indian public opinion, media and Parliament highly obliged to the Chinese neutrality. When India and China narrowly avoided the Kargil crisis, another disturbing matter erupted in Tibet. The spiritual leader, 17th Karmapa escaped from Tibet and sought for political asylum in India. China asked India to stay away from interfering into the internal matters of China. India reached out to Beijing and discussed the issue with Chinese leadership. India also did not let the issue to escalate and played down the issue within and outside the parliament. As a result, the issue was resolved within the diplomatic fronts without damaging the relationship further.

The Indian parliament as a whole was apparently in favor of pro-talks and constructive relation with China during the period of reengagement. There was not much objection in the parliament from the opposition parties towards the government's decision to reestablish ambassadorial level diplomatic relation. All sections of the house apparently supported this development, though there was some objection in the parliament from Jan Sangh and Socialist party. There was a visible consensus among all the sections of the Parliament towards improvement of relationship with China and the government's efforts to normalize relationship with China were supported by majority of parties. Hence, the high level visit from both the sides was welcomed by majority of the members of the Parliament. However, there used to be pressure over the government for the settlement of outstanding disputes. The process of normalization of relationship got another set beck when, Deference Minister George Furnades termed China as the potential threat number one and the government of India conducted nuclear test citing Chinese threat as the prime reason. In 12th General Election of 1998, BJP led NDA government came into power through the national security reform manifesto and George Furnades became the Defense Minister of India. George Furnades, one of the front line leaders who openly criticized by Chinese leadership for Tibetan human right violation on many occasions, labeled China as the threat number one in a media interview. It sparked another debate in the Indian parliament, despite Vajpayee's rejection to this irresponsible remark. Furnades's statement was condemned by various political leaderships and the opposition parties such as Congress, CPI and CPI-M demanded his resignation for this statement. Government of India soon came into action in rejecting the statement and sought friendly relation with China. Looking at the large scale opposition to Fernandez's statement and Vajpayee's commitment to improve the bilateral relationship, China sent the PLA chief for a bilateral visit to India. But the goodwill did not last for a long time. India tested the nuclear weapons on May 13, 1998. In his letters to US President, Prime Minister Vajpayee tried to justify India's nuclear programme by citing the increasing Chinese threat for the recent test. China reacted strongly to this statement and all those efforts to improve the relationship had gone in vain. In the Parliament, the opposition parties, especially CPI, CPI-M and Congress party criticized the nuclear test and government's China policy. They also criticized the government for its no first use policy and its decision for the partial acceptance of the CTBT and NPT. The relation between India and China remained in freeze for nine months, since the reestablishment of official dialogue in February 1999. While the official dialogue was in process to normalize relationship, the war between India and Pakistan broke out in the Kargil region of the state of Jammu and Kashmir. International community condemned Pakistan's draconian strategy for violating the line of Control. China remained neutral in this war, though the Chinese civil society and media apparently supported Pakistan. Indian Parliament appreciated the Chinese neutrality and there was wide feeling among the members to resolve the outstanding border issues peacefully with China. While the relationship between India and China was in the process of improvement, another crisis emerged in Tibet. The 17th Karmapa fled from the Tibet and reached India on January 5, 2000. He approached India for political asylum, which put India in difficult situation. India could not have another confrontation with China, which seemed like looking at the past episode of Dalai Lama incident. But, India kept the issue low profiled and reached Chinese authority for discussion. The timely discussion to resolve the differences did not let the issue escalate. In the parliament the matter was also given a low profile and was ignored by most of the Parliamentarians, including the communists block. However, some questions were raised for the safety and security of the spiritual leader and the government of India's decision towards the political asylum issue. The government gave limited information in the Parliament in lip locked manner, with the intension to play down the situation.

Therefore, the period between 1976 and 1999 was one of the important episodes of India China relationship. During this period both the nations reestablished their diplomatic relationship and took enormous steps to normalize the relationship. This period also witnessed the major difficult times of the India China relation and major incidents such as the India's nuclear tests, Kargil war the issue of Karmapa crisis. Except for some occasions, the attitude of the Parliament was constructive, supportive and it supplemented to government's normalization efforts. However, during time of nuclear test it criticized the government. To conclude, it can be stated that, the Parliament was most favorable towards India's China policy during this period.

The relationship between India and China during the first decade of 21st century witnessed several ups and downs. The Indian president visited China to ease the tension that erupted following India's nuclear detonation and the Karmapa incident. Since then, both the countries have taken several measures to improve their relation and several high level visits have exchanged. Few important agreements also have been signed between New Delhi and Beijing to facilitate the growing bilateral trade, including the agreement to open the Nathu La pass. The India-China cooperation also reached a new high when both the countries decided to go for the joint bidding and to co-operate each other in international oil exploration. However, the promises deemed low as the two countries slowly entered into competition in many areas.

During this period the attitude of Indian parliament towards India's China policy was mostly cooperative as well as cautious. While most of the constructive initiatives, such as the improvement of relationship and promotion of trade between India and China were appreciated by the members of the parliament. But matter that affects India's national interest, including the Sino-Pakistan Nuclear cooperation and the visa issues with China has been opposed by parliament as whole. The Indian parliament, at large has been encouraging greater Sino-Indian trade and economic engagement and also encouraged the opening of the Nathu La pass for border trade. However, there was a little hesitation among the members of the parliament about the attitude of China towards India and the growing gap between volume of importing and exporting in the bilateral trade with China. There was overall consensus among all sections of the parliament for greater relation with China and no political party, whether ruling party or oppositions have opposed to improve relation with China.

After analysing the Parliamentary debates, it has been observed that, during the hectic debate of India-China relation around 700 members of twenty five political parties have participated in the Parliamentary debate. While congress party has been running the government from the second Lok Sabha to fifth Lok Sabha under the Prime Ministership of Jawaharlal Nehru, Lal Bahadur Shastri and Indira Gandhi, PSP, San Sangh, Socialist, CPI, CPM, GP, RPI, MKP, RSP, HM, JP, ML, Congress–O, Forwards Bloc, Utkal Congress, Dravida Munnetra Kazhagam (DMK), Jharkhand Party, SSCP, HLP, SSP and MGJP were the principal opposition parties that participated in the Parliamentary debate on India-China relations between 1959 and 1975. About 89 debates have been raised on various issues of India's China policy in Indian Parliament. While around 32% of the 708 participated members have supported the government China policy, about 68% members have criticised it. While the emergence India-China war attracted maximum number of (120) members in the Parliamentary debates, the Sikkim crisis has least number of (only 14) participation. Similarly, the debates during the 'era of confrontation' were around 32% higher than the 'era of hostility', due to the sensitivity and intensity of the issues that have been discussed.

Out of the total 708 participant members, 278 members belong to the ruling Congress party alone, which is about 40% of the entire participants. The overall stand of the congress party was divided, where around 55% members supported the government's China policy against around 45% who opposed. With 123 participated members, PSP emerged as the largest opposition party in debating India-China relations between 1959 and 1975, followed by Jan Sangh with 72 participated members. The attitude of the other non-communist oppositions, such as SP, PSP, BJS, Swatantra, GP, RPI, MKP, RSP, HM, JP, ML, Congress–O, Forwards Bloc, Utkal Congress, DMK, Jharkhand Party, SSCP, HLP, SSP and MGJP was largely critical of the government's China policy. Similarly, over 90 percent of the independent members also rejected India's foreign policy towards China. However, the attitude of the Communist fronts during the debate on India's China policy was apparently diverged, though both parties largely backed the government's overall China policy. While CPI did not hesitate to criticise the government's rigid stand towards China, the CPM extended its full support to the government's overall China policy irrespective of the issue. The analysis also finds that, majority of the participated members of the Parliament (around 67 %) criticised the government's policy, whereas only 33% members supported it. Hence, the overall attitude of the Indian Parliament towards India's foreign policy towards China was apparently critical of India's foreign policy towards China. The research also reveals that, there is significant attitudinal deference between ruling and opposition parties; and communist and non-communist parties. Though the differences between the ruling and opposition parties have been common in the Parliamentary democracy, the overwhelming support of the opposition front like communist parties towards the government's China policy was a new phenomenon. It is also noticeable that, the overall support of the communist bloc was 25% more than the overall support of the ruling Congress party, which was running the government. This overwhelming support towards India's China policy was mostly motivated by the party's pro-communist ideology and manifestos. Hence there is a positive correlation between the party ideology and the stand of the political parties in foreign policy decision making.

The researcher has chronologically analysed all the major issues between India and China and studied the attitude of various political parties and the overall approach of the Parliament on each of these issues. Based on the analysis it is observed that, the first hypothesis which states "the role of Parliament is very minimal when compared to other matters" is strongly accepted, given the fact that the Foreign Policy is mostly an interplay between the cabinet and bureaucracy and the voice of the Parliament is hardly considered as essential for the approval and rejection of any matters of foreign policy.

The study reveals that the stance of any particular party has been correlated to its party ideology and party manifesto. The Communist Party of India, for example, always stands for greater cooperation with China and blames the Indian government for jeopardizing the Sino-Indian relations, clearly because of its pro-communist ideology. It is also noticeable that, the overall support for better Sino-Indian relations by the communist bloc was 25% more than the ruling congress party. This overwhelming support towards India's liberal China policy was mostly motivated by the party's pro-communist ideology and manifestos. Similarly, the Jan Sangh always remains critical towards China due to its nationalist ideology.

It has been noticed during the research that the debates and discussions in the Parliament are hardly associated with pragmatism and mostly based on ideological arguments of India's Foreign Policy. The present study reveals that the members of the Indian Parliament are gaining more and more maturity gradually in debates and discussions on the topic of India's Foreign Policy in general and India's China policy in particular. India is a transitional largest democracy. Obviously most of the members lack expertise in the matters related to Foreign Policy while members have been paying larger attention towards the issues related to their respective constituencies or more domestic issues only. Therefore most of the members express ad-hoc as well as emotional opinions without any clarity. However, they explicitly express their opinion towards India's China Policy and the issues of other countries whose policies and programmers are affecting India's national Interest.

Policy Suggestions

The Indian Parliament as an institution has little formal power to influence India's Foreign Policy and it does not wield any power beyond questioning the government and overseeing financial accounts. Yet, the Parliament reigns substantial authority in democracy like India and any closed loop policy making by executive committees would be tantamount to the basic philosophy of 'popular will'. By shedding light on the role of Indian Parliament this research has sought to illuminate how Indian legislature moves towards establishing a procedural control over the executives. A procedural and operational control over the government on foreign and strategic affairs by the Members of the legislature has important consequences and as this research is concluded in the end, the changing dynamics of Indian polity and governance requires a pro-active and a critical legislature concentrating more on analysing or defending the Indian policy's motivations and achievements than on describing events factually or polemically. The following are some of the policy suggestions to the government for improving the Parliamentary involvement in India's foreign policy.

1. To Establish Parliamentary Research Services akin to Congressional Research Services of the United States which would provide qualitative research for the members of the Parliament to substantially debate on the floor of the house.
2. The members of the Indian Parliament must have compulsory training / refresher courses every year in Indian Politics, Foreign Affairs, Economics and Sociology with almost exhaustive coverage of contemporary and historical lessons.
3. Members of the Parliament must be conscious of the long term strategy of India and must by consensus request the government to release yearly strategic doctrines and Foreign Policy reviews.
4. Members of the Parliament must break the inherent secrecy on India-China War and the government has to publish the Henderson Brooks report. The report has to be placed in the floor of the Parliament for debate.
5. The Parliament has to become more assertive in its role as policy making institution and must demand that the government must submit to the Parliament all international treaties and agreements for approval.
6. Academicians, think tanks and independent policy analysts must be given adequate space to advise the government, and the existing bureaucratic dominance must be done away with. Provision must be made for lateral entry to important portfolios in the government.
7. Finally an attitudinal change has to come from within and the members of the Parliament should be broad minded to accept and practice change.

This study on the *Parliament and Foreign Policy Decision Making in India* is basically an investigation to analyse the attitude of the Indian

Parliament in making India's China policy and to theorize the attitude of different political parties and the attitude of the Indian Parliament as a whole towards India's external relation with China in various important issues. The most important aspects of the research is that, it has attempted to see India's foreign relation with china through the lens of Indian Parliamentary debates and discussions. While other studies on India's Foreign Policy towards China would comprehend the foreign, defence or strategic priorities, this research provides useful insights on the role of legislature on all the three areas and attempts to further delve into the dynamics of Parliament's evolution from passivity to veracity in foreign policy decision making. Further research in this area needs to understand the institutional incapacities of Parliament by modelling rational structures to the changing conditions of modern times. Model building and theoretical development in accordance with the Indian politico-administrative set up would bring about a paradigm shift rather than mindlessly incorporating the western model of governance.

Bibliography

Abraham, Itty. *TheMaking of the Indian Atomic Bomb: Science, Secrecy and the Postcolonial State*. London: Zed Books, 1998.

Agrawal, S. P. *Information India: 1997-98 and 1998-99: Global View*. New Delhi: Concept Publishing Company, 2002.

Alagappa, Muthiah (Ed.) *Coercion and Governance: The Declining Political Role of the Military in Asia. Stanford:* Stanford University Press, 2001.

Alastair J. Johnston and Robert S. Ross (Ed.) *New Directions in The Study of China's Foreign Policy*. Stanford: Stanford University Press.

Alkhafaji, Abbass F. *Strategic Management: Formulation, Implementation, and Control in a Dynamic Environment.* Haworth Press, Presently Routledge, 2003

Allen, Louis A. *The Management Profession. New York:* McGraw-Hill, 1964.

Allison, Graham. and Philip Zelikow. *Essence of Decision: Explaining the Cuban Missile Crisis, Second Edition*. New York: Addison-Wesley Longman. 1999.

Allison, Graham. *Essence of Decision: Explaining the Cuban Missile Crisis*, First Edition. Boston: Little Brown, 1971.

Alvi, Hayat, and Nikolas K. Gvosdev (Ed.), *Case Studies in Policy Making, 12th Edition*. Newport, US: Naval War College, 2010.

Appadorai, A.*Select Documents on India's Foreign Policy and Relations*. New Delhi: Oxford University Press, 1982.

Arpi, Claude.*1962 and the McMahon Line Saga*. Atlanta: Lancer Publishers, 2013.

Arpi, Claude. *Born in Sin: The Panchsheel Agreement: The Sacrifice of Tibet*. New Delhi: Mittal Publications, 2004.

Babu, D. Shyam. "National Security Council: Yet another Ad Hoc Move?" In *Security Beyond Survival*, Edited by P.R. Kumaraswamy. New Delhi: Sage, 2004.

Bajpai, G. S. *China's Shadow over Sikkim: The Politics of Intimidation*. New Delhi: Lancer Publishers, 1999.

Bakshi, Parvinrai Mulwantrai, and Subhash C. Kashyap, *The Constitution of India.* New Delhi: Universal Law Publishing, 2002.

Balabanova, Ekaterina. *Media Wars and Politics: Comparing the Incomparable in Western and Eastern Europe*. Hampshire, England: Ashgate Publishing, 2013.

Bandyopadhaya, J. *The Making of India's Foreign Policy: Determinates, Institutions, Process and Personalities, 3rd Edition.* New Delhi: Allied Publishers, 2003.

Bargh, John A., Peter M. Gollwitzer and Gabriele Octtingen, "Emotion", in *Handbook of Social Psychology - Volume 2*, Edited by Susan T. Fiske, Daniel T. Gilbert, Gardner Lindzey. Hoboken, New Jersey: John Wiley & Sons, Inc., 2010.

Basu, D.D. *Introduction to the Constitution of India, 19th Edition*. New Delhi: Wadhwa and Co. Law Publishers, 2001.

Basu, Partha Pratim. *Press and Foreign Policy in India,* New Delhi: Lancer Books, 2003.

Beach, Lee R. *Terry Connolly, The Psychology of Decision Making.* Thousand Oaks: People in Organizations, Sage, 2005.

Behera, Navnita Chadha. *Demystifying Kashmir.* Delhi: Pearson Education, 2007.

Bennett, W. Lance, and David L. Paletz. *Taken by Storm: The Media, Public Opinion, and US Foreign Policy in the Gulf War.*University of Chicago Press, 1994.

Benvenisti, Eyal.*The International Law of Occupation*. Oxford: Oxford University Press, 2012.

Betsill, Michele Merrill, and Elizabeth Corell, *NGO Diplomacy: The Influence of Nongovernmental Organizations in International Environmental Negotiations.* Cambridge: MIT Press, 2008.

Bimal N. Patel (ed.), *India and International Law: Introduction, Vol.2*. Leiden, The Netherlands: Martinus Nijhoff Publishers, 2008.

Boyer, Pascal. *Religion Explained: The Evolutionary Origins of Religious Thought*. New York: Basic Books, 2013.

Boynton, G. Robert. "The Expertise of the Senate Foreign Relations Committee," in *Artificial Intelligence and International Politics*, edited by Valerie Hudson. Boulder, CO: Westview, 1991.

Brahma Challeney, *Asian Juggernaut*. New Delhi: Harper Collins, 2006.

Brecher, Michael, and Jonathan Wilkenfeld, *A Study of Crisis*. Michigan: University of Michigan Press, 1997.

Brecher, Michel. *Nehru's Mantle: The Politics of Succession in India*. New York: Frederick A. Praeger, 1966.

Brigitte Lebens Nacos, Robert Y. Shapiro, PierangeloIsernia. *Decision making in a Glass House: Mass Media, Public Opinion, andAmerican and European Foreign Policy in the 21st Century*. Maryland: Rowman & Littlefield, 2000.

Budania, Rajpal. *India's National Security Dilemma: The Pakistan Factor and India's Policy Response.* New Delhi: Indus Publishing, 2001.

Carlsnaes, Walter, Thomas Risse, and Beth A. Simmons (ed.), *Handbook of International Relations*. London: Sage, 2002.

Carlsnaes, Walter. "Foreign Policy", in, *Handbook of International Relations,* Edited by Walter Carlsnaes, Thomas Risse and Beth A. Simmons. London: Sage, 2002

Carlsnaes, Walter., Thomas Risse-Kappen, Thomas Risse, Beth A Simmons, *Handbook of International Relations*. London: SAGE, 2002.

Cashman Greg, *What Causes War?: An Introduction to Theories of International Conflict*. Lanham, Maryland: Laxington, 2013.

Cassese Antonio. (ed), *Parliamentary Control Over Foreign Policy*. Alphen aan den Rijn, Nederlands: Sijthoff & Noordhoff, 1980.

Cecil V. Crab jr., *American Foreign Policy in the Nuclear Age, 3rd ed.* New York: Harper and Row, 1972.

Chary, M. Srinivas *The Eagle and the Peacock: U.S. Foreign Policy Toward India Since Independence.* Westport, US: Greenwood Publishing Group, 1995.

Chengappa, Bidanda M..*India-China relations: Post Conflict Phase to Post Cold War Period.* New Delhi: APH Publishing Corporation, 2004.

Christie, Daniel J. (Ed.), *Foreign Policy: The Encyclopedia of Peace Psychology, 1st Edition*. Blackwell Publishing, 2012.

Chung, Tan, *Across the Himalayan Gap: An Indian Quest for Understanding China*. New Delhi: Gyan Publishing House, 1998.

Chung, Tan, Zhang Minqiu and Ravni Thakur, *Across the Himalayan Gap: A Chinese Quest for Understanding India*. New Delhi: Gyan Publishing House, 1998.

Cohen, Bernard C. *The Public's Impact on Foreign Policy*. Boston: Little, Brown, 1978.

Cohen, Bernard Cecil. *Democracies and Foreign Policy: Public Participation in the United States and the Netherlands*. University of Wisconsin Press, 1995.

Cohen, Stephen P. and Sunil Dasgupta, *Arming Without Aiming: India's Military Modernization.* Washington DC: Brookings Institution Press, 2010.

Crab Jr. Cecil V. *American Foreign Policy in the Nuclear Age, 3rd edition*. New York: Harper and Row, 1972.

Cresswell, Julia. *Oxford Dictionary of Word Origins*. New York: Oxford University Press, 2010.

Daalder Ivo H. and I.M. Destler, "How National Security Advisor See Their Role", in *The Domestic Sources of American Foreign Policy: Insights and Evidence*, Edited by Eugene Robert Wittkopf, James M. McCormick. Lanham, U.S.: Rowman& Littlefield, 2008.

D'Anieri, Paul, *International Politics: Power and Purpose in Global Affairs.* Boston: Wads Warth, Cengage Learning, 2012.

Das, S.K. *Encyclopaedic Dictionary of Public Administration, Vol. 2.* New Delhi: Sarup & Sons Publication, 2000.

Dasgupta, Sunil. "India: The New Militaries", in *Coercion and Governance: The Declining Political Role of the Military in Asia,* Edited by Muthiah Alagappa. Stanford: Stanford University Press, 2001.

DeConde, Alexander. *Ethnicity, Race, and American Foreign Policy: A History*. Boston, MA: Northeastern University Press, 1992.

Deepak, B.R. India and China 1904-2004: A Century of Peace and Conflict. New Delhi: Manak Publication, 2005.

Denhardt, Robert B. *Theories of Public Organization*. Boston: Wodsworth Cengage Learning, 2010.

Deogaonkar, S.G. *Parliamentary System in India,* New Delhi: Concept Publishing Company, 1997.

Diamond, Jared. The *Third Chimpanzee: The Evaluation and Future of Human Animal*. New York: Harpet Perennial, 1992.

Dudley, Geoffrey, and Jeremy Richardson, *Why Does Policy Change?: Lessons from British Transport Policy 1945-99*. London: Routledge, 2001.

Duncan, W. Raymond. Barbara Jancar-Webster and Bob Switky, *World Politics in the 21st Century*. Boston: Houghton Mifflin, Cengage Learning, 2008.

East, Maurice A., Stephen A. Salmore, and Charles F. Hermann (ed.) *Why Nations Act*. Beverly Hills: Sage, 1978.

Easton, David. *The Political System*. New York: Alfred Knopf, 1953.

Edwards, Paul M. *The Korean War*. Westport: Greenwood Publishing Group, 2006.

Elkin, Jerrold. "India", in *The Defense Policies of Nations: A Comparative Study*, 3rd Edn. edited by Douglas Murray, Paul R. Viotti. London: John Hopkins University Press, 1994.

Entman, Robert M. *Projections of Power: Framing News, Public Opinion, and US Foreign Policy*. Chicago: University of Chicago Press, 2004.

Epstein, Leon D. "*British Foreign Policy" as quoted in Naheed Murtaza, Parliament and Foreign Policy: Reflection on India-China Relations*. New Delhi: CADPLAN Publisher, 1998.

Eugene R. Wittkopf. *Faces of Internationalism: Public Opinion and American Foreign Policy*. Durham, N.C.: Duke University Press, 1990.

Fazio, Silvio. *The Harmonization of International Commercial Law*. AH Alphen aan den Rijn, Netherlands: Kluwer Law International, 2007.

Feinstein, Andrew. *The Shadow World: Inside the Global Arms Trade*. New York: Picador, 2011.

Femenia, Nora. 'Emotional Actor: Foreign Policy Decision Making In The 1982 Falklands/Malvinas' War in *Social Conflicts And Collective Identities*. Edited by Patrick G. Coy and Lynne M. Woehrle. Lonham, Mariland: Rowman & Littlefield, 2000.

Fiske, Susan T., Daniel T. Gilbert, and Gardner Lindzey, *Handbook of Social Psychology - Volume 2*. Hoboken, New Jersey: John Wiley & Sons Inc., 2010.

Foyle, Douglas C. *Counting the Public in: Presidents, Public Opinion, and Foreign Policy*. Columbia University Press, 1999.

Frankel, Joseph. *International Relations in a Changing World, Revised Edition*. New York: Oxford University Press, 1988.

Frankel, Joseph. *International Relations in a Changing World*, Revised edn. New York: Oxford University Press, 1988.

Frey, Karsten. *India's Nuclear Bomb and National Security*. Oxon: Routledge, 2007.

Frey, Karsten. *India's Nuclear Bomb and National Security*. Oxon: Routledge, 2007.

Fritz Gaenslen, "Decision-Making Groups." In *Political Psychology and Foreign Policy*, Edited by E. Singer and V. Hudson. Boulder, Colorado: Westview Press, 1992.

Gaur, Mahendra.*Foreign Policy Annual, 2001 : Events And Documents*. New Delhi: Gyan Publishing House, 2005.

George, A. *Bridging the Gap: Theory and Practice in Foreign Policy*. Washington, DC: U.S. Institute of Peace, 1993.

Geva, Nehemia. Alex Mintz, *Decision Making on War and Peace: The Cognitive-Rational Debate*. Colorado: Lynne Rienner Publishers, 1997.

Ghose, Sankar. Jawaharlal Nehru: A Biography, Allied Publishers, 1993) 264;

Ghosh, Anjali , Tridib Chakraborti, A.J. Majumdar, and Shibashis Chatterjee . *India's Foreign Policy*. New Delhi: Pearson Education India, 2009. Print.

Gibson, Hugh. *The Road To Foreign Policy*. New York: Doubleday, 1944.

Gilbert, D., S. Fiske, and G. Lindsay (Ed.), *Handbook of Social Psychology, 5th Edition*. New York: McGraw, 2010.

Glassner, Martin Ira *Political Geography, 2nd Edition*. New York: John Wiley & Sons, 1996.

Goldberg, David Howard. *Foreign Policy and Ethnic Interest Groups: American and Canadian Jews Lobby for Israel*. Westport, CT: Greenwood Publishing Group, 1990.

Goldstein Joshua S., and John C. Pevehouse, *International Relations (9th Edition)*. New York: Pearson, 2010.

Goldstein, Joshua S. and John C. Pevehouse, *International Relations*, 9th Ed. New York: Pearson, 2010.

Government of India.*The Gazette of India*, Part I, Section I, 19 April 1999.

Government of India.*The Gazette of India*, Part I, Section I, 22 September 1090.

Gupta K.R., and Vatsala Shukla, *Foreign Policy of India, Vol. 1*, New Delhi: Atlantic Publishers, 2009.

Gupta, U. N. *Indian Parliamentary Democracy*. New Delhi: Atlantic Publishers, 2003.

Halperin, Morton H. Bureaucratic *Politics and Foreign Policy*. Washington, D.C.: Brookings, 1974.

Hanrieder, James F. *Comparative Foreign Policies: Theories, Findings and Methods*.New York: John Wiley and Sons, 1974.

Hardgrave Jr., Robert L. Stanley A. Kochanek, *India: Government and Politics in a Developing Nation: Government and Politics in a Developing Nation*. Boston: Thomson Wadsworth, 2008.

Harrison, Jeffrey S., and Caron H. St. John, *Foundations in Strategic Management, 5th Edition.* Mason, Ohio: South-Western, Cengage Learning, 2009.

Headley, James, and Jo-Ansie van Wyk."Debating the Public's Role in Foreign Policy." In *Public Participation in Foreign Policy*, edited by James Headley, Andreas Reitzig, Joe Burton. New York: Palgrave Macmillan, 2012.

Heitzman, James, and Robert L. Worden (ed.), *India: A Country Study*, (Federal Research Division: Library of Congress, 1995.

Hermann, Charles F. "Decision Structure and Process Influence on Foreign Policy" in *Why Nations Act*, Edited by M.A. East, S.A. Salmore and C. F. Hermann. Beverly Hills: Sage, 1978.

Hermann, Charles F. "Foreign Policy Behavior: That Which Is to Be Explained," in *Why Nations Act*, ed. Maurice A. East, Stephen A. Salmore, and Charles F. Hermann (Beverly Hills: Sage, 1978) 25.

Hill, Christopher. *Changing Politics of Foreign Policy*. Hampshire: Palgrave Macmillan, 2003.

Hoffmann, Steven A. *India and the China Crisis.*Berkeley: University of California Press, 1990.

Hollis, Duncan B. *The Oxford Guide to Treaties*. Oxford: Oxford University Press, 2012.

Holsti, Ole R. *Public Opinion and American Foreign Policy*. Ann Arbor: University of Michigan Press, 1996.

Holsti, Ole Rudolf.*Public Opinion and American Foreign Policy, Revised Edition.* Michigan: University of Michigan Press, 2009.

Holtom, Paul Mark Bromley, Pieter D. Wezeman and Siemon T. Wezeman, *Trends in International Arms Transfers, 2011*, SIPRI Fact Sheet, March 2012.

House of Lords. *Report of the Leader's Group on Working Practices: Report, Session 2010-12*. Great Britain: House of Lords, 2011.

Hoyt, P., & Garrison, J. "Political Manipulation in the Small Group: Presidential dvisers in the Carter Administration". In *Beyond Groupthink: Political Group Dynamics and Foreign Policymaking*, Edited by P. Hart, E. Stern, & B. Sundelius Ann Arbor, MI: University of Michigan Press, 1997.

Hudson, Valerie M. "The History and Evaluation of Foreign Policy Analysis" in *Foreign Policy: Theories, Actors, Cases,* Edited by Steve Smith, Amelia Hadfield, Tim Dunne. Oxford: Oxford University Press, 2012.

Hudson, Valerie M..*Foreign Policy Analysis: Classic and Contemporary Theory*. Lanham, Maryland: Rowman & Littlefield, 2013.

Jackson, Robert H. *Georg Sorensen, Introduction to International Relations: Theories and Approaches.* New York: Oxford University Press, 2007.

Jain R.K. *China South Asia Relations 1947-1980, Vol. 1 (India).* New Delhi: Radiant Publications, 1981.

Jain, Girilal. *Panchsheela and After: A Re-appraisal of Sino-Indian Relations in the Context of the Tibetan Insurrection*. Bombay: Asia Pub. House, 1960.

Jain, Lal Kumar. *Parliament and Foreign Policy in India*. Jaipur: Printwell Publishers, 1956.

Jain, R. B. *Public Administration in India: 21st Century Challenges for Good Governance.* New Delhi: Deep and Deep Publications, 2001.

Jain, Satya Bhusan. *India's Foreign Policy and Non-alignment.* New Delhi: Anamika Publishers, 2000.

James D. Morrow, "A rational Choice Approach to International Conflict" in NehemiaGeva, Alex Mintz, *Decision Making on War and Peace: The Cognitive-Rational Debate*. Colorado: Lynne Rienner Publishers, 1997.

James, Simon. *British Cabinet Government, 2nd Edition.* London: Routledge, 2002.

Janis, Irving Lester. *Victims of Groupthink: A Psychological Study of Foreign-Policy Decisions and Fiascoes*. Boston: Houghton Mifflin Company, 1972.

Jayapalan, N. *Foreign Policy in India*. New Delhi: Atlantic Publishers, 2001.

Jayapalan, N. *Indian Administration,* Vol. 1. New Delhi: Atlantic Publishers, 2001.

Jensen, Lloyd. Explaining Foreign Policy (Englewood Cliffs, NJ: Prentice-Hall, 1982) 13-14.

Jetly, Nancy.*Indian China Relations, 1947-77: A Study of Parliament's Role in the Making of Foreign Policy*. New Delhi: Radiant Publishers, 1979.

John P. MacKintosh, *TheBritish Cabinet, 3rd Edition*. London: Methuen & Co., 1981.

Johnston, Alastair I., and Robert S. Ross, *New Directions in the Study of China's Foreign Policy*. Stanford: Stanford University Press, 2006.

Jones, Roy E. *Analyzing Foreign Policy: An Introduction to some Conceptual Problem*. London: Routledge and Kegan Paul, 1970.

Jorgensen, Knud Erik. Aasne Kalland Aarstad, Edith Drieskens, Katie Laatikainen, Ben Tonra, *The SAGE Handbook of European Foreign Policy*. London: SAGE, 2015.

Jost, John T., and Jim Sidanius (Ed), *Political Psychology: Key Readings in Social Psychology*. New York: Psychology Press, 2004.

Kapur, Ashok. *India - From Regional to World Power*. New York: Routledge, 2013.

Kashyap, Subash.*Our Parliament*. National Book Trust, New Delhi, 2007.

Kashyap, Subash. *Parliamentary Procedure: Law, Privileges, Practices and Precedents Vol.1*. New Delhi, Universal Law Publishing Company, 2000.

Kaufman, Joyce P. *A Concise History of U.S. Foreign Policy*. Lanham, Maryland: Rowman & Littlefield, 2010.

Kaul, Brij Mohan. *The Untold Story*. New Delhi: Allied Publishers, 1967.

Kaul, T.N. *Diplomacy in Peace and War:Recollections and Reflections*. New Delhi: Vikas Publishers, 1978.

Kegley Jr., Charles W. *Shannon Lindsey Blanton, World Politics: Trend and Transformation*. Boston: Wodsworth, Cengage Learning, 2011.

Keltner, D. and J. S. Lerner. 'Emotion', In D. Gilbert, S. Fiske, & G. Lindsay (Eds.), *Handbook of Social Psychology*, 5th Ed. New York: McGraw, 2010.

Khong, Yuen Foong. *Analogies at War: Korea, Munich, Dien Bien Phu, and the Vietnam Decisions of 1965*. Princeton: Princeton University Press, 1992.

Kickert, Walter J M, Erik-Hans Klijn, and Joop F M Koppenjan (ed.) *Managing Complex Networks: Strategies for the Public Sector*. London: Sage, 1997.

Knutsen, Torbjorn L..*History of International Relations Theory*. Manchester: Manchester University Press, 1997.

Koontz, Harold. *Cyril O'Donnell, Principles of Management: An Analysis of Managerial Functions. Tokyo:* McGraw-Hill Kogakusha, 1972.

Kubálková, V. *Foreign Policy in a Constructed World*. New York: M.E. Sharpe, 2001.

Kumaraswamy, P.R. *Security Beyond Survival*. New Delhi: Sage Publication, 2004.

Kurian, Nimmi. *Emerging China and India's Policy Options*. New Delhi: Lancer Publishers, 2001.

Laird, Thomas. *The Story of Tibet: Conversations with the Dalai Lama*. New York: Grove Press, 2007.

Lal, Dinesh. *Indo-Tibet-China Conflict*. New Delhi: Kalpaz Publications, 2008.

Lal, Rollie. *Understanding China and India: Security Implications for the United States and the World*. Westport, US: Greenwood Publishing, 2006.

Lama, Dalai.*My Spiritual Autobiography*. Noida: Random House, 2011.

Lanther, Howard H. Foreign Policy Analysis. Columbus: Merrill Publishing, 1974.

Lawrance, Alan. *China's Foreign Relations Since 1949*. Oxen: Routledge, 2007.

Laxmikanth, M. *Public Administration,* New Delhi: Tata McGraw-Hill Publication, 2011.

Lee, Dong Sun. *Power Shifts,Strategy, and War: Declining States and International Conflict*. New York: Routledge, 2008.

Lempert, Michael. *Discipline and Debate: The Language of Violence in a Tibetan Buddhist Monastery*. Berkeley: University of California Press, 2012.

Lok Sabha Secretariat.*Rules of Procedure and Conduct of Business in Lok Sabha, 14th Edition*. New Delhi: Lok Sabha Secretariat, 2010.

Lok Sabha Secretariat. *The Ninth Lok Sabha, 1989-1991: A Study*. New Delhi: Northern Book Centre, 1992.

Lok Sabha Secretariat.*The Rules of Procedures and Conduct of Business in Lok Sabha, 14th Edition*. New Delhi: Lok Sabha Secretariat, 2010.

Louden, Robert B. *The World We Want : How and Why the Ideals of the Enlightenment Still Elude Us*. New York: Oxford University Press, 2007.

MacKenzie, W.J.M. *Power, Violence, Decision*. New York: Peregrine Books, 1975.

Macridis, Roy C. (ed.), *Foreign Policy and World Politics, 5th Edition*. Englewood Cliffs, NJ: Prentice-Hall, 1976.

Maheshwari, S.R. *The Administrative Reform Commission*. Agra: Laxmi Narain Agarwal, 1972.

Maheshwari, Shriram. *Indian Administrative Year Book 1990*. New Delhi: Concept Publishing Company, 1992.

Maldonato, Mauro. *Decision Making: Towards an Evolutionary Theory of Human Action*. Sussex: Academic Press, 2010.

Malone, David M. *Does the Elephant Dance?: Contemporary Indian Foreign Policy*. Oxford; Oxford University Press, 2011.

Mathur Krishan D., and P.M. Kamath, *Conduct of India's Foreign Policy*. New Delhi: South Asian Publishers, 1996.

Maxwell, Neville. *India's China War*. Dehradun: Natraj Publishers, 2010.

McGrew, Anthony G. and Michael John Wilson (ed), *Decision Making: Approaches and Analysis*. Manchester: Manchester University Press, 1982.

McKay, Vernon. *African Diplomacy, 2nd Edition*. Praeger, New York, 1996.

Mehra, Ajay K..and Gert W. Kueck (Ed.) *The Indian Parliament: A Comparative Perspective*. New Delhi: Konark Publishers, 2003.

Michael, Arndt. *India's Foreign Policy and Regional Multilateralism*. Hampshire: Palgrave Macmillan, 2013.

Ministry of External Affairs, *Foreign Affairs Record*, Ministry of External Affairs, Government of India, 1965.

Ministry of External Affairs, Government of India. *Annual Report 2010-12*. New Delhi: Ministry of External Affairs, Government of India, 2013.

Ministry of External Affairs, *Notes, Memoranda and letters Exchanged and Agreements signed between The Governments of India and China, White Paper I*. Ministry of External Affairs, Government of India, New Delhi, 1959. (Hare after cited as While Paper).

Ministry of External Affairs, *Official Report of the SummitVol. 6*. New Delhi: Ministry of External Affairs, Government of India, 1960.

Ministry of External Affairs, *Prime Minister on Chinese Aggression*. New Delhi: Ministry of External Affairs, Government of India, 1963.

Ministry of External Affairs, *White Paper II*. Ministry of External Affairs, Government of India, New Delhi, 1959.

Ministry of External Affairs, *White Paper III*. (New Delhi: Ministry of External Affairs, Government of India, 1960).

Ministry of External Affairs, *White Paper IV*. New Delhi: Ministry of External Affairs, Government of India, 1960.

Ministry of External Affairs, *White Paper IV*. New Delhi: Ministry of External Affairs, Government of India, 1960.

Ministry of External Affairs, *White Paper V*, New Delhi: Ministry of External Affairs, Government of India, 1961.

Ministry of External Affairs, *White Paper VI*. New Delhi: Ministry of External Affairs, Government of India, 1962.

Ministry of External Affairs, *White Paper VII*. New Delhi: Ministry of External Affairs, Government of India, 1962.

Ministry of External Affairs, *White Paper VIII*. New Delhi: Ministry of External Affairs, Government of India, 1962.

Ministry of External Affairs, *White Paper VIII*. New Delhi: Ministry of External Affairs, Government of India, 1963.

Ministry of External Affairs, *White Paper XII*. New Delhi: Ministry of External Affairs, Government of India, 1963.

Mintz, Alex, and Karl DeRouen Jr. *Understanding Foreign Policy Decision Making*. New York: Cambridge, 2010.

Mishra, Keshav. *Rapprochement Across the Himalayas: Emerging India-China Relations Post Cold War Period (1947-2003)*. New Delhi: Gyan Publishing House, 2004.

Mitchell, David. *Making Foreign Policy: Presidential Management of Decision – Making Process*. Hants, England: Ashgate Publishing, 2005.

Modelski, George.*A Theory of Foreign Policy*. London: Pallmall Press, 1962.

Mookerjee, R. K. *Local Government in Ancient India*. New Delhi: Oxford University Press, 1920.

Moran, Michael, Martin Rein, and Robert E. Goodin (Ed) *The Oxford Handbook of Public Policy*. New York: Oxford Handbooks Online, 2008.

Morgan, Patrick M. *Deterrence Now*. Cambridge: Cambridge University Press, 2003.

Motions and Resolutions in Parliament. New Delhi: Lok Sabha Secretariat, 2009.

Muni, S. D., and Tan Tai Yong (Ed.), *A Resurgent China: South Asian Perspectives*. New Delhi: Routledge, 2011.

Murray, Douglas, and Paul R. Viotti (Ed.) *The Defence Policies of Nations: A Comparative Study*, 3rd Edition. London: John Hopkins University Press, 1994.

Murthza, Naheed. *Parliament and Foreign Policy: Reflection of India-China Relations* New Delhi: CADPLAN Publisher, 1998.

Nacos, Brigitte Lebens, Robert Y. Shapiro, and Pierangelo Isernia (ed.), *Decision making in a Glass House: Mass Media, Public Opinion, and American and European Foreign Policy in the 21st Century*. Maryland: Rowman & Littlefield, 2000.

Nadkarni, Vidya. *Strategic Partnerships in Asia: Balancing without Alliances*. New York: Routledge Publication, 2010.

Naidu, S.P. *Public Administration: Concepts and Theories.* New Delhi: New Age International, 2005.

Neff, Stephen C. "A Short History of International Law", in *International Law*, Edited by Malcolm D. Evans. Oxford: Oxford University Press, 2014.

Northedgeed, F.S. *The Foreign Policy of The Powers*. London: Faberand Faber, 1968.

Norton, Richard J. "Understanding the Policy-Making Process: A Guide to Case Analysis", in *Case Studies in Policy Making*, 12th Edition, Edited by Hayat Alvi and Nikolas K. Gvosdev. Newport, US Naval War College 2010.

Nownes, Anthony J. *Interest Groups in American Politics: Pressure and Power*. New York: Routledge, 2013.

Official Report of the Government of India and China on Boundary Question. New Delhi: Ministry of External Affairs, Government of India.

Olson, William C. and A. J. R.Groom, *International Relations Then and Now*. London: Routledge, 1991.

Orton, Anna. *India's Borderland Disputes: China, Pakistan, Bangladesh, and Nepal*. New Delhi: Epitome Books, 2010.

Panda, Pramoda Kumar.*Making of India's Foreign Policy:Prime Minister and Wars.* New Delhi: Raj Publications, 2003.

Patel, Bimal N. ed., *India and International Law: Introduction*, Vol.2. Leiden, The Netherlands: Martinus Nijhoff Publishers, 2008.

Patnaik, Saroj K., Jaya KrushnaBaral, and Jagdish Prasad Sharma (Ed.) *United Nations India and The New World Order*. New Delhi: Mittal Publications, 2004.

Patrick G. Coy and Lynne M. Woehrle (Eds.) *Social Conflicts and Collective Identities*. Lonham, Mariland: Rowman & Littlefield, 2000.

Paylee, M.V. *Constitutional Government in India, 4thEdition.* New Delhi: S. Chand & Co., 1984.

Perkovich, George. *India's Nuclear Bomb: The Impact on Global Proliferation.* Berkeley: University of California Press, 1999.

Prakash, A Surya. "Parliamentary Questions as Instruments of Accountability" in *The Indian Parliament: A Comparative Perspective,* Edited by Ajay K. Mehra and Gert W. Kueck. New Delhi: Konark Publishers, 2003.

Prasad, S.N. (ed.), *History of the Conflict with China, 1962* (Unpublished Report). New Delhi: History Division, Ministry of Defence, Government of India.

Prys, Miriam.*Redefining Regional Power in International Relations: Indian and South African Perspectives.* Oxon: Routledge, 2012.

Quattrone, George A. and Amos Tversky, "Contrasting Rational and Psychological Analysis of Political Choice" in *Political Psychology: Key Readings in Social Psychology*, edited by John T. Jost, Jim Sidanius. New York: Psychology Press, 2004.

Quinn, Adam. *US Foreign Policy in Context: National Ideology from the Founders to the Bush*. New York: Routledge, 2010.

Raghavan, Srinath. *War and Peace in Modern India: A Strategic History of the Nehru Years*. Ranikhet, India: Permanent Black, 2010.

Rai, Ajai K., *India's Nuclear Diplomacy after Pokhran II*. New Delhi: Pearson Education India, 2009.

Rajya Sabha Secretariat. *Rajya Sabha at Work*. New Delhi: Rajya Sabha Secretariat, 2006.

Rana,Krishna S. *Inside Diplomacy*. New Delhi: Manas Publication, 2000.

Ray, Jayanta Kumar. (Ed.), *Aspects of India's International Relations, 1700 to 2000: South Asia and the World*. New Delhi: Pearson Education India, 2007.

Renshon, Jonathan. and Jennifer S. Lerner, Decision - Making, the Role of Emotions in Foreign Policy, in *The Encyclopaedia of Peace Psychology, First Edition,* Edited by Daniel J. Christie. Oxford: Blackwell Publishing, 2012.

Robinson, Piers. *The CNN Effect: The Myth of News, Foreign Policy and Intervention*. London: Routledge, 2002.

Rocher, Guy. *Introduction to Sociology*. Kolkata: Academic Publishers, 2004.

Rosati, Jerel A. "Congress and Interbranch Politics." In *The Politics of United States Foreign Policy*. Belmont, CA: Wadsworth/Thomson Learning, 2004.

Rosenau, James N. "Comparing Foreign Policies: Why, What, How," in *Comparative Foreign Policies: Theories, Findings and Methods*, Edited by James F. Hanrieder. New York: John Wiley and Sons, 1974.

Rosenau, James N. *Domestic Sources of Foreign Policy*. New York: Free Press, 1967.

Rosenau, James N. *Public Opinion and Foreign Policy: An Operational Formulation*. New York: Random House, 1961.

Rosenau, James. 'Pre-theories and Theories of Foreign Policy', excerpt in *Classics of International Relations, 3rd Edition*, Edited by J. Vasquez. New Jersey: Prentice Hall, 1996.

Roth, Byron M. and John D. Mullen, *Decision Making: Its Logic and Practice*. Savage, Maryland: Rowman & Littlefield, 2002.

Sahukar, Behram A. "Intelligence and Defense Cooperation in India" in *Intelligence Cooperation Practices in the 21st Century: Towards a Culture of Sharing*, edited by Musa Tuzuner. BG Amsterdam, Netherlands: IOS Press, 2010.

Said, Abdul Aziz. *Ethnicity and US Foreign Policy*. New York: Praeger Publishers, 1981.

Sali, M. L. *India-China Border Dispute: A Case Study of the Eastern Sector*. New Delhi: APH Publishing, 1998.

Sarkar, Siuli. *Public Administration in India.* New Delhi: PHI Learning, 2010.

Schultz, David A. *Encyclopaedia of Public Administration and Public Policy*. New York: Infobase Publishing, 2009.

Schultz, David A. *Encyclopaedia of Public Administration and Public Policy*. New York: Fact on File Inc, 2004.

Sen, Chanakya. *Tibet Disappears*. Bombay: Asia Publishing House, 1960.

Sethi, S.K. "India and the UN: the Indira Gandhi Era". In *United Nations India and The New World Order*, edited by Saroj K. Patnaik, Jaya KrushnaBaral, and Jagdish Prasad Sharma. New Delhi: Mittal Publications, 2004.

Sharma, B.K. *Introduction to the Constitution of India.* New Delhi: PHI Learning, 2007.

Sharma, Shalendra D. *China and India in the Age of Globalization.*Cambridge: Cambridge University Press, 2009.

Sharma, Shri Ram. *India-China Relations, 1947-1971: Friendship Goes with Power, Part 1.* New Delhi: Discovery Publishing House, 1999.

Shipley, Joseph Twadell. *The Origins of English Words: A Discursive Dictionary of Indo-European Roots*. London: JHU Press, 2001.

Simonin, Herbert A. *Administrative Behavior; A Study of Decision-Making Processes in Administrative Organization.* New York: Macmillan, 1947 .

Singh, Hoshiar. *Indian Administration.* New Delhi: Pearson Education, 2011.

Singh, Hoshiar. *Public Administration: Theory and Practice*. New Delhi: Pearson Education India, 2012.

Singh, Ravinder P. *Arms Procurement Decision-making Processes: China, India, Israel, Japan, South Korea and Thailand*. New York: Oxford University Press, 1998.

Singh, Swaran. "India and China: Confidence Building Through Crisis" in *Living with China: Regional States and China Through Crises and Turning Points*, edited by Shiping Tang, Mingjiang Li, AmitavAcharya. New York: Palgrave Macmillan, 2009.

Singh, Swaran. "Three Agreements and Five Principles between India and China", in *Across the Himalayan Gap: A Chinese Quest for Understanding India*, edited by Tan Chung, Zhang Minqiu and Ravni Thakur. New Delhi:Gyan Publishing House,1998.

Sismanidis, Roxane D.V. "Foreign Relations (of India)", in *India: A Country Study*, edited by James Heitzman and Robert L. Worden. Washington DC.: Federal Research Division, 1995. http://lcweb2.loc.gov/cgibin/query/r?frd/cstdy:@field(DOCID+in0168).

Sisodia N.S., and Sujit Dutta, *India and the World: Selected Articles from IDSA Journals, Volume 1.* New Delhi: Institute for Defence Studies and Analysis and Bibliophile South Asia, 2005.

Sisson, Richard, and Leo E. Rose, *War and Secession: Pakistan, India, and the Creation of Bangladesh*. Berkeley: University of California Press, 1999.

Smit, Pieter Johannes, T. Brevis, G.J. De J. Cronje, M.J. Vrba and P.J. Smit, *Management Principles: A Contemporary Edition for Africa.* Cape Town: Juta and Company, 2007.

Smith, Steve, Amelia Hadfield, and Tim Dunne (ed.), *Foreign Policy: Theories, Actors, Cases*. Oxford: Oxford University Press, 2008.

Smith, Tony. *Foreign Attachments: The Power of Ethnic Groups in the Making of American Foreign Policy*. Harvard University Press, 2000.

Smith, Warren W. *Tibet's Last Stand: The Tibetan Uprising of 2008 and China's Response*. Lanham, Mary land: Rowman & Littlefield, 2010.

Snyder, Glenn H. *Alliance Politics.* New York: Cornell University Press, 2007.

Snyder, Richard C., HW Buck and Burton Sapin.*Decision Making as an Approach to Study of International Politics*. Princeton: Foreign Policy Analysis Project, Princeton University, 1954.

Sondhi, M. L. *Foreign Policy and Legislatures - An Analysis of Seven Parliaments*. New Delhi: Abhinav Publications, 2014.

Stein, Janice Gross. "Foreign Policy Decision-Making: Rational, Psychological, and Neurological Models", in *Foreign Policy: Theories, Actors, Cases* edited by Steve Smith, Amelia Hadfield, and Tim Dunne. Oxford: Oxford University Press, 2008.

Stein, Janice Gross. "Psychological Explanations of International Conict", in *Handbook of International Relations*, Edited by Carlsnaes, Walter, Thomas Risse, and Beth A. Simmons. London: Sage, 2002.

Tan, Chung. *Rise of the Asian Giants: The Dragon-Elephant Tango*. New Delhi: Anthem Press, 2009.

Tang, Shiping, Mingjiang Li, Amitav Acharya (Ed.), *Living with China: Regional States and China through Crises and Turning Points*. New York: Palgrave Macmillan, 2009.

Tellis, Ashley J. *India's Emerging Nuclear Posture: Between Recessed Deterrent and Ready Arsenal*.Santa Monica, US: Rand Corporation, 2001.

Terry, Janice. *US foreign policy in the Middle East: the Role Of Lobbies and special Interest Groups*. Pluto Press, 2005.

Tharoor, Shashi. *PaxIndica: India and the World of the Twenty-first Century.* London: Penguin UK, 2013.

Thomas, John Clayton. *Public Participation in Public Decisions: New skills and strategies for Public Managers*. San Francisco, CA: Jossey-Bass, 1995.

Thompson, Kenneth W. and Roy C. Macridis, " Comparative Study of Foreign Policy" in Foreign Policy and World Politics, Fifth Edition, edited by Roy C. Macridis. Englewood Cliffs, NJ: Prentice-Hall, 1976.

Todd, Paul, and Jonathan Bloch, *Global Intelligence: The World's Secret Services Today*. London: Zed Books, 2004.

Tuzuner, Musa. (Ed), *Intelligence Cooperation Practices in the 21st Century: Towards a Culture ofSharing*. BG Amsterdam, Netherlands: IOS Press, 2010.

Tzou, Byron N. *China and International Law: The Boundary Disputes*. New York: Praeger Publishers, 1990.

Vang,Pobzeb.*Five Principles of Chinese Foreign Policies.* Bloomington: Author House, 2008.

Verma, S. K. *An Introduction to Public International Law.* New Delhi: PHI Learning, 2004.

Vertzberger, Y. *The World in Their Minds: Information Processing, Cognition, and Perception in Foreign Policy Decision Making*. Stanford, CA: Stanford University Press, 1990.

Walt,Stephan M. *The Origins of Alliances*. New York:Cornell University Press, 1987.

Wittkopf, Eugene R., Christopher Martin Jones and Charles W. Kegley, Jr., *American Foreign Policy: Pattern and Process, 7th Edition*. Belmont: Thomson Wadsworth, 2008.

Wittkopf, Eugene R., Christopher Martin Jones and Charles W. Kegley, Jr. American Foreign Policy: Pattern And Process, Seventh Edition. Belmont: Thomson Wadsworth, 2008.

Wittkopf, Eugene Robert and James M. McCormick (Ed.) *The Domestic Sources of American Foreign Policy: Insights and Evidence*. Lanham, MD.: Rowman & Littlefield, 2008.

Allison, Graham T. and Morton H. Halperin, "Bureaucratic Politics: A Paradigm and Some Policy Implications", *World Politics* 24, (Supplement 1972): 40-79.

Baum, Matthew A., and Philip BK Potter."The Relationships Between Mass Media, Public Opinion, and Foreign Policy: Toward a Theoretical Synthesis."*Annual Review of Political. Science* 11 (2008): 39-65.

Baumann, A, and Deber R. "Limits of Decision Analysis for Rapid Decision Making in ICU Nursing." *Image: Journal of Nursing Scholarship* 21, no. 2 (1989): 69-71.

Brown, Judith. "Foreign Policy Decision Making and the Indian Parliament", *Journal of Constitutional and Parliamentary Studies* 3, no. 2, (April-June 1969): 15-52.

Brown, Reva. "Consideration of the Origin of Herbert Simon's Theory of 'Satisficing' (1933-1947)". *Management Decision* 42, no.10 (2004): 1240–1256.

Cao, Xiaoxia, and Paul R. Brewer."Political Comedy Shows and Public Participation in Politics." *International Journal of Public Opinion Research* 20, no. 1 (2008): 90-99.

Cato, A. C. "Fijians and Fiji-Indians: A Culture-Contact Problem in the South Pacific". *Oceania* 26, no.1 (September, 1955): 14-34.

Cherry, P.R. "India's Nuclear Doctrine: Confused Ambitions", *The Nonproliferation Review* 7, no. 3 (Fall Winter 2000): 123-35.

Clark McCauley, "The Nature of Social Influence in Groupthink: Compliance and Internalization", *Journal of Personality and Social Psychology* 57, no. 2 (Aug 1989): 250-260.

Delbecq, André L., and Andrew H. Van de Ven, "A Group Process Model for Problem Identification and Program Planning", *Journal of Applied Behavioral Science* 7, no. 4 (July 1971): 466-492.

Dumbrell, John, and David M. Barrett, "Non-Governmental Organizations: The Voice of People". *U.S. Foreign Policy Agenda* 5/1 (March 2000): 28-32.

Fearon, James D. "Domestic Politics, Foreign Policy, and Theories of International Relations". *Annual Review of Political Science* 1 (1998): 289 -313.

Gilboa, Eytan. "Global Communication and Foreign Policy." *Journal of Communication* 52, no. 4 (2002): 731-748.

Grande, Edgar. "The State and Interest Groups in a Framework of Multilevel DecisionMaking: The Case of the European Union." *Journal of European Public Policy* 3, no. 3 (1996): 318-338.

Haass, Reshard N. "Think Tanks and US Foreign Policy: A Policy Maker's Perspective", *Foreign Policy Agenda*, 7/3 (November 2002): 5-8.

Haney, Patrick J., and Walt Vanderbush. "The Role of Ethnic Interest Groups in US Foreign Policy: The Case of the Cuban American National Foundation." *International Studies Quarterly* 43, no. 2 (1999): 341-361.

Hermann Margaret G. and Thomas Preston, "Presidents, Advisers, and Foreign Policy: The Effect of Leadership Style on Executive Arrangements", *Political Psychology,* 15/1 Special Issue: Political Psychology and the Work of Alexander L. George (Mar., 1994) 75-96.

Hinnebusch, Raymond. "The American Invasion of Iraq: Causes and Consequences", *Perceptions*, (Spring 2007): 9-27.

Holsti, Ole R. "Public Opinion and Foreign Policy: Challenges to the Almond-Lippmann Consensus Mershon Series: Research Programs and Debates." *International Studies Quarterly* (1992): 439-466.

Jain, R.B. "Parliament and Policy in India", *Asian Journal of Public Administration*, 6/ 2 (1984): 127-152.

Jian, Chen The Tibetan Rebellion of 1959 and China's Changing Relations with India and the Soviet Union, *Journal of Cold War Studies* 8/3 (Summer 2006): 54–101.

Kaarbo, Juliet. "Power and Influence in Foreign Policy Decision Making: The Role of Junior Coalition Partnersin German and Israeli Foreign Policy". *International Studies Quarterly* 40/ 4 (December, 1996): 501-530.

Kashyap, Subash. "Executive Legislature Interface in the Indian Polity", The Journal of *Legislative Studies* 10/ 2 (2004) 278-294.

Khilnani, Niranjan M. "The Role of Parliament of foreign Affairs" *Journals of Constitutional and Parliamentary Studies* 6, no.4 (1972): 32-38.

Lowi, T. J. "Four Systems of Policy, Politics and Choice", *Public Administrative Review*, 32, no. 4 (1972): 298-310.

Madhok, Balraj. "Parliament's Influence on the Conduct of Foreign Policy" *Journals of Parliamentary Information* 15, no.2 (October 1969).

Manning, Bayless. "Goals, Ideology and Foreign Policy", *Foreign Affairs 54* (January 1976): 278.

Martin, Paul. "The Role of Canadian Parliament in the Formulation of Foreign Policy".*Parliamentarian* 50 (October 1969): 259-66.

Mearsheimer, John J., and Stephen M. Walt. "The Israel Lobby and US Foreign Policy." *Middle East Policy* 13, no. 3 (2006): 29-87.

Mitchell, David. "Centralizing Advisory Systems: Presidential Influence and the U.S. Foreign Policy Decision-Making Process." *Foreign Policy Analysis* 1, no.2 (2005): 181-206.

Moller, Kay. "Diplomatic Relations and Mutual Strategic Perceptions: China and the European Union", *China Quarterly* 169, no1 (March, 2002): 10-32.

Muni, S.D. Parliament and Foreign Policy in India" *Indian Journal of Politics* 10, no. 1 (June 1976): 48-60

Narashima Rao, P.V. Parliament and Foreign Policy," *Journals of Parliamentary Information* 27, no. 4 (December 1981): 385-92.

Naveh, Chanan. "The Role of the Media in Foreign Policy Decision-making: A Theoretical framework." *Conflict and Communication Online* 1, no. 2 (2002): 1-14.

Origins, Humble British."Government, Interest Groups and Policy Change."*Political Studies* 48 (2000): 1006-1025.

Page, Benjamin I., and Robert Y. Shapiro. "Effects of public opinion on policy." *American Political Science Review* 77, no. 01 (1983): 175-190.

Pilote, Alain. "Reflections on the War in Iraq, The Real Motives: Oil and Money". *Michael Journal* (March-April, 2003).

Powlick, Philip J., and Andrew Z. Katz. "Defining the American public opinion/ foreign policy nexus." *Mershon International Studies Review* 42, no. 1 (1998): 29-61.

Radcliffe, Liat. "A Muslim Lobby at Whitehall?Examining the Role of the Muslim Minority in British Foreign Policy Making." *Islam and Christian–Muslim Relations* 15, no. 3 (2004): 365-386.

Ratnam, P. "Policy-making and Parliamentary Accountability with Particular Reference to India's Foreign Policy" *Journals of Constitutional and Parliamentary Studies* 9, no.1 (March1975): 73-78.

Redd, Steven B. "The influence of Advisers and Decision Strategies on Foreign Policy Choices: President Clinton's Decision to Use Force in Kosovo". *International StudiesPerspectives* 6, no.1 (February, 2005): 129–150.

Risse-Kappen, Thomas. "Public Opinion, Domestic Structure, and Foreign Policy in Liberal Democracies" *World Politics* 43, no. 4 (1991): 479-512.

Robinson, Piers. "The CNN Effect: Can The News Media Drive Foreign Policy?." *Review of International Studies* 25, no. 02 (1999): 301-309.

Robinson, Piers. "Theorizing the Influence of Media on World Politics Models of Media Influence on Foreign Policy." *European Journal of Communication* 16, no. 4 (2001): 523-544.

Robinson, Piers. "The CNN Effect: Can the News Media Drive Foreign Policy?". *Review of International Studies* 25 (1999): 301–309.

Rosati, Jerel A. "Developing a Systematic Decision-Making Framework: Bureaucratic Politics in Perspective", *World Politics* 33, no. 3 (1981): 234-52.

Russett, Bruce. "The Calculus of Deterrence", *Journal of Conflict Resolution* 7, 21 (1963) 97-109.

Salameh, Mamdouh G. "The Oil "Price Rise Factor in the Iraq War: A Macroeconomic Assessment". *International Politics* 2, no. 3 (Winter & Spring 2009): 43-57.

Saluja, A.R. "Indian Intelligence Organization: Need for a Comprehensive Knowledge Management", *Indian Defence Review* 16, no 2 (Jan-Mar 2008): 82-88.

Simonin, Herbert A. "Rational Choice and the Structure of the Environment", *Psychological Review* 63, no.2 (1956): 129-138.

Singh, Dinesh. "The Indian Parliament and Foreign Policy" *The Parliamentarian: Journal of the Parliaments of Commonwealth* 51, no. 3 (July 1970): 157-60.

Singh, Swaran. "The Kargil Conflict: Why and How of China's Neutrality?", *Strategic Analysis*, 23/7 (1999):1083-1094.

Soroka, Stuart N. "Media, Public Opinion, and Foreign Policy." *The International Journal of Press/Politics* 8, no. 1 (2003): 27-48.

Tower, John G. "Congress versus the President: The Formulation and Implementation of American Foreign Policy." *Foreign Affairs* 60, no.2 (1981): 229-46.

Index

E

F

G

H

J

K

N

O

P

Q

R